D1047365

# STRATEGIC DATABASE Marketing

The Masterplan
for Starting
and Managing
a Profitable,
Customer-Based
Marketing Program

**Arthur M. Hughes**

**PROBUS PUBLISHING COMPANY**
Chicago, Illinois
Cambridge, England

© 1994, Arthur M. Hughes

ALL RIGHTS RESERVED. No part of this publication may be reproduced, stored in a retrieval system, or transmitted, in any form or by any means, electronic, mechanical, photocopying, recording, or otherwise, without the prior written permission of the publisher and the author.

This publication is designed to provide accurate and authoritative information in regard to the subject matter covered. It is sold with the understanding that the author and the publisher are not engaged in rendering legal, accounting, or other professional service.

Authorization to photocopy items for internal or personal use, or the internal or personal use of specific clients, is granted by PROBUS PUBLISHING COMPANY, provided that the U.S. $7.00 per page fee is paid directly to Copyright Clearance Center, 222 Rosewood Drive, Danvers, MA 01923, USA; Phone: 1-508-750-8400. For those organizations that have been granted a photocopy license by CCC, a separate system of payment has been arranged. The fee code for users of the Transactional Reporting Service is 1-55738-551-3/94/$00.00 + $7.00.

ISBN 1-55738-551-3

Printed in the United States of America

BB

2 3 4 5 6 7 8 9 0

Probus books are available at quantity discounts when purchased for business, educational, or sales promotional use. For more information, please call the Director, Corporate/Institutional Sales at (800) 998-4644, or write:

Director, Corporate/Institutional Sales
Probus Publishing Company
1925 N. Clybourn Avenue
Chicago, IL 60614
PHONE (800) 998-4644    FAX (312) 868-6250

*For Lydia, Robin, David, and Bill*

Also by Arthur Middleton Hughes

*The Complete Database Marketer*
Probus Publishing Company: 1991

*The American Economy*
Norvec Publishing Company: 1968

# Contents

# Preface

In the three years since *The Complete Database Marketer* appeared, database marketing has made major strides. At that point, most marketers had heard of database marketing, but very few were doing anything about it. Since then, virtually every large corporation in the United States has added a position of director of database marketing. All direct marketing magazines are devoting major space to this subject. Throughout industry, many successful database projects have been undertaken.

Unfortunately, many mistakes have been made. In a few cases, millions of dollars have been wasted on database projects that did not survive. A number of projects touted as new trends by industry leaders sank like stones months after the accolades. The reasons for these failures are many, but they center on one central fault: the inability of marketers to develop a logical, practical, and winning strategy for their database programs.

Building a database is not difficult. Making money with a database is the real challenge. Keeping it going, building relationships with customers, reducing attrition, increasing sales over a multiyear period have proved to be very difficult for some, while others have mastered the art.

Clearly, as an industry, we need to look closely at the available data, study success and failure, and from this research, come up with some sound principles that can guide strategy development onto safer ground in the future. That is the purpose of *Strategic Database Marketing*.

This book is written to speak directly to the people in any corporation who are concerned with customer-based marketing and prospecting for new business: database marketers and direct marketers. This book will be of great interest to executives of the many organizations that work with and service the direct response (DR) industry, including DR agencies, advertising agencies, service bureaus, telemarketing services, statistical modelers, and consultants.

Within corporations, it should be highly useful to executives in customer service, technical support, advertising, management information systems

(MIS), and sales—since most good database marketing ends up involving these units in a very intimate way.

For those who have no idea what database marketing is, *The Complete Database Marketer* will give you a solid grounding in the subject. For those who already know something about database marketing, but want to know how to turn a database into a profit center, this is the book. It is your next step up.

The book you are reading is designed to give marketers some practical, workable, theoretical underpinnings of the marketing strategies needed to create successful relationship-building database projects. The concentration is not with the mechanics of database construction, which is found in *The Complete Database Marketer*. The focus is on the theory that will tell you whether an idea will work before millions have been spent.

The key to strategy development is computation of customer lifetime value. This procedure, which used to be considered somewhat mysterious and complicated, has been transformed in this book, with the help of techniques developed by Professor Paul Wang of Northwestern University, to a simple set of numbers that can be mastered by any competent marketer.

Lifetime value analysis enables a database marketer to know—in advance—whether a strategy holds the promise of success. Using this technique, database marketing can soon become a highly successful and established marketing tool, rather than what it is today: an experimental curiosity that everyone feels might work, but is still poorly understood.

Database marketing is fun. It is exciting. It is a challenge. Done correctly, it holds the promise of making customers happy and loyal, and companies profitable. It will make the United States a more satisfying place to live in the 21st century.

## Acknowledgments

Virtually all the ideas that you will read in this book have occurred to me as a result of stimulating contact with the many master database marketers quoted in these pages. I particularly want to acknowledge a debt of gratitude to several who helped me in special ways:

Paul Wang, Assistant Professor of Marketing, Northwestern University. Paul taught me the lifetime value techniques that are basic to modern database marketing strategy development.

Thomas Lix, President and CEO of MarketPulse, Inc. Tom has the imagination to see what relationship marketing can do, where others see only names and data.

Brian Woolf, President of the Retail Strategy Center, Inc., Author of *Shrinking the Corporate Waistline*, and former Chief Financial Officer of Food Lion, Inc. Brian is a knowledgeable and enthusiastic marketer who provided tremendously useful help on the editing and organization of this book.

Terry Vavra, President of Marketing Metrics and Author of *After Marketing*. Terry is an expert marketing strategist and educator whose ideas have helped many to understand this new media.

# Part One: What Is Database Marketing?

# Introduction

Lydia McCabe had just received her new cellular phone. No bigger than a calculator, it fit easily in the purse beside her in her Land Rover as she drove to her office. When she glided to a stop in the parking lot, a strange man approached the car. He tapped on the window with a metal rod. Her adrenaline began flowing fast: This was a moment of decision.

Making sure that all the doors were locked, she restarted the engine and shoved it into reverse. In a moment, she was out of the lot and turning around in the street. In her rear view mirror, she could see the man, running in the opposite direction. Her instincts were right! But what to do now? She did not want to drive back into that parking lot.

Pulling to a stop in a safe area, Lydia opened her purse and reached inside to make her very first call on the new phone. Who to call? The dealer's written instructions were taped to the front of the instrument: "First call: * 611 SEND." She entered the commands.

"Hello. Is this Lydia McCabe? Welcome to U S West Cellular Phone Service," a friendly voice said.

"Boy, am I glad to hear your voice," Lydia replied. "I'm scared to death. A strange man approached me in my office parking lot. I'm afraid to go back in there. I need help."

"Where are you now?"

"Lambert and Van Cleave."

"I'll have the police over there right away. You're driving your Land Rover, license plate MCC200?"

"That's right. Please hurry!"

Lydia was the beneficiary of database marketing as it is being practiced today: personal, helpful service that inspires loyalty and repeat business. Is it possible that in a few weeks she will shift to another cellular telephone company when she receives a special discount offer? Not on your life.

The police arrived a few moments later, and escorted her into her office. As she tucked her portable phone back into her purse, she realized that she had purchased more than a telephone. She had bought friendship, service, and security.

### The Land Rover

Lydia had bought her Land Rover as a family car: a luxury outdoor vehicle that would hold everyone comfortably. What she didn't realize was that in buying the car, she also bought into an exclusive club. The check-out program was called a Royal Welcome. It included a tour of the dealership and introduction to key personnel, and the presentation of a British picnic basket with mugs, napkins, tablecloth, tea, crackers, and fruit.

The welcome was followed up by telephone calls to be sure that everything was going well. A couple of weeks after taking delivery, she received an extensive survey questionnaire asking her about her reactions to every aspect of the vehicle, and the service that came with it. Soon thereafter, the dealer called her to remind her to come in for regularly scheduled maintenance. When she arrived, an attendant drove her to work and picked her up at the end of the day—free of charge. Lydia and her husband, Jack, soon discovered that being in the Land Rover database meant much more than service calls, however.

Lydia and Jack were invited to a reception at the golf club the following month, sponsored by the Land Rover agency. New in town, they were pleased to meet a number of the leading figures in the city at the reception, in addition to some of their nearby neighbors. Shortly thereafter, they decided to join the golf club.

The Land Rover database kept them busy. Their daughter Sarah was invited to a yacht club race, sponsored by the agency, and a year after they bought the car, Lydia and Jack traveled to Scotland to attend the world famous Land Rover Off Road driving school—a chance to get out of a rut and travel.

### Strategies that Reached Lydia

This is a book about marketing strategy. It explains how companies in the 1990s can adapt their marketing approaches to the new customers, new products, new delivery methods, and new information processing techniques of the 1990s.

We have seen the results of several strategies as we reviewed Lydia McCabe's experiences. What marketing problems and solutions lay behind these successful database programs?

## Cellular Phones

The problem: Customers switching to another provider to take advantage of a temporary price drop, a situation known as churning.

The solution: Use a database to build a bond of trust, loyalty, and service that will inoculate the customer against discounts.

## Land Rover Cars

The problem: Ensuring that existing customers buy another Land Rover when their three or four years of ownership is up, and that they recommend the car to their friends.

The solution: Use a customer database to provide super service; extensive surveys and communication; and to create events, clubs, and dialogue, making customers feel comfortable with Land Rover as an institution, besides being a super car. Make the transition to the next Land Rover a matter of course.

## The Message of This Book

The message of this book essentially is this: In most free-market transactions, both parties to a transaction, the buyer and the seller, profit. If you want transactions to happen, you must find out what the buyer considers profitable. It may not be a low price; it may be better service, information, reliability, higher quality, helpfulness, friendship, or simply personal recognition. Each buyer may have different subjective values. By discovering each buyer's personal requirements, you can better fill these and complete more transactions. In the process, you will make your customers happier, keep them buying for a lifetime, and make your company profitable.

This book also contains a second message, different from but related to the first: How do we use the information we have gained from building a relationship with our customers to locate and win over prospects who resemble our most profitable customers? The answer to this second question can be found in analytical work with our database: adding survey information, appending external data, doing modeling, and conducting controlled tests. The results of this analysis will help us to find new customers in a very cost-effective way.

A third message is built in to the other two: Detailed cost accounting should be performed for every step in database marketing. Calculation of lifetime customer value is an idea that everyone talks about, but few people actually ever compute. This has got to stop. Presented in this book is a fairly universal way of calculating lifetime value that should become standard practice in any database marketing situation. Using this method, all innovations in marketing can be tested before serious money is committed.

We will be elaborating on these themes throughout the rest of this book. In the meantime, let's return to Lydia McCabe and her experiences with database marketing.

## Grocery Shopping

A year ago February, Lydia and Jack both came down with the flu. Resting up in bed, Lydia decided to experiment with the new Grocery Express service widely advertised at the time. With both Lydia and Jack sick, the personal computer (PC) software for Grocery Express arrived at the perfect time. Both children watched as Lydia maneuvered her electronic shopping cart up and down the Grocery Express aisles, buying needed items.

Today, a year later, Grocery Express is a household fixture. Logging on to Grocery Express, Lydia enters a video supermarket, pushing her electronic shopping cart with her PC mouse. As she goes up one aisle and down the next, she can see the products displayed on each side—just like a regular supermarket. When she turns her mouse towards the cereal display, the boxes enlarge and fill up the screen. She clicks on a box of Kellogg's Frosted Flakes and clicks the Nutrition Information field. Looking at the calorie, fat, protein, and carbohydrate content, she makes a quick decision: "The kids are right. This is good stuff. I'll put two in the cart."

As two boxes jump into her electronic cart, a small cash register in the corner of her screen displays $6.14. She moves on to the meat department. Here she can pick up standard items—packaged chicken, pork chops, steaks, hamburger, or various cuts of roast beef—or, for something special, she can signal for a live butcher, which she does. The butcher discusses her needs with her and makes up a special order for her immediately. The special order drops into her cart, and the register jumps to $20.88.

As she rounds the last aisle, with a loaded cart, Lydia wonders: "Have I forgotten anything?" She has many clues to help her remember. A click of her mouse brings up last week's purchases. The items that she bought then but didn't buy this week are highlighted in yellow. "Aha, toilet paper." Another click brings up the weekly specials. If she sees something better than an item in the cart, a click puts the special into her cart. Another click sends any unwanted items back to the shelf.

To leave the store, she enters her secret personal identification number, and verifies the total by retyping it herself. The complete order will be waiting for her on the porch, as she requested, when she gets home. Delivery charge? $9.95—all charged to her credit card.

Lydia is now wedded to the system. She doesn't know what she would do without it. All told, it saves her about two hours a week—hours that she can spend with her family. When she is really busy, she can just make a phone call and say "Send me the same as last week, except for the salmon." Grocery Express has her whole history in its database. Grocery shopping takes her about 10 minutes a week.

## Gift Service

Lydia has more than 20 birthday and Christmas presents to buy, wrap, and dispatch to parents, grandparents, brothers, sisters, nieces and nephews, neighbors, and friends, not counting Jack and the children.

More than a year ago, trying to be more organized, she responded to a direct mail offer from Harald's department store about its Family Club program. She spoke with Andrea, a personal gift counselor there. Together, they collected information on the names, addresses, sexes, and ages of all the friends and relatives that Lydia was responsible for. Lydia also told Andrea about her relatives' lifestyles and interests. All this information was tucked away into Lydia's record in Harald's customer database.

Since that time, every month, Lydia gets a letter from Andrea reminding her of the upcoming birthdays. Included is Andrea's list of suggested gifts for each person. If Lydia does nothing, the presents and birthday cards are delivered by UPS to each recipient, charged to her store credit card. She can cancel any gift by checking a box and returning the letter. Or she can call Andrea and change the addresses, recipients, or gifts.

The Family Club service is made possible by Harald's customer marketing database. Through this database, Andrea handles 2,000 different clients similar to Lydia. Andrea and five other gift counselors at Harald's together generate more than $5 million a year in sales.

The database, of course, does all the thinking and heavy lifting. Using information furnished by Lydia, inventory reports from the merchandise department, and creative ideas from the marketing department, the database automatically generates a suggested gift for every person on Lydia's list. The software also draws on profiles developed for Lydia's recipients, Andrea's ideas, and database records showing Lydia's previous gifts to each recipient.

How useful is this service for Lydia? "A godsend," she replied recently. How important is this service to Harald's? "We can point to a 12 percent growth in sales to Family Club members from purchases they made unrelated to the Family Club system!" explained the marketing manager. The club itself has proved to be a major winner.

*Home Entertainment*

Years ago, Jack used to swing by Blockbuster Video to rent a video several nights a week. No longer. Nowadays, when Jack and Lydia want to watch a movie, they use their telephone and a program from U S West. By direct connection from the TV, they can call up and see any film in the immense Warner Brother's video library. They never have the frustration of finding the latest titles checked out of the video store. Since U S West has all these titles on disk, thousands of people can watch the same film the same night—but on different schedules—every evening. The U S West database knows what Jack and Lydia like to watch. How? Because they answered a survey. Titles of interest to them can be previewed on their TV.

## Is This Buck Rogers?

Lydia may seem to be ahead of her time. But virtually everything that she is doing is a marketing reality in the 1990s or near future. This is where we are going today, spurred on by several facts:

- Technology is moving faster and faster. No one can keep track of where it is going, or even where it is today. Computers and software are becoming so advanced that it is possible to say, "If you can imagine it, it probably already exists."
- Affluent consumers in developed countries are firmly in charge of the free market system. They are asking for new services and products, and entrepreneurs are listening. The race is on to find out what consumers want and to give it to them.
- Marketing is changing with the customer. Providers of services are realizing that they must run very fast, providing new products and services, and new ways of delivering their products, or they will soon be swept aside.

## What Customers Want

What has been happening to Lydia is that the companies competing to meet her needs are doing so increasingly through database marketing. Instead of making one product and trying to sell it, they are finding out what their customers want, and selling them that. It is customer-based marketing. But it is really more than that.

Customers' wants can be summed up in a few general concepts:

- Recognition: Customers want to be recognized as individuals, with individual desires and preferences. They like being called by name.
- Service: Customers want thoughtful service provided by sales staff, delivery personnel, billing, customer service, and technical support.
- Diversity: People want a wide variety of products and are no longer content with mass market merchandise. Providers need to find a way to offer a huge assortment of styles, shapes, colors, fragrances, and sizes to meet diverse customer requirements.
- Information: Customers are more literate today than ever before. They read the labels. They look at fat content, calories, fiber, sodium, calcium, sugar, and protein—and they base their purchases on what they read. Technical information is as important to many of them as the product itself.
- Identification: People like to identify themselves with their products (their cars) and their suppliers (their country clubs and condominiums). Companies can build on that need for identification by providing customers with a friendly, helpful institution to identify with.

## The Importance of Price

In this enumeration, I haven't mentioned price. Of course, price is today—as it has always been, with some exceptions—the most important single factor influencing customers in their product selection. When Compaq drastically lowered its prices in 1992, the company sold more computers per month than ever before in its history, and turned its bottom line around.

Drastic price reductions, however, also can be self defeating. The airline industry went through a series of destructive price wars that not only eliminated some carriers, but also brought huge losses to major airlines. In most highly competitive industries, constant price reductions cannot be a successful long-range strategy. Companies today are seeking a way of building up customer loyalty and reducing attrition so that drastic price reductions are not necessary to maintain or increase their market share.

Central to such a strategy is relationship marketing, or, as we call it in this book, database marketing. The idea is this: The company collects in a relational computer database as much information about each customer as it finds relevant and profitable for successful marketing strategy. Access to the information is provided to all parts of the company involved in customer contact and to those who design products, services, or marketing programs. The database is used to assist in the following:

- Providing knowledgeable customer service
- Fashioning products and services tailored to individual preferences

- Developing individualized targeted marketing programs
- Conducting one-on-one dialogues with each customer
- Enlisting loyal customers in referral programs
- Classifying customers by interests and profitability so as to lavish special attention on those who are most likely to build the bottom line
- Devising effective marketing programs to new prospects
... and much, much more.

From the earliest days, merchants have known that customers return to them again and again for reasons other than simply low prices. People like helpful, friendly service. People like a clean, well-organized store. There is often more to the experience of shopping than the acquisition of goods. People go to a mall to learn what there is, to be amused, educated, informed. They go to see and meet other people. When they find a store they like, they will return. What do they like about a particular store? It may be the items for sale, of course. It also may be the helpful and friendly attitude of the salespeople.

The first step in relationship marketing is recognizing that there is more to customer desires than price alone. The second step is finding out what those desires are, and how they can be satisfied by the actions of the merchant. In a small store, the owner can find out these things very directly by talking to his customers on a daily basis. If they don't like a product or service, he will quickly sense this. If they want something that he does not have, this can be easily learned.

From 1960 to 1990, many popular products were delivered by mass marketing. Suppliers figured out what the vast majority of people wanted, made it well and inexpensively, and advertised it widely in print and on TV. It worked. Mass marketing created intense competition, low prices, and a wide variety of goods. Mass marketing was good: It increased real consumer income through better products at lower prices.

During this same time, however, retailers, dealers, agencies, hospitals, insurance companies, and other service providers, have become so huge through successful mass marketing that they have lost the ability to touch their customers and learn their views. They need a way to accumulate, manipulate, and extract knowledge from the data on hundreds of thousands or millions of customers. In earlier days store owners were able to accumulate, manipulate, and extract information about their customers intuitively in their heads. Database marketing today provides that same result through computer technology.

Database marketing, as described in this book, and in my earlier book *The Complete Database Marketer* (Chicago: Probus Publishing Company, 1991), is primarily aimed at making customers happy and loyal. It is built on the theory that if—in addition to providing a quality product at a reasonable price—you can find a way to provide recognition, personal service, attention, diversity, and information to your customers, you will build a bond of loyalty that will keep them coming back for a lifetime. Database marketing, therefore, is a way of providing service that is focused on the customer, not on the product.

Modern computer technology is used to create a relational database that stores a great deal of information on each household (or company, in the case of a business-to-business product). Such information includes:

- The client's name and address
- Complete purchase history
- Customer service calls, complaints, returns, inquiries
- Ongoing marketing promotions and responses
- Results of customer surveys
- Household (or business) demographics: income, age, children, home value and type, etc.

Each customer record in the database, in other words, permits the marketer to know almost everything about the customer that is relevant to the product or service the company provides.

## Where We Are Going

Although database marketing was invented in the late 1970s, cost reductions for computerized data storage and retrieval made it an active part of major U.S. corporations only in the late 1980s. The National Center for Database Marketing held its first conference in 1988. Since that time it has educated more than 1,000 executives per year in its sessions. Scores of other conferences on the same subject have been held by the Direct Marketing Association, Direct Marketing to Business, *Target Marketing* magazine, the *Canadian Direct Marketing News*, and others. The first World Database Marketing Seminar was held in Tokyo in October 1992, and similar events have been held in Europe. Most large corporations, and many small ones, have begun building customer databases.

If you want a short definition of database marketing, it is this:

> Managing a computerized relational database system that collects relevant data about our customers and prospects that enables us to provide better service and establish a long-term relationship with them. Successful use of the database has the effect of building loyalty, reducing attrition, and increasing customer satisfaction and sales. The database is

used to target offerings to customers and prospects, enabling us to send the right message at the right time to the right people—increasing our response rate per marketing dollar, lowering our cost per order, building our business, and increasing our profits.

*The Complete Database Marketer* explains the concepts involved in database marketing: history; hardware; software; Recency, Frequency, Monetary (RFM) analysis; construction of profiles; clustering; demographics; psychographics; telemarketing; fulfillment; economics; and many other key subjects that every database marketer must know.

In the three years since *The Complete Database Marketer* was written, it is obvious that one factor above all is missing from database marketing as it is being practiced in the early 1990s. That factor is strategy. We have learned how to build customer databases, how to store information, and how to retrieve it at will. What most companies have not yet learned is how to make money with a database. That is the main objective of this book. In these pages we will show how companies can successfully build profitable relationships with their customers. We will explain, at some length, exactly how to compute customer lifetime value, and how to use it to evaluate strategies before thousands or millions of dollars are wasted.

## A Sense of Balance

Something else is needed, which this book provides: a sense of balance. Database marketing is not helpful for every product and service. There are some products for which it will not work and should not be attempted. In these pages you will find many examples of failure, as well as methods of determining in advance whether your great strategy will succeed or fail.

This book, therefore, concentrates on the strategy that underlies database marketing. Those of you who read *The Complete Database Marketer* are familiar with the distinction between constructors and creators. A constructor is interested in building a database: cleaning the names, designing the format, and providing instant access and data retrieval. A creator develops strategies for making money with the database. You need both types for database marketing, of course. But creators are the hardest to find.

There is a reason for this. Database construction has become an honorable profession. Many service bureaus have developed a good deal of valuable experience in building databases for clients. When they are doing this, the job is much the same whether the database is for baby food, insurance, software, or automobiles. Creating a successful database strategy, however, has proved to be much more difficult. The strategy for each of these four industries, for example, is quite different.

## Advanced Marketing Strategies that Reached Lydia

Let's return to Lydia McCabe and sum up the additional strategies that have been employed to make her happy and loyal.

### *Grocery Shopping*

The problem: Providing a service for a standard task (grocery shopping) that stands out from similar services and keeping customers by providing personal service, not discounts.

The solution: Stay ahead of the competition by constantly improving an extremely high-tech software ordering system, linked to a database that gives customers real value (memory of previous transactions) that they cannot get in any other way.

### *Gift Service*

The problem: Increasing the customer retention rate and annual sales to existing customers in a cost-effective way.

The solution: Use a database to open up a new method of selling products and services that already exist by providing a service to customers that does not currently exist for them, and that will save them time and build their loyalty to the store at the same time.

### *Home Entertainment*

The problem: Telephone lines connected to every customer in the country are costly to install and maintain. They have, however, the potential to deliver much more than conversations. There is a world of profit for the company that can build on this investment by providing extended services.

The solution: Use technology to deliver a useful product and a database to increase its relevance to each customer.

## Conclusion

Each strategy is really quite different from the other ones, and is also quite different from scores of other strategies that are discussed throughout the rest of this book.

Database marketing is here. It is being widely adopted. Your company is already making moves in this direction—one important step is the acquisition of this book. Your next step must be the development of a marketing strategy that uses a database. No one will serve this to you on a silver platter. You must think it up yourself. This book, however, should provide you with some ideas.

Database marketing is not just a way to increase profits by reducing costs and selling more products and services, although that is, and must be, one of its results. It is a tool that provides management with customer information. That information is used in various ways to increase customer retention and increase customer acquisition rates—the essence of business strategy. The database provides both the raw information you need and a measurement device essential for the evaluation of strategy.

Viewed from the customers' point of view, database marketing is a way of making customers happy and of providing them recognition, service, friendship, and information. In return, they will reward you with loyalty, reduction in attrition, and increased sales. Genuine customer satisfaction is the goal and hallmark of satisfactory database marketing. If you are doing things right, your customers will be glad that you have a database and that you have included them in it. They will appreciate the things that you do for them. If you can develop and carry out strategies that bring this situation about, you are a master marketer. You will keep your customers for life and be happy in your work. You will have made the world a better place to live.

# 1

## Strategic Database Marketing: An Overview

*I do believe that database marketing, if it's done correctly, is a discipline of its own ... What distinguishes database marketing from direct is the amount of up-front work that has to be done to come to grips with who your customers are and who your customers are not. I think direct marketing is a form of mass marketing with a name on it, which may offend some, but I think it's true. Database marketing is true individual marketing in which we try to come to grips with the needs and wants of individual customers, and then try to come up with products and services most likely to meet those needs and wants on an individual basis.*

*—John Travis, Hudson's Bay Company*

**D**atabase marketing has arrived. Recognized as a good idea in the late 1980s, it has become a growing reality in the 1990s. Most large corporations now have a position with a title like director of database marketing. That doesn't mean, however, that they are practicing database marketing. It means that corporate America has discovered that this marketing method exists, and that it holds out the promise of building customer loyalty, increasing sales, reducing marketing costs, and reaping bigger profits. This book focuses on what it takes to get from the concept to the reality of profitable database marketing.

The fact is that database marketing is difficult to accomplish. It needs a number of basic inputs that are tough to arrange in most corporations. Among them are the following:

- Strategic Plan: A long-range creative plan for maintaining an ongoing relationship with customers needs to build loyalty, reduce attrition, and increase sales. Most marketers are still learning how to create and sell such plans. Few understand how to justify them in terms of customer lifetime value.

- Long-Range Budget: Successful database marketing doesn't happen overnight. Two to three years is a minimum time for database marketing, in most cases, to affect customer behavior. The budget usually has to be carved out of some other corporate function, and the carving process is painful.
- Corporatewide Commitment: Maintaining a relationship with customers takes more than just newsletters and statement stuffers. Database marketing, when done correctly, involves customer service, technical support, advertising, marketing, and sales, to mention just a few areas. Database marketing requires the integration of a number of different marketing tactics into a broad system focused on the customer.
- Leadership and Teamwork: Marketing must provide strong leadership and build a team that includes internal units like management information systems (MIS), customer service, and sales plus, in many cases, an external direct response agency, a service bureau, a telemarketing service, and a fulfillment house.

## The Two Uses for Database Marketing

Database marketing involves building a computer database that contains information about customers and can be easily accessed. The two key uses for database marketing are:

- Marketing to Customers: Maintaining a close relationship with customers by providing them with special services and recognition, resulting in increased loyalty, reduced attrition, and increased sales.
- Marketing to Prospects: Using the knowledge developed in the database to understand customer motivation, leading to finding prospects that match the profile of profitable customers, resulting in expanding the customer base in a cost-effective way.

These two uses are illustrated in Figure 1-1.

Every marketing database is distinct and is used in quite different ways by various companies. These dissimilarities are due to the varying imagination and skill levels of the marketers in each corporation, not just to varying circumstances in each company and diverse competitive environments.

The fact that these differences occur makes database marketing a much more difficult skill to learn than direct marketing. While direct marketing is often complex, each campaign usually stands on its own. In database marketing, each marketing initiative builds on previous customer contacts and usually influences the course of subsequent customer retention and sales.

**Figure 1-1: Two Uses for Database Marketing**

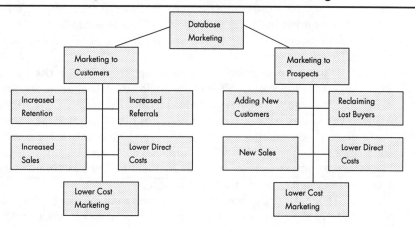

Database marketing involves two very different types of professionals:

- Constructors: People who know about computers and software; who understand merge/purge, postal pre-sort, segmentation, data enhancement, coding, modeling, and profiling. These people are fascinated with personal computers, cross tabs, relational databases, and data management. You really can't do database marketing unless somebody understands these things.
- Creators: People who understand the motivation of customers and how to use a database to build relationships with them, leading to increased loyalty and repeat sales. These people are fascinated with the strategy and tactics of database marketing: learning about customer lifetime value; Recency, Frequency, Monetary (RFM) analysis; affinity tables; and attrition analysis. They come up with the great ideas that create profits. You really can't be successful at database marketing unless you have at least one very capable creator who has authority and a long-term budget.

Both of these professional types must understand the data needed for successful database marketing and the objectives of the program.

## Why Things Are Moving Slowly

Despite the widespread acceptance of the concept of database marketing, there is very little database marketing being done. There are several reasons for this:

- Construction problems. It should not take more than six months to build a functioning customer database containing a million names. In fact, most companies take two or three years to build one. The delays occur because of uncertainties concerning the location, budgets, and staff.

  *Location:* Most companies begin by wanting to build their databases in-house. After they start, they find that their MIS departments are not skilled at database construction, and often put the marketing department at the end of a long queue of program revisions. They also find that personal computer solutions tend to involve much more costly marketing staff time than they had anticipated. As a result, they eventually turn to outside service bureaus. By this time, two or three years have been wasted exploring other alternatives.

  *Budgets:* Database marketing requires a minimum of three years to show real payoff in terms of increased customer loyalty, reduced attrition, and increased sales. The budget for such activities has to come from somewhere, such as the advertising budget. Funds are seldom transferred without a fight. It is a catch-22: you can't demonstrate the value without a long-term effort; you can't justify the long-term budget without some immediate results. You must have some short-run successes or you will never make it.

  *Staff:* There is a shortage of experienced database marketing people. Even the directors of database marketing in most corporations today are, of necessity, retreads from other disciplines. These people need time to understand their jobs and develop winning strategies. It can't be done overnight.

- Strategy Problems. There are a lot of very clever marketers who know how to develop individual tactics involving dialogues with customers, loyalty building programs, referral programs, and surveys. What is rare are people who can put a number of these tactics into a long-range coherent strategy. Without a strategy, however, a marketing database is all dressed up with no place to go. Developing a strategy has proved to be much more difficult than the rather understandable process of building the database. It is this strategy development process that forms the central theme of this book.

## Understanding Customer Lifetime Value

The key to strategy development is customer lifetime value analysis. This method is the standard by which strategies can be appraised before serious money is spent on them. There are established procedures involving control groups and test groups that permit careful investigation of each strategy initiative in terms of its effect on customer lifetime value.

Database marketing looks at customers as long-term assets. Lifetime value is used to weigh changes in the value of these assets. In brief, customer lifetime value is the net present value of the profit that you will realize on the average new customer during a given number of years. The number of years over which it is measured varies with the industry and the product. For example, it is longer for a utility than for a dress manufacturer.

Database marketing can augment lifetime value in five ways:

- Retention Rate: It is easier to keep existing customers than to find new ones. Customers, however, tend to slip away. It is possible to create strategies that increase the retention rate. This increase builds lifetime value and, hence, boosts profits.
- Referral Rate: Existing customers influence others to become customers. Word of mouth is a powerful marketing tool. Carefully crafted database marketing strategies can influence this process and expand the referral rate through a system of rewards and motivations.
- Sales Volume: Loyal customers tend to buy more. They will buy upgrades, companion products, and new products. Database marketing can influence the total buying patterns of existing customers. The key is making the right offer to the right people at the right time. You can do this by learning more about individual customers and using that knowledge appropriately.
- Direct Costs: In many cases, database marketing can reduce direct costs by changing the channels of distribution or affecting the renewal process. Insurance companies, credit card companies, and cellular phone companies have found that proactive database marketing not only improves the retention rate, but also reduces their direct costs. Software companies routinely sell upgrades to existing customers, retaining 90 percent of the revenue, while the same product sold through retailers yields only 50 percent or less.
- Marketing Costs: Database marketing often makes it possible to reduce marketing costs to existing customers or prospects selected by modeling and profiling. Companies that routinely mail millions of offers a year find that profits increase by mailing to targeted prospects, just a fraction of their lists. Prospects are chosen by RFM analysis, testing, and modeling. Strategies can be tested on a small scale before the rollout.

## How Strategy Is Developed

Database marketing strategy begins with understanding the customers. All marketers try to do that, of course, but database marketers have an edge.

They are able to store in their computer databases a vast amount of information about each customer that can be used in marketing operations. This information includes:

- Purchase behavior (dates, dollars, products, responses)
- Demographics (age, income, family size, etc.)
- Location (city, state, ZIP, market area, proximity to dealer)
- Opinions (survey results, complaints, inquiries, etc.)

### Analyzing the Customer Database

The beauty of a customer database is the information that you can extract from it with sophisticated analytical techniques. Here are some of the methods that are covered in this book:

- Ad Hoc Queries: A good database can permit marketers to ask any question that comes into their heads, and receive the answer on their personal computers in a few seconds. The days when programmers were needed to produce hard copy reports are about over in database marketing. Ad hoc queries enable marketers to do "what if" scenarios, putting data into lifetime value tables and gaining real knowledge from the wealth of detail that is at their fingertips.
- Recency, Frequency, Monetary (RFM) Analysis: This analysis provides the ability to predict, with some precision, the response rate and dollar sales to customers of a promotional offer before the offer is mailed. The significance of this ability is that groups whose predicted response is low will not receive any mailings at all. High responding groups will be targets of promotions more often. The result: lower costs and lower total revenue, but higher profits.
- Customer Profiling: The database makes it possible to deal one-on-one with individual customers. As part of that process, it is also useful to segment the customer base into affinity groups, lifestyle groups, and geographic groups. As a result, customers find that communications from your company are more relevant to their needs. This builds loyalty and increased sales, and also reduces marketing costs.
- Testing and Evaluation: Database marketing is a highly accountable art. Skilled marketers use their databases to set up control groups and test groups. The test groups receive promotional offers, telephone calls, newsletters, membership cards, surveys, and other communications. The exactly matched control groups do not receive these communications. By comparing the purchasing activity of the two groups, it is possible to know precisely the effect that each promotion has on sales

volume, customer retention, referral rates, etc. This type of analysis can be done only with a database.

- Customer Lifetime Value Calculation: The final step in any evaluation of strategy is to measure its effect on customer lifetime value. A standard method for calculation of this measure is explained in Chapter 3, Lifetime Value: The Criterion of Strategy. It can be used for all marketing databases whether for consumers or business-to-business.

The key use of customer lifetime value is to show how given strategies affect long-term profits. Strategies have revenue effects (such as increasing annual sales or retention rate) and cost effects (for customer service calls, mailings, premiums, discounts, etc.). Each of these effects can be shown on a lifetime value chart, both in terms of the immediate impact and the long-term impact. Using such charts, marketers can calculate whether a new strategy could work before they actually test it. Whether it will work, of course, depends on the effectiveness of execution, and whether the planning process was adequate.

Customer lifetime value is a measure of the net present value of future profits to be received from the average customer over a period of several years. While the wording sounds quite financial and formidable, the calculation method (using a spread sheet) is quite simple and within the grasp of any marketer. The process goes this way:

"If we issue membership cards to our customers, track sales to cardholders, and give special benefits to members who use their cards, the program will have certain costs and certain benefits."

The costs will be:
- Card issuance
- Promotion to get members to use the cards
- Capturing and storing purchase information
- Premiums given for card use

The benefits can be estimated as well:
- Increase in the retention rate as cardholders accumulate equity
- Increase in annual sales to card members
- Increase in referrals of new customers by cardholders

The estimated costs and benefits are entered into a lifetime value chart that shows how lifetime value will change as a result of the program. In some cases, such programs will decrease lifetime value, because the costs outweigh the benefits. That can be calculated. In such situations, the strategy is a loser, and should not be introduced. In other cases, the lifetime value goes down in the short run (from the promotional costs for the strategy) and up in the long run. The issue then is whether the company can afford to wait.

Database marketing to existing customers must be based on incremental profits. In most cases, goods are being sold through awareness advertising, display in stores, and general availability. The purpose of database marketing is to make incremental increases in these sales and profits. Properly stimulated with database activities, customers will be retained longer, spend more money, and refer friends and neighbors.

Since database marketing is incremental, it must be justified on incremental grounds: not on how much customers will buy, but on *how much more* they will buy as a result of the database activities. This incremental analysis is difficult, but essential. It is the reason why lifetime value is so important.

### Benefits to the Customer

In free market transactions, both parties make a profit—both the buyer and the seller—because they receive something that they value more than what they give up. To assure many transactions (sales), therefore, marketers need to be sure that their potential customers are making what they consider to be a profit.

In today's world, profit for the customer is not necessarily measured in dollars. For most of today's busy customers, time—even leisure time—has a high value. In many cases, customers value convenience and time-saving delivery processes more than a lower price. Database marketing can help determine the best delivery method for different groups of customers, and, in some cases, can be the vehicle by which the products are delivered.

As mentioned earlier, today's customers also place a high value on such benefits as recognition, service, diversity, information, and identification.

To meet these needs, the database provides a number of useful techniques that help to build the customer dialogue. Among these are:

- Event-Driven Programs: Marketing databases can be programmed to send announcements of affinity products whenever a particular product is ordered, or to create very personal communications. Department stores may send letters to a husband before his wife's birthday, suggesting the perfect gift—based on data supplied by the wife when she made some other purchase. Or, to take an example from the insurance industry:

"As you know, Mr. Sawyer, you have been a customer of ours since 1976. The cash value of your policy has now grown to more than $28,000. In view of this ..."

- Satisfaction Surveys: Companies have been conducting customer satisfaction surveys for many years. In most cases, the results of the surveys are discarded once they are tabulated. With marketing databases, however, the survey results can be stored in the computer and used to build a relationship with each individual customer. The overall results are less important than the use of the survey to open up a dialogue with each respondent.

## Why Databases Fail

It is not all fun and games in the database marketing world. There have been some notable failures involving hundreds of millions of dollars, plus scores of smaller database projects that have not panned out as planned.

This book provides a large number of case studies in retailing, packaged goods, financial services, and business-to-business enterprises that document the successes and the failures. More importantly, this book includes an analysis of why databases fail, and what you, as a marketer, can do to avoid failure in your work.

Failures come from both faulty planning and faulty execution. Planning success comes from creative strategy development based on sharp-pencil lifetime value calculation. Execution success comes from a variety of detailed steps including:

- Outsourcing most database functions to experienced professionals
- Building your first database rapidly, on an appropriate scale so that you learn by experience before major mistakes are made
- Building a database team with a forceful leader who has a long-term budget

## The Emergence of an Industry

Database marketing came about in the 1980s independently in a dozen different places: American Express, American Airlines, Reader's Digest, insurance companies, and garden tool manufacturers, to mention a few. Wherever it occurred, the idea was basically the same: find a way to use the power of modern computer technology to begin one-on-one dialogues with thousands of customers, to learn what they want, and to supply them with individualized products and services that meet their needs.

Based on the idea that it is easier and more profitable to keep the customers you already have than to search for new ones, the concept worked. Many of those who tried it found that a little money spent on building a database, in customer correspondence, surveys, customer and technical support services with toll-free telephone numbers, recognition, and personalized fulfillment could build loyalty, reduce attrition, and make a major long-term improvement in their bottom line.

It wasn't until 1987 that many in the industry looked around, realized what was happening, and gave it a generally accepted name: database marketing. In that year the National Center for Database Marketing was established by Skip Andrew to "provide a forum for database marketing experts to exchange ideas, stimulating growth in innovative applications of database technology." Now owned by Cowles Business Media, the twice annual conferences attract more than 1,000 people a year—the top database marketers, suppliers of services, and newcomers to the business.

While several successful customer databases have been constructed, there are many that have been built but never used to increase profits. Lacking is a sense of how to develop effective strategies to turn a profit with relationship marketing. That is the central purpose of this book: to outline the method whereby marketers can develop strategies for using a database to build relationships with customers that will make the customers happy and loyal, reduce attrition, boost sales, and increase profits.

# 2

## "The Vision Thing"

*We used to look for the unique selling proposition (USP) to articulate an important feature that distinguished a product from all others. Today, similar technologies and bottom line pressures have hampered innovation. It's harder to discover the USP in a product that has no discernible difference from its competitors.*

*Yet, even if products have become blander, there is still inherent drama in brands. But brands must do more than articulate their tangible benefits. Today, the unique selling proposition is borne of the consumer, not the product. It answers the question, "What are the needs of my target audience that could be met by my brand?" This is our key to successful advertising.*
    —*Ronald J. Davis, CEO of Biggs/Gilmore Communications*

**W**e have all heard that mass marketing in its traditional sense is no longer as effective as it was. Everyone is saying it. Mass marketing is changing to "integrated marketing." But why is it changing? What happened to it and the comfortable world that we built up around it?

We also have heard that database marketing is starting to replace some mass marketing. But how does database marketing work? And why is it better, in some situations, than mass marketing?

This chapter is aimed at answering these questions. We will be taking a broad look at the customer's situation today, in contrast with the situation in earlier times decades and centuries ago. We are going to attempt to place database marketing in its historical perspective as an evolutionary forward step. This chapter is what former President George Bush would have called "the vision thing."

Compared to the rest of the chapters, which describe practical applications of database strategy, this chapter is filled with history and philosophy, and my personal views, which may well be wrong. Personally, I love to explore the ideas of the past, wonder about how we got where we are now, and speculate about what future generations will think about what we marketers are doing today. So that is what we will be doing.

Let's settle back, and view ourselves as painted figures on a grand historical canvas leading from the earliest Sumerian traders of 5000 B.C., through the Industrial Revolution, past the electric age, the automobile age, the nuclear age, the jet age, the computer age, and into the 21st century.

## What Drives Industry?

Let's begin with a basic question: What drives industry: production or marketing? In general, are products manufactured first and then marketed? Or are they marketed, and then manufactured to fill the needs of the market?

This is an important question for economists and for marketers. It goes to the heart of the whole philosophy of marketing, and particularly of database marketing. To answer it, let's go back to the Industrial Revolution—an epoch that changed the production system and led to our present affluence. Let's examine the role of marketing in this revolution.

### The Industrial Revolution

For thousands of years before 1760, productivity in industry and agriculture was stagnant. Roughly the same number of bushels of grain per acre or bolts of cloth per worker per year were produced in A.D. 1700 as were produced in 1700 B.C. Production stayed the same from year to year and from century to century.

In the period after 1760, however, an unusual series of events occurred in England that changed the world forever. For the first time, entrepreneurs began to combine significant amounts of capital—machinery and raw materials—with labor, in large factories devoted to the mass production of goods. By 1800, thousands of people were organized into enterprises that mass-produced cotton thread, iron products, and other items.

For the first time in history, mass production, making extensive use of capital, increased productivity and brought the price of consumer goods down dramatically. It led to England's dominance of world trade for a century. Due to this system, the average person in developed countries today can expect to live at a much higher level than the average person has ever been able to live since the world began.

Why have we become so wealthy in the last two centuries? Is it our production methods or our marketing skills? Most writers have concentrated on the factories as the places that have produced the wealth. In concentrating on products alone, however, they have overlooked the main reason that the Industrial Revolution was possible: the expansion of the market system and trade.

Adam Smith pointed out in 1776 that mass production was the product of the division of labor: many people working together successfully in a common enterprise, producing much more than the same people could produce working independently. But Adam Smith said something else: "The division of labor is limited by the extent of the market." Where the market is small, the gains from the division of labor are correspondingly small. The larger the market, the more efficiencies are possible, the greater productivity, the greater profits, the greater affluence.

Marketing is the key. Producing a million pounds of cotton thread would not have been possible if marketers had not found a way to sell a million pounds of cotton thread. Marketing is not something that happens after the goods are produced. Marketing is the reason the goods are produced in the first place.

The reason why cellular phones, fax machines, VCRs, and personal computers have been manufactured in the tens of millions is not primarily because of the activity of inventors and investors—although they are essential to the process—but primarily because of the activities of the marketers that have made the public aware of the products, created the demand for them, and set up the distribution channels.

New and unknown products—plus new versions of old ones—have to be introduced to the public in a way that creates the orders for the factories. Marketing comes first.

### The U.S. Market

From 1900 to the present time, the United States has had the largest single market on earth. Everywhere else, political systems or physical boundaries combined with poor transportation to limit most markets to comparatively small areas. The United States has spent the last 200 years breaking down barriers and building the waterways, railroads, telegraph, telephone and electronic communications systems, superhighways, airports, and massive delivery systems that link all parts of our market together in a freely competitive order.

The result has been the greatest outpouring of production, affluence, and personal freedom ever known. The process has not been directed or controlled by government. Instead, the driving force has been free competitive market activity—each entrepreneur trying to satisfy the public best so as to realize a personal dream.

Marketing has been the means whereby the division of labor has expanded. Individual marketing heroes have provided the leadership. From 1812 to 1860, Frederic Tudor, one of our first mass marketers, built his fortune by shipping blocks of ice from Boston to the south and to the outside world. He taught the middle class how to store ice and to preserve food. He changed the way people ate and drank. A hundred years later, another hero, Frank Perdue, taught us, "It takes a tough man to make a tender chicken." His chicken empire was not so much a triumph of production—which was superb—but of marketing, which was even better. Americans as a people are master marketers. Our marketers have educated the public, and provided the means whereby fantastic new products can be developed, mass produced, and delivered at lower and lower prices.

## The Growth in Mass Marketing

From 1950 to 1980, mass marketing predominated. The growth of television built on the solid foundation of national print ads and radio to create mass audiences for national advertising. National brands, sold in supermarkets, department stores, fast food restaurants, and franchised outlets everywhere, homogenized the contents of the American home. Mass marketing made possible mass production. This combination resulted in a constant reduction in the cost and improvement in the quality of most products, and a vast increase in the real income of the average American consumer, as shown in Figure 2-1.

### Figure 2-1: Per Capita Disposable Income 1960–1990

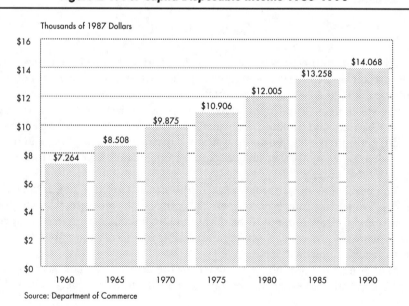

Source: Department of Commerce

The growth in real income shown in Figure 2-1 conceals a very real trend that is hard to display in graphic form; the products that Americans were buying with their income became significantly more efficient and sophisticated.

Products today work better. Automobiles work much better than they did 40 years ago. Tires last longer and rarely get flat. Toothpaste has reduced the problem of cavities. Television sets rarely need repair. Photocopying machines, fax machines, computers, and air conditioning make offices much pleasanter to work in and much more productive. Life expectancy has grown. Many diseases, including pneumonia, measles, mumps, chicken pox, diphtheria, tuberculosis, smallpox, and malaria, have been virtually eliminated from the average person's life.

One result of this productive system is that the middle class has grown from being about 15 percent of the population in 1920 to being 85 percent of the population in 1990. While a significant proportion of the American people still lives at the poverty line, the vast majority of Americans are affluent, compared to their grandparents. They have the money to buy the products produced by American industry.

We have arrived at the situation where more than 80 percent of the American households have discretionary income: not all their take-home pay is required to pay for food, clothing, rent, and transportation. People's basic needs are met. They want something more.

## What the Market Consists of Today

We are not at the end of a long evolutionary process. Instead, we are today right in the middle of a vast program of change leading us on to new levels of wealth and affluence. Our market is still expanding. Look at some of the features of this market:

- New products are being created at an accelerating rate. If you look at the U.S. market in the last two centuries, there is a steady acceleration in innovation. Figure 2-2, a graph of patents issued during the past 200 years, shows a staggering increase in patents during the 1980s, which some have called the "decade of greed." There were more patents issued from 1980 to 1990 than in the first 100 years of our nation.

Before 1850, we began our age of steam and mechanized agriculture. Early progress in industry was slow as we concentrated on exploring and extending our nation over the entire continent. The Industrial Revolution was just beginning to take root here. From 1850 to 1900, we developed electricity, railroads, photography, and the telephone. From 1900 to 1950,

**Figure 2-2: Patents Issued 1790–1990**

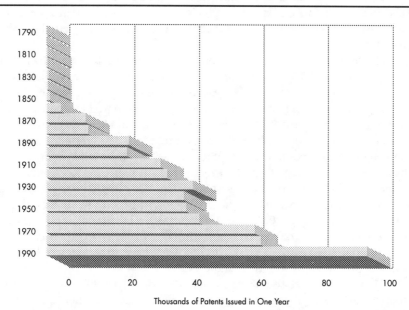

Thousands of Patents Issued in One Year

the automobile and radio radically changed our way of living. From 1950 to 1990, the progress was amazing: development of the television, VCR, fax, photocopier, jet travel, interstate highway, and computer; tremendous advances in medicine, nuclear power, and space travel.

The pace of new product introduction and expansion is staggering. It is not possible for anyone to keep on top of even a small percentage of the new developments today. As a result of this constant innovation, the market is much more complex for the consumer than it once was.

- The world is far more impersonal than it used to be. As Frank Rizzo, the late mayor of Philadelphia, once said, "The streets of Philadelphia are safe. It's only the people that make them unsafe." Everywhere we look today, we face an increasingly impersonal and unfriendly world. In our anxiety to provide freedom and equal treatment to all races, nationalities, religions, and sexual preferences, we have tended to lose a sense of values, belonging, identification, and family. Children become sexually active in their teens and become independent of their parents. Food stamps and welfare are always available if children want to leave home. The elderly don't expect their children to take care of them.

The public schools have, in some cases, become places of violence and fear. Drugs and guns are everywhere. Government grows more powerful and more intrusive in the interest of advancing equality and protecting minorities.

Most of these changes are caused by well intentioned programs and policies created by legal and democratic means. In the process, however, they have tended to reduce the authority of parents and leave us without some of the institutions that once held Americans together: the family, the church, the school, and neighborhood businesses. People are looking for something to identify with in a world without strong family ties and local institutions.

- Consumers have very little time. In most households today, the adults all are working. There are few people who have the leisure to shop around to find the latest products at the lowest prices. People search for repair personnel who will work without someone having to take a day off from work to wait for them. The choice of products is usually conducted in an atmosphere of lack of information and ignorance. Leisure time has a high value to most people. They will pay money to avoid having to waste it in the search for products and services.

## What Motivates Customers

To summarize what we have discovered: We have affluent consumers, most of whom work very hard, have little time to shop, and who expect and are prepared to pay handsomely, for new, high quality products.

To understand the market, we must understand the customers. What is motivating them to buy, or not buy?

- Customers buy products to reduce uneasiness. Why, after all, does anyone buy anything? There is one basic reason that is always true: People purchase products because they think that their life will be better with the products than it was without them. This is true of both consumer or business customers. They don't know that their life will be better with the products. They just make that assumption. Sometimes they are wrong.
- The value of products is subjective. The market value of products and services is determined primarily by the customers. A computer, for example, has no value at all unless someone wants it. The money that went into its production is totally ignored by potential customers. They simply see it as a way to relieve uneasiness. If a competing product will be better at relieving their uneasiness, they will not buy the

computer, and it will have, essentially, no value at all for them. Obsolescence is an ever-present worry for any business holding inventory. Constant obsolescence is the result of constant innovation.

- Customers experience diminishing marginal utility. Every time customers acquire a new product, it normally tends to reduce their need for more of that same product. The satisfaction, utility, or uneasiness reduction power of the next computer, for example, is less than that of the previous computer purchased. This is a limiting factor on buying behavior. At the same time, as customers buy one product, the relative utility of other possible products tends to go up (in relation to the one purchased). They want to acquire, say, a computer and a camera. The utility to them of each one is about equal. If their desire for the computer is slightly greater, they will buy that. After the purchase, their desire for the camera (its marginal utility for them) is now greater (relative to another computer) than it was. Their next major purchase will probably be a camera, as a result.

- Money also has marginal utility. Every time you buy something, your stock of money decreases. The marginal utility of the money you have left (in relation to the usefulness of possible goods and services) tends to go up. When the utility to you of the money you have left is greater than the utility of any possible purchase, you will stop buying.

- In free market exchanges, both parties make a profit. It is often overlooked that the consumer makes a profit as well as the supplier. Each party to a trade typically gives up less than each gets—or why would they trade? If you sell a consumer a computer for $1,000, it must be worth more to the consumer than $1,000, or the consumer would never buy it. For you, the computer must be worth less than $1,000, or why would you sell it?

- Purchase decisions cause internal conflicts in potential customers' minds. All customers are torn between their desire for a product or service on the one hand, and their desire to retain their money stock on the other. Acquiring a product tends to reduce uneasiness; dissipation of one's personal money stock tends to increase uneasiness. Life is a balancing act between the two desires.

- The internal struggle affects different sides of the brain. Recent research on the hemispheres of the brain has made us aware that we possess two different and complementary ways of processing information—a linear, step-by-step style that analyzes the parts that make up a pattern (the left hemisphere) and a spatial, relational style that seeks and constructs patterns (the right). The left hemisphere controls our language. It is here that we do our mathematics, and calculate prices and bank account balances. The right brain constructs patterns and recognizes relationships. It is most efficient at visual and spatial processing. It is here that we visualize what our life would be like if we were to acquire a new product. It is the source of our imagination and our desire.

It is the complementary functions of both sides of the brain that give the mind its power and flexibility. We do not think with one hemisphere or the other; both are involved in the decision-making process.

Any significant decision is often preceded by a good deal of logical, linear thinking as a person defines and redefines a problem. This linear, verbalized thinking goes on in the left hemisphere, then an answer presents itself in a moment of insight. This answer occurs when the right side combines all the pieces together into an image of the solution to the problem. Finally the mind tackles the difficult job of evaluating the insight and putting it into a form in which it can be communicated and applied to the problem. Figure 2-3 illustrates the purchase decision process for the left and right hemispheres of the brain.

### Figure 2-3: The Purchase Decision Process

**Right Hemisphere**

Patterns and relationships. Visual and spacial processing. Imagination and desire.

"If I had that product, I would be handsome, cultured, sophisticated, and popular. I must have it."

**Left Hemisphere**

Language, linear thinking. Mathematics, accounting, and logic.

"I have only $X in my bank account as a result of yesterday's extravagance. I must resist the right side's customary exuberance."

- Advertising can appeal to either side of the mind. It is well known in retailing that "buy one get one free" performs better than "50 percent off." Why should that be? There seem to be several reasons. 1) A consumer can get the 50 percent reduction by buying only one, instead of two, so purchases could prove to be less. 2) Even today, many people are insecure about the meaning and method of computation of percentages. Everyone, however, understands the meaning of free; it's a wonderful word. 3) Wanting products is a right brain function. Calculating charges is a left brain function. The 50 percent off notice

requires a left brain calculation plus a right brain stimulus: a complicated mental sleight of hand that is hard to process. "Buy one get one
free" is pure right brain. You not only get what you want, you get two
of them.

## Recapitulation

Let's summarize where we are thus far.

Affluent consumers with very little leisure time face a rapidly changing
marketplace containing ever improving new products without adequate
knowledge or information about what is available. They purchase products
to reduce feelings of uneasiness, but are torn between the desire for goods
and the desire to maintain their cash balances. The decision-making
process goes on in their minds, which, in addition, are divided into a left
brain that keeps track of the money, and a right brain that visualizes the
benefits that can come from acquisition of new products and services.

Marketers are faced with a dilemma on the approach. Should they base
their message on the price (a left brain argument), or on the benefits of the
product (which appeals to the right brain)?

### Prices and Products Tend to Be the Same

There is a problem with both marketing approaches today. Prices tend
to become similar as each airline, computer company, and cigarette manufacturer rushes to match every price move of the competition. The consumer knows that price changes are temporary, and seldom fundamental.
Many consumers, moreover, being affluent, are less interested in price than
in quality and service.

Product quality also tends to be uniform. Avis, Hertz, National, Budget,
Dollar, and Alamo all rent brand new cars. Detergents, yogurts, canned
goods, tires, televisions, phones, and toilet paper are getting more perfect
and similar; each manufacturer produces equally good, high quality products that do the same things. Every improvement is immediately matched
by the competition.

### The Importance of Time

Price and quality have been the staples of marketing for years. Today,
there is a new dimension entering consumer decision-making that is of
equal importance: time. People have less and less time available for shopping (or for anything).

Products that can be purchased for $100 and a one-hour roundtrip to the supermarket are perceived to cost more than the same products that can be purchased for $110 and a telephone call. Our leisure time has acquired a monetary value that it never had before.

To the monetary cost of any transaction, therefore, we must add the cost of the time involved in completing the transaction. If we can make a purchase more convenient and less time consuming for customers, we make the product more attractive to them. They are more likely to buy it. In many cases, making this purchase more convenient costs us less than the increased value to the consumer; both of us make a profit by the change in delivery methods.

Self-service gasoline stations have been making a quiet revolution in the past decade. At first, it was thought that the public would not be able to (or willing to) pump their own gas (hence, the popular humorous book *Real Women Don't Pump Gas*). That thought proved to be entirely wrong. Most gas today is pumped by the customer.

Self-service gas is less expensive in two ways: it is about four or five cents cheaper, and it usually takes less time than waiting for a full-service attendant to show up. Time, today, is worth more.

A new innovation introduced around 1990 further reduced the time. A credit card gas purchaser swipes a credit card through a slot, and pays for self-service gas without ever talking to an attendant. The advantage to the customer: another three or four minute reduction in the time required to fill a car with gasoline. People used to this service seek out such stations. It beats waiting in line at the payment window. The service also reduces labor costs for the gasoline company; both parties make a profit.

What we marketers are selling today, therefore, is the product, plus the delivery method. The convenience and service is part of what we are selling. The real decision-making process required for a purchase (from the customer's point of view) looks something like this:

$$\text{Customer Profit} = a(\text{utility of product}) - b(\text{money cost}) - c(\text{time})$$

The coefficients a, b, and c are weights that vary with each customer. Lower income customers place a higher value on b and a lower value on c (since money is worth more to them, and time is worth less). Busy people place the highest value on c. This was illustrated in the 1970s during the energy crisis. Gasoline prices were controlled at low levels by the government. As a result there were regional gasoline shortages and long lines at the gasoline stations. Across the Texas border in Mexico gasoline cost much more, but there were no lines and unlimited supplies. For months, Texans drove south of the border to fill up their gas tanks at high prices, while Mexicans came north to wait in lines for the cheap gas.

## Why the Mass Marketing Process Is Changing

Mass marketing became dominant from 1950 to 1980 because we had newly affluent consumers, many of whom had lived through the bleakness and despair of the depression, and the shortages and rationing of World War II and the Korean War. At last, for the first time in two decades, the consumers had jobs and money, and were in a position to spend their money. The consumers were so grateful to find full shelves in the stores, as well as new homes, automobiles, washers, dryers, kitchens, telephones, and televisions, that they took what they could get, and loved it.

Mass marketing worked because a deprived mass suddenly had the wherewithal to spend, and a business community was ready to provide the many things desired in common by millions.

Why did mass marketing lose its effectiveness for some products? Because of diminishing marginal utility. We have finally reached the point where most people have acquired the minimum. They have enough food, clothing, and medical care, plus a home, a car, a phone, a TV, a washer and dryer, and air conditioning. The basics are covered. They have become more discriminating. In effect, they have discretionary income for the first time, and they have decided to use their discretion in spending it.

For the producers of some products, the mass market, as we have known it, seems to be slipping away. While there still are emerging minorities who are moving up to the middle class and will respond to straight mass marketing during their journey, they are minorities. The majority of our consumers today have grown up with an abundant economy. They know that they can get anything that they want. What they want is something quite different from what previous generations have wanted. They are looking for more than the basics, which they already have. They seek recognition, personal attention, service, diversity, and information, and they are prepared to pay for these things.

Today, most marketers are looking at integrated marketing as a solution. Rita Aldridge of Biggs/Gilmore Communications says:

*Integrated marketing combines the strengths of both mass advertising and direct marketing ... Without direct marketing, an advertiser may never come to closure with a customer or prospect. The marketer may pique interest, but most people need an added incentive to take action. Without mass advertising, a marketer may never gain credibility. A fantastic offer may get a response, but brand preference keeps a loyal customer.*

## Providing Information

The fact that the market today is filled with change, uncertainty, lack of information, and ignorance is a wonderful opportunity for marketers. I recently refinanced my condominium for 8 percent, down from 9 3/4 percent. I felt that I had made a profit even though I had to pay 3 points. I learned later that I could have gotten 7 percent and paid no points if I had waited two more months. "If I had only known," was my thought. How many of us have had that same thought about market transactions. It is universal in any free market. If you were selling refinancing arrangements, you could happily make a profit by educating me, and I would make a profit by listening to you.

The American market is not only huge, it is gigantic. It is filled with millions of businesses and millions of consumers, all looking out for themselves, pursuing subjective goals of their own. No one can possibly know all the commodities and services that are available, their respective benefits and features, and the prices at which they can be obtained. We can only scratch the surface of available information.

The significance of this fact is that you, as a marketer, have available to you some vital information that your customers need in order to make decisions about their purchases and their lives. Through well-organized marketing activity, you can not only help customers to make a profit, you can also relieve them of some of their anxiety about the marketplace: what is available, what they are missing out on, and how much it costs. You are an information provider. If you concentrate on giving customers information that they need, you will make them happy, they are more likely to purchase, and you will be successful.

## Providing an Institution for Loyalty

People like to be loyal. Look at the support given to local baseball and football teams. Look at the fans rooting for basketball teams. The loyalty of military personnel to their units is legendary. The dedication of alumni to their colleges is often life-long.

For years, my father bought nothing but Fords. He was intensely loyal to Ford. Was Ford loyal to him? They didn't know about him, or care about him. That didn't matter. He loved Fords. We all know many people like him: people who love their Steinway piano, their adidas shoes, their Rossignol skis, their Camel cigarettes. And why not? It is wonderful to have something that endures, that lasts, that you can believe in and hang on to, that you can identify with.

The growing need to identify with institutions is shown by the explosion of nonprofit institutions.

As shown below in Figure 2-4, nonprofits are growing five times as fast as the population is growing. The urge to identify with causes and institutions has never been stronger.

### Figure 2-4: Growth of Nonprofit Institutions

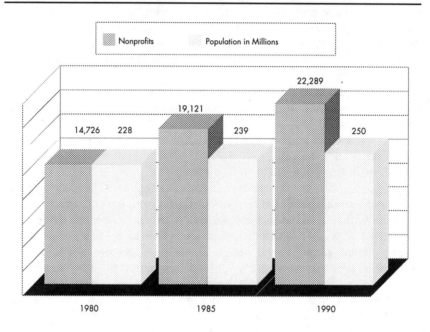

What does this mean for U.S. corporate enterprises? They can either play ball, or sit this one out. Database marketing provides a mechanism for taking advantage of this urge to identify by giving your customers a warm, friendly, stable institution to identify with. "Like a good neighbor, State Farm is there." It is easy, inexpensive, and it builds loyalty. Why reject it?

## How Database Marketing Solves Customers' Problems

Database marketing solves the information problem: it provides recognition, personal service, and a profit to the customer.

Database marketing is possible, of course, because of the development of computers with advanced software. We can store thousands of facts about every customer, and retrieve them in seconds when we need them to provide information and services to each customer. This information is badly needed by customers. It is worth money to them, and they will reward you for it.

At the same time, being the one to provide that information to the customer is very profitable for you. Let's take a concrete example, suggested by the ideas of Thomas Lix, president and CEO of MarketPulse Inc. Read this letter: *

---

Ridgeway Fashions
123 Main Street
Leesburg, VA 22090

October 25, 1995

Dear Mr. Hughes:

I would like to remind you that your wife's birthday is coming up in two weeks on November 5th. We have the perfect gift for Helena in stock.

As you know, she loves Liz Claiborne clothing, and we have an absolutely beautiful new suit in blue, her favorite color, in a 12, her size, priced below typical retail value of $290 at $232.

If you like, I can gift wrap the suit at no extra charge and mail it to you next week so that you will have it in plenty of time for her birthday, or, if you like, I can put it aside so that you can come in to pick it up. Please give me a call within the next 48 hours to let me know which you'd prefer.

In any event, I appreciate your business and hope to hear from you soon.

Sincerely yours,
Tracy Anderson, Store Manager

---

What would be my reaction to this letter? If the store has done its homework, and the database has the correct information in it (about Helena's tastes and my pocketbook), I will snap at the opportunity.

A letter like this would be a godsend for me. Helena has two birthdays a

---

* Tom Lix's original letter was included in *The Marketing Revolution* by Kevin Clancy and Robert Shulman, published by HarperBusiness.

year. Her saint's day is August 18th. Her birthday is November 5th. What do I get for her? She is a very stylish, fashion-conscious business woman who always wears the latest clothes. I, on the other hand, am color blind, and have no idea what to buy for her. Would that I knew of a store with the database and chutzpah of Tom Lix's example!

This is what database marketing is all about: reducing ignorance and lack of information, bringing a very particular buyer with unique subjective goals together with a specialized solution to the customer's problem.

Database marketing, of course, is not a universal solution. It will be effective only in situations in which a continuing relationship between a seller and a buyer is profitable for both parties. If either or both find that they can do better without the relationship, the database project will fail—and it should.

### Event-Driven Personal Communications

Tom Lix's idea is excellent strategy. To produce this type of customer service selling, you need to include client topologies in the database using survey questions obtained when the customer is visiting the store. They can include such things as:

| | |
|---|---|
| Suitable gift | Women's apparel |
| | Tropical weight business suits |
| | Casual outdoor clothing |
| Decision algorithms | Quality conscious |
| | Price conscious |
| | Fashion conscious |
| Magical dates | Birth dates, anniversaries, graduations |
| | Trips planned, moves in progress |
| Personal specifications | Dress and suit sizes |
| | Color, style, and manufacturer preferences |
| | Personal coloring |
| | Measurements |
| | Face and body shape |
| Demographics | Gender, birth date, education |
| | Income, financial situation |
| | Home ownership |
| | Children |

| Sociographics | Shopping role |
| --- | --- |
| | Occupation and marital status |
| | Spouse's name and birth date |
| | |
| Shopping history | Shopping behavior |
| | Dollar expenditures: total and by department |
| | Store and brand preferences |
| | Hobbies, interests, activities |
| | Lifestyle characteristics |

What the software will do:

- Sweep the database weekly to determine targets for communications
- Determine which product type represents a match
- Calculate the expected value of each target, recipient, merchandise, and occasion combination
- Select the winning possibility
- Generate inputs for the communication package
- Monitor the results of each communication and update the database

## Lifetime Value

Building the database necessary to send that letter to Arthur Hughes was not cheap. The store had to collect a lot of information about Helena and me: sizes, styles, birthdays, budgets, ages, fashions, interests, and preferences. The software had to use all that information to match this data with the products that Helena has already bought at the store and the thousands of products currently available, so as to produce the perfect letter at the right time to the right person.

Capturing the information has a cost. Maintaining the database and producing the monthly output has a cost. Mailing the letters has a cost. Most of the letters will not result in sales. Balancing all these costs are the potential profits that will come from the actual sales (less the returns) that the system produces.

For those market situations in which a continuing relationship is possible and desirable between the buyer and the seller, it is advantageous for the seller to compute the lifetime value of each customer. Lifetime value permits the seller to figure out the amount of money practical to expend on maintaining its relationships with its customers.

The way to know whether you have built a successful database marketing system is to compute the lifetime value of the Hughes family, and all the other families in your database. Each time you introduce another innovation (sending out a gift suggestion before a wedding anniversary or college graduation, for example), you recompute the lifetime value. If the value goes up, you should do it. If it goes down, you should not.

In the next chapter, we will build a lifetime value table for Ridgeway Fashions to show how you would go about costing out Tom Lix's idea, to determine whether it will pay dividends.

## Does Database Marketing Always Work?

No, it definitely does not. There are tens of thousands of products, particularly packaged goods for which database marketing will never work. This is spelled out in detail in Chapter 11, Packaged Goods Databases: Don't Lose Your Shirt. Too many articles have been written implying that database marketing is a panacea, and that those who fail to use it are blockheads. Don't be fooled. Work out the economics. The next chapter, which focuses on lifetime value, will give you a solid tool to determine whether database marketing will work in your situation.

### Is Mass Marketing Ending?

Of course not; it is alive and well. Combined more often with direct marketing, it is becoming integrated marketing. Mass marketing always will be essential to make the public aware of new products and old products for which database marketing and direct marketing cannot be used. Will most toothpastes ever be sold by direct marketing or database marketing? Never. They will be using mass marketing long after the people reading this book are gone.

## Summary

The United States is unique and fortunate. Working in a land of freedom and opportunity, a nation of immigrants built a continental market with few political and economic restrictions. For the last century we have had the largest and freest market on earth.

In this free market, entrepreneurs and marketers seek better ways of making customers happy. Customer happiness means purchases, and purchases mean profits for both the buyer and the seller. The size of our market has resulted in economies of scale from mass production, constantly lower prices, constantly increasing per capita income.

Mass marketing came about because of a special combination of circumstances. A whole generation, deprived from a decade of depression, followed by a decade of war, was finally able to produce and purchase in peace. This coincided with the birth of television as a marketing medium. Mass marketing assumed that everyone wanted the same things. From 1950 to 1980, that was a correct assumption.

Since that time, the very success of mass marketing has brought about its decline for certain products. Most people today have all the basics. Increasingly since 1980, customers are using their massive discretionary income to buy a wider variety of products. With most adults working, there is less time to shop. With the expanding marketplace, there is so much more to know, and so little time to learn about it all. Customers today value service, time, and information as highly as they used to value quality and price. Competition has pushed the quality of most products up to a uniformly high standard. Competition continues to push prices down to uniformly low levels.

At the same time, the breakdown of family and community institutions has combined with increased affluence to produce an explosion in non-profit institutions. People want something to believe in, to be loyal to, to identify with. Stable and caring profit-making enterprises can play a part.

Consumers in the 1990s have all the basics. What they want now is recognition, service, diversity, information, and identification. Database marketing is the most efficient way of providing all these things.

Database marketing is aimed at the customer's right brain. Instead of being bombarded with discounts, the customer is showered with attention, recognition, friendship, and service. Why these things? Because that is what the customer wants. Furthermore, database marketing is the only way to start a two-way dialogue in which customers are able to tell you what is on their minds, and you are able to react to their thoughts by varying your services and product mix.

Database marketing works for some products because it is singly qualified to meet the requirements of today's customer, just as mass marketing was the ideal marketing solution for these same products in previous decades. Companies that recognize this shift and take advantage of it will prosper. The others may be consigned to the dustbin of history.

## Executive Quiz 2

"What are these quizzes doing in this book?" you may ask. "Is this supposed to be a textbook?" No, the quizzes are in here for fun. Some people like crossword puzzles; others like quizzes. If you are one of them, try your luck. The answers can be found in Appendix B. If you don't like quizzes, ignore them. Database marketing is supposed to be fun for the customers. *Choose the best answer to complete each statement.*

1. Mass marketing today
   a. is ending.
   b. is being replaced by database marketing.
   c. is the best way to sell certain products.
   d. is growing in importance.
   e. provides recognition and diversity.

2. The left brain
   a. computes mathematics.
   b. sees spatial relationships.
   c. does most of our thinking.
   d. controls the right brain.
   e. is poor at languages.

3. In free market transactions
   a. buyers often fail to make a profit.
   b. sellers often fail to make a profit.
   c. information is often lacking.
   d. price is more important than quality.
   e. government sets price guidelines.

4. From 2000 B.C. to A.D. 1700, the annual rate of productivity gain in industry was closest to
   a. 0 percent.
   b. 0.1 percent.
   c. 0.5 percent.
   d. 1.0 percent.
   e. 1.5 percent.

5. Of all the following, the key reason why the American economy has been so successful is because of
   a. natural resources.
   b. protective tariffs.
   c. our monetary system.
   d. environmental regulations.
   e. the extent of our market.

6. Average Americans today
   a. have higher incomes than their parents.
   b. can no longer afford the housing of their parents.
   c. live increasingly in poverty.
   d. resist innovation.
   e. have the same income as previous generations.

7. The impersonal world we live in today
   a. hinders market development.
   b. provides a marketing opportunity.
   c. is being reduced by government programs.
   d. does not affect marketing.
   e. is desired by most consumers.

8. The value of most products
   a. is set by the cost of production.
   b. is set by the cost of imports.
   c. does not change from day to day.
   d. is determined by the customer.
   e. is set by government regulations.

9. Diminishing marginal utility means that
   a. products become obsolete.
   b. money is being replaced by plastic.
   c. you stop buying some products after acquiring a few.
   d. some products are always scarce.
   e. companies cannot count on sales.

# Part Two: Strategy Development

# 3

# Lifetime Value: The Criterion of Strategy

*In the information-intensive marketplace of the '90s, marketers'*
*success will not only depend on the extent to which they collect*
*information about their current customers but also on how well*
*they use the information they collect. Marketers who sell big-ticket*
*items and who routinely collect information on their customers*
*will adapt to the new information-intensive marketing relatively*
*easily. Marketers who sell low-ticket items, such as consumer pack-*
*aged goods, will find adaptation more challenging. But the efforts*
*of both marketers in forming customer information files will be*
*rewarded by increased loyalties from their customers.*

*The promise of the customer information file is immense. Com-*
*petitors can outspend, underprice, and over distribute a company,*
*but if that company has achieved a strong database-implemented*
*relationship with its current customers, it is unlikely to be immedi-*
*ately vulnerable. As [retailer] Marshall Field said:*

"Goodwill is the one asset the competition cannot undermine
or destroy."

*—Robert M. Smith, Focal Point, Inc.*

**M**ost marketers today talk about lifetime value. Some understand it, but very few have actually calculated it or used it in marketing strategy. There are a number of reasons for this, which we will explain. You don't need to feel left behind if you are one of the multitude who has not used it yet. It takes an understanding of some basic concepts which are not difficult, once you know them, but until you do seem quite arcane.

In this chapter you will find a complete explanation of how lifetime value can be calculated. When you get through, you will be able to use it in your marketing planning. This chapter is detailed. If you stick with it to the end, however, it will change your life as a marketer and make you a better person. Who could ask for anything more?

## Definition of Lifetime Value

First, a definition: Lifetime value is the net present value of the profit that you will realize on the average new customer during a given number of years. Lifetime value can be used in the development of marketing strategy and tactics. At any given time it is a specific number, but it will change from month to month. Many different factors cause lifetime value to change, some of which are under your control, most of which are not.

One expert on lifetime value is Paul Wang, assistant professor of marketing at Northwestern University. Paul serves as a consultant to a number of companies, besides teaching graduate students who go on to do marketing for some of the United States' most successful companies. Many ideas throughout this chapter and book are based on Paul's concepts.

### Why Lifetime Value Is Seldom Used in Marketing Today

Few marketers use lifetime value today for a number of valid reasons:

- They do not understand it. That problem is easily solved, and we will solve it in this chapter. In general, marketers don't understand lifetime value because it involves several marketing and financial concepts that people with advertising backgrounds have not learned in school. They are not difficult to learn.
- They do not have a database—also easily solved. It costs less to build a database than many people think, and you can have a useful database built in six months or less. Lifetime value cannot be converted into a concrete number without a database that keeps track of customer behavior over a period of time. If you have not yet gathered customer data and stored it in a database that provides you the ability to count and select, you really cannot come up with a valid lifetime value number, although you can use the concept in your planning (as we shall see below).
- They are under pressure to produce. This is the hardest problem. To get any sort of specificity in lifetime value, you usually have to do some testing. You have to keep track of customer behavior over a period of time. The problem that marketers have to face is: "What marketing programs are we going to carry out right now?" Management expects action from its marketing staff, not just a series of extended tests. If you use the methods in this chapter, however, you will find that it is possible in many cases to use lifetime value in planning your current marketing strategy. You will have the time.

## Analyzing a Lifetime Value Table

Let's begin with a basic lifetime value table. After you understand it, we will explain:

- How you can modify it
- How you can use it to test strategy
- Some of the technical details

For this table, we are going back to Tom Lix's example at the end of the previous chapter. We will look at Ridgeway Fashions before and after they adopted the new strategy of writing letters to husbands before their wives' birthdays. We will see how they costed this out, and determined whether the strategy would work, using the lifetime value table, shown in Table 3-1.

### Table 3-1: Customer Lifetime Value

| | Revenue | Year1 | Year2 | Year3 | Year4 | Year5 |
|---|---|---|---|---|---|---|
| A | Customers | 1,000 | 400 | 180 | 90 | 50 |
| B | Retention Rate | 40 | 45 | 50 | 55 | 60 |
| C | Average Yearly Sale | $150 | $150 | $150 | $150 | $150 |
| D | Total Revenue | $150,000 | $60,000 | $27,000 | $13,500 | $7,500 |
| | **Costs** | | | | | |
| E | Cost Percent | 50 | 50 | 50 | 50 | 50 |
| F | Total Costs | $75,000 | $30,000 | $13,500 | $6,750 | $3,750 |
| | **Profits** | | | | | |
| G | Gross Profit | $75,000 | $30,000 | $13,500 | $6,750 | $3,750 |
| H | Discount Rate | 1 | 1.2 | 1.44 | 1.73 | 2.07 |
| I | NPV Profit | $75,000 | $25,000 | $9,375 | $3,902 | $1,812 |
| J | Cumulative NPV Profit | $75,000 | $100,000 | $109,375 | $113,277 | $115,088 |
| K | **Lifetime Value (NPV)** | $75.00 | $100.00 | $109.38 | $113.28 | $115.09 |

In this table we are looking at a group of customers over a five-year period. In the first year (Year1), 1,000 new customers are attracted to Ridgeway Fashions, Ltd. which has a chain of shops for upscale women. They have issued proprietary credit cards to their customers so that they can keep track of the activities of their customers. They have built a database using the data collected.

Line B shows the retention rate. Ridgeway tends to lose customers. After the first year, only 40 percent of the original customers come back. Of those who do return, the retention rate gradually improves from year to year as shown in Line B.

Line A, therefore, shows those customers remaining from the original 1,000. There are, of course, many other customers who come in to shop but are not in the database. We are not concerned with them at this point. We are just looking at what happens to the original database-tracked group over a five-year period. In your table, you don't need to select only 1,000 as your group for study. You could select 100,000 or more. The only requirement is that we are taking snapshots of the performance of a specific group over its first five years as a customer.

## Annual Sales

Line C shows the average amount spent by each customer each year. This amount can be computed easily by dividing total retail sales by the total number of customers. In this example, Ridgeway's annual sales per customer are projected as being a flat $150 per year. That doesn't mean that Ridgeway's sales are not growing—they could be, if the stores attract more customers each year. It simply means that their sales per customer are not growing.

Line D shows total revenue from the customers still remaining from the original group. It is customers (Line A) times average yearly sale (Line C).

## Costs

Direct costs can be figured in any way that makes sense in your company. It can include the cost of the materials, the cost of overhead, advertising, etc. Ridgeway Fashions has computed it as a percentage of revenue—in this case 50 percent. Line E, therefore, shows 50 percent, and is multiplied by Line D, the revenue, to get Line F, the total costs.

Computation of costs does not need to be made into a major problem. If you have one number, such as 50 percent or 80 percent, and stick to it consistently, that is all you need. The reason? We are going to look at the effect of a new strategy on lifetime value. If both tables use the same cost percentages, that percentage may not be of crucial importance.

## Profits and Net Present Value

Gross profits (Line G) is easy. It is total revenue (Line D) less total costs (Line F). We need to spend some time on the discount rate in Line H, however, since that is the most complicated part of the entire lifetime value analysis.

The reason for the discount rate (Line H) is simple: The profits you receive from your customers come in over several years. Money received in future years is not worth as much today as money received today. You will have to discount the amounts that you expect to receive in the future, in order to calculate their net present value (NPV), which is the way lifetime value is calculated.

How much should you discount future revenue? There is an easy answer: You use the market rate of interest. If I were to offer you $1,000 in a year's time as a payment for $1,000 that I owe you today, you would probably object. You would insist on interest for waiting for a year for the money. The rate of interest varies with the market. As I write this today, 8 percent seems like a reasonable interest rate. Ten years ago, businesses paid 12 percent. The amount varies with the general market conditions. You may use any number you wish. In this book, I am using 10 percent throughout, a nice round number.

In reality, however, I am doubling that 10 percent to get 20 percent. Why is that? Because I am including risk. In any long-term business transaction, such as lifetime customer value, there is always serious risk. What are the risks?

- Interest rates could go up.
- Obsolescence. Your product could become obsolete in the next few years and wipe out your possibility of further sales.
- Competition. In most industries, competitors always make marketing a risky business. They could steal your expected customers.
- Other business risks. In each business situation, there are many different factors that can easily go wrong. Your business is no exception.

For these reasons, I double the interest rate to get the discount rate. You may argue with this, and use some other rate. Fine, use it. You must use some rate.

### Computing the Discount Rate from the Interest Rate

Once you have decided on an interest rate—such as the 20 percent that I have used—you need to compute the discount rate that applies to amounts to be received in each year. There is a simple formula that is used to compute the discount rate. It is:

$$D = (1 + i)^n$$

Where $D$ = discount rate, $i$ = interest rate, and $n$ = number of years that you have to wait. The discount rate in Year4 (three years from now), for example, is computed like this:

$$D = (1.20)^3 = 1.728$$

It is possible to be much more precise in your discount rate calculation. You can worry about whether the profits will be realized in the first part of the year, or later in the year, and make n into a fractional amount, such as 3.25. You are welcome to do this. In this book, I have tried to keep the process simple.

## NPV Profits

Once you have the discount rate, each of your expected profits must be discounted to arrive at the net present value of these future profits. The process is a simple one:

NPV Profits = Profits ÷ Discount rate

The net present value of the $13,500 profits expected in Year3 is $9,375 (Line I), the result of dividing $13,500 by the discount rate of 1.44.

## Cumulative NPV Profit

Line J adds together the net present value of all the profits in the present year, and each previous year. The net present value of profits realized by Year3, for example, is equal to the net present value of the profits in Year1 + Year2 + Year3.

## Lifetime Value

The lifetime value, Line K, is simply Line J divided by the original group of customers (in this case 1,000). The NPV lifetime value really represents the average profits that you can expect to receive, after a given number of years, from every new customer that you can sign up.

The present lifetime value of the average new customer for Ridgeway Fashions after four years is $113.28. This is a very important number. It and the other figures on the bottom line are the most important numbers in your entire database. They can be used to develop your entire marketing strategy.

## Strategy Development

Developing your customer lifetime value table is the first step in the development of strategy. The second step is to get a great idea and test it out—in theory—on your lifetime value table. Let's do that right now.

Strategy always begins with some assumptions: "If we do this, then the customer will do that." We will learn that customer relationship building strategy can affect five (and only five) basic things:

1. **Retention Rate.** Building relationships increases customer loyalty and augments the retention rate.
2. **Referrals.** Database activities can lead customers to suggest your products to their friends and relatives.
3. **Increased Sales.** Database activities can lead to increased cross-selling, upgrades, or simply more buying by existing customers.
4. **Reduced Direct Costs.** Database activities can reduce costs, in some cases, by changing the channel for distribution.
5. **Reduced Marketing Costs.** Well-planned database activities are often much more cost-effective than mass advertising. Few companies realize this yet, but it is a possible strategy.

For Ridgeway Fashions, let's imagine a creative director of database marketing who we will call Robin Baumgartner. Robin decides to test a possible strategy: to build a database, collect survey information on female customers, and write personal communications to husbands (before their wives' birthdays or anniversaries), mothers (for their daughters' graduations), etc. Table 3-2 shows what Robin's idea might do to Ridgeway Fashions' lifetime value:

### Table 3-2: Customer Lifetime Value with Database Marketing

|   | Revenue | Year1 | Year2 | Year3 | Year4 | Year5 |
|---|---|---|---|---|---|---|
| A | Referral Rate | 5 | 5 | 5 | 5 | 5 |
| B | Referred Customers | | 50 | 28 | 17 | 11 |
| C | Total Customers | 1,000 | 550 | 331 | 216 | 151 |
| D | Retention Rate | 50 | 55 | 60 | 65 | 70 |
| E | Average Yearly Sale | $180 | $200 | $220 | $240 | $260 |
| F | Total Revenue | $180,000 | $110,000 | $72,820 | $51,840 | $39,260 |
|   | **Costs** | | | | | |
| G | Cost Percent | 50 | 50 | 50 | 50 | 50 |
| H | Direct Costs | $90,000 | $55,000 | $36,410 | $25,920 | $19,630 |
| I | Database Activities | $10,000 | $5,500 | $3,310 | $2,160 | $1,510 |
| J | Total Costs | $100,000 | $60,500 | $39,720 | $28,080 | $21,140 |
|   | **Profits** | | | | | |
| K | Gross Profit | $80,000 | $49,500 | $33,100 | $23,760 | $18,120 |
| L | Discount Rate | 1.00 | 1.20 | 1.44 | 1.73 | 2.07 |
| M | NPV Profit | $80,000 | $41,250 | $22,986 | $13,734 | $8,754 |
| N | Cumulative NPV Profit | $80,000 | $121,250 | $144,236 | $157,970 | $166,724 |
| O | **Lifetime Value (NPV)** | $80.00 | $121.25 | $144.24 | $157.97 | $166.72 |

This table is similar to the previous one with some significant additions.

## Referrals

Line A is the Referral Rate, estimated at 5 percent. This means that Robin is assuming that she can use database activities to encourage customers to recommend Ridgeway to other customers. Her assumption is that this program will result in a 5 percent increase in the customer base each year. In Year1 there were 1,000 customers. If these 1,000 customers mention Ridgeway to their friends and families, the assumption is that 50 new customers will make purchases in Year2 as a result of referrals.

In Year2, there are only 550 customers (including these 50 referrals). These will also be encouraged to get others to patronize Ridgeway. That will result in 28 (5 percent) new referrals in Year3.

Is Robin correct? Can her activities increase referrals by 5 percent? Who knows? That depends on many things, including the success of Ridgeway as a store, the execution of the marketing plan, etc. But it is certainly a reasonable goal to build into a marketing plan. It is also a testable proposition. If the plan does produce 5 percent new customers, the database will show it. If it brings in 12 percent, or only 3 percent, the plan can be modified. This is the beginning of good strategy development.

## Retention Rate

In the previous example, the retention rate for Ridgeway began at 40 percent, based on historical patterns for this store. Robin makes the assumption that her programs can increase that to 50 percent—with further increases as the remaining customer base becomes composed of more and more loyalists (Line D). The resulting customer base is shown in Line C, which is 50 percent of last year's customers, plus 5 percent new referrals (Line B). This is certainly a reasonable assumption. If her programs are well designed, she might beat that goal.

What determines the retention rate? A great many things, only some of which are under the marketer's control. Factors that marketers usually cannot control include:

- Type of product and the speed with which customers use it
- Strength of the competitor's marketing strategy
- Saturation of the market for this product
- Public perception of the product, compared with other things to buy
- Macroeconomic trends such as recessions, booms, or changes in interest rates that affect the overall demand for most products

The factors that marketers can control that affect the retention rate, however, are quite impressive:

- Type of promotion used to attract customers
- Price charged for the product
- Efforts made to get the customer to buy again
- Relationship-building efforts made with the customer

### Average Yearly Sale

Here, in Line E, Robin has gone out on a limb. She is assuming that as a result of her database activities, the average customer will buy $180 worth of clothing in Year1 instead of the $150 they are buying now, a 20 percent increase in sales. She may be too ambitious. Of course, some database programs have done better than that. It is, clearly, a testable proposition.

Her assumptions in Line E in Years2–5 are less questionable. Those loyal customers who are still shopping at Ridgeway in subsequent years will probably buy more than the average new customer in Year1. Robin is assuming that average annual purchases will go up by $20 per year.

Total revenue (Line F) is simply average yearly sale (Line E) times the number of customers (Line C).

### Database Costs

In planning her database activities in Line I, Robin is on somewhat surer ground. She can budget her database costs with some precision, which she does at $10 per customer per year.

You can actually buy quite a lot of database work for $10 each. This will buy the database, data entry of the customers' names, capture of the purchases from the point-of-sale (POS) system, plus a newsletter and outgoing personalized communications on birthdays, anniversaries, holidays, etc. It will also pay for some telemarketing to the best customers.

### Resulting Lifetime Value

Lines K through O have the same function as Lines G through K on the previous table. Table 3-3 helps us compare the bottom line on both tables:

The difference between lifetime value before and after Robin's plan was implemented is shown here. Robin has increased lifetime value after five years by $51.63. Just what does that mean?

To explain the meaning, assume that Ridgeway Fashions has 200,000 customers. Robin's database marketing program, if as successful as her

**Table 3-3: Customer Lifetime Value with and without Database Marketing**

|                     | Year1       | Year2       | Year3       | Year4       | Year5        |
|---------------------|-------------|-------------|-------------|-------------|--------------|
| Without Database    | $75.00      | $100.00     | $109.38     | $113.28     | $115.09      |
| With Database       | $80.00      | $121.25     | $144.24     | $157.97     | $166.72      |
| Increase            | $5.00       | $21.25      | $34.86      | $44.69      | $51.63       |
| 200,000 Customers   | $1,000,000  | $4,250,000  | $6,972,000  | $8,938,000  | $10,326,00C  |

plan, will have increased the net present value of long-term (five year) profits by more than $10 million dollars.

## Lessons Learned

What lessons can we draw from what we have learned already?

- Lifetime value is a practical, hardheaded technique for determining the effectiveness of various marketing strategies. It can and should be applied to any marketing program to test it before any significant amount of money is spent. Before we act on our hunches and prejudices, we can do our homework and prove, at least theoretically, whether any proposed program has the possibility of success.
- Lifetime value is future profits computed in today's dollars using the net present value calculation method.
- Lifetime value grows with the number of repeat customers.
- Lifetime value increases with the number of years that customers continue to buy.

The basic idea is to come up with strategies that increase lifetime value as much as possible. If we set up a matrix showing lifetime value each year for five years (as we have already done), then we can use our imagination, and do "what if" analyses to see what we can do to increase lifetime value. The results of each possible action can be calculated to determine whether the effect on lifetime value is worth the effort that went into it.

## Looking at Customers as Assets

Most businesses list buildings, machinery, and cash as assets. But when a business is sold, good will is often what the buyer pays the most for. Good will is nothing other than the value of the customer base that the company has built up over the years and currently is holding on to. Lifetime value is a way of quantifying the value of the good will represented by the existing customer base.

Economists and accountants often talk as if the main problem of any business is to find the most efficient way to produce products and services. It's not. The main problem of any business is to find the most efficient way to sell its products and services. Customers provide the cash flow that keeps any business alive.

By building up customer lifetime value, we will be building up the key assets of the business—assets that are essential to the business's survival.

## The Computation Period

In this example, we have shown the results of lifetime value after one, two, three, four, and five years. Which is the right number of years to look at? Throughout the industry there is a lot of confusion over this question. When you think about it, however, it is not that complicated.

Some customers stay with you for years. Others buy once and drop out. The remainder drop out at various intervals—and some drop out and then come back. The lifetime value is a function of the length of time that you use for measurement. The longer period of time you use, the greater the lifetime value. That being the case, which is the correct length of time?

If you read the literature on this subject, you will see various periods of time used. Some, like Donald Libey, president of Libey Consultancy, Inc., use two years as the period. Others use three or four years. Which is right?

Paul Wang has what I consider to be the best answer: All of them are correct. Lifetime value, for Paul, is always tied to a number of years: Lifetime value after two years is X; lifetime value after three years is Y. You look at all the numbers, and say: "How long can we afford to wait?" If, for instance, you are selling personal computers with 286 chips, computing a five-year lifetime value is self-delusion. No one will be selling new personal computers with 286 chips five years from now.

You have to look realistically at your product, your competition, and the market and say, "How long can we continue in this business?" After that you ask, "How long can we afford to wait?" The answer will be quite different for each product in each industry.

Our company, ACS, sells a mainframe software product called MarketVision that is used to count and select customer records from large mainframe files using a personal computer front end. It is the best product on the market in 1994 for this purpose. But how long will there be a market for such a product? That depends on the direction taken by database marketing in general, the capabilities of personal computers to do the work of mainframes, the future of the mainframe, and the skill and persistence of competitors who may come up with a better product at any time in the near future. Realistically, we cannot use a five-year lifetime value for our strategy planning. It is unlikely that this product and its market will last that long without some sort of drastic change.

For that reason, of course, we are hard at work on research and development to produce new releases incorporating features that will help us to stay ahead of the market. In addition, we are building a one-on-one relationship with our customers to keep them loyal and buying.

The lesson: Compute lifetime value for each of several years. Use the period of time that makes the most sense to you based on your particular product situation.

### What Is Your Product and Who Is Your Customer?

Lifetime value also can vary depending upon how you define your product. If you are selling gasoline, the product and customer are pretty obvious. If your company is a department store, it is not as clear. Do you determine the lifetime value of all customers or just women's wear customers?

By lumping them together, you may miss a lot of detail that would be important to your marketing program. Upper income women may be attracted by the style of your clothing; lower income shoppers may like the values; do-it-yourself types may like your hardware department. Lumping them all together to determine the lifetime value of all of them at once may lead you to false strategies that may turn off some while turning on others.

The lesson: Segment your file by department or type of customer, and compute the lifetime value for each different segment.

## Possible Strategies

What can you do to increase your profits by increasing customer lifetime value? Throughout this book, we will explore several techniques including:

### Retaining Existing Customers

- Increase the number of efforts to get customers to renew.
- Build a relationship with customers to make them more loyal.
- Segment the database and target the company's relationship to the appropriate groups of customers, rather than treating them all alike.
- Establish special groups, a president's club or a gold card group, to build loyalty and encourage people to buy more to belong.
- Set up a frequent buyer/flyer/traveler/shopper club.
- Increase renewal or reactivation efforts.

## Adding New Customers

- Attract the type of customer most likely to stay with the seller.
- Determine the customer acquisition budget with more precision.
- Profile existing customers and use the profiles to find new customers.
- Use the database to qualify prospects.
- Study the lifetime value of customers obtained from different sources. Concentrate on the best sources.

## Increasing Renewal Efforts

Magazine publishers have renewal down to a science. *Newsweek,* for example, grips its customers like a pit bull. Before a subscription is due to expire, a series of reminders and increasingly strident warnings of impending doom are sent. After the subscription has expired, a series of reactivation messages are continued. The publisher just cannot accept the idea that anyone would ever want to drop a subscription to *Newsweek.*

This is great marketing. Most companies don't do this because they don't know how to do it. Magazines do it because they are in the habit of corresponding with their customers and have developed lifetime value down to a fine science.

Supermarkets have begun to do this. Ukrops, in Richmond, Virginia, has a frequent shopper program with membership cards that customers use to get discounts whenever they shop. Ukrops analyzes its customer base regularly. When it looks as if a regular shopper has dropped the supermarket, it goes after the shopper with letters and telemarketing. Does it pay off? Well, Ukrops has been doing this for five years. It must be producing results.

## How to Do Your Own Calculation

Lifetime value calculation as a base for strategy development is not as difficult as you may have thought. Follow these simple steps:

- Use your database to select a group of customers, all of whom came on board at about the same time in the past. Depending upon the size of your customer base, you could use 1,000, 10,000, or more.
- Determine how many of these customers are still buying a year later to figure your retention rate. If you have enough data, determine the second-year retention rate as well. If not, estimate it for subsequent years. Attrition of 50 percent is not unusual.
- Estimate the money that you spent acquiring these customers by

advertising, direct mail, promotions, etc.

- Determine the average amount of money that these customers spend with you in a single year to compute your revenue.
- Determine the discount rate that applies to your business. To include risk, you may want to double the market rate of interest.
- Put all this data into a spreadsheet like Lotus 1-2-3 or Microsoft Excel, and project your customer lifetime value for five years.
- Try out some "what if" scenarios, experimenting with the costs and effects of relationship-building activities. The goal should be to build the long-term customer value to as high a level as possible. Predict the results of each major marketing initiative before you implement it.
- Keep your spreadsheet active. After you have tried a few marketing initiatives, check their results against your spreadsheet. Improve your predicting ability. Become a master marketer. If you need help creating your spreadsheet, see the Technical Assistance section in Appendix A in this book.

## Summary

1.   Few marketers have computed lifetime value for their customers because they don't understand the concept, don't have a database, or are so busy marketing they cannot do strategic planning.

2.   Net present value is a way of determining the value today of money that you will receive or expend at some date in the future. It results in discounting future money by the assumed market rate of interest. The formula is:

$$NPV = Amount \div (1+i)^n$$
where: $i$ = the interest rate
   $n$ = the number of years

3.   The marketplace is always filled with uncertainty and lack of information. There are no eternal truths. Customer Lifetime Value, for example, must be recalculated from month to month, because conditions are always changing: competitors come up with new initiatives, products become obsolete, and the market becomes saturated.

4.   The retention rate is a measure of how many of last year's customers are still buying from you this year. It varies with things you cannot change such as type of product, competitor's strength, public perception, and macroeconomic trends. There are many things you can do to

affect your retention rate: type of promotions, pricing, renewal efforts, and relationship building.

5. The computation period defines how far you must go to define the lifetime customer value. It varies by industry. The longer the period, the greater the lifetime value.

6. Lifetime value may be different for different products and different types of customers. You should think this through before you lump all products and customers together.

7. For lifetime value purposes, you need to estimate your direct costs. The easiest method is to compute them as a percent of revenue. The amount depends on your industry. Direct costs (for this purpose) include everything except marketing costs.

8. To compute lifetime value for a given group of customers, you add together the net profit from prior years to the net profit from the current year. This gives you the cumulative profit up to that year. This number is divided by the original number of customers.

9. Customers are assets, the same as buildings or cash. Another name for lifetime value is good will.

10. Customer lifetime value calculations also will help to determine how much effort to put into getting lost customers to come back.

11. Customer lifetime value also helps to determine the cost and the value of database marketing relationship-building efforts.

12. Each new strategy, such as gold cards, president's clubs, and newsletters, can and should be tested by measuring lifetime value before and after. If your calculations do not show an increase after your computation period, drop or modify your strategy before it is too late.

## Executive Quiz 3

Answers to quiz questions can be found in Appendix B. The quizzes are for fun. Do them if you enjoy quizzes. Ignore them if you don't.
*Choose the best answer to complete each statement or question.*

1. What is the net present value of $4,000 to be received in three years? The rate of interest is 8 percent.
   a. $2,175.32
   b. $3,175.33
   c. $4,000.00
   d. $4,175.32
   e. None of the above

2. Why is lifetime value not used more by marketers today?
   a. They do not have a database
   b. They do not understand it
   c. They are under pressure to produce
   d. All of the above
   e. None of the above

3. The rate of interest is 14 percent. You have to wait four years for your money. What is the discount rate (not including risk)?
   a. 1.00
   b. 1.22
   c. 1.69
   d. 1.82
   e. 2.07

4. Retention rate is calculated by dividing the number of customers at any one time this year by
   a. the number of customers in some original period several years ago
   b. the number of customers one year ago
   c. the market rate of interest plus the risk
   d. the expected referral rate
   e. None of the above

5. You began with 2,000 customers last year. This year you have 1,060. What is your retention rate?
   a. 43
   b. 53
   c. 63
   d. 73
   e. 83

6. In Year4 the discount rate is 1.8. The revenue is $142,846. What is the net present value of that revenue?
   a. $257,122
   b. $157,122
   c. $142,846
   d. $79,359
   e. None of the above

7. Revenue is $50,000. The direct cost ratio is 80 percent. What are the direct costs?
   a. $10,000
   b. $20,000
   c. $40,000
   d. $50,000
   e. $60,000

8. There were originally 1,000 customers. After Year4, there are only 200 left. The cumulative NPV profit in that year from this group is $48,210. What is the NPV lifetime value per customer in Year4?
   a. $241.05
   b. $141.05
   c. $96.42
   d. $46.42
   e. $48.21

# Strategy: How to Build Profits with a Database

*The greatest obstacle to growth is not ignorance, but the illusion of knowledge. To sound a bit radical, the information age as we know it does not exist. What does exist is the non-information age, the age of information anxiety and information overwhelm. We have so much data and information available to us that instead of making better, more informed decisions, the exact opposite is occurring. Guesswork is the norm and success the exception. We are trying to keep up with an endlessly increasing base of information. And the fact is, we will never keep up ...*

*The illusion of knowledge exists because large amounts of data provide security. The reality, though, is that the data are never looked at or used. Why? Because most times there is no technology in place that can do anything meaningful with the data or find the patterns in the data that will energize it and make it come alive to answer our questions. Data alone are not enough. This suggests strongly that we need to change the way we think about and look at information.*

*By thinking of database marketing in broader terms, you can integrate into your business decision-making based on new technology that finds the patterns in your information, that gives you, with laser-beam precision, a complete understanding of where you are in your marketplace, what your prioritized opportunities are, why they are best for you and how and who to target for maximum return. And maybe most importantly, you get the ability to answer those questions now!*

*—Robert Posten, The Landis Group*

This is a chapter about the development of strategy. As you know by now, the main reason why database marketing has not been more successful to date is that few people know how to create and implement strategy. They know how to build databases, but that is not enough. Without a profit-making strategy, it is all money wasted.

## What Strategy Means in Database Marketing

The word strategy is a military term, derived from the Greek word *strategia*—a military general. The definition of strategy closest to our usage appears in the *American Heritage Dictionary*: "the art or skill of using stratagems in politics, business, courtship or the like" with *stratagem* being defined as "a deception." As used in marketing today, these definitions are clearly way off the mark.

What marketers mean by strategy is something like "a method of designing and putting into practice a profitable marketing program, one that increases sales, reduces costs, or both." The military definition of strategy relates to deceiving an enemy. In marketing, I suppose, the enemies are the competing firms. Database marketing, however, really ignores the competition. Database marketing is aimed at the mind of the customer. Strategies are devised to build long-term relationships with the customers resulting in an extended period of mutually profitable exchanges of products, services, and money. There is no deception involved if database marketing is done correctly. The stratagems, rather than being deceptions, are initiatives such as a club, a newsletter, technical support, or frequent shopper rewards.

### Choosing a Marketing Strategy

All marketing involves some strategy, even if it is as simple as providing quality merchandise at low prices in a convenient location. For many years, TROY-BILT had the strategy of coming out with a new model Roto Tiller each year, concentrating on a better and better product with more and more features. The strategy failed. The company went on the rocks in the late 1950s. In 1962, the new managers developed a different strategy: focus on what customers can do with the product, reaching them directly. The new strategy, based on database marketing, turned the company around.

How can you decide on the best marketing strategy for your product? No single answer has universal validity. For some products, mass marketing through retail stores is the best possible strategy. For some business-to-business products, telemarketing and sales calls beat all other methods.

There are thousands of situations, however, where database marketing—relationship building—in conjunction with other methods, is the most profitable solution. If you have such a product or service, you must devise an effective method of using your database to build profits. This chapter contains guidance on the development of this strategy.

## *What a Strategy Can Accomplish*

While there are scores of different database marketing strategies being pursued by different companies, they all have something in common. They all are designed either:

- To increase customer lifetime value of existing customers, or
- To find new customers by a targeted approach.

We can develop some general principles that apply to both of these database marketing objectives.

## Increasing Customer Lifetime Value

Customer lifetime value is defined as the net present value of the profit that you will realize on the average new customer during a given number of years. There are five methods in which database marketing can improve lifetime value of existing customers:

1. Increase the retention rate (customers remaining loyal buyers).
2. Increase the referral rate (customers recruiting other customers).
3. Increase the average annual purchases of each customer.
4. Decrease direct costs by changing the distribution method.
5. Decrease marketing costs.

To develop a workable strategy, each marketer must come up with clever ideas, using, among other things, the hundreds of ideas being tested by others. Each clever idea should be examined to determine to what extent it will affect one or more of the five methods listed above.

Any initiative has costs. A newsletter, membership card program, or survey will increase marketing costs. Whether the strategy is useful will be determined by finding out whether the benefit from improvements in the five methods will exceed the costs of the strategy. This determination can be made on paper before any funds have been expended. The determination can then be tested on a small scale before major expenditures have been made.

Only after the paper calculations and the tests are over is it necessary to commit serious marketing dollars to a database project. At that point, you will know that your strategy will succeed. This is the customer strategy development process.

## Finding New Customers

The other objective of database marketing is targeted marketing to new prospects. While there are scores of different strategies, they all have the same three-step procedure in common:

1. Profile the existing customer base together with a test mailing to determine the characteristics of those people who respond best or who are the most profitable customers. If you have no existing customers, you can still use the method by doing a test mailing, and determining the profile of the respondents versus the nonrespondents.
2. Clone these desirable (responsive or profitable) people by matching these profiles to outside lists of prospects that match the characteristics of the respondents or profitable people.
3. Market to these clones using methods that have been shown to be effective in tests.

To carry out these methods, it is necessary to survey your existing customers to ask them demographic questions (age, income, presence of children, or other factors relevant to your marketing situation and likely to be coded on external rented lists). You also can overlay the existing customer base or a test mailing with external data relevant to separating the respondents from nonrespondents (or heavy users from light users). Once the overlay process is complete, it is necessary to do ad hoc cross tabulations or neural network modeling to find out which of the pieces of data (overlaid and existing) are relevant to the problem of separating the respondents from the nonrespondents. Then you must go out and rent names that match the profile of the heavy respondents. You develop targeted marketing programs to segments of these lists.

If you have done your profiling, overlaying, and targeting correctly, you will know that your strategy will succeed. This is the prospect strategy development process.

## Understanding the Customer

The role of a database is to provide a place to store and retrieve data about customers and prospects. Manipulation of this data is the method whereby we gain knowledge and understanding of the customers. It is this understanding that permits us to select the right strategies. There are a number of problems involved in developing this understanding that must be dealt with before adequate strategy development can take place. They are:

- The information problem
- The profit problem
- The focus problem
- The identification problem
- The hardware problem

Let's discuss these problems, and see how we can devise strategies that deal successfully with them.

### The Information Problem

A few years ago, my son-in-law Jack Baumgartner, my daughter Robin, and the children were visiting for the weekend. Jack had just lost 35 pounds on a no fat diet. I was amazed. He looked great. Jack and Robin explained to me exactly how the diet works: You don't eat low fat, you eat no fat.

I decided to try it. I began to read the labels of foods. I found that almost everything is labeled with the fat content. I also discovered that besides all the vegetables and fruit, you can get no fat margarine, cheese, sour cream, eggs, yogurt, bread, cake, pizza, spaghetti sauce, cereal, and cookies.

There is a whole world of no fat out there that I was unaware of. In the space of nine months, I lost 20 pounds and two inches from my waist, and have kept them off ever since.

The point of this personal note: Where were the manufacturers? I am a reasonably well-read person who does all the shopping in our household. (Helena is very busy making movies.) Why did I have to find out about this from Jack and Robin?

The answer: The American marketplace is a very complex, confusing clutter with too much data and not enough information. There was a time, not so long ago, when grocers had a few hundred products on their shelves, and everyone knew what they were. Today there is a constantly changing mix of 30,000 products in the average supermarket, and no one can possibly really know much about more than a fraction of them.

People want information, and they don't know how to get it. Manufacturers want to supply it, but they aren't doing a very good job of it. They are barraging us with so much advertising, that most of us are missing the important information—if it is there at all.

The problem is not confined to food. We have today dozens of competitive markets that require specialized knowledge to function as a customer, let alone as a supplier:

- Computer hardware and software
- Videos and VCRs

- Music records, tapes, compact discs
- Office, home, and cellular phones; faxes; answering machines
- Mortgages, home equity, credit cards, personal loans
- Stocks, bonds, mutual funds, partnerships

The biggest problem in all these marketplaces is information. For customers the problem is understanding what is out there, how it works, how we could use it to our advantage, how much it costs, and what we should buy. For suppliers, the problem is how to get the word out, how to let people know what they have, how it works, how it would benefit them, and where they should buy it.

Most people are missing important information in the market because they don't know how to get it—and because they are unaware that they are missing it!

To make things even more confusing, the market is changing very, very rapidly. No one can keep up with the new products produced in the computer and software industries, to mention one. It is almost impossible to make a purchase without the virtual certainty that somewhere out there is a product that is better for your application, or a similar one that is less expensive than what you bought. It is just too difficult and too expensive to do the research to find it.

If your strategy is to be successful, it must find a way to solve the information problem: to make your customers aware of what you have. "Well, the best way to do that is mass marketing!" I can hear you saying. Not necessarily. Mass marketing just adds to the cacophony out there that's not getting through to the right people.

Database marketing can solve the information problem by helping you learn what customers want, and then telling them about that. How do you do that?

- Through surveys (see Chapter 7, Building Relationships with Surveys) and storing the results of the surveys in your database
- Through profiling to segment your customers into affinity groups (senior citizens, working mothers, sports enthusiasts, couch potatoes—see Chapter 6, Using Customer Profiles in Marketing Strategy) and designing messages specifically for them
- Through newsletters and personal communications targeted to the right people

This does not, of course, exhaust the list. It is just a start. Your job is to recognize the problem and figure out how you can use your database to solve it.

## The Profit Problem

We have learned the first lesson in strategy development for database marketing: The market is filled with change, ignorance, and lack of information. To have a successful strategy, we must help the customer solve this problem. The second problem concerns the importance of profit.

The market is an exchange process. Everyone is trading something that they value less for something that they value more. The implication of the principle of exchange is this: If you, as a supplier, want to consummate market exchanges, you must figure out a way to be sure that your trading partner makes a profit. People will not trade unless they do make a profit. You must put yourself in the customer's shoes and say, "If I were the customer, why would I want to be in this company's database? What's in it for me? What good could come of my having a relationship with those guys?" If there is no good answer to this question, any database marketing strategy in this situation will fail.

How do you solve the profit problem? The first step is to determine, through your database, what your customers consider as profit. Is it discounts, delivery method, customer service, technical support, recognition, identification? Different customers have different ideas of profit. You can deal differently with each customer once you know what he or she wants.

Surveys will help to determine what each customer wants. Only a small percentage of your customers will respond to the surveys, however. Once you have surveys from 5 percent of your customers, you can match the survey results to profiles you have developed and ascribe the opinions of the respondents to the nonrespondents. It isn't perfect, but it is much better than nothing.

Once you know what people want, your next job is to figure out how to give it to them. You have begun to execute what should be a profitable and customer-based strategy.

## The Focus Problem

The third problem concerns the focus of your business: the products versus the customers. Many companies focus their attention on the products. Whoever first said "If you can build a better mousetrap, the world will beat a path to your door" certainly did not understand today's marketplace. Thousands of wonderful services and products, including mousetraps, fail every year because the makers cannot get the word out. The companies go bankrupt; employees are laid off. The problem today is not how to make it, but how to sell it.

It is often said, with great truth, that it is easier to sell products to existing customers, than it is to find new customers in the marketplace. Why, then, do companies focus their attention on products and services and not on the cultivation of their relationships with existing customers? The answer is that most companies do not know how to focus on customers.

Shortly after writing *The Complete Database Marketer,* I sent a letter to Lee Iacocca, then Chrysler's CEO, complaining about the fact that Chrysler did not have a customer database and made no attempt to cultivate me as a customer, even though I had bought three new Chrysler cars in the previous five years. I didn't get a letter from Lee. Instead I got a telephone call from Chrysler's director of sales for the Eastern region in Baltimore. He assured me that Chrysler did have a customer database, and that I was on it. That was almost three years ago. I have never heard a word from them since, by mail or phone, with the exception of a legal recall notice for engine exhaust emissions.

Does Chrysler need me as a customer? Of course. They have been offering cash back, zero percent financing, and multiyear warranties to everyone who would listen. But those messages are directed at the general public. They have never directed any one of those messages to me as a loyal and valued customer. The message I have received from Chrysler is that I am not a valued customer at all. I am nobody special, and should content myself with the same messages that everyone else gets from Chrysler.

This is a very foolish way to run a company in today's marketplace. Database marketing is not that difficult. It is not that expensive, and it pays rich dividends. It requires, however, a fundamental rethinking of the focus of the company. Chrysler, like many others, will have to stop focusing exclusively on the product they are trying to sell, and start concentrating on the customers they are trying to do business with.

*Saying* you are customer focused is not *being* customer focused. The strategy of focusing on the customer really involves changing the attitudes and working habits of a large number of people in your company. You will have to go to the top to get approval to do what is needed. Backed up with hard data from your database, you should be able to prove to top management what a shift to customer-based marketing will cost, and will do to the company profits. Customer focus should not be done because it is a nice way to operate, only if it is the most profitable way to operate. You have the tools to determine whether it is profitable.

## The Identification Problem

It is a lonely world out there. The American family system is breaking up. There are more and more divorces and single parent homes. Children leave home at an early age and never come back. Grandparents and aunts and uncles rarely move in with their families. Children move to distant cities. The family gets together—if at all—only a few times a year. The telephone is in. Personal visits are out. Family values are taking a beating.

Compared to the family, communities seem even worse. The village shopkeeper, letter carrier, druggist, police chief, librarian, and mayor no longer know the people they serve. People move in and out of communities without ever getting to know their neighbors or the established leaders (whoever they are).

Yet many people feel the need to belong to something. Americans today define themselves by where they work and what they do.

> "I'm a programmer. I work for Microsoft."
> "I'm a broker. I work for Merrill Lynch."

People like to identify themselves with some institution larger than themselves. Membership in nonprofit institutions is at an all-time high.

In many cases, people want to identify themselves with products that they own or use. Products say something about them and their taste.

> "I drive a Saturn."
> "I fly American."
> "We are a Macintosh shop."
> "I believe in Nordstrom."

Companies that want to survive will provide their customers with something for them to identify with: an institution that stands for something, that has a vision of what the world should be like, that they and their customers can share.

Is this a basis for strategy, or is this just maudlin nonsense? Ask the companies that have successfully developed this idea, sold it to their customers, and kept the faith by living by it. If you have a good product and a good company, people want to identify with you, if you will let them.

How do you provide an institution to identify with? There are dozens of ways, beginning with integration of your advertising message with your database marketing, as State Farm tried to do. Give your customers something to hold in their hand that helps them to identify with you. Ask for their opinions on how your business is run. Set up advisory panels, president's clubs, charter memberships. When people respond to your overtures, go back with a thank you, and tuck the information in the database. Refer to their helpfulness again and again in personal correspondence. Keep the bonding going. Your database must become super active.

Will identification pay off in terms of profits? Use lifetime value charts to determine whether it will increase the retention rate, referral rate, or annual sales rate. You can measure the results of identification efforts. If your analysis shows that identification, in your case, will not work, then forget about it. Database marketing is about profits, not about "nice ideas."

### The Hardware Problem

There is an important fifth concept that affects the other four: computer technology is racing ahead, and computer costs have been in a free fall for almost a decade. It is now possible to do wonderful things to build relationships with customers that were impossible or prohibitively expensive 10 years ago. We can keep track of our customers, store mountains of data, retrieve it in seconds, and develop event-driven software that can generate direct one-on-one communications with the greatest of ease.

The problem is that few companies have had the imagination to exploit this medium.

> While database marketing was made possible by rapid advancements in computer technology, the concept relies upon creativity and analysis, and a willingness to innovate. Without a conscious effort, no hardware, software, or marketing capabilities can be fully utilized ...
>
> No canned package can analyze competitive strengths and weaknesses, or design marketing strategies. Hint: Your mindset and your ability to design and produce meaningful analyses must provide the bridge between your software package and the implementation of an integrated database marketing program.
> —Jeffrey Parnell, Overton's Inc.

Only a handful of the tens of thousands of companies in the United States that could be building relationships with their customers are doing so today. The reason is that cited by Jeff Parnell: a lack of creative imagination in the development of strategy, and the selection of data upon which to build the strategy.

We can sum up the hardware problem in this way: Modern computer technology makes database marketing possible, but it also diverts marketers' attention from the marketing problem. It leads them to play with computers instead of dreaming up strategies to build relationships with their customers.

Playing with computers has a significant cost. The computers and software are comparatively inexpensive. What is not inexpensive is the staff time that must be devoted to maintaining databases on personal computers, backing up, fixing bugs, restarting systems, loading new software, etc. This cost is estimated at $6,000 per user per year. Worse than the direct cost is the indirect cost. Marketers who are supposed to be developing and executing profitable marketing strategies by building customer relationships are diverted into make-work activities. The cost to the marketing program is sometimes significant.

## The Lifetime Value Focus

"Focus on the customer" is a nice sounding phrase. It has a nice ring to it. But what does it really mean? How can we justify taking real dollars out of the advertising budget to devote to relationship building. How can we show that customer communications designed to strengthen customer loyalty translate into the standard measures of corporate success: expanded sales, reduced costs, and increased profits?

To be justifiable, strategy has to contain a measurement technique that can tell us how much should be allocated to it, and how much can we expect it to accomplish.

This is where lifetime value comes in. Let's show by a practical example how customer lifetime value ties together all the building blocks listed above into a clean and clear guide to strategy development.

### A Customer Newsletter

We are selling software. Let's assume that we have about 500,000 customers at any given time. It is proposed that we start a newsletter to our existing customers designed to:

- Describe how the product is being used by others
- Tell about new features coming out in new releases
- Help customers to form user groups
- Supply fixes and tricks to solve problems
- Encourage users to call the technical hotline with their problems
- Get users to suggest improvements in the software and service
- Get more nonregistered users to register through amnesty programs

The real purpose, of course, is to affect lifetime value. It is expected that the newsletter will:

- Encourage customers to buy the annual upgrades
- Encourage customers to buy related products

- Encourage referrals of new customers through user groups and incentive programs
- Keep customers from shifting to the competition

The newsletter, in other words, is much more than a newsletter. It is a shorthand way of referring to many marketing activities built up around the idea of regular customer correspondence.

This is what is meant by strategy. Whether the strategy is effective is measurable. We know how many customers we have on the database. We know (or can estimate) the average amount they spend on our products—even though the purchases are made at retail stores and mail order houses. Let's see how we can estimate the customer lifetime value before and after the newsletter is introduced.

The present situation is this: The software sells for about $300 retail, of which about 20 percent is profit. Half of the customers desert the software each year. Of those who remain, only about half purchase the annual upgrades and associated products, spending an average of about $24 per year.

According to Table 4-1 below, the lifetime customer value rises from $60 per year in Year1 to $63.62 in Year5. Multiplying that by 500,000 customers gives a net present profit picture of $31,810,000.

### Table 4-1: Lifetime Value of Software Customers without Newsletter

|    | Revenue | Year1 | Year2 | Year3 | Year4 | Year5 |
|----|---------|-------|-------|-------|-------|-------|
| R1 | Customers | 1,000 | 500 | 275 | 165 | 107 |
| R2 | Retention Rate | 50 | 55 | 60 | 65 | 70 |
| R3 | Average Yearly Sale | $300 | $24 | $24 | $24 | $24 |
| R4 | Total Revenue | $300,000 | $12,000 | $6,600 | $3,960 | $2,568 |
|    | **Costs** | | | | | |
| C1 | Cost Percent | 80 | 80 | 80 | 80 | 80 |
| C2 | Total Costs | $240,000 | $9,600 | $5,280 | $3,168 | $2,054 |
|    | **Profits** | | | | | |
| P1 | Gross Profit | $60,000 | $2,400 | $1,320 | $792 | $514 |
| P2 | Discount Rate | 1.00 | 1.20 | 1.44 | 1.73 | 2.07 |
| P3 | NPV Profit | $60,000 | $2,000 | $917 | $458 | $248 |
| P4 | Cumulative NPV Profit | $60,000 | $62,000 | $62,917 | $63,374 | $63,623 |
| L1 | **Lifetime Value (NPV)** | $60.00 | $62.00 | $62.92 | $63.37 | $63.62 |

You can sum up the situation by saying that the big money is in the new customers. Those existing customers who make further purchases do not add very much. It is a self-fulfilling prophecy. The advertising manager is (correctly) putting all his money into general advertising, aiming at attracting new customers and ignoring those who have already signed up.

## Impact of the Newsletter

The newsletter and the other activities associated with the newsletter are designed to change the situation radically. They are aimed at reducing the attrition rate and increasing referrals, the participation in annual upgrades, and cross sales possibilities. Table 4-2 shows what could happen:

**Table 4-2: Lifetime Value of Software Customers with Newsletter**

|    |                        |          |          |          |          |          |
|----|------------------------|----------|----------|----------|----------|----------|
|    | **Revenue**            |          |          |          |          |          |
| R1 | Referral Rate          | 5        | 5        | 5        | 5        | 5        |
| R2 | Referred Customers     |          | 50       | 35       | 26       | 20       |
| R3 | Total Customers        | 1,000    | 700      | 525      | 394      | 296      |
| R4 | Retention Rate         | 65       | 70       | 70       | 70       | 70       |
| R5 | Average Yearly Sale    | $300     | $60      | $70      | $80      | $90      |
| R6 | Total Revenue          | $300,000 | $42,000  | $36,750  | $31,520  | $26,640  |
|    | **Costs**              |          |          |          |          |          |
| C1 | Cost Percent           | 80       | 50       | 50       | 50       | 50       |
| C2 | Direct Costs           | $240,000 | $21,000  | $18,375  | $15,760  | $13,320  |
| C3 | Newsletter ($3.20)     | $3,200   | $3,360   | $3,472   | $3,555   | $3,619   |
| C4 | Related Activities ($2)| $2,000   | $1,400   | $1,050   | $788     | $592     |
| C5 | Total Costs            | $245,200 | $25,760  | $22,897  | $20,103  | $17,531  |
|    | **Profits**            |          |          |          |          |          |
| P1 | Gross Profit           | $54,800  | $16,240  | $13,853  | $11,417  | $9,109   |
| P2 | Discount Rate          | 1.00     | 1.20     | 1.44     | 1.73     | 2.07     |
| P3 | NPV Profit             | $54,800  | $13,533  | $9,620   | $6,599   | $4,400   |
| P4 | Cumulative NPV Profit  | $54,800  | $68,333  | $77,953  | $84,553  | $88,953  |
| L1 | **Lifetime Value (NPV)** | $54.80 | $68.33   | $77.95   | $84.55   | $88.95   |

Several significant things have happened. As a result of the newsletter, current customers are referring new customers at the rate of about 5 percent per year. These new customers come in at a special reduced rate, including compensation to the current customers for referring them. As a result, the retention rate of customers has increased from 50 percent per year to 60 percent the first year and 70 percent thereafter. The sales of product to remaining customers including the new referrals has increased from $24 per year to $60 per year, growing to $90 to the loyalists still hanging on after five years.

Against this, we must increase the expenses by $3.20 per customer per year for the newsletter and $2 per customer for associated marketing activities. You will note that the company continues to mail the newsletter to the original 1,000 customers, plus the new referrals, even though by Year5 only 274 are still left. Why beat a dead horse? This is a testable strategy. Divide the customer base into two groups: continue to send the newsletter to nonrespondents in one group, and drop the newsletter to nonrespondents in the other group when they fall by the wayside.

The effect of the newsletter associated activities is to increase the lifetime value of customers from $63.62 to $88.95. The five-year net present value of profits from the 500,000 customer base is now $44,475,000 instead of $31,810,000, an increase of $12,665,000. Not a bad result for a newsletter.

How do we know that the newsletter will accomplish all these things? We don't. No one knows. But we have a plan. We have worked it out. It is possible that the newsletter could have this impact, and be produced for these costs. Nothing ventured, nothing gained.

Each year, as we go along, we will test to see what is happening. Perhaps the retention rate is not as good as we had hoped. Perhaps the annual sales increase to current customers is not as great as we had anticipated. Perhaps the referral rate is not as substantial as we hoped, and needs to be fine tuned. Fine, redo the calculations. If the newsletter is not pulling its weight, revise it or scrap it.

I am not illustrating here the benefits of a newsletter (which may, in fact, be worthless), but the benefits of a hard-headed method of evaluation of strategy in advance by careful calculations.

### What the Newsletter Strategy Does

In this example, the newsletter with its associated activities accomplishes a number of the basic strategy imperatives outlined in this chapter.

- It provides information to our customers who are operating in a confusing marketplace filled with ignorance and doubt.
- It provides a profit to our customers for being in the database. Information may not cost us much, if anything. We already know all about our software, but the customers don't. Finding out something new about a product they use every day is worth real money to them.
- It reduces our costs. Notice that the direct costs go from 80 percent down to 50 percent. Why is that? Because we are now selling our upgrades and supplementary products directly to the customer. We are able to keep half of what the customer spends, instead of only 20 percent of it.
- It assists in defining the institution so that customers can identify with it. Saying "Weyerhaeuser, the tree growing company" in awareness advertising is great. Even greater, however, is providing the same message personally to Weyerhaeuser customers in a way that helps them to identify with the mission and vision of the company.
- It increases the customer base through referrals and through reduced attrition.

## How Strategy Is Developed

Presented later in this chapter and throughout this book are examples of database marketing strategies being developed or in active use in companies during the 1990s. How do these companies think up all these ideas?

There are a series of steps that any company can go through that should work if applied rigorously.

- Put yourself in your customers' shoes. Figure out what your customers want that you might be able to provide. Is it technical information, repair service, spare parts, creative ideas for use of the product, or customer service? The ideas will work to solve the information problem, the profit problem, the focus problem, or the identification problem. Come up with a shopping list. This is the beginning of the strategy.
- Work out the costs and benefits. Each strategy that you have devised will have some benefits in terms of customer actions. It should increase the number of customers, reduce attrition (lengthen customer time with you), increase annual sales per customer, reduce your direct costs, or reduce your marketing costs.

All this is quantifiable. At the same time, the costs of each strategy are also quantifiable.

- Do a lifetime value analysis. When you know the costs and benefits, the effect of the strategy on lifetime value can be calculated. Some strategies will make lifetime value decrease; they will be harmful, even though they sound great. Scrap these ideas fast.

## Examples of Strategies

Following are a small group of successful strategies to pique your imagination. They are by no means comprehensive. There are scores of others presented in the remaining chapters of this book.

### Customer Referral Programs

The MCI Friends & Family program is brilliant database marketing in several different ways. Under this program, MCI customers furnish the names and telephone numbers of friends and family members that they call frequently. These supplied names, of course, are MCI's prospect database. This program creates a club and a club within a club (identification). It enlists the member to help with the marketing, and it helps MCI to identify their competitors' customers by comparing the names suggested by members with the MCI subscriber base.

Prospects in the database are sent a check (see Figure 4-1) and a letter, which links the prospect to the customer who first supplied the name.

***Figure 4-1: Check from MCI Friends & Family***

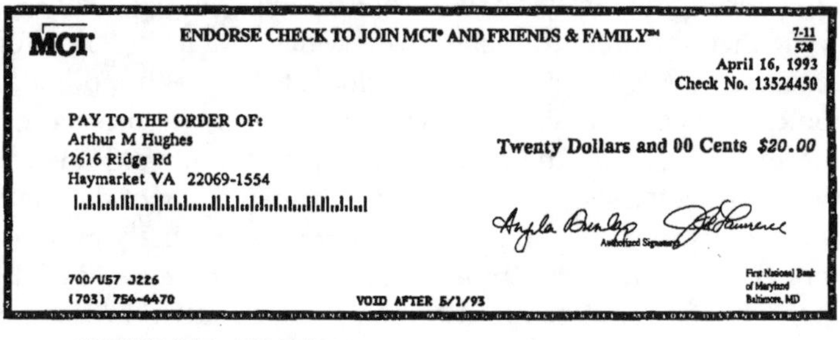
MCI
ENDORSE CHECK TO JOIN MCI® AND FRIENDS & FAMILY℠
7-11
520
April 16, 1993
Check No. 13524450
PAY TO THE ORDER OF:
Arthur M Hughes
2616 Ridge Rd
Haymarket VA 22069-1554
Twenty Dollars and 00 Cents $20.00
Authorized Signature
700/U57 J226
(703) 754-4470
VOID AFTER 5/1/93
First National Bank of Maryland Baltimore, MD
⑈13524450⑈ ⑆052000113⑆ 425⑈2640 6⑈

The wording that goes with the check is interesting:

> Important: Mr. Jack Baumgartner has nominated you for membership in MCI and Friends & Family.
> Action Needed: Sign and cash your $20 check and call 1 800 688-2336 Ext. 2260 to join MCI and save.
> Arthur M. Hughes: Important Notice ...
> The attached check is real. We've sent it to you because you've been nominated by Mr. Jack Baumgartner to join MCI's popular Friends & Family long distance savings program ... Mr. Jack Baumgartner already enjoys the extra 20 percent savings benefit of Friends & Family when calling Circle members who are MCI customers. And so can you ...
> Questions? Please read the back of this page ... talk with Mr. Jack Baumgartner ...

What was the effect on me? I wanted to participate because I felt that by joining I would help Jack Baumgartner (my son-in-law) in some way. There is no wonder that the program built MCI's business like gangbusters.

The Carnation Perform Program for door-to-door delivered premium dog and cat food also included a customer referral program. When customers referred a neighbor or friend, customers received credit on their next orders if the referred person purchased the product. Veterinarians and breeders also received credit when their customers purchased Perform directly by calling a toll-free number for Carnation's Perform animal nutrition specialist.

For such programs to work, the customer doing the work for you has to make a profit. Some of them will do it for free, of course, but you should not count on that. The profit they make does not have to be in cash. It could be recognition:

> "You are now a member of our 'Sponsor's Club.' We look to our sponsors to advise us on products and services so as to make Molly's Candies the best in the world."

### Development of Niche Markets

Database marketing is the opposite of mass marketing. With database marketing, you can offer different products to different people. You can serve a variety of different tastes, which is not possible with mass marketing. By consulting the customers and using your database, you can discover what these niches are. This is an effective strategy.

Jeffrey Parnell of Overton's, a master marketer, suggests a technique. Suppose your primary audience is men. You discover by analysis that certain products you offer are purchased mainly by women. What are these products? What can we conclude about this audience's demographics and psychographics? Can you spin off a specialty catalog featuring only that type of product, and send it exclusively to the women in your database?

You may think that for a certain product, your primary audience is young couples with children. Lo and behold, there are a number of senior citizens who buy the product. Why? Are they grandparents? Or is there some other reason? Telemarketing, or surveys of these older buyers, may disclose a valuable and overlooked niche. Knowing of this niche can help you to target your offers specifically to this group, rather than to your customer base in general.

How can you find these niches? The answer comes about from constant experimentation with the customer database using ad hoc queries. Assuming that you have captured or overlaid the database with lots of information (age, income, sex, education, purchasing behavior, products purchased, dates, dollar amounts, cluster codes, presence of children, etc.), you begin to ask questions of your database:

```
IF (PRODUCT IS A,B) AND (BUYDATE WITHIN 9401, 9404)
COUNT PRODUCT BY AGERANGE
```

If that does not show you anything important, try it again with:

COUNT PRODUCT BY SEX
COUNT PRODUCT BY CHILDREN
COUNT PRODUCT BY YTDSALES

... and so on. Eventually, if there is a niche there, you will discover it. If you have good software, each query will take 10 or 15 seconds.

Figure 4-2 shows an example of the results of running one of these queries with modern software. It took six seconds to run across a customer database of 2.7 million customers.

### Figure 4-2: Customers for A and B by Age Range

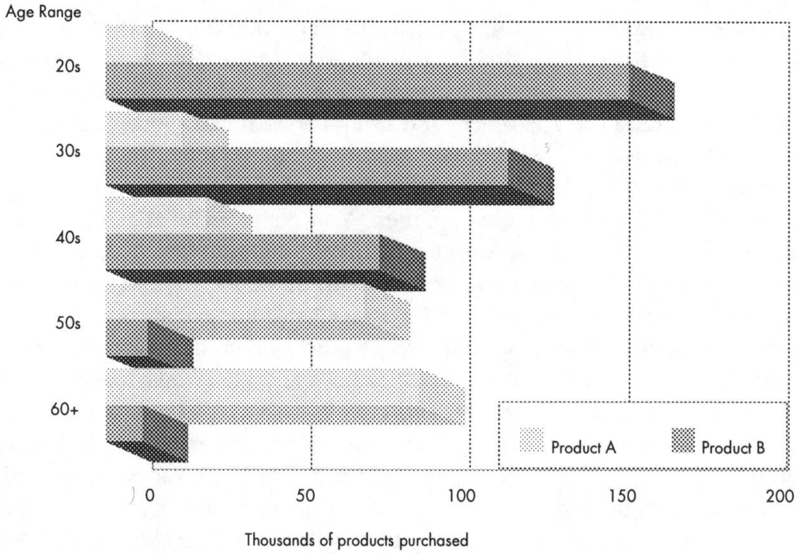

Thousands of products purchased

In this query, Product B clearly outsold Product A. In addition, Product B appealed to younger people. Can you use that information in developing a strategy? There is something else interesting here. Product A sells much better than Product B with older people. In people over age 50, Product A outsells Product B by nine to one. Product A should be sold to older people, and Product B to younger people.

Once you have identified your niche, you can take your analysis one step further. How do the sales of the two products vary by income levels? Figure 4-3 shows the same sales of the two products, but arranged by income instead of age. Look at the huge sales of Product B to lower-income people. Clearly, the niche for this product is for lower-income people in their 20s!

**Figure 4-3: Customers for A and B by Income Level**

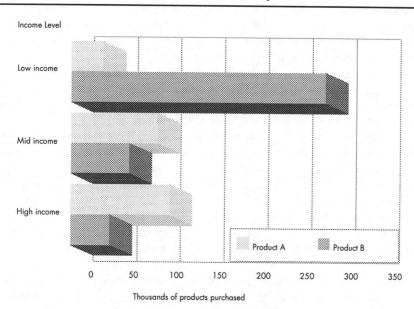

This is the beginning of knowledge, the precursor to the development of a strategy.

You can, and should, run ad hoc queries like this all day until you really understand your customer database: what makes them buy what they buy? Your next step is the intuitive one: "How can we use this information to help these customers to know more about products and services that they are obviously interested in?"

A niche is not a selling opportunity. It is a service opportunity. By offering something that someone is interested in, and wants to buy, you are providing a valuable public service that will make the customers happy and more loyal. If your strategy can result in providing services to your customers that they want and will take advantage of, the profits will take care of themselves.

## Integration of Marketing Processes

Databases can be used to integrate processes that once were taken separately and unconnectedly. The result of such integration can be to create the mechanism to improve relations with customers, build loyalty, and repeat sales.

Everyone knows the person most likely to buy from us again is the person that just bought something from us. We know that, but very few companies have put in place any means of making it easy for the customer to do just that. GeGe Mix, vice president of database marketing systems at Maritz, Inc., in Fenton, Missouri, described how they were able to put the pieces together for an electronics manufacturer.

Before Maritz began, the manufacturer had the traditional approach to customer relations. A self-mailing warranty card was included with each product. A very small proportion of all cards were actually returned. When the cards were received, they were keypunched and retained on a customer list. No action was taken, because the products were sold through electronics stores. There was no direct channel, and no intention of developing one. The manufacturer was convinced that recommendations by store personnel were crucial to its overall success rate. It did not want to weaken the loyalty of the local dealers by offering an alternate channel.

Maritz began by estimating customer lifetime value based on the system then in place. Then Maritz designed an effective and comprehensive program to stimulate sales and loyalty that took the following steps:

1. Day One: The manufacturer placed national ads for the product on television and in print. The ads suggested calls to a toll-free number to receive literature and a coupon for a substantial product discount.
2. Week One: Those calling the number were added to a growing database, and sent a direct mail package including the coupon. The responses were used, as well, to monitor responses to the various media used for the program.
3. Week Two: Customers took the coupons to their local electronic stores to buy the product. The coupons entitled the customer to a discount and the dealer to an equal rebate to make up for the discount. To get the reimbursement, the dealer had to get the purchaser to fill out the warranty card, which was returned to the manufacturer together with the coupon for the dealer's reimbursement. The warranty card contained household demographics and other information. From these coupons, the manufacturer also was able to build a dealer database, subsequently used for relationship-building purposes.
4. Month One: Outbound telemarketing to the customer (using the telephone number supplied on the warranty card) provided feedback to the manufacturer on the service provided by the dealer and the acceptance by the customer of the product design features. A certain amount of customer service training also was provided in the telephone calls, plus research on product features. Feedback was provided to dealers on any compliments or complaints received.
5. Year One: Outbound telemarketing was conducted to determine the

owner's intention to purchase new products. The satisfaction survey was designed to boost loyalty and encourage repeat sales. Incentives were provided by those indicating an interest in further purchases.

The program was designed to:

- Increase dealer loyalty
- Improve product design and positioning
- Change the media mix to develop two-way communication
- Build customer loyalty and lifetime value

After the program had been in place for more than a year, Maritz could make a revision in customer lifetime value estimates.

### Selecting the Appropriate Communications Channel

What is the best way to communicate with customers? Different people and different messages work better through one channel than another. Some like telephone calls at work; others prefer home. Some don't want any phone calls at all. Some like direct mail.

GeGe Mix suggests using the database to analyze response compared to effort, which tells us the correct media to use. It could include:

| | |
|---|---|
| Direct mail | Television |
| Print | Sales promotion |
| Telemarketing | Interactive electronic media |
| Outdoor advertising | Event marketing |
| Sponsorships | Point-of-sale |
| Newsletters | Fulfillment offers |
| Public relations | Image advertising |
| Dealer programs | |

Every time the database is used to carry out strategy, track customer behavior, or tie in dealership programs, you should analyze the results and refine the existing intelligence in the database. The customer lifetime value should be recomputed and stored in the database. This improves profits and helps customers by reaching them through a method that they favor.

### Media Buying for Long-Term Customer Acquisition

If you build a database and keep track of the sources of your customers, you may discern differences between the long-term value of people attracted by different media. Table 4-3 shows the results of a typical customer acquisition process for a company that casts a wide net for customers. This company sells a food-related product that assumes repeated sales over a period of years.

### Table 4-3: Media Cost Calculations

| Media | Cost per 1,000 Exposures | Buyers per 1,000 Exposures | Acquisition Cost per Buyer |
|---|---|---|---|
| TV (30 sec.) | $5.40 | 0.30 | $18.00 |
| Infomercials | $10.00 | 0.50 | $20.00 |
| Newspaper | $16.00 | 0.70 | $22.86 |
| Magazines | $24.00 | 1.00 | $24.00 |
| Food Magazines | $26.00 | 1.10 | $23.64 |
| Radio | $5.00 | 0.20 | $25.00 |
| Direct Mail | $350.00 | 18.00 | $19.44 |

Analysis of this table shows that the most economical method of attracting new customers appears to be 30-second television commercials. The acquisition cost is determined by a simple formula:

$$AC = CPM \div BPM$$
where:   AC = acquisition cost
CPM = cost per 1,000 exposures
BPM = buyers per 1,000 exposures

An entirely different picture emerges when the company considers the retention factor of newly acquired customers. Looking at those customers who are still buying the second year after their initial acquisition, the picture looks like Table 4-4:

### Table 4-4: Media Cost Calculations for Two Years

| Media | CPM Exposures | Buyers per 1,000 | Acquisition Cost Year1 | Retention Rate | Acquisition Cost Year 2 |
|---|---|---|---|---|---|
| TV (30 sec.) | $5.40 | 0.30 | $18.00 | 10 | $180.00 |
| Infomercials | $10.00 | 0.50 | $20.00 | 12 | $166.67 |
| Newspaper | $16.00 | 0.70 | $22.86 | 20 | $114.29 |
| Magazines | $24.00 | 1.00 | $24.00 | 30 | $80.00 |
| Food Magazines | $26.00 | 1.10 | $23.64 | 40 | $59.09 |
| Radio | $5.00 | 0.20 | $25.00 | 15 | $166.67 |
| Direct Mail | $350.00 | 18.00 | $19.44 | 50 | $38.89 |

As you can see, the retention rate of the television buyers is only about 10 percent, whereas the rates are 40 percent from food magazines and 50 percent from direct mail.

The formula for acquisition cost of Year2 buyers is:

$$AC_2 = (CPM \div RPM) \div RR$$
where RR = Retention Rate (in decimals)

The acquisition cost for television buyers in Year2, thus is:

$$AC = (\$5.40 \div .3) \div .10 = \$180.00$$

From a long-term perspective of two years, the television acquisition method changes from being the most economical to being the most expensive. Direct mail and food magazines turn out to be the best long-term acquisition method.

### Discovery of Strengths and Weaknesses

If your growth rate is slipping due to market saturation, increasing competition, or a poorly conceived campaign, Jeff Parnell suggests that this may be the ideal time to use database marketing to solve your problems by identifying profitable niches that can be served by a different marketing approach.

If analysis shows that average order and response rates have dropped, look more closely to see what segment of your database is primarily responsible for the fall off. Suppose, for example, that it appears that your losses come mainly from people who in the past have purchased product X. Let's assume that product X is dress slacks.

Look at your competition's offerings of dress slacks. By comparing their prices and qualities with yours, you may find that:

- Wool slacks are the competitor's loss leader. Assign these products a competitive code of A in your database.
- With polyester slacks, you and the competitor are about equal. Assign a code of B.
- With cotton slacks, your product has little competition. Assign a code of C.

By comparing what customers bought in the past with what they are buying now, by competitive code, you can determine which customers are being lost to the competition and which ones are lost somewhere else versus the ones who have stayed with you.

With this knowledge, you have in hand the information necessary to determine a shift in your products and pricing. You also can target special offers to particular customers based on their propensity to purchase competitive items. Don't offer discounts to people who are not price sensitive.

Do offer discounts to those who are.

Careful testing can open up a whole new world of marketing that was impossible before you developed the database.

### Provide Super Customer Services

On Tuesday, Helena ordered a dress from The Very Thing (TVT) in Meredith, New Hampshire. She paid $138 by credit card. It arrived at our house in Virginia the next day. She wore it to a dinner party that night. TVT says in its catalog, "If you want to wear any of these exciting new TVT looks tomorrow, simply order by phone, toll free, today! All orders delivered overnight!" All purchases are shipped via Airborne Express. The shipping and handling charge includes the overnight service.

How easy is it for The Very Thing to do this? It is incredibly difficult. Arranging a contract with Airborne Express was the easy part. The hard part was getting their act together so that every order could be entered and credit card processed; and items selected, packed, addressed, and made ready in a few hours for the Airborne pickup.

Will Helena order from The Very Thing again? After the first dress arrived, her first impulse was to order something else to see if this fantastic experience was just a fluke, or was the real thing.

Is this just a gimmick, or is it a sound marketing strategy? I leave it to readers to decide.

The short sampling of strategies listed here does not do justice to the hundreds of creative ideas that are bubbling forth in database marketing staffs today. To get a better idea, attend the database marketing conferences given twice a year by Cowles Communications and the Direct Marketing Association, or one of the many others sponsored by the *Canadian Direct Marketing News* and other groups. To succeed in this field, you really have to get around the country and find out what other people are doing and thinking.

### Summary

1.  A database really has only two uses:

    • To market to existing customers, building loyalty and improving sales
    • To find new customers by profiling customers and finding prospects that match the profiles of the best customers

2.  Most database marketing failures stem from the inability of marketers to devise effective strategies for marketing to customers. The correct

route is found by solving some fundamental customer problems: providing information, helping the customer make a profit, focusing on the customer rather than the product, and giving the customer an institution to identify with. In the quest for a method of marketing to customers, marketers must avoid getting bogged down in computers and missing the customer strategy development process completely.

3. For database marketing to claim a share of the advertising dollar, it must prove itself. Customer lifetime value is the method whereby this can be done. The methods are: finding more customers, reducing attrition, selling more to each customer, and reducing costs. Lifetime value calculations measure all four.

## Executive Quiz 4

Answers to quiz questions can be found in Appendix B. The quizzes are for fun. Do them if you enjoy quizzes. Ignore them if you don't.
*Choose the best answer to complete each statement.*

1. In the free market process of today
   a. there is not enough data to make decisions.
   b. most participants know what is available and what it costs.
   c. suppliers have a hard job getting information into the hands of customers.
   d. most customers today do a good job of competitive shopping.
   e. product information is easily compared.

2. In a free market exchange
   a. both parties always make a profit.
   b. many customers are exploited by their suppliers.
   c. the main problem is production.
   d. the problem is one of scarcity of inputs.
   e. people often act without regard to their own self interest.

3. Companies focus on the product and not the consumer because
   a. it is more profitable to do that.
   b. federal regulations dictate this approach.
   c. that is what the competition is doing.
   d. most companies don't know how to focus on the customer.
   e. the public will reward the best products, not the best marketing methods.

4. The identification problem is this:
   a. family cohesion is very strong in the United States today.
   b. unions keep workers from identifying with their employers.
   c. people want to identify with institutions whose visions they share.
   d. most companies have no vision with which customers can identify.
   e. None of the above

5. The hardware problem is this:
   a. some marketers consider playing with computers a substitute for developing a marketing strategy.
   b. PC technology is not advancing rapidly enough.
   c. the cost of computers and software today is skyrocketing.
   d. most marketers don't understand computers.
   e. there are too many creators and not enough constructors.

6. Database marketing increases long term profits by
   a. finding more customers.
   b. getting customers to buy more.
   c. reducing attrition.
   d. reducing costs.
   e. All of the above

7. In the newsletter example, the newsletter reduced
   a. the retention rate.
   b. the sales/customer/year.
   c. the direct cost percentage.
   d. the lifetime value.
   e. None of the above

8. The newsletter
   a. provided a profit for customers.
   b. cost more than it was worth.
   c. discouraged user groups.
   d. reduced the retention rate.
   e. All of the above

# 5

# Building Profits with Recency, Frequency, Monetary (RFM) Analysis

*Being measured continually is a tough lesson. In direct [market-ing], it's cost per lead or cost per sale, not some art director's squin-ty-eyed aesthetic standard, that counts. And you learn very quickly that you can be wrong about how you think people will react. When you put it on the line this way, you become a different kind of creative person.*

*—Mike Slosberg, Wunderman Worldwide*

**M**ost companies treat their high-volume customers better than their low-volume customers. This makes sense. Someone who does a million dollars worth of business should be treated differ-ently from someone who spends only $100. Marketing efforts, customer service, and technical support of that million dollar customer are sound, logical, important ways of building company profits.

Few companies, however, go beyond that to categorize all their cus-tomers by behavior, making major efforts to retain their profitable cus-tomers and not wasting promotion and retention dollars on less valuable customers. These same companies, in addition, often continue to mail offers to nonrespondents year after year, pouring millions of promotional dollars down the drain. Those that use Recency, Frequency, Monetary (RFM) analysis can save these wasted dollars and build their profits. This chapter is about RFM analysis.

## RFM Calculation

RFM is a method of categorizing the records in a customer database so that you can know who are the most recent buyers, the most frequent buyers, and the biggest spenders. It is a way of profiling by behavior. RFM can be used only for customers. It is of little use for prospects, since you rarely have the needed data about them. RFM, also, is not possible if you don't have a database. The RFM data is derived from data (on purchases and responses) kept in the database, and RFM codes are stored in customer records in the database. Use of RFM analysis (with the associated testing) always improves the responses and profits in a rollout direct-response mailing. It is better than any model. It is the most powerful segmentation method you can use with a database.

### Recency

Recency is the most powerful of the three measures. Someone who has made a purchase from you quite recently is much more likely to buy from you again than someone who bought from you several months or years ago. It is for this reason that every time you deliver a product to a buyer or receive a registration card, you should bounce back with a catalog or flier on some other product that you have for sale. Hit them while they're hot. In that momentary rush of enthusiasm for the new product and your company, they are most likely to buy something else. They will welcome the opportunity to do business with you again.

All database records must include a field that indicates the date of the most recent purchase so records can be selected by recency.

In addition, each record should have a code for recency quintile, which is recomputed each time the database is updated. A quintile is one-fifth of the database. You can use codes composed of quintile numbers like 5, 4, 3, 2, 1 (with 5 being the most recent). To compute these codes, the entire customer database is sorted by last date order and divided into quintiles (five equal groups) from most recent to most ancient. Quintile 5 is the 20 percent of your customers who have purchased the most recently. Quintile 4 is the 20 percent with next most recent purchasers, etc.

These recent buyers—Quintile 5—are your most responsive customers, as shown by Figure 5-1. As a general rule, direct marketers have found that the most recent buyers will always respond better than any other group in your database. You can plan your marketing programs around use of that code, and become much more successful in your marketing than you would by ignoring recency.

Here are examples of strategies using recency:

- If you have budget money left after a campaign, use the money to mail a second time to recent buyers. It will be the best use of your money.
- The customers in Quintile 1—the ones who purchased from you a long time ago—should be the subject of reactivation marketing, designed to get them to come back, or perhaps dropped from your regular marketing efforts.

**Figure 5-1: Response by Recency**

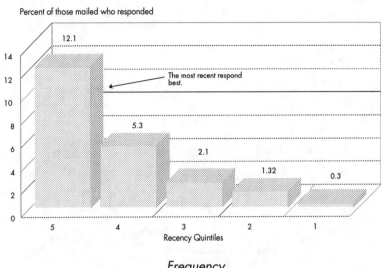

Percent of those mailed who responded

Recency Quintiles

## Frequency

The second most powerful factor in customer purchase behavior is frequency: the number of times that a person makes a purchase from you. This measure should be stored in all customer records. A quintile breakdown is essential here, too (use 5 through 1). Those coded 5 will respond better to any promotion than those lower down in the quintiles, as illustrated in Figure 5-2.

Frequency is useful in marketing. Rewards can be given to Quintile 5. That fact can be advertised to Quintile 4, encouraging them to get the benefits accorded to Quintile 5 by making just a few more purchases.

Frequency has to be combined with recency to understand customer behavior properly. Members of Quintile 1 in frequency can be excellent customers if they are also in Quintile 5 in recency. A brand new customer always will be a Quintile 5 in recency and a Quintile 1 in frequency. Given time, their frequency may move up, while their recency may move down.

Any time you need quick, and almost assured responses, reach out to the "55" group: most recent and most frequent. They are your most loyal customers, and the best responders to almost anything.

## Monetary Amount

The third measure is created by calculating the total dollar amount purchased by each customer since they first joined your database. This amount

### Figure 5-2: Response by Frequency

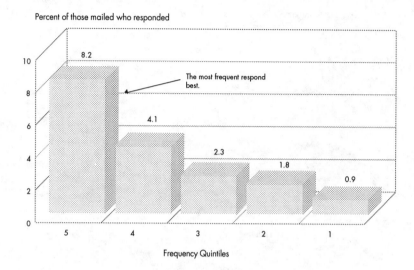

Percent of those mailed who responded

should be stored in a field in each record. Sort your database by monetary amount during each update, divide it into quintiles, and create a 5 through 1 code showing the group that spends the most money, the next group, etc.

Figure 5-3 shows that the biggest spenders respond better. Monetary amount is not as powerful a predictor as recency, however, for a simple reason: It takes time to get to Quintile 5. A monetary amount of 1, therefore, is not necessarily bad. This person just may be a new customer.

## Storing the RFM Codes in the Customer Record

Depending on your business, RFM can be a very powerful method of profiling. The combination of the three measures (R, F, and M), when put together, categorizes each customer as a 555 through a 111, with 125 possible combinations in all. You will soon learn to predict the response to any promotion by means of RFM. Here's how to code your file:

1. With each update of your file, create a list of the most recent contact (or purchase) date of each customer.
2. Sort the list from newest to oldest date.
3. Divide the list into five equal parts (quintiles).
4. Assign a 5 to the top group, 4 to the next, etc.
5. Put the quintile number into each customer record. The number will change with each update.

**Figure 5-3: Response by Monetary Amount**

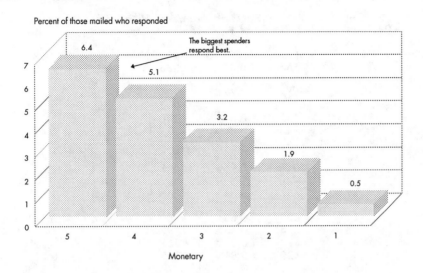

6. Repeat steps 1 through 5 for frequency and for monetary amount (total purchases since the database was started). You will have three numbers in every customer record.

7. Set up reports for every marketing program to existing customers categorizing them by RFM code. There will be 125 lines in each report.

Table 5-1 shows what a report could look like. Let's examine this chart in some detail. Shown below is a portion of the entire table which has 125 lines, showing the response to RFM cells from 555 down to 111. To do the mailing, the entire customer base of one million was coded with three-digit RFM cell codes (Column B). Once this was done, the percentage of the file represented by each cell code was computed (Column C). An exact cross-section sample (called an Nth) of the entire file of one million was taken, pulling out 30,000 for the mailing. The number mailed in each RFM cell (Column D) was an exact representation of the larger universe.

Altogether, 474 people responded to the mailing (Column E), representing 1.58 percent of the entire mailing of 30,000. The response rate (Column F) was compiled by dividing the number of responses in each RFM cell by the number mailed. As you can see, some cells did better than others. In general, the trend in response is downward from 555 to 111, but there are always exceptions, which may become important later, as we shall see.

**Table 5-1: Results of Test Mailing to 30,000**

| Cell Position A | RFM Cell B | Percent of File C | Number Mailed D | Number of Responses E | Response Rate F |
|---|---|---|---|---|---|
| 1 | 555 | 0.79% | 238 | 19 | 7.98% |
| 2 | 554 | 0.81% | 244 | 12 | 4.92% |
| 3 | 553 | 0.83% | 250 | 12 | 4.80% |
| 4 | 552 | 0.77% | 231 | 8 | 3.46% |
| 5 | 551 | 0.81% | 244 | 5 | 2.05% |
| 6 | 545 | 0.80% | 240 | 9 | 3.75% |
| 7 | 544 | 0.74% | 221 | 12 | 5.43% |
| 8 | 543 | 0.81% | 243 | 7 | 2.88% |
| 9 | 542 | 0.89% | 267 | 10 | 3.75% |
| 10 | 541 | 0.96% | 287 | 7 | 2.44% |
| ... | ... | ... | ... | ... | ... |
| 39 | 432 | 0.84% | 253 | 5 | 1.98% |
| 40 | 431 | 0.77% | 230 | 2 | 0.87% |
| 41 | 425 | 0.63% | 189 | 4 | 2.12% |
| 42 | 424 | 0.64% | 192 | 3 | 1.56% |
| 43 | 423 | 0.84% | 253 | 3 | 1.19% |
| 44 | 422 | 0.81% | 243 | 2 | 0.82% |
| 45 | 421 | 0.75% | 224 | 4 | 1.79% |
| 46 | 415 | 0.84% | 253 | 3 | 1.19% |
| ... | ... | ... | ... | ... | ... |
| 87 | 234 | 0.89% | 267 | 2 | 0.75% |
| 88 | 233 | 0.96% | 287 | 0 | 0.00% |
| 89 | 232 | 0.66% | 199 | 3 | 1.51% |
| 90 | 231 | 0.78% | 234 | 3 | 1.28% |
| 91 | 225 | 0.84% | 253 | 2 | 0.79% |
| ... | ... | ... | ... | ... | ... |
| 121 | 115 | 0.84% | 253 | 0 | 0.00% |
| 122 | 114 | 0.81% | 243 | 1 | 0.41% |
| 123 | 113 | 0.78% | 234 | 0 | 0.00% |
| 124 | 112 | 0.84% | 253 | 1 | 0.40% |
| 125 | 111 | 0.92% | 277 | 0 | 0.00% |
| Total | 125 | 100.00% | 30,000 | 474 | 1.58% |

## The Offer and the Profit from the Test

To take our example further, let's look at the financial side of this mailing. We will assume that the mailing offered a product that sold for $100, of which $65 was the cost of the product and the fulfillment. The net profit on each unit sold was $35. The mailing cost $0.55 per piece. The overall results, therefore, looked something like Table 5-2.

As such, the test mailing was not much of a success. A $90 profit on an investment of $16,500 is hardly worth the effort. However, the test mailing has given us vital information about the offer and our customer's reaction, which will enable us to turn this miserable test into a magnificent profit.

**Table 5-2: Results of Test Mailing**

|  | Quantity | Rate | Amount |
|---|---|---|---|
| **Revenue** | | | |
| Sales | 474 | $35.00 | $16,590 |
| **Costs** | | | |
| Mailing | 30,000 | $0.55 | $16,500 |
| **Profit** | | | $90 |

Since we now know the response of each RFM cell to the offer, we will design our rollout mailing to drop the losing RFM cells and include all the profitable RFM cells so as to maximize our profit. Let's see how we go about doing that.

## Rollout Predictions Must Be Discounted

In planning our rollout mailing to selected prospects from the one million customer universe, we will make the assumption that the test response is representative of the rollout (major mailing) response for each RFM cell. Is this a reasonable assumption? Absolutely yes. If the test names were selected based on an across-the-board Nth from the total universe, the behavior of the customers in each RFM cell in the rollout should be almost identical to the behavior of the customers in each RFM cell in the test, with one difference.

The overall response to the test was 1.58 percent. Will the rollout do as well? Answer: probably not. While there are exceptions, of course, in general rollouts never do as well as the test. How much worse? That varies, of course. To be safe, we will assume that the rollout response will be only 85 percent as good as the test (a 15 percent reduction in response rate).

To see how the rollout will look, let's use the test results, discounted by 15 percent, to predict our rollout response. This is shown as Table 5-3.

If the test response rate is discounted by 15 percent, there will be 13,432 responses to the rollout if we mail all the RFM cells. Let's explain some of the new columns shown below.

The Rollout Universe (Column D) is simply the number of customers in each RFM cell. We have not excluded the 30,000 mailed in the test mailing, although we could have. The Cumulative Mailed Rollout (Column E) is a column included by many marketers. It is based on the assumption that we will plan our final mailing from the top down, mailing the most responsive cells and working our way down through the RFM cells to less and less responsive ones until we decide to stop. This is not the best way to use

### Table 5-3: Prediction of Rollout Response

| Cell Position | RFM Cell | Percent of File | Rollout Universe | Cum. Mailed Rollout | Response Rate | Rollout Resp. Rate | Rollout Response |
|---|---|---|---|---|---|---|---|
| A | B | C | D | E | F | G | H |
| 1 | 555 | 0.79% | 7,933 | 7,933 | 7.98% | 6.78% | 538 |
| 2 | 554 | 0.81% | 8,133 | 16,066 | 4.92% | 4.18% | 340 |
| 3 | 553 | 0.83% | 8,333 | 24,399 | 4.80% | 4.08% | 340 |
| 4 | 552 | 0.77% | 7,700 | 32,099 | 3.46% | 2.94% | 226 |
| 5 | 551 | 0.81% | 8,133 | 40,232 | 2.05% | 1.74% | 142 |
| 6 | 545 | 0.80% | 8,000 | 48,232 | 3.75% | 3.19% | 255 |
| 7 | 544 | 0.74% | 7,367 | 55,599 | 5.43% | 4.62% | 340 |
| 8 | 543 | 0.81% | 8,100 | 63,699 | 2.88% | 2.45% | 198 |
| 9 | 542 | 0.89% | 8,900 | 72,599 | 3.75% | 3.19% | 284 |
| 10 | 541 | 0.96% | 9,567 | 82,166 | 2.44% | 2.07% | 198 |
| ... | ... | ... | ... | ... | ... | ... | ... |
| 39 | 432 | 0.84% | 8,433 | 313,097 | 1.98% | 1.68% | 142 |
| 40 | 431 | 0.77% | 7,667 | 320,764 | 0.87% | 0.74% | 57 |
| 41 | 425 | 0.63% | 6,300 | 327,064 | 2.12% | 1.80% | 113 |
| 42 | 424 | 0.64% | 6,400 | 333,464 | 1.56% | 1.33% | 85 |
| 43 | 423 | 0.84% | 8,433 | 341,897 | 1.19% | 1.01% | 85 |
| 44 | 422 | 0.81% | 8,100 | 349,997 | 0.82% | 0.70% | 57 |
| ... | ... | ... | ... | ... | ... | ... | ... |
| 120 | 121 | 0.64% | 6,400 | 957,992 | 1.04% | 0.88% | 56 |
| 121 | 115 | 0.84% | 8,433 | 966,425 | 0.00% | 0.00% | 0 |
| 122 | 114 | 0.81% | 8,100 | 974,525 | 0.41% | 0.35% | 28 |
| 123 | 113 | 0.78% | 7,800 | 982,325 | 0.00% | 0.00% | 0 |
| 124 | 112 | 0.84% | 8,433 | 990,758 | 0.40% | 0.34% | 29 |
| 125 | 111 | 0.92% | 9,233 | 999,991 | 0.00% | 0.00% | 0 |
| **Total** | **125** | **100.00%** | **999,991** | **999,991** | **1.58%** | **1.34%** | **13,432** |

RFM, however, as we will soon see.

The Response Rate (Column F) is the rate for each cell derived from the test mailing. The Rollout Response Rate (Column G) is the rate in Column F discounted by 15 percent. This is the rate we can conservatively count on for our rollout mailing. The Rollout Response (Column H) then is the number of people from each cell who will buy our product if we mail to them.

### How Many Should We Mail?

Knowing our response rate, the question becomes, "How many of our universe of one million should we mail to?" The answer has to be, "Mail in such a way that you maximize your profits." If we were to mail to our entire one million names, the picture would look like Table 5-4:

### Table 5-4: Results of Rollout Mailing

| Assuming All Names Mailed | Quantity | Rate | Amount |
|---|---|---|---|
| **Revenue** | | | |
| Sales | 13,432 | $35.00 | $470,120 |
| **Costs** | | | |
| Mailing | 1,000,000 | $0.55 | $550,000 |
| **Loss** | | | ($79,880 |

Mailing to all one million names would be a disaster. What we want to do is to pick and choose among the RFM cells to select those that are profitable and drop those that are not. Let's see how we determine our maximum profit mailing plan.

## Mailing Only to Profitable Cells

The secret to successful RFM marketing is to mail only to those cells that you know will be profitable. How can you know that? By determining the break-even response rate for each cell, and mailing to all cells that do better than the break-even rate. Figure 5-4 shows the number of profitable RFM cells versus the number of unprofitable cells—the ones that produce a response rate lower than the break-even rate.

### Figure 5-4: Predicted Cell Response in Rollout

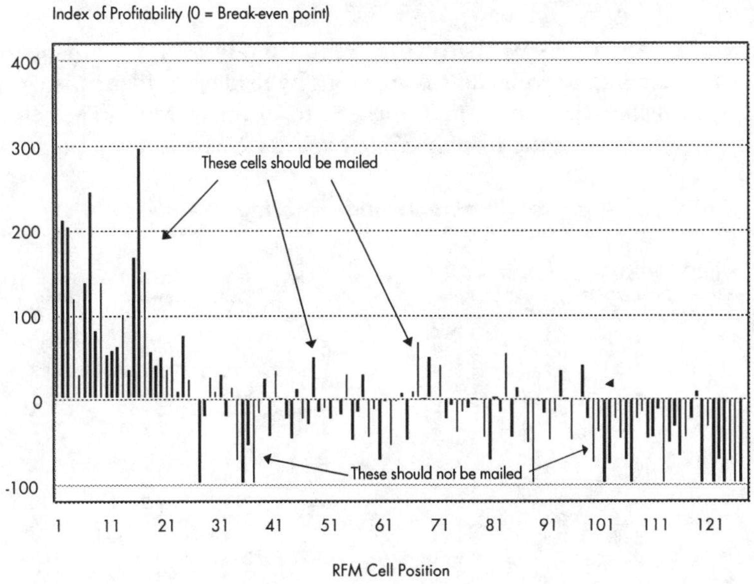

Index of Profitability (0 = Break-even point)

These cells should be mailed

These should not be mailed

RFM Cell Position

## Break-Even Response Rate

The break-even point occurs when the profit from a cell is exactly zero. Mailing to any cell that produces a positive profit adds to the total profit. To determine which cells are profitable, we need to determine the response rate that just breaks even. This occurs when the cost of mailing to the cell is equal to the net revenue from sales to members of the cell.

Break-even response rate occurs when:
Mailing costs to cell = net revenue from cell
Where NM = number mailed
      MC = cost per piece
      R = break-even response rate
      NR = revenue per sale
$$NM \times MC = (NM \times R) \times NR$$

Solving this formula for R (the break-even response rate) leads to:

$$R = MC \div NR$$

In our example:

$$R = \$.55 \div \$35$$
$$R = 1.57\% \quad \text{This is the break-even response rate.}$$

This calculation tells us that if the response rate to any cell is greater than 1.57 percent, we will add to our profit by mailing to that cell. We can use a spreadsheet, as shown in Table 5-5, to examine each RFM cell and select those for which the response rate exceeds the break-even point.

### Table 5-5: Profitable and Unprofitable Cells

| Cell Position A | RFM Cell B | Rollout Universe C | Resp. Rate D | Cell Position A | RFM Cell B | Rollout Universe C | Resp. Rate D |
|---|---|---|---|---|---|---|---|
| 1 | 555 | 7,933 | 6.78% | 64 | 332 | 7,800 | 1.45% |
| 2 | 554 | 8,133 | 4.18% | 65 | 331 | 8,433 | 0.67% |
| 3 | 553 | 8,333 | 4.08% | 66 | 325 | 7,667 | 1.48% |
| 4 | 552 | 7,700 | 2.94% | 67 | 324 | 6,300 | 2.25% |
| 5 | 551 | 8,133 | 1.74% | 68 | 323 | 6,400 | 1.33% |
| 6 | 545 | 8,000 | 3.19% | 69 | 322 | 8,433 | 2.01% |
| 7 | 544 | 7,367 | 4.62% | 70 | 321 | 8,100 | 1.40% |
| 8 | 543 | 8,100 | 2.45% | 71 | 315 | 7,467 | 1.90% |
| 9 | 542 | 8,900 | 3.19% | 72 | 314 | 8,433 | 1.01% |
| 10 | 541 | 9,567 | 2.07% | 73 | 313 | 9,233 | 1.22% |
| 11 | 535 | 6,633 | 2.13% | 74 | 312 | 7,033 | 0.81% |
| 12 | 534 | 7,800 | 2.18% | 75 | 311 | 7,700 | 1.11% |
| 13 | 533 | 8,433 | 2.69% | 76 | 255 | 9,600 | 1.18% |
| 14 | 532 | 7,667 | 1.84% | 77 | 254 | 8,467 | 1.33% |
| 15 | 531 | 6,300 | 3.60% | 78 | 253 | 8,200 | 1.39% |
| . . . | . . . | . . . | . . . | . . . | . . . | . . . | . . . |
| 56 | 345 | 7,700 | 1.11% | 119 | 122 | 6,633 | 0.00% |
| 57 | 344 | 8,133 | 1.74% | 120 | 121 | 6,400 | 0.88% |
| 58 | 343 | 8,000 | 0.71% | 121 | 115 | 8,433 | 0.00% |
| 59 | 342 | 7,367 | 1.16% | 122 | 114 | 8,100 | 0.35% |
| 60 | 341 | 8,100 | 0.35% | 123 | 113 | 7,800 | 0.00% |
| 61 | 335 | 8,900 | 1.28% | 124 | 112 | 8,433 | 0.34% |
| 62 | 334 | 9,567 | 0.60% | 125 | 111 | 9,233 | 0.00% |
| 63 | 333 | 6,633 | 1.28% | | | | |
| | | | | Total | 125 | 1,000,000 | 1.34% |

As you can see from Table 5-5, some cells have a rollout response rate of more than 1.57 percent and many have a lower predicted response rate. Our job is to select the winning cells, and mail to them, leaving out the remaining cells.

How can we pick out these winning cells rapidly? If we have constructed a spreadsheet similar to the one shown here using Lotus 1-2-3 or Microsoft Excel, we merely have to add a column that identifies the profitable cells. The Lotus language for such a selection is:

```
@if(+D4>0.0157,C4,0)
```

Assuming that column D contains the response rate, column C contains the quantity of that cell available to be mailed. The result will be placed in a new column E. This yields a table similar to Table 5-6.

### Table 5-6: Mailing Only to Profitable Cells

| Cell Position | RFM Cell | Rollout Universe | Rollout Resp. Rate | Profitable Cells | Rollout Response |
|---|---|---|---|---|---|
| A | B | C | D | E | F |
| 1 | 555 | 7,933 | 6.78% | 7,933 | 538 |
| 2 | 554 | 8,133 | 4.18% | 8,133 | 340 |
| 3 | 553 | 8,333 | 4.08% | 8,333 | 340 |
| 4 | 552 | 7,700 | 2.94% | 7,700 | 226 |
| 5 | 551 | 8,133 | 1.74% | 8,133 | 142 |
| 6 | 545 | 8,000 | 3.19% | 8,000 | 255 |
| 7 | 544 | 7,367 | 4.62% | 7,367 | 340 |
| 8 | 543 | 8,100 | 2.45% | 8,100 | 198 |
| 9 | 542 | 8,900 | 3.19% | 8,900 | 284 |
| 10 | 541 | 9,567 | 2.07% | 9,567 | 198 |
| 11 | 535 | 6,633 | 2.13% | 6,633 | 141 |
| 12 | 534 | 7,800 | 2.18% | 7,800 | 170 |
| 13 | 533 | 8,433 | 2.69% | 8,433 | 227 |
| 14 | 532 | 7,667 | 1.84% | 7,667 | 141 |
| 15 | 531 | 6,300 | 3.60% | 6,300 | 227 |
| 16 | 525 | 6,400 | 5.31% | 6,400 | 340 |
| 17 | 524 | 8,433 | 3.36% | 8,433 | 283 |
| 18 | 523 | 8,100 | 2.10% | 8,100 | 170 |
| 19 | 522 | 7,467 | 1.90% | 7,467 | 142 |
| 20 | 521 | 8,433 | 2.01% | 8,433 | 170 |
| 21 | 515 | 9,233 | 1.84% | 9,233 | 170 |
| 22 | 514 | 7,033 | 2.01% | 7,033 | 141 |
| 23 | 513 | 7,700 | 1.47% | 0 | 0 |
| 24 | 512 | 9,600 | 2.36% | 9,600 | 227 |
| 25 | 511 | 8,467 | 1.67% | 8,467 | 141 |
| 26 | 455 | 8,200 | 1.39% | 0 | 0 |
| 27 | 454 | 7,933 | 0.00% | 0 | 0 |
| 28 | 453 | 8,133 | 1.05% | 0 | 0 |
| 29 | 452 | 8,333 | 1.70% | 8,333 | 142 |
| 30 | 451 | 7,700 | 1.47% | 0 | 0 |
| 31 | 445 | 8,133 | 1.74% | 8,133 | 142 |
| ... | ... | ... | ... | ... | ... |
| 125 | 111 | 9233 | 0 | 0 | 0 |
| **Total** | **125** | **1,000,000** | **1.34%** | **290,763** | **7,394** |

In short, we will mail to only 290,763 people (29 percent of the file) and make only 7,394 sales. Our profit, however, will far exceed that if we mailed to the entire file as shown by Table 5-7.

**Table 5-7: Comparison of Test, Full File, and RFM Selected Mailings**

|  | Test | Full File | Selected by RFM |
|---|---|---|---|
| **Revenue** |  |  |  |
| Response Rate | 1.58% | 1.34% | 2.54% |
| Responses | 474 | 13,432 | 7,394 |
| Net Revenue | $16,590 | $470,120 | $258,790 |
| **Costs** |  |  |  |
| Mailing | 30,000 | 1,000,000 | 290,763 |
| Total Costs | $16,500 | $550,000 | $159,920 |
| **Profits** | $90 | ($79,880) | $98,870 |

We have turned a $79,880 loss into a $98,870 profit by use of RFM break-even cell selection.

Is this a fluke? A classroom example cooked up for this book, but not possible in real life? Not at all. It is an example that every reader of this book can emulate, provided that:

• You have a database that contains customer data, including recency, frequency, and monetary amounts.
• You create the necessary RFM codes from the data.
• You do a test mailing to an Nth of the file. (It is surprising how difficult it is to get marketers to do test mailings. They always want to rush out too early with what they assume is a knockout mailing.)
• You create a spreadsheet with the test mailing results, discounting the rollout percentage by an appropriate amount.

Once you have a customer database, you hold in your hands a powerhouse profit generator that always will work if you use it properly. Furthermore, you don't need statisticians, neural network modelers, or external consultants. All you need are a spreadsheet and the knowledge of how to use it. If you need additional help, see the Technical Assistance section in Appendix A of this book.

## Why Quintiles?

Dividing your database into five equal parts (quintiles) for the purpose of analysis seems rather arbitrary. Why not divide it into quartiles (four parts) or deciles (10 parts)? Wouldn't deciles, for example, be more accurate?

Actually, the answer is no. With deciles, accuracy tends to go down. Using RFM with deciles gives you a total of 1,000 RFM cells (10 x 10 x 10), instead of the 125 cells you get with quintiles. With a test mailing to 30,000 and an average response rate of 2 percent, you will get an average of only 0.6 respondents per cell with deciles. This is such a small number that the law of chance becomes much more important than the law of consumer behavior (the concept that underlies RFM analysis). Each person responding to your promotion makes his cell seem like a winner (since 1.0 is greater than the average of 0.6), when in reality, the cell may be a real loser in the rollout.

To get a prediction with deciles that is as accurate as a 30,000 mailing using quintiles, you would have to send each test mailing to 240,000 people. This is such a large test mailing that it makes extensive testing uneconomical in most cases.

On the other hand, using a smaller division than quintiles, such as quartiles, reduces the accuracy in another way. With quartiles, you have only 64 cells (4 x 4 x 4). The fewer cells you have, the more you mix different consumer behaviors together and thereby lose the pinpointed predictive accuracy that you get with a larger number.

For these reasons, I suggest that you stick with quintiles and learn how to use them in your marketing.

## Qualifications of RFM Analysis

Can we be safe in assuming that there is always a relationship between what the test group did and what the full file will do? Absolutely. RFM, if done correctly, is the most reliable method of predicting response known to marketers. It is more reliable than any survey or any model based on such demographics as age, income, and home value. Why is that? Because RFM is a measure of behavior, and what we are trying to predict is behavior. If the test group is a true Nth, then the master customer base will perform in a similar way, assuming that the time period is the same, the offer and creative the same, etc.

## Going Beyond Profits

With an in-house customer base that has the ability to track responses and purchases, RFM is the most efficient, most effective, and least costly method of targeting mail to maximize profits. What about building a relationship with our customers? Does RFM analysis relate to relationship building or simply short-term profits?

Profits are the surest way of knowing that the customer is satisfied. People can say they are happy in surveys, but when they spend money you have proof that they are happy. However, the fact is that 97 percent of the customers are not responding to our offer, which means they are not thrilled with what we are mailing to them. What should we do about that?

## Beginning a Continuing Dialogue

With a house file, it is a good idea to build a dialogue. For the 97 percent who see your letter and do not respond, why not make it worth their while to open the envelope to see what is inside? Put a newsletter and a survey in with the offer. The newsletter tells the customer what you are doing, what is new or coming up, and how others are using your product. The survey asks their opinion about the offer, what products they would like to have news about, and what they think about your company. Why throw away $159,919 in mailing material that gets trashed, when with a little imagination, a significant percentage of the mail could be opened and read?

What good could come from the newsletter and the survey? Building lifetime customer value. Every time a customer opens your envelope and sees something of no interest, the chances of the customer opening the next envelope are diminished. By providing something of value—beyond the rejected product offer—you expand the dialogue, and open up the possibility of sales in the future.

In effect, by adding $X to the cost of each mailing by including a newsletter and a survey, you are increasing the response rate to future mailings by Y percent. This is where lifetime value comes in to the calculation. You must measure the lifetime value of the customer base, not just the response to each individual mailing.

Another way of saying the same thing is this: if this mailing of 290,763, instead of being an isolated offer, were part of a continuing dialogue, expected and welcomed by the customer base, the response would not be 2.54 percent but some higher figure—even though the package sent and the recipients were identical!

Will adding additional material increase the cost of the mailing? Of course. Will it reduce the response to this particular offer by diluting the impact? Possibly. This is testable with controls.

## What about the Unmailed Universe?

RFM analysis usually results in the elimination of a large portion of the customer base from promotional mailings. In this case, 709,237 customers were not mailed to at all because their RFM cells had response rates less than the break-even rate. How can you maintain a dialogue with these

700,000 people if you never mail to them?

The answer to this question depends upon your type of business:

- If you are in a business that mails monthly bills, the dialogue is maintained in the monthly statements.
- If you have a quarterly newsletter including surveys and offers, this can be your dialogue method.
- If you have neither of these options, you may want to use your promotional mailing to make an offer to losing RFM cells, just to maintain the dialogue.

In most cases, however, I believe that you will find that it is a mistaken strategy to mail to people who are unlikely to respond. Database marketing is meant to be profitable for both the buyer and the seller. If you lose money, it is not profitable for you. If your customers do not respond, you have wasted their time, sending them something that they do not want. You have cheapened your reputation and relationship with them, forcing them to reject you. You become like the boy who too often cries "wolf." When he really sees a wolf, no one believes him. Save your promotional dollars for situations in which both you and your customers are likely to win. It is a favor to both the buyer and the seller.

Imagine a friend or an associate at work who tells you about a good thing, perhaps a vacation spot that you visit. Later, however, he begins to suggest other ideas that are not so helpful. He invites you to play poker every Thursday night. He tries to convince you to buy a time-share condominium. His wife tries to sell you life insurance. He wants to play handball or golf two times a week. You politely turn down each of these offers, but you are getting a little sick of them. You try to avoid eye contact when you run across him and dread that he is calling when the phone rings. This isn't a relationship; it's a damn nuisance.

This is what it is like to be on the receiving end of a large string of unwanted offers from your company. Don't do it. Use RFM to save money and your customers' time, while building goodwill with other customers by sending them offers that they appreciate.

## Calculation of Lifetime Value by RFM Cell

Lifetime value is much more useful if it is calculated by RFM cell. It will give you a real handle on the value to be attached to such benefits as gold cards, preferred customer programs, etc. Figuring out the lifetime value by RFM cell is really quite simple. Table 5-8 is an example of the calculation for a single cell.

**Table 5-8: Calculation of Lifetime Value by RFM Cell**

| | | |
|---|---|---|
| Total Annual Sales for this RFM Cell | $1,920,000 | |
| Total Number of Customers in Cell | 6,126 | |
| Average Annual Sales per Customer | $313.42 | |
| Direct Cost Percentage | 70.00% | |
| Retention Rate for this Cell | 60.00% | |
| Referral Rate for this Cell | 2.00% | |

| | Gross Profit | Discounted Profit | Lifetime Value |
|---|---|---|---|
| Year1 | $94.03 | $94.03 | $94.03 |
| Year2 | $58.30 | $48.58 | $142.61 |
| Year3 | $36.14 | $25.10 | $167.70 |
| Year4 | $22.41 | $12.95 | $180.66 |
| Year5 | $13.89 | $6.71 | $187.37 |

The calculation method is quite straightforward. Use the database to determine the annual sales of all customers in each RFM cell. Divide by the number in the cell. Determine the direct cost percentage, retention rate for each cell, and referral rate for each cell.

These numbers will quickly yield profit rates for the next five years, which, discounted, will produce lifetime values.

These values will change with each update of your database. Built into each update program should be software that updates the lifetime value as well, and stores it in each customer record.

RFM cells change with every update, as do lifetime values. Measuring what happens to people's RFM cells can be as interesting as what happens to their lifetime values as a result of your relationship-building activities.

## Is RFM for Direct Mail Only?

This example given above shows the increased profits from a direct mail offer using RFM. That is not the only use of RFM. Once you have classified your customer base by RFM, you can use the knowledge to create other marketing initiatives. For example, you can establish a preferred customer group, using RFM as the criteria. Preferred customers get special cards, special invitations to test new products or preview your new releases, and consultation via surveys or telephone calls. There are many marketing initiatives that are too costly to be attempted with one million customers, but will work just fine with the top 200,000. Use RFM to discover who those top 200,000 are, and test your ideas at 20 percent of the original cost.

If your database has purchase and promotion history information stored in it, you can and should do RFM analysis of your customers, and their direct response promotions. You will learn a great deal about your customers from this analysis. You will become an expert at predicting response. You will discover how to save millions of dollars by mailing smarter. RFM is the most powerful analytical tool available to database marketers—more powerful than any demographic model. It is a basic building block of strategy.

After you have coded your database with RFM quintiles, you should become adept at putting each promotion into a spreadsheet, which can be used to predict responses and segment your customer base. If you need help in this process, see the Technical Assistance section in Appendix A.

## Summary

1.  RFM stands for Recency, Frequency, and Monetary analysis. People who have purchased from you most recently are the most likely to purchase from you again. For this reason a recency code should be added to every database record, showing the quintile (20 percent grouping) to which each household belongs (when arranged in order of recency).

2.  Frequency refers to the number of times that a person buys from you. This also can be coded by quintiles. Monetary amount is a measure of total spending with you during a lifetime, which again may be coded in reference to all other customers.

3.  Mailing smarter means testing, followed by a revised mail plan based on the results of the test. Better targeting will improve profits. It will also build lifetime customer value by not bothering customers with unwanted communications.

4.  The first step in RFM analysis is coding your entire database by RFM quintiles: one score for recency, one for frequency, and one for monetary. Second step is a test mailing. Break the responders down by RFM. From the results of the mailing, determine the response rate from each RFM cell. Discount that by a fixed percentage (15 to 25 percent). This is your discounted response rate that will apply to any rollout.

5.  For each promotion, you should determine your break-even response rate. The formula for this is:

    $R = MC \div NR$
    where:

R = break-even response rate
MC = mailing cost per piece
NR = net revenue (sales less nonmailing costs) from each respondent

You should mail to every RFM cell that has a discounted response rate greater than the break-even response rate.

6.  In mailing to a house file, use the occasion to begin a dialogue. Ask survey questions. Send out a newsletter. It may not improve the response to this mailing, but it may build the overall relationship, resulting in better response to later mailings.

## Executive Quiz 5

Answers to quiz questions can be found in Appendix B. The quizzes are for fun. Do them if you enjoy quizzes. Ignore them if you don't.
*Choose the best answer to complete each statement or question.*

1. Customers in your oldest recency quintile should probably be
   a. dropped from your regular mailing.
   b. receiving a reactivation mailing.
   c. considered lapsed buyers.
   d. All of the above
   e. None of the above

2. Which of these RFM cells will probably have the best response rate to a mailed promotion?
   a. 311
   b. 444
   c. 231
   d. 211
   e. 333

3. If you mailed to one group of 30,000 and 510 responded, what is the response rate?
   a. 510
   b. 58.8
   c. 1.7
   d. 2.7
   e. 170

4. Which best predicts the response of existing customers to your next promotion?
   a. modeling based on demographics
   b. mailed customer survey results
   c. affinity analysis
   d. RFM analysis
   e. telephone surveys

5. In predicting response using RFM, in most cases,
   a. frequency is the most powerful predictor.
   b. total monetary spending is the most important.
   c. recency is the most powerful predictor.

d. frequency and monetary override recency.
   e. None of the above

6. To create a single RFM predictive number for each customer, you will have to
   a. use demographic modeling.
   b. use the response rate of the customer's RFM cell.
   c. discount the customer's RFM cell test response rate by a fixed percentage.
   d. determine the break-even rate for each customer.
   e. None of the above

7. RFM analysis
   a. can be used best on prospect files.
   b. can be used on either prospect or customer files.
   c. does not require testing prior to rollout.
   d. requires help from an outside consultant.
   e. None of the above

8. If a mailing costs $.83 per piece and the average profit from a successful response is $42, what is the break-even response rate?
   a. .98 percent
   b. 1.4 percent
   c. 1.98 percent
   d. 2.98 percent
   e. 3.98 percent

# 6

# Using Customer Profiles in Marketing Strategy

*To develop a relationship program, you still have to put individu-*
*als into groups, and develop products and strategies that will keep*
*them loyal. That, in my opinion, is where companies have the most*
*difficulty. We come across this problem every day with our clients.*
*Even when you say to them, "I can help you identify your key cus-*
*tomer segments," they respond, "Well, great, but tell me what to do*
*with them once they're identified? How do I manage each*
*segment?" Many marketers are not yet sophisticated enough to*
*know what to do with the information.*
*—Stephen Shaw, vice president, Spectrum Decision Sciences*

I n earlier chapters, we have been talking about one-on-one dialogue with
the customer. With one million customer names on our database, however, we cannot really have one million separate and different dialogues.
Instead, what we seek to do is to develop customer profiles—dividing customers into groups of similar tastes and purchasing habits, so that we can
offer each group what it is looking for. This, at least, is the way that a dialogue can be started.

How do you go about creating customer profiles? There are a number of
valid and useful methods. The most powerful method is Recency, Frequency, Monetary (RFM) analysis discussed in the previous chapter. In this
chapter, we will discuss five additional methods that can be used in situations when RFM is not possible:

1. Profiling by product affinity
2. Profiling by demographics
3. Profiling by cluster coding
4. Profiling by lifestyle overlays
5. Profiling by geography and mapping

## Profiling by Product Affinity

Affinity analysis starts from a customer's perspective. You look at what customers are buying, how often and when, and use this analysis as a way of classifying customers.

One obvious type of product affinity analysis would be to check everyone who buys baby diapers and baby food. Here is a household with a single preoccupation. Baby clothes, strollers, and crib toys are likely promotion items. You would be unlikely to offer these people golf clubs or yachting apparel without some other indication.

Another affinity could be someone who buys lawn fertilizer, lawn mowers, and garden hoses. Should you try to sell them lawn furniture, shrubbery, weed whackers, and insect repellent? Go to it!

If they buy an executive briefcase, how about a portable computer? An unlikely offering for such a household would be a food processor or a TV recliner.

If they take out a home equity loan, you might offer them a credit card, auto loan, or traveler's checks. They might not be the best candidate for a certificate of deposit.

This type of analysis is difficult to do. It requires a lot of thought, and analysis of customer purchasing habits. It requires, of course, data about purchases in a database. Without the data, the analysis is impossible.

One of the experts in affinity analysis is Richard J. Courtheoux, president of Precision Marketing Corporation. He shows how the purchasers of one product can be cross tabulated against the buyers of another product for analysis purposes. Table 6-1 shows one example:

### Table 6-1: Cross Buying Rates Between Products A and B

| A | B–No | B–Yes | Total |
|---|---|---|---|
| No | 268,431 | 8,328 | 276,759 |
| Row % | 96.99% | 3.01% | 100.00% |
| | | | |
| Yes | 27,023 | 12,444 | 39,467 |
| Row % | 68.47% | 31.53% | 100.00% |
| | | | |
| Total | 295,454 | 20,772 | 316,226 |
| Row % | 93.43% | 6.57% | 100.00% |

From this table you can conclude that: Product A buyers are 10.5 times as likely to buy Product B as people who have not purchased Product A $(31.53 \div 3.01 = 10.5)$.

The computer can be used to calculate the cross buying rates between any number of products in a similar way to that shown above. Based on these numbers, an affinity matrix such as Table 6-2 can be constructed that shows the likelihood of each group of buyers of one product being buyers of another product.

**Table 6-2: Affinity Matrix**

|  | Product A | Product B | Product C | Product D |
|---|---|---|---|---|
| **Product A** | • • • | 10.50 | 2.40 | 4.50 |
| **Product B** | 10.50 | • • • | 9.00 | 1.10 |
| **Product C** | 2.40 | 9.00 | • • • | 3.00 |
| **Product D** | 4.50 | 1.10 | 3.00 | • • • |

Once you know the likelihood of people buying a certain product who already have bought another product, you can use this information in your segmentation for mailings or statement stuffers. You can test whether this type of affinity ranking works by setting up control groups. If you have done your homework properly, mailings to people offering Product B will do better to people who have already purchased Product A or C than they will to people who have purchased Product D.

## How to Go about Affinity Profiling

On the assumption that you have a database that contains purchase information sufficient to do the analysis (true on only a small proportion of databases), how can you produce the affinity matrix?

You can use ad hoc queries from your database to get the data, and enter the results into a spreadsheet. For details see the Technical Assistance section in Appendix A.

If you don't want to do the work yourself, the normal method is to ask a programmer from your service bureau to write a program that results in the matrix shown above. After a day's work, most programmers should be able to do the job. The programmer will have several problems, however.

- You have to decide what to do about quantities and prices. If Product A is snow tires ($300 a set), and Product B is sewing supplies ($20 per average purchase), do you equate $300 with $20 and call each one a purchase? It is possible to shift the equations and base the affinity matrix on dollars rather than number of purchases. You might try it both ways, and see which one makes the most sense.

- A more serious difficulty is the sheer problem of numbers. If you work for a bank with 10 products, the matrix will be very neat and understandable. You can match home equity customers with credit card holders and with savings account owners, and come to some valid and useful conclusions.

If, however, you are a department store with 10,000 products, your matrix may contain 100 million cells, and take tens of thousands of pages to print out. It will be totally useless to you. Beware of letting the computer do your thinking for you. The computer is not an intuitive machine. It cannot think. It will just follow orders, blindly. If you tell it to do something stupid, it will do so, hour after hour after hour.

This points out one advantage of doing computations on a personal computer. A laser printer cannot easily print out 10,000 sheets of paper. It will take days, and wear out the laser printer. Someone will ask you if it is really necessary, before the job is finished. For a mainframe, 10,000 sheets of paper is an hour's work.

### How to Handle a Massive Affinity Matrix

What should you do if you have too much data? You have to use your head. Purchases should probably be organized by department, not by product. That could cut the matrix down to a much smaller number, depending on the number of departments. Even that may be too big, if it results in more than 50 possible groups. For affinity to be useful, it should be limited to a maximum of about six groups on a side or less. You can achieve that by combining similar departments.

Don't place too much reliance on an elaborate computer-constructed affinity matrix. Common sense can often tell you as much or more. For example, affinity analysis may tell you that:

- People who buy snow tires are more likely to buy hardware than sewing supplies.
- People who have large savings accounts are more likely to buy money market accounts than people who have large credit card balances.
- People who buy children's books are more likely to buy encyclopedias than people who buy books on sports.

But you knew all this already. The advantage of an affinity matrix is that it can start you thinking about relationships that might not have been obvious, but which may become clear to you after you analyze the data.

Depending on your product, it is possible to work out a customer lifetime table, recording significant events that can be used to build a relation-ship. Know your customer's age, birthday, anniversary, and ages and gradu-ation dates of children and grandchildren. Moving to a new home is a very important date for new purchases. The birth of a new child often changes the entire family focus. Empty nests occur when the last child goes off to college, and retirement opens up new opportunities for the customer and for the supplier. All of these lifetime events are triggers for an intelligently organized affinity program built around a database.

Other examples developed from an affinity matrix include:

- What do female skiers purchase to wear when they aren't skiing?
- What is the best product to offer to someone who has just taken out a long-term care policy?

Conclusion: If you have the data, you should experiment with building an affinity matrix to see what it can teach you. Based on the analysis, you may develop an entire marketing strategy based on the affinity results.

## Profiling by Demographics

Profiling really depends on the comparison of two types of measurable vari-ables: behavior and demographics. Behavior concerns factors such as the amount of purchases, amount of responses, or length of time as a cus-tomer. These are actions of our customers that we can record in the data-base. RFM and affinity are measures of behavior.

Demographics refers to facts describing people that we can determine, measure, and record. Demographics includes income, age, presence of children, housing type and value, ethnicity, sex, marital status, type of auto-mobile, occupation, and a hundred other similar facts. There are, of course, many other things that affect purchasing behavior: whether parents are lib-eral or conservative, and whether children have to earn their own pocket money or receive lavish allowances from their parents. But these things are more difficult to learn and cannot be readily used in marketing analysis.

There are 328 different pieces of 1990 census information that can be inserted in your database. They include age, education, bank balance, department store average balance, family members who work, occupa-tions, cars per household, age of housing, income level, type of housing, housing owned or rented, property value, travel time to work, and urban-rural nature of neighborhood.

Where does this demographic information come from? There are two sources: Survey questions answered directly by the households concerned and U.S. census data attributed to the household.

Survey data is probably the most accurate. You can ask your own customers questions on satisfaction surveys, application forms, contests, and in other ways. National survey companies such as Carol Wright or National Demographics and Lifestyles have compiled a great deal of specific information from survey questions that you can match against your customer base if you don't want to ask your customers directly.

A winter resort collected a lot of data about their skiers in a new way. Every winter it holds a sweepstakes with a Jeep as the prize. Entrants have to fill out a survey form contained in wooden boxes on each table in the cafeterias at the base of the ski lifts. The boxes contain forms, pencils, and a place to put the completed forms. A hundred thousand are filled out (including many duplicates because skiers like Jeeps). The resort key-punches the information, eliminates the duplicates (following the fine print on the contest rules), and awards the Jeep every spring. In the process the resort builds up its valuable database, loaded with demographic data, family composition, skiing experience, and future winter sport plans.

Census data are the second best source. Every 10 years the Census Bureau finds out an amazing amount of information about U.S. households. Everyone is asked his or her age. Every seventh household is given the "long form" to fill out, which asks for about 200 other pieces of information, including income, occupation, housing type, etc.

To protect the privacy of Americans, the Census Bureau does not release any information about a single household. Instead, they furnish to the public only the long form answers from a block (an area of about 14 houses). Marketers use this information, and assume that everyone in the block has the same demographics as the two families that filled out the long form. It is, obviously, wrong in some cases, but probably right in most cases and better than nothing.

This data are purchased directly from the Census Bureau by private list compilers such as Donnelley, Polk, MetroMail, Claritas, Equifax, and others. These firms package the data attractively, and resell it to marketers for appending to their customer and prospect files.

If you haven't looked into buying such data, you should. Demographics is a useful tool in marketing and an essential tool in modeling.

There are many other sources of demographic data besides the census and surveys. Polk purchases driver's license and registration data from the states that sell such data (about half of them do), and has compiled useful information from the other states. Driver's licenses provide an exact date of birth, which is probably as accurate as you can get.

Overlaid data is seldom very accurate. Take all estimates of age, income, and home value with a huge grain of salt. They can be totally wrong. However, they are often all that is available, and usually, better than nothing.

## Applicant Data

Banks and insurance companies are sitting on a gold mine that they rarely make use of. To obtain a loan or an insurance policy, people have to fill out a great deal of information. This information is private, of course, and should not be rented outside of the institution. There is no reason, however, why the financial institution that receives this information from their applicants cannot use it to better target their promotional mailings to these same applicants.

In fact, very few banks keypunch the valuable data that is submitted on loan applications. The loan processing staff sees no point in spending the money to do the data entry (since they are not marketers). When marketers try to get such data, they find that it is stored away in legal folders in some bank archive and too costly to extract. Many insurance companies, however, are making effective use of applicant data for marketing purposes.

Is this legitimate? Well, why not? Think about it. If you tell a banker that you have $100,000 to put in a savings account, would you think it wrong for the banker to say to you: "You could make more money by putting that same money into a certificate of deposit (CD)"? Of course not. It would be a very helpful favor. Why, then, would it be wrong for the bank marketer to do the same thing?

In a free market transaction, both parties always make a profit. The investor who puts money into a CD makes a profit. At the same time, the financial institution that issues the CD also makes a profit. That's why they have CDs. Any time you, as a marketer, persuade people to buy your products, you are doing them a favor and helping them to make a profit. The market is characterized by ignorance. Millions of people pass up profitable opportunities because they don't know what is available. You, as a marketer, are playing a key role in the market by reducing ignorance, and hence, helping millions to make profitable use of their resources.

The lesson: Use any information you can get to help your customers and prospects to learn what is available. You are doing them a favor.

## How Significant Is Demographic Information?

Are age, income, or presence of children important to develop a profile of your customer? Maybe yes, and maybe no. For some products—batteries, tires, wallpaper, dog food, garden supplies—these factors may show no correlation at all. For other products—insurance, bank products, encyclopedias, vacation property—demographics may be powerful profiling tools. In all cases, you should test overlays with a small sample of your file to determine whether there is any correlation between profitability or response, and the demographics.

## Profiling by Cluster Coding

Claritas, Donnelley, CACI, and Equifax have gone one step beyond demographics. For some time, they have been grouping demographic data about blocks and block groups into clusters, groups of people that have similar lifestyles. While each company has its own proprietary system, each ends up dividing all the people in the United States and Canada into about 40 to 50 different clusters. Claritas began it, and others have copied the idea of giving each cluster a catchy name that describes it and helps you to remember it. Some of Claritas's names have become household words: Shotguns and Pickups, Pools and Patios, Furs and Station Wagons, Money and Brains.

Each cluster has a number, from 01 to 48. The lower numbers are usually the more affluent. Each cluster comes with a useful description that provides a lot of information about their education, age, and family composition; how they live; what they buy; what media they read, watch, or listen to; and what their housing is like. It is much easier to work with 48 different groups than data on 7.5 million blocks, which is what the census data provides. Table 6-3 is provided by Michael Phillips of Equifax Marketing Decision systems, using MicroVision Plus cluster information.

The sources in the MicroVision Plus program include questionnaire respondents, mail-order buyer new issues, local government records, homeowner data, driver's license information, new movers, and mail order buyers with bank cards. The 150 million names are located in 93 million households.

In this table, the buying power is estimated by percentages. For the first category, Upper Crust, 90 percent have a high buying power, and only 1 percent have a low buying power. When you get down to category 38, Rustic Homemakers, only 1 percent have a high buying power, and 76 percent have low buying power.

Don't assume that people with a high buying power will have a high response rate. Marketers have found that groups with a high buying power often respond very poorly when promoted. Why is that? Probably because, with their affluence, they are subjected to hundreds of unwanted solicitations. They are used to tossing out mail unopened.

Each cluster represents a segment of society that has relatively similar lifestyles and purchasing habits. To illustrate that, here are the definitions of a few of them:

## Table 6-3: MicroVision Consumers

| | | | Percentages of Buying Power | | | Card |
| --- | --- | --- | --- | --- | --- | --- |
| | | | High | Mid | Low | Holder |
| 1 | Upper Crust | 1,330,568 | 90 | 9 | 1 | 92 |
| 2 | Lap of Luxury | 2,717,105 | 68 | 30 | 2 | 91 |
| 3 | Established Wealth | 4,699,784 | 55 | 40 | 5 | 90 |
| 4 | Mid Life Success | 1,742,966 | 64 | 32 | 4 | 92 |
| 5 | Prosperous Ethnic Mix | 4,902,093 | 45 | 50 | 5 | 90 |
| 6 | Good Family Life | 2,738,947 | 25 | 67 | 8 | 90 |
| 7 | Comfortable Times | 1,260,538 | 34 | 56 | 10 | 89 |
| 8 | Movers and Shakers | 4,217,356 | 45 | 44 | 11 | 88 |
| 9 | Building a Home Life | 1,167,165 | 35 | 59 | 6 | 87 |
| 10 | Home Sweet Home | 10,753,480 | 24 | 67 | 9 | 89 |
| 11 | Family Ties | 7,545,667 | 9 | 80 | 11 | 57 |
| 12 | A Good Step Forward | 2,863,444 | 39 | 46 | 15 | 70 |
| 13 | Successful Singles | 700,299 | 3 | 89 | 8 | 95 |
| 14 | Middle Years | 202,308 | 28 | 55 | 17 | 84 |
| 15 | Great Beginnings | 5,835,825 | 23 | 64 | 13 | 88 |
| 16 | Country Home Families | 8,263,528 | 3 | 68 | 29 | 43 |
| 17 | Stars and Stripes | 3,320,967 | 3 | 56 | 41 | 67 |
| 18 | White Picket Fence | 10,597,585 | 3 | 67 | 30 | 69 |
| 19 | Young and Carefree | 902,607 | 18 | 57 | 25 | 71 |
| 20 | Secure Adults | 2,816,758 | 7 | 52 | 41 | 68 |
| 21 | American Classics | 871,483 | 11 | 43 | 46 | 58 |
| 22 | Traditional Times | 4,139,545 | 2 | 54 | 44 | 38 |
| 23 | Settled In | 7,345,358 | 5 | 57 | 38 | 65 |
| 24 | City Ties | 2,754,509 | 2 | 39 | 59 | 41 |
| 25 | Bedrock America | 4,061,734 | 3 | 41 | 56 | 47 |
| 26 | The Mature Years | 2,443,265 | 1 | 39 | 60 | 43 |
| 27 | Middle of the Road | 638,050 | 11 | 39 | 50 | 56 |
| 28 | Building a Family | 1,914,150 | 4 | 34 | 62 | 36 |
| 29 | Establishing Roots | 560,239 | 4 | 64 | 32 | 41 |
| 30 | Domestic Duos | 1,540,658 | 8 | 52 | 40 | 61 |
| 31 | Country Classics | 882,376 | 1 | 33 | 66 | 43 |
| 32 | Metro Singles | 2,845,213 | 5 | 37 | 58 | 49 |
| 33 | Living off the Land | 2,956,818 | 1 | 31 | 68 | 45 |
| 34 | Books and New Recruits | 1,727,404 | 8 | 32 | 60 | 39 |
| 35 | Buy American | 6,971,865 | 1 | 25 | 74 | 33 |
| 36 | Metro Mix | 1,462,846 | 2 | 23 | 75 | 28 |
| 37 | Urban Up & Comers | 778,110 | 7 | 61 | 32 | 71 |
| 38 | Rustic Homesteaders | 7,423,169 | 1 | 23 | 76 | 25 |
| 39 | On Their Own | 4,295,167 | 7 | 56 | 37 | 65 |
| 40 | Trying Metro Times | 3,890,550 | 1 | 30 | 69 | 41 |
| 41 | Close Knit Families | 964,856 | 1 | 19 | 80 | 19 |
| 42 | Trying Rural Times | 3,475,039 | 1 | 23 | 76 | 21 |
| 43 | Manufacturing USA | 373,492 | 1 | 17 | 82 | 19 |
| 44 | Hard Years | 482,428 | 2 | 26 | 72 | 30 |
| 45 | Struggling Metro Mix | 1,626,250 | 4 | 36 | 60 | 48 |
| 46 | Difficult Times | 2,598,887 | 1 | 11 | 88 | 15 |
| 47 | University USA | 824,796 | 6 | 33 | 61 | 44 |
| 48 | Urban Singles | 1,078,460 | 5 | 26 | 69 | 38 |
| | Total | 149,505,707 | | | | |

Upper Crust is a middle-aged segment (ages 45 to 54), predominantly white. Almost half have college or graduate degrees. They primarily work in managerial and professional fields, with the highest income in the nation. The majority of these families, with teenagers, own homes built in the '60s and the early '70s. Their financial activity is high, with installment account balances much higher than the national average. City dwellers, they watch morning news programs, read the Wall Street Journal, attend live theater, and travel to foreign lands. Aerobics and jogging keep them fit and trim. Ninety-two percent have a bank card and 90 percent have a high buying index.

Home Sweet Home segment is urbanite parents with teenage children. Most have an academic background (some with college degrees, most having attended a few classes). They are in the technical and sales fields. With a head of household age-range of 35 to 64 years old, the majority are homeowners, earning a medium-high combined income (two workers). Their financial behavior is typical of the nation. They keep abreast of world events by reading the *Wall Street Journal* and listening to talk radio. Living just outside of metropolitan areas, they play video games and work out at the health club for excitement. Eighty-nine percent have bank cards. Most of them (67 percent) have a mid-range buying power index.

White Picket Fence are young families in their late 20s or early 30s with young children (0–4). They live on the borders of metropolitan areas. Their education level is low to medium and income levels are medium. The heads of household work in precision production, craft and repair occupations, as well as operations, fabrication, and labor. The majority own single family homes, built between 1960 and 1974. The average household has three persons. They enjoy billiards, bowling, and golf. Only 69 percent have bank cards. Their buying power index is 67 percent mid range and 30 percent low range.

Settled In are empty-nesters, mostly 55 to 64 years of age. They are predominantly of Northern European ancestry. These households have an average education and are in the middle income bracket, with occupations such as technical, sales, and administrative support and services. They tend to live in their own houses, which were built before 1939 and located on the fringe of metropolitan areas. The average household has two individuals. These individuals' financial behavior is less than average. At the same time, they have had many accounts open for more than two years. Up-to-the-minute information is important to them. Sixty-five percent own a bank card, and their buying power is mid range (57 percent) to low (38 percent).

*How to Get Cluster Information Appended to Your Database*

Today, the easiest way to get cluster information appended to a customer or prospect file is to run the names through a program that appends ZIP+4 coding (nine-digit ZIP codes). Licensed service bureaus have look-up tables that equate the nine-digit ZIP codes to the appropriate cluster codes. For about $12 per thousand, you can have your entire database cluster coded.

Don't expect to get a match on all your data. For a consumer list, you can expect to get between 90 and 95 percent matched, depending upon the completeness of the vendor's database, the matching logic applied, the recency of your names, and the demographics of your list. Cluster coding cannot be used for a business-to-business file because census data, on which it is based, counts only residences, not businesses. Don't make the mistake of trying to use clusters where they have no validity.

Overlaying cluster codes may be very useful, or it may be a waste of money. The decision depends upon the product you are selling and the size of your customer base. In the ideal situation, you can learn that your product appeals to Young and Carefree and Successful Singles, but it goes nowhere when marketed to American Classics or Bedrock America. This type of knowledge is dynamite. You can use it to purchase new prospect names from the right clusters, and avoid getting names from the wrong clusters. It should pick up your response rate by a significant amount—by far more than the cost of the appended information.

On the other hand, such breakthroughs are few and far between. If marketing by cluster were that easy, everyone would be doing it. In most cases, the lift from using clusters is marginal, and not much more valuable than the cost of appending the cluster information. Here, however, is one case in which it really paid off.

## The Globe and Mail

Big city dailies are under extreme profit pressure all over the United States and Canada. Declining ad revenues and a reluctant subscriber base— plus diehard trade unions—are threatening the long-term existence of the business. In Toronto, the *Globe and Mail,* Canada's national newspaper, decided to do something about its problems using database marketing.

Like most dailies, 75 percent of the *Globe's* newspaper revenue comes from advertising. A demographically desirable subscriber base is essential to maintaining the advertising sales. The *Globe* determined that to maintain an adequate ad revenue, they needed a minimum paid circulation of 310,000, which results in approximately one million readers daily.

The revenue from selling newspapers does not cover the cost of paper, ink, and distribution. Subscriptions, however, produce more revenue per copy than newsstand sales. Selling subscriptions and maintaining existing subscribers, therefore, is critical. To gain new readers and to persuade readers to renew their subscriptions when they expired, the *Globe* spent in the late 1980s $7 million per year on a telemarketing program that made calls all day and into each evening. Ninety percent of new subscriptions were gained by outbound telemarketing to telephone lists selected from upper-income census tracts. The callers dialed manually on a random basis. The offer was invariably a 50 percent discount.

The system was not working well. There was a very low retention rate and high rate of churn. Because of the way lists were rented, upper income households were contacted repeatedly, and despite an effort at merge/purge, there were many calls to current subscribers. The system was expensive.

Nigel Pleasants, director of marketing at the *Globe*, decided to set up the newspaper's first marketing database to solve the subscription problem. The prospect database was coded with Mosaique cluster codes provided by Dan Huck of the Canadian Marketing Analysis Centre, and included fields to show each contact, and the reason for refusal to subscribe.

Pleasants's first strategy decision was to eliminate the discounts. He reasoned that people should subscribe to the *Globe and Mail* because it was the best paper in Canada, not because it offered to cheapen itself. The idea was that if people bought the paper for the right reason, they would tend to stick with it when renewal time came around. The strategy was sound, but like all strategies, it had its down side: it was harder for the telemarketers to close on a sale without the sweetener of a discount.

The second strategy was to move customers to a "'Til Forbid" system in which the paper was automatically charged monthly to the subscriber's credit card, unless the subscriber called up to cancel.

The third strategy was to install a predictive dialing system—equipment that cost $400,000. The dialing was directed by a model using the data in the prospect and customer database.

### Which Is Best: Penetration or Cluster Data?

At first, prospects were selected for outbound calls based on the penetration of the *Globe* into a particular postal walk (based on the six-digit ZIP code). If the database showed that a particular postal walk had a high percentage of subscribers already, the remaining holdouts were considered fair game for a call. The success rate was better than a random control, but relatively low. Then Pleasants experimented with using the Mosaique clusters as his predictors. Clusters, as you know, rank people by income and lifestyle. Pleasants chose people for calls who lived in clusters that contained the highest percentage of current subscribers. The results were much more successful.

Four months after the new system was installed, the predictive dialer had paid for itself in terms of reduced costs per subscription sale. The elimination of the discount further increased the newspaper's profits. Within a year the *Globe* had:

- Cut its telemarketing budget in half (a savings of $3.5 million per year).
- Increased the retention rate of new subscribers from 10 to 40 percent.
- Learned why prospects were not subscribing and why subscribers were not renewing, so that the *Globe* could accurately predict what was happening to its subscriber base.
- Decreased contacts with prospects from once every four months to once every year.
- Switched from calling the top third of Mosaique segments to calling the top two-thirds of selected prospects.
- Widened its choice of telephone lists to include new movers and new directory listings, since these lists were shown to produce excellent results.

Why did it work? Because Pleasants had a well thought out marketing plan that he modified as the project developed. Without the plan, the database would have been of little use.

How can you tell whether you should use cluster data in your situation? There is an easy answer, which is always correct: test. Get cluster information appended on 50,000 customers or so, and see what you discover. Split your next marketing program: half selected using cluster information and half selected without using clusters. See which provides more profit (after deducting the cost of the clustering).

## Profiling by Lifestyle Overlays

Grouping customers by a combination of sex, age, income, presence of children, and cluster codes makes a lot of sense. Messages to 65-year-olds should not be the same as those addressed to customers in their 20s. Customers like to be treated individually. The marketing results of such individual treatment can usually be demonstrated in dollars and cents.

Going beyond demographics to hobbies and interests can prove, in some cases, to be a winning approach. Surveys of customers can bring out ways of classifying customers that make better sense for marketing purposes than either RFM or demographics. Compiled lifestyle information from companies like National Demographics and Lifestyle (NDL) can be overlaid on a customer file to produce the answers that might take much longer or cost more if done by a direct survey. As explained by Don Hinman, vice president of NDL:

*National Demographics and Lifestyles was founded by Jock Bickert using a simple idea: he would collect and keypunch the customer registration forms sent in by customers of national manufactured products. The forms ask many questions about the product, questions about the customer (age, income, etc.), and questions about the customer's lifestyle: book reading, foreign travel, interests in gardening, golf, real estate, etc. NDL owns the names and is able to offer them to marketers. Over the years, more than 100 manufacturers have signed up for the service. There are more than 25 million customers recorded in the database.*

Figures 6-1 and 6-2 show information available on these individuals. Once the names are available, they can be used for several purposes:

### Figure 6-1: Lifestyle Selector Counts by Income

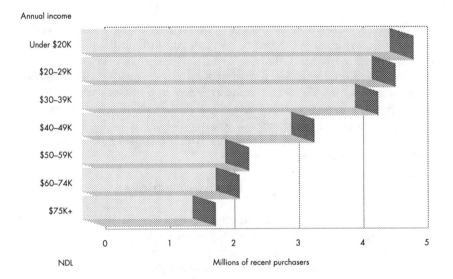

- Overlay: Marketers can have their house files overlaid with NDL data to show whether their customers are more likely or less likely than the national average to have certain interests or hobbies.
- Purchase: Marketers can purchase names of people who are interested in the specific product or service they are selling.

The lifestyle interests available from NDL include:

**Figure 6-2: Lifestyle Selector Counts by Age**

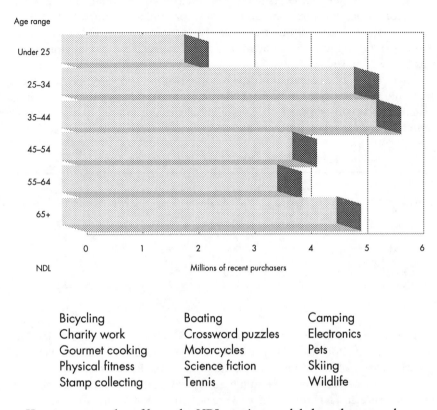

Age range

NDL    Millions of recent purchasers

| Bicycling | Boating | Camping |
| Charity work | Crossword puzzles | Electronics |
| Gourmet cooking | Motorcycles | Pets |
| Physical fitness | Science fiction | Skiing |
| Stamp collecting | Tennis | Wildlife |

Here are examples of how the NDL scoring models have been used:

- A sporting goods merchandiser had a universe of more than three million names, but was unable to make it work. By using the NDL scoring model, the number was refined to a profitable universe of more than one million names.
- A book continuity series used the scoring model to expand its total universe from 900,000 inconsistently responsive names to a universe of more than two million successful names.
- A women's upscale catalog was mailing to 250,000 NDL names. After matching its successful customers against the NDL file, its universe was expanded to 400,000 names.

Consider this example showing the value of lifestyle coding as a way of understanding your customer base and improving your marketing to it.

Suppose that you plan to mail an offer to one million households for a particular product that costs about $50. Before you commit the funds for the promotion, you run a test on an Nth (representative sample) of 25,000, and you get a disappointing response: 1.6 percent, which is below break-even. How can you turn the situation around so that your one million name mailing will be successful?

There is a way that can almost guarantee results. Suppose that you code your file with lifestyle codes from NDL, and use those to redo your mailing list. For example, suppose that your initial mailing looked like Table 6-4, when coded for seven different lifestyles:

### Table 6-4: Results of Test Mailing to 25,000

| Lifestyle | Percent Mailing | Number Mailed | Number Responding | Response Rate | Index of Response |
|---|---|---|---|---|---|
| A Athletic | 32.00% | 8,000 | 40 | 0.50 | 31 |
| B Blue Chip | 8.00% | 2,000 | 6 | 0.30 | 17 |
| C Cultural | 8.00% | 2,000 | 12 | 0.60 | 38 |
| D Do-It-Yourself | 20.00% | 5,000 | 90 | 1.80 | 113 |
| E Domestic | 3.60% | 900 | 30 | 3.33 | 208 |
| F Fitness | 24.00% | 6,000 | 198 | 3.30 | 206 |
| G Good Life | 4.40% | 1,100 | 24 | 2.18 | 136 |
| Total | 100.00% | 25,000 | 400 | 1.60 | 100 |

The net revenue on each sale is $25, or $10,000 for the 400 sold. The cost of the mailing is $450 per thousand, or $11,250. The test has lost $1,250. On a rollout of one million, the project would be a disaster.

Looking more closely at the numbers, however, it is obvious that lifestyle codes Athletic (A), Blue Chip (B), and Cultural (C) are losers. Their response is way below the group average of 1.6 percent. These households should not be mailed in the rollout, because they will result in a loss of revenue. What should be done?

A solution would be to code the entire one million name file with similar lifestyle codes and use these codes to exclude codes A, B, and C. As a result, as shown in Table 6-5, the mailing drops to 520,000.

This will produce sales of 13,680 at $50 each, of which $25 is the gross profit totaling $342,000. The mailing will cost $450 per thousand or $234,000, a net profit of $108,000.

That is not the end of the story, however. The lifestyle coding costs money. How much can you afford to spend on external data plus processing costs? Clearly the maximum is $108 per thousand names (which would consume your entire $108,000 net profit). Fortunately, this type of lifestyle coding can be applied by most service bureaus for a cost of about $10 to $15 per thousand names.

**Table 6-5: Predicted Results of Mailing to 520,000**

| | Lifestyle | Number Names | Test Rate | Rollout Rate ** | Rollout Responders |
|---|---|---|---|---|---|
| A | Athletic | 320,000 * | 0.50 | | |
| B | Blue Chip | 80,000 * | 0.30 | | |
| C | Cultural | 80,000 * | 0.60 | | |
| D | Do-It-Yourself | 200,000 | 1.80 | 1.53 | 3,060 |
| E | Domestic | 36,000 | 3.33 | 2.83 | 1,019 |
| F | Fitness | 240,000 | 3.30 | 2.81 | 6,744 |
| G | Good Life | 44,000 | 2.18 | 1.85 | 814 |
| | Total | 520,000 | 1.60 *** | 2.24 | 11,637 |

\*     Not mailed
\*\*   Discounted by 15% for rollout.
\*\*\* Response at test rate if all 1,000,000 were mailed.

There is an additional cost, however. You rented one million names, but used only 520,000 for mailing. Most list houses also will charge you for the unused names—perhaps not full price, but not zero. Suppose you have to pay them $40 per thousand for names rented but not mailed. This will further reduce your profit.

There is a final cost that you should figure in. Rollouts never do as well as tests. Why this should be, no one knows. But it almost always happens. Let's assume that your rollout does only 90 percent as well as the test.

Here are your final results:

| | |
|---|---|
| Cost of the Product | $307,800 |
| Cost of Mailing of 520,000 | $234,000 |
| Cost of Unused 480,000 Names | $19,200 |
| Cost of Lifestyle Coding ($15 x 1M) | $15,000 |
| Cost of Selecting (@$2 x 1M) | $2,000 |
| Total Costs | $578,000 |
| Gross Revenue | |
| ($50 x 13,680 x 90%) | $615,600 |
| Net Profit | $ 37,600 |

Figure 6-3 shows in graph form the costs from this targeted mailing: What can we learn from the above example?

- Knowing more about your customer or prospect base can improve your profits significantly.
- Advance testing can turn a loser into a winner.
- Cluster or lifestyle coding can be very valuable in database marketing.

**Figure 6-3: Costs from Targeted Mailing**

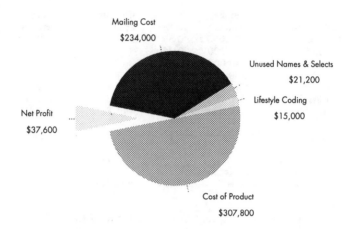

Mailing Cost
$234,000

Unused Names & Selects
$21,200

Lifestyle Coding
$15,000

Net Profit
$37,600

Cost of Product
$307,800

13,680 Sales of $50; Total Revenue $615,600

On the other hand, it is also possible that the coding may not prove anything at all. In many cases, coding does not show the kind of differences in response rates that will enable you to justify the cost. The cost of coding only 25,000 test names is minimal. It should always be done to make sure that you are not passing up any obvious methods of improving your return. Whether you go on to spend the money to code the one million names depends on the results of the test. In the example cited, it really paid off. Whether it will pay off for you can be known only by testing yourself.

Once you have your own customer base coded for lifestyle, demographics, or clusters, you can and should consult these codes in connection with any marketing activity. At this point, the money has been spent. You should try to get as much value out of it as possible. Why send letters to your customers offering them products and services that they probably don't want? It will reduce your company's value to them and waste your money. The better you can target your message, the better you will be received by your customers and the more profitable you will be. Coding with lifestyle, demographics, and clusters helps.

## Profiling by Geography and Mapping

For many marketing applications, geography is crucial. Database analysis using geographical coordinates can tell us:

- Where to locate our next branch.
- What our trading area consists of.
- The extent to which we have penetrated our market.
- Where our competition is going.
- What is the most efficient delivery route.
- Where to look for prospects.

During the 1990s all database marketing based on geography will be organized around TIGER, the U.S. Census Bureau's computerized map of all 50 states. TIGER is a computerized database maintained by the Census Bureau on 42 CD-ROM disks available to the public for $250 per disk. Before you rush off to buy one, pause a minute. The disks are almost useless without proper software processing and updating based on expansion of the population and economy since the census was taken in 1990. Fortunately, many marketing service organizations have done this processing, and can sell you the information you need in a form that you can use.

TIGER provides maps and codes that enable you to link together several different data sources, including:

- Census data, organized by block, block group, and census tract. More than 328 pieces of data are included on each census subdivision besides the number of people and their ages. You can learn income, type of housing, home value, ethnic makeup, etc.
- Geographic coordinates, specifically latitude/longitude, and address ranges. These coordinates permit computers to pinpoint locations on a computer map and to determine distances from a specific point.
- Topographic information including connectivity and adjacency. From this information, it is possible to determine the nearest cross streets or intersections near a business or customer location.
- Postal information, specifically, streets and ZIP codes. Any name and address file can be coded with ZIP+4. Several companies have built cross reference tables from ZIP+4, which automatically locate a dwelling or business in TIGER.

### Mapping Your Database

You can map the customers or prospects on your marketing database with relative ease. The first step is to geocode each database record. Using commercial software from Group 1, LPC, Donnelley, or Polk, you can get a service bureau to append ZIP+4 and geocodes to any name and address record. This information includes latitude/longitude and also can include census demography. Geocodes are the census numbers for the various blocks, block groups, and census tracts used by the Census Bureau for the 1990 census. Once your customer data is geocoded, it can be fed into a mapping program to display customer information on a computer map. Mapping software programs are available from a dozen capable vendors.

All these systems can be used to color or shade geographic areas based on numeric values (level of sales, number of affluent homes, etc.) They can pinpoint specific locations of customers. Many of them can show the actual streets on which your customers live or work. Most of them can show all houses or businesses within a given radius (3 miles, 10 miles, etc.)

### Expanding Branch Markets

Let's look at one example in more detail. Jeff Knebel of Donnelley Marketing Information Services described a project illustrating banks' typical use of DMIS's Cluster PLUS and CONQUEST mapping software.

*A community bank with 20 branches in Philadelphia used direct mail and in-branch applications to promote its bank credit card. It wanted to:*

- *Reduce the number of inactive card accounts.*
- *Do a better job of targeting new customers.*

*As a first step, the bank profiled both active and inactive card holders. DMIS geocoded the database and appended key household information such as age, income, length of residence, number of credit lines, and Cluster PLUS lifestyle codes. Looking at the credit lines, the bank pinpointed the inactives that already had another credit card. These were dropped from the prospect database and not sent more promotional mail.*

*The second step was to profile the active card holders. This analysis disclosed that 11 of the 47 Cluster PLUS segments accounted for most of the high-percentage users. The bank then used CONQUEST to draw maps of their market area, showing the concentration of people living in one of the 11 high-user cluster codes.*

The map in Figure 6-4 shows the ZIP codes in which these users were concentrated. The locations of the bank's branches are shown. Using CONQUEST's TradeMarket Model, these branches were ranked to identify those six branches that had the highest potential for development of high-activity credit card customers.

This target market potential for each branch is shown in Figure 6-5.

## Figure 6-4: Concentration of Target Market by ZIP Code

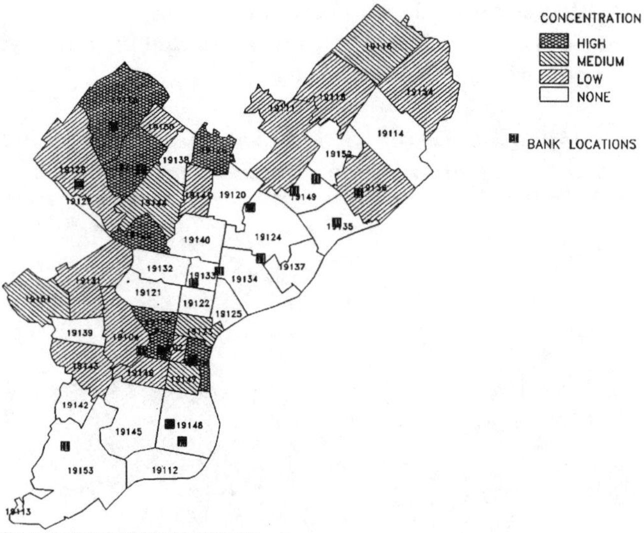

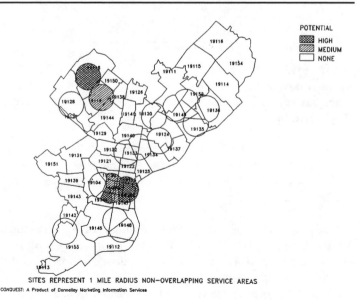

CONQUEST: A Product of Donnelley Marketing Information Services

## Figure 6-5: Target Market Potential by Branch

SITES REPRESENT 1 MILE RADIUS NON—OVERLAPPING SERVICE AREAS

CONQUEST: A Product of Donnelley Marketing Information Services

To further refine their targeting, the bank was able to identify those ZIP+4 areas within each of the six branch's trading areas that contained the highest potential for credit card user cultivation.

Figure 6-6 shows the ZIP+4 areas with selected branch service areas that meet the primary target market profile.

### Figure 6-6: ZIP+4s within Selected Branch Service Areas
### Meeting Primary Target Market Profile

CONQUEST: A Product of Donnelley Marketing Information Services

Aimed now at very specific target areas, the bank used Donnelley Marketing's residential database to get a list of those households in the targeted ZIP+4 areas that:

- Fit the profile and do not have a bank card.
- Lie in the trade area of one of the six branches.
- Are not serviced by one of the branches, but have a medium to high potential.

A mailing was done to the selected households. As responses came in, the bank used CONQUEST's Byways geocoding module to append geocodes and coordinates to the respondent's addresses and create maps showing the respondents.

Figure 6-7 illustrates the respondents within a branch service area.

The bank was able to reduce printing costs for applications by knowing

**Figure 6-7: Respondents within Selected Branch Service Area**

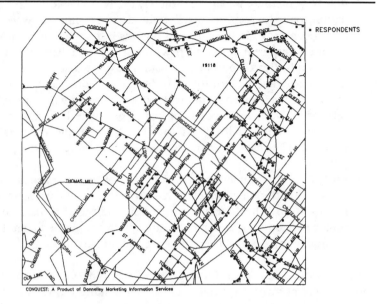

CONQUEST: A Product of Donnelley Marketing Information Services

the number of application forms most likely to be used by branches, and to identify areas in Philadelphia where new branches should be developed.

These case studies show state-of-the-art use of maps in the service of database marketing. Software to draw the type of maps shown can be obtained for less than $50,000 from a number of sources. Drawing maps is not quick, even with a very fast PC. Setting up, creating, and printing any of the maps shown above usually takes from five to 15 minutes or longer. A single marketer can probably create less than 20 maps a day.

The other serious mapping problem is the assumption that the residence of the customer should be near your branch office. In fact, because so many people are employed, many, if not most people bank, buy gas, and buy other products near their work, rather than near their home. Planning your branches near people's homes may not be the smartest move. At the same time, however, I don't know of any way in which you can get a list of people by their work location.

## Evaluation

How useful is mapping in database marketing? This is an important question, because the investment in mapping software and staff resources is not trivial. There are really two answers:

- Understanding and communication: A picture is worth a thousand words. Sometimes a map is absolutely the best way to understand a situation, or to explain it to someone else. Mapping software systems have been growing by leaps and bounds in the past decade. Mapping programmers cannot keep up with customer demand for more and more sophisticated output products. I suspect that this will continue to be a growing field for the next decade or more. Computing latitude and longitude is essential in many cases. Knowing where people are in relation to your branches is of key importance in marketing. Using software such as CONQUEST to see maps of neglected areas where profits can be made is often essential to a full understanding of market potential.
- Analysis and action: When the point has been made and the explanations given, the time for action has arrived. Maps may not be as useful in this step. Why? Because, once you use these maps to convince senior executives that some definite action should be taken, they will invariably say, "Wow. There they are. Great! Now get me a list."

In evaluating your need for and use of mapping software, you should look closely at your requirements for understanding, communication, analysis, and action. In some cases, maps are essential to seeing the situation and making your point. In other cases, you can reach the same conclusions by using software like CONQUEST to view cross tabulations, reports, and graphs.

Balance the benefits and costs in your particular marketing situation.

### Summary

1.  Profiling is a way of dividing your customer base into segments with similar attributes—either purchasing behavior, demographics, or lifestyle. It is useful because you can engage in relationship building better if you talk about things that interest customers. It is also useful because you can vary your marketing programs based on the segment you are dealing with, and improve your success rate.

2.  There are five different types of intuitive profiling methods, consisting of information or data that you can add to a database to assist in construction of meaningful segments. They are: product affinity codes, demographics, cluster codes, lifestyle codes, and geography.

3.  Product affinity is a useful way of classifying customer behavior. By comparing purchasing behavior of different customers, useful seg-

ments can be created (parents of babies, automotive repair hobbyists, sewing specialists) that can be the start of a dialogue or a way of improved marketing.

4. An affinity matrix can be constructed on a computer to measure the propensity of people who buy certain products to buy other products. Be careful not to go overboard with affinity matrices. Computers can generate thousands of pages of data—overkill in marketing.

5. Demographics can be applied to any file. The 1990 census listed 328 different pieces of data such as income, presence of children, and house value, which can be inserted into any database record to which ZIP+4 coding has been applied. The demographics can be used to develop profiles of a customer database.

# Executive Quiz 6

Answers to quiz questions can be found in Appendix B. The quizzes are for fun. Do them if you enjoy quizzes. Ignore them if you don't.
*Choose the best answer to complete each question.*

Given the information in Table 6-6, fill in the blanks showing how much you could improve the response rate and profit by eliminating the mailing to Young Suburbia.

*Table 6-6*

|  | Number | Responses | Response Rate | Index of Response |
|---|---|---|---|---|
| Furs & Station Wagons | 43,980 | 836 | 1.90 | 126.70 |
| Shotguns & Pickups | 80,970 | 1,296 | 1.60 | 106.70 |
| Pools & Patios | 20,145 | 766 | 3.80 | 253.30 |
| Young Suburbia | 140,220 | 1,262 | 0.90 | 60.00 |
| Total | 285,315 | 4,160 | 1.50 | 100.00 |

Cost of Mailing @$0.80   $228,252
Net Revenue @ $60.00   $249,600
Profit   $21,348

**Revised Mailing Prediction Eliminating Young Suburbia**

|  | Number | Responses | Response Rate | Index of Response |
|---|---|---|---|---|
| Furs & Station Wagons | 43,980 | 836 | (1) | 95.00 |
| Shotguns & Pickups | 80,970 | 1,296 | (2) | 80.00 |
| Pools & Patios | 20,145 | 766 | (3) | 190.00 |
| Total | 145,095 | 2,898 | (4) | 100.00 |

Cost of Mailing @$0.80   $ (5)
Net Revenue @ $60.00   $ (6)
Profit   $ (7)

8. A company markets 40 different SKUs. They want to construct a cross-buying affinity matrix. How many different cells will it have?
   a. 40
   b. 80
   c. 120
   d. 400
   e. 1,560

9. The break-even point for a direct mail promotion is 2 percent. A test mailing to 20,000 has an average response rate of 1.2 percent and an overall loss. Overlaying NDL lifestyle groups shows response rates varying from 5.8 percent to 0.3 percent. What should you do for the rollout?
   a. Give up. The test was a failure.
   b. Mail all NDL groups with 2 percent or better response rates.
   c. If cost of NDL, unused names, and mailing to greater than 2 percent results in a profit, mail rollout.
   d. Retest. It may have been a fluke.
   e. Redo the offer, change lists, and rollout.

# 7

# Building Relationships with Surveys

*Someone recently asked me why Marlboro is in so much trouble if Philip Morris is so sophisticated at direct marketing. Philip Morris has been intent on gathering names, but they haven't done much with them. They are now cutting prices across the board—a typical mass marketer reaction. There are people out there who are still willing to pay full price for Marlboros. The problem is, Philip Morris doesn't know who they are.*
*—Don Schultz, Northwestern University*

Relationship marketing begins with a dialogue. You talk to your customer or prospect, and get the person to respond to you. You exchange information, opinions, desires, and friendship. One of the best ways to begin this dialogue is with a survey. Sometimes when you can't reach a customer or prospect with a promotional letter, you can get him or her to respond to surveys. This is particularly true with business-to-business correspondence.

Surveys tell you more personal information about each customer than you could ever get from overlays or models. Many people like to be asked their opinions or desires, particularly when they think that someone will pay some attention to what they say. That last part, of course, is the key to success in surveys.

Surveys are used with profit in almost every business. They are common in dialogues with automobile owners, cellular phone prospects, winter resort customers, prescription drug purchasers, cruise line passengers, and hundreds of others.

## Statistical Limitations

Statisticians will argue that customer questionnaires are biased: You will only hear from customers who like to fill out forms, and these folks may not represent a cross section of your customer base. With a mailed survey, you can't construct a control group (of nonquestioned customers) to test the validity of your questionnaire, since the only way to test the validity of your conclusions would be, ultimately, to survey your control group. Another problem cited by experts: The customers may not tell the whole truth.

All these quibbles are sound. But they overlook the main point: to begin a dialogue with each customer or prospect, not to collect statistics. The dialogue builds a relationship, and the relationship translates into reduced attrition, cross-selling, and repeat sales.

Don't confuse database marketing with market research. Many marketers fail to see the fundamental difference between these two disciplines. Market researchers don't really care about the customer, or even the success of the business. Their interest is in getting their hands on truth: Some scientifically accurate statement about the market that will hold up under scrutiny. Database marketers, on the other hand, are looking for ways to build the bottom line by building relationships with customers.

## The Hawthorne Effect

In the early 1960s, Western Electric Co. performed industrial efficiency experiments in its Hawthorne Works assembly plant. One of the researchers came up with the idea of determining whether the introduction of the new fluorescent lighting would improve productivity. Since Western Electric was one of the pioneers with this type of lighting, success in the experiment could be used in sales promotion.

The researchers replaced the incandescent lighting in an assembly area with fluorescent lights. They studied the workers' output per hour, stationing engineers in white coats in strategic places throughout the area who asked the workers their reactions, writing the results of their observations neatly on clipboards. They discovered that production rose by a significant percentage! To prove that they had discovered something important, they yanked the new lights out, and replaced them with the old incandescent bulbs. They watched the workers' reactions.

Amazingly, production went up again! They replaced the bulbs with smaller wattage bulbs. The astounded engineers in the white coats reported another improvement in output at the plant. What was happening here?

The researchers finally concluded that the workers were producing more because someone was paying attention to what they were doing and asking their opinions. They felt that their opinions were important to the company. Someone cared about what they thought and did. In this atmosphere, they willingly applied themselves with full vigor and imagination to their assembly tasks.

The Hawthorne effect applies to database marketing as well as to assembling electrical devices. People will become interested in you, if you become interested in them. Some of the most interesting people to talk to are people who just listen to what you have to say. Psychiatrists learned that 50 years ago. Patients willingly pour out their hearts on the couch to doctors who say little or nothing, but listen and make notes.

## Defining the Purposes

Before you begin any effort involving a survey, write down its objectives. There should be only a few, and they should be clearly understandable to you and to the people being surveyed. Examples include:

- To begin or continue a dialogue with a customer or prospect
- To find out how your product or service is being received, with an eye to improving the product, the method of delivery, the advertising, etc.
- To find out if the customer or prospect needs further products or services that you might provide, determining what is needed, by when, and how you can help with the purchasing decision

These are good objectives. Here are examples of bad objectives (for database marketing) that will not help your business:

- To gather data on people using your product, such as their demographics or their business, without bothering to ask why they've purchased your product or how it satisfies their needs
- To gather the data solely for the purpose of selling the information collected to other companies
- To make people think you will do something with the results of the survey, when you have no intention of doing anything at all

Why are these bad reasons? Because they are not honest, friendly dialogue; they are self-centered impositions, which, in the long run, will weaken or destroy the relationship you are trying to build.

This is not to say that you cannot rent out your database, with the information it contains. This is a perfectly legitimate use of data that you have collected. What's wrong is to collect the information only for the purpose of selling it. It is also not wrong to collect demographic or company information about your customers. The data collection should be a by-product of some relationship-building activity, not a purpose in itself.

A survey is like any other market transaction: Both parties must make a profit, or the transaction will not take place. Figure out what profit you will make from the survey, and what profit your respondents will make. If either side's benefits are slim, redo your survey until both parties win. You do this when offering products for sale; do the same thing for your surveys.

Victor Hunter of Hunter Direct points out that some studies show that the number of contacts, not their length or medium, is a prime determinant of customer satisfaction. For this reason, substituting surveys by mail or phone for sales visits can save money without reducing the perceived level of service.

## The Beginning of a Dialogue

Questionnaires are one of the least costly ways of developing a dialogue. The customer does all the work. All you have to do is to tabulate the response, and then use it as a basis for further actions.

Make clear in your cover letter or explanation the reasons why the customer would benefit from answering your questionnaire. Here are several points that you should explain:

- The benefit to the respondent: Make clear in the first sentence why the person receiving this questionnaire would want to respond to it.
- The objective of the survey: Why are these questions being asked? What will be done with the results?
- How the respondent was selected: How did we happen to choose the reader, and why?
- The importance of the survey: Besides the benefit to themselves, people like to feel that they are playing a part in a larger effort that will shower goodness upon others. Make that clear.
- The confidentiality and privacy involved: Make clear that respondents do not need to worry that their names would be used in any way other than what you intend and state in the letter. Provide safeguards.
- The identity of the sponsor: Who is asking these questions? Are they a recognized authority or household word? If you are not well known, perhaps you can get a trade association or larger group to sponsor your survey.
- Where to send the result: The address and date should be on the questionnaire. Ideally, there should be a business reply envelope. Don't forget to put the address on the cover letter as well.
- The deadline: Don't leave it vague. "The survey must be returned by March 15th" will prompt people to act. March 15 does not have to have any special significance, but if you provide a survey without any deadline, your response will be depressed.

## The Satisfaction Survey

One of the best ways of conducting a dialogue with customers is the satisfaction survey. Some automobile companies have made this a fine art: asking about dealerships and their services, vehicles and their features, customers and their preferences. People are usually in a good mood when they have just received a new car, and it is an ideal time to get information from them.

Cruise lines can survey their passengers while they are cruising. Besides asking them how they like the ship, the survey can ask what friends might benefit from such a cruise.

Equipment manufacturers all have owner registration programs with survey questions. Asking customers how they liked the product will often help you learn about customers as well as about the product itself.

What do you do with a satisfaction survey? Most companies haven't a clue. They file them away. Wrong. What you do with a satisfaction survey is to store the information in a database, and use it immediately as a part of an overall relationship-building strategy. The strategy may be directed at several possible avenues:

- Making sure that the customer purchases a replacement model at the appropriate time
- Making sure that the customer comes back to you for spare parts, service, or consumables
- Alerting the customer to other products that you sell. Your satisfied customer is your best prospect for future sales.

The strategy needs to be worked out in advance before the survey is even drawn up. Each question should be designed with the strategy objective in mind. The appropriate response to the survey needs to be worked out and put in place. The cost of the survey should be built into a customer lifetime value model.

### A Good Idea Gone Wrong

Here is one example of what not to do:

A major company collected data by means of an interactive diskette packed with each of its products. The diskette asked more than 100 questions of the customer: name, age, occupation, income, why the product was purchased, how it was to be used, etc. Each customer had to spend more than a half hour entering all the data. A thousand are completed every business day and sent to a central collection agency, where they are gathered into a database.

Good idea, right? Bad idea. The company used the data for market research purposes and for product design. There was no communication back to the customer. No one ever responded to complaints (although they were solicited). The customer got absolutely no value in return for the half hour of work, except automatic entry in a quarterly sweepstakes to win a valuable prize.

No one at this company ever sat down and wrote the objectives of this survey. If they had, the survey would have been completely redesigned. The usefulness to the company would have been vastly improved, and the relationships with the customers would have been strengthened. In reality, the questionnaire was designed for and used by market researchers, not by marketers. The millions of dollars that were spent on it were largely wasted, as far as relationship building is concerned.

### Cruise Line Case Study

Now, let's take a look at a very different survey strategy. This shows what could happen when a cruise line considers building a customer database and using it to improve its profits.

To begin with, cruise lines normally have a terribly low retention rate. Cruises are expensive. Unlike airplane trips, which are made to get somewhere else, most cruise trips end up back where they started. They are strictly for pleasure. Many people take only one cruise in their entire lives. Many of the remainder who do cruise more than once will take their second cruise on another cruise line. The situation is a difficult one for loyalty building—or we might say, it is an opportunity for a creative loyalty-building program.

Table 7-1 shows the picture facing a sample cruise line. As you can see, the retention rate is only 6 percent. Of 1,000 cruise line passengers this year, only 60 of them will come back again next year. The lifetime value that begins at $200 is only up to $211.18 five years later. A heavy penalty—$300 per customer—must be paid in advertising costs to attract a constant new stream of vacationers.

How could a customer satisfaction survey change that situation? Let's say that the cruise line trains its cruise directors to be sure that all travelers fill out a comprehensive satisfaction survey while they are onboard. The survey has a lot of important data. In particular, it identifies the travel agent who recommended the cruise and asks people to suggest a number of friends who might enjoy coming on such a cruise with them next year. We find out about their anniversaries, their birthdays, their children, their par-

### Table 7-1: Lifetime Value of Cruise Line Customer

|   |   | Year1 | Year2 | Year3 | Year4 | Year5 |
|---|---|---|---|---|---|---|
| | Revenue | | | | | |
| R1 | Customers | 1,000 | 60 | 7 | 1 | 1 |
| R2 | Retention Rate | 6 | 12 | 18 | 24 | 30 |
| R3 | Yearly Sales | $2,000 | $2,000 | $2,000 | $2,000 | $2,000 |
| R4 | Total Revenue | $2,000,000 | $120,000 | $14,000 | $2,000 | $2,000 |
| | Costs | | | | | |
| C1 | Direct Cost Percent | 75 | 75 | 75 | 75 | 75 |
| C2 | Direct Costs | $1,500,000 | $90,000 | $10,500 | $1,500 | $1,500 |
| C3 | Advertising | $300,000 | $18,000 | $2,100 | $300 | $300 |
| C4 | Total Costs | $1,800,000 | $108,000 | $12,600 | $1,800 | $1,800 |
| | Profits | | | | | |
| P1 | Gross Profit | $200,000 | $12,000 | $1,400 | $200 | $200 |
| P2 | Discount Rate | 1.00 | 1.20 | 1.44 | 1.73 | 2.07 |
| P3 | NPV Profit | $200,000 | $10,000 | $972 | $116 | $97 |
| P4 | Cum. Profits | $200,000 | $210,000 | $210,972 | $211,088 | $211,184 |
| L1 | Lifetime Value | $200.00 | $210.00 | $210.97 | $211.09 | $211.18 |

ents, their jobs, their hobbies, their income, their lifestyle.

While the cruisers are still on the ship, the director faxes the survey forms by radio back to the cruise line headquarters. The data is key-punched and entered into the cruise line database. When the cruisers return to their home, there is a gift waiting for them: a video of the cruise they were just on, a basket of tropical fruit, and a check for $X to provide refreshment for a party that the cruisers can throw for their friends to show the video and tell them how great the cruise was.

Meanwhile, over at the travel agency, the names of the friends who have been recommended for cruises have been sent to the particular agent involved, with a suggestion that the agent call them. A letter is sent to the cruisers telling them that, if their friends do decide to cruise, the cruisers will get a 20 percent reduction on their own next cruise. The database will keep track of this, sending out letters and certificates.

The entire program is followed up by a post-cruise satisfaction survey, phone call, and reminder letters a few months later on the occasion of anniversaries and birthdays. This is a full court press.

What can be the result? No one knows for sure. One possibility would be a major change in the retention rate, and, for the first time, a significant referral rate. Table 7-2 shows what it might look like.

A referral rate of 8 percent is projected here—eight passengers out of 100 suggest someone else who actually takes a cruise. The retention rate doubles from 6 percent to 12 percent. What does all this cost? Projected here is a total of $70 per passenger. This covers the database, the surveys, the phone calls, the video, the fruit basket, the post cruise party. Where does the money come from? From the advertising budget.

**Table 7-2: Lifetime Value of Cruise Line Customers with Databases**

|     |                      | Year1        | Year2      | Year3      | Year4      | Year5      |
|-----|----------------------|--------------|------------|------------|------------|------------|
|     | **Revenue**          |              |            |            |            |            |
| R1  | Referral Rate        | 8            | 8          | 8          | 8          | 8          |
| R2  | Referred Customers   |              | 80         | 16         | 4          | 1          |
| R3  | Customers            | 1,000        | 200        | 52         | 16         | 6          |
| R4  | Retention Rate       | 12           | 18         | 24         | 30         | 36         |
| R5  | Annual Sales         | $2,000       | $2,000     | $2,000     | $2,000     | $2,000     |
| R6  | Total Revenue        | $2,000,000   | $400,000   | $104,000   | $32,000    | $12,000    |
|     | **Costs**            |              |            |            |            |            |
| C1  | Direct Cost Percent  | 75           | 75         | 75         | 75         | 75         |
| C2  | Total Direct Cost    | $1,500,000   | $300,000   | $78,000    | $24,000    | $9,000     |
| C3  | Survey & DB Cost     | $10,000      | $4,000     | $1,040     | $320       | $120       |
| C4  | Retention & Referral | $60,000      | $12,000    | $3,120     | $960       | $360       |
| C5  | Renewal Discounts    | $0           | $16,000    | $3,200     | $800       | $200       |
| C6  | Advertising          | $230,000     | $46,000    | $11,960    | $3,680     | $1,380     |
| C7  | Total Costs          | $1,800,000   | $316,000   | $82,160    | $25,280    | $9,480     |
|     | **Profits**          |              |            |            |            |            |
| P1  | Gross Profit         | $200,000     | $84,000    | $21,840    | $6,720     | $2,520     |
| P2  | Discount Rate        | 1.00         | 1.20       | 1.44       | 1.73       | 2.07       |
| P3  | NPV Profit           | $200,000     | $70,000    | $15,167    | $3,884     | $1,217     |
| P4  | Cum Profits          | $200,000     | $270,000   | $285,167   | $289,051   | $290,268   |
| L1  | **Lifetime Value**   | $200.00      | $270.00    | $285.17    | $289.05    | $290.27    |

Is this realistic? Can we expect this type of result from a survey and database program? Who knows? It depends on the situation, the aggressiveness of the marketer, the market, the product, the agents, etc. What is certain is that this type of analysis has to be done before the survey program is launched if you are serious about your customers and your business.

A test group can be created that receives all these goodies, while a control group is set aside that receives none of these things. After a year or two, it will be possible to know with certainty what is working and what is not working. This is an excellent opportunity for creative database strategy testing. Certainly doing nothing, assuming that practically no one will ever come back, and ignoring the possibilities for change doesn't seem like a creative solution.

If the referral rate can be pegged at 8 percent and the retention rate increased to 12 percent, what will be the results on overall company profits? This can be estimated by multiplying by the number of passengers. Let's assume that this cruise line has 200,000 passengers per year. Table 7-3 shows the results of the changes:

If our homework is done correctly, the five-year effect of the database program will be to increase profits by more than $15 million. Before you get too ecstatic, against this we must charge the reduction in awareness advertising of $70 per passenger—a hefty reduction from $300. This will certainly reduce the number of new recruits and therefore reduce profits. Will the increased retention and referrals by existing customers be greater,

**Table 7-3: Changes Resulting from Database Programs**

|    |                        | Year1 | Year2       | Year3        | Year4        | Year5        |
|----|------------------------|-------|-------------|--------------|--------------|--------------|
| L1 | Value Without DB       | $200.00 | $210.00   | $210.97      | $211.09      | $211.18      |
| L2 | Value With DB          | $200.00 | $270.00   | $285.17      | $289.05      | $290.27      |
| L3 | Difference             | $0.00 | $60.00      | $74.19       | $77.96       | $79.08       |
| P1 | With 200,000 Customers | $0    | $12,000,000 | $14,838,889 | $15,592,646 | $15,816,801 |

the same, or less than the reduction in new customers due to reduced awareness ads? Only testing will tell. In many cases, resistance by the advertising manager to having the advertising budget cut would doom such a database program in its cradle. There are ways around this, of course. Let's see what one of them might be:

The overall ad budget before the database was $60 million per year. If we were to run a test of the survey and database on 20,000 passengers per year, it would reduce the budget by only $70 each or $1,400,000, a cut of only 2.3 percent. No one can measure the change in effectiveness in awareness ads by budget changes as small as 2 percent, but the database managers can certainly measure precisely the impact of the $1.4 million. A two- to three-year test would appear to be warranted.

Of course, the survey alone did not do any of these things. The survey simply gathered the information into the database, which was essential for all these programs to become possible. Added to the survey were training of cruise personnel, a fax and keypunching system, telemarketers, fruit basket dispatchers, direct mail, and discounts for repeat passengers.

Suppose that you do this analysis and you discover that there is no way that the survey could possibly pay for itself. What do you do then? Scrap the survey! We are not doing these things as a public service. The idea of a survey is that we will make a profit from it. This is how you prove that you are making a profit.

## How to Get Them to Respond

There are a great many old wives' tales about secret methods of assuring a response to a survey. Some of them are valid; many of them are not. Presented here are the good and the bad, with some comments:

- Provide a definite incentive. Some of the best (in order of normal success rate) are: a dollar bill included in the survey envelope, the promise of a specified and clearly valuable premium sent by return mail, and automatic entry in a sweepstakes drawing for some large premium in the near future. (Be sure to specify the drawing date and the odds of winning; this is one of the best.)

- Provide a copy of the results of the survey (tends to be weak).
- Provide a postage paid return envelope—a must. If you doubt this, send half with and half without. You will soon see that it pays.
- A longer questionnaire often works better. Many people assume that the response is inversely related to the length of the questionnaire. Completely wrong. If you develop an interesting questionnaire with clear benefits, you will usually get better results from a four-page questionnaire than you would with a two-page questionnaire. The reason: People like to feel as if they are participating in something well designed and comprehensive. After they finish the first page, they have an investment in the survey and will go on to the end. A small questionnaire with only a few questions may not be considered important enough to bother with. These comments really relate to two- and four-page questionnaires. Whether they work for larger questionnaires depends on the audience, the interest, and the type of survey.
- Select the audience carefully. As in all direct response work, the list is the most important factor. If your survey is directed at prospects, you will make more progress by buying the best lists and carefully screening the names to be sure that they are totally qualified for the products or services involved than any other possible thing you could do to improve response. If you are surveying your customers, the list is of even greater significance.
- Don't ask the same people the same questions over and over again. You will not only reduce response, you will infuriate your customers. In talking to a friend, you cannot get away with asking him what his wife's name is every day. It will soon become obvious that you haven't listened, don't care, or have no memory whatsoever. These customers are supposed to be your friends. If you are intent on developing a relationship, once you have asked a question once, tuck the information in your database. Next time you send a survey to this person, ask something else. Easy to do if your survey methods are well designed.
- Don't ask questions that are irrelevant. You know which customers bought model B, C, and D. Don't ask model D customers questions that apply only to model B (even if you excuse yourself by saying something like "if you don't have model B, go on to the next question"). In talking to a friend you would not say, "How do you like your Cadillac?" when you know that she drives a Toyota. Why do this to your customers?
- Don't survey customers who have made a specific complaint or suggestion until you have responded to their complaint or suggestion.

Let me provide a personal example of this. A few years ago, I was asked in a personal letter (at least I thought it was a personal letter) by the dean of my graduate school to come back for my 35th reunion. I had not been back in more than 20 years. I wrote the dean a two-page letter explaining in detail some grievance I had with the school about 20 years before.

I never received an answer. The following year, I received a similar personal letter from the dean's successor, inviting me to come back for my 36th reunion. No mention was made of my previous letter. It became obvious to me that these personal letters were the product of an active computer, and that the responses to the letter went quickly to the trash. Needless to say, my graduate school is not high on my list of charities to which I donate money.

Why send such letters when they just infuriate people? There is no way of asking the dean this question, of course, because any letter that he receives is automatically trashed unread. But in your company, where relationship building is important, responding is vital. Not communicating at all, until you have responded, should be a cardinal rule.

- Make an advance screening call. If the survey is of any size, when you get your list ready, have a telemarketing firm check 40 names at random to be sure that the selected people are really who you think they are, and have the interests you think that they should have. If the telephone calls do not prove the value of your list, don't mail the survey. Go back to the drawing board, and get a new list.
- Send advance communication. Many successful surveys start with a teaser letter saying that the survey is coming next week, and asking people to be on the lookout for it. This should improve response by a measurable percentage. You can prove this by not mailing the teaser letter to a third of your list, and keeping track of who got what.
- Follow up with calls to nonrespondents. If the survey is going to big ticket purchasers, a telemarketing follow-up may be justified and greatly improve response. Be prepared to ask the survey questions over the telephone if the respondents prefer it that way.
- Personalize your cover letter and questionnaire. Here is where you can really use your database. If the recipient is a customer, you should use this opportunity to reminisce.

> As you know, you are one of our oldest customers, having been with us steadily since 1972. We were particularly grateful for your comments in 1989, which were useful in helping us with our redesign of Release 6.0. I am writing this time to ask your ideas in making improvements in ...

Can anyone doubt that this letter will not only receive an answer, but will be another link in a chain that binds this customer to your company? Does your database permit you to create such letters? If it is well designed, it does. It is not expensive to create this type of personalization. It just takes advance planning. Even letters to prospects can be personalized, if you do the job right. Realtors do this all the time:

> Two houses on Bull Run Mountain sold last month for over $200,000. One of them was on your street, Ridge Road. If you are interested in finding out more about what your house at 2616 Ridge Road is worth right now, I would be glad to ...

Is it worthwhile to do this type of personalization? You can prove whether this effort works by not personalizing a certain percentage and measuring the difference.

Here are several factors that probably are less important:

- The day of the week the questionnaire is dropped in the mail
- The size of the envelope and the color of the paper
- First class versus bulk rate postage. Here, the difference is the stamp. Bulk rate with a live stamp often pulls as well as first class.

But don't take my word for it. Always do a test with different timing, envelopes, or postal classes to be sure.

## Hidden Agenda

Most questionnaires have a hidden agenda. If you are engaging in a dialogue with automobile owners, the big question you want them to answer may be, "When will you trade in your present car, and what make and model are you thinking about?"

Asking the question directly may reduce the response and the value of the dialogue to the responder. Try wrapping your key questions in a soft cocoon of easy ones that are also useful:

- What do you like best about your present car?
- What is the main disadvantage of your present car?
- How long should a person keep a new car before the declining value and increased repair bills make a change economical?

## Should Questionnaires Be Anonymous?

If you are doing a statistical survey, a blind questionnaire may be useful. It may improve response. It may be more objective. But if you are developing a dialogue with your customers and prospects, you have to know who they are. You will want to store their responses in your customer marketing database. There is very little you can do with an anonymous questionnaire. Don't get sidetracked from your main objective. In some cases, it is possible to encode an anonymous questionnaire with an inconspicuous number or barcode that will help track the respondent.

Better practice is to come right out and print recipients' names on the questionnaire so that they will know at once that it is not anonymous. Most people don't mind giving their opinions openly to a friend, and that is the relationship you are shooting for.

## How to Organize Your Questions

There are several basic rules that have been developed over the year and seem to produce the best results:

- Ask the easy questions before the hard ones. Let respondents glide easily into the questionnaire and get so much invested in terms of interest and time that they won't want to back out when they come to the tough questions that require memory, thinking, or research.
- Ask nonthreatening questions before threatening ones. If you really want to know why a customer dropped your product, ask first to hear some good things about your product and some questions about the economy in general.
- Ask general questions before specific ones. Place a question such as:

    Will the climate for air conditioning installations in the United States be better next year than it was this year?
    before:
    How many units will you install next quarter?

- Keep the content of each block of questions in the survey logical— don't jump around. You may precede each block with a short sentence such as:

    The following questions relate to the merits of vinyl versus concrete as a lining for swimming pools:

- Put the demographics at the end. Your last questions should be the ones where the respondent checks off annual income, sales, home value, or number of children. These should never be put in the beginning of a questionnaire. They will depress response in that position.
- Create several versions to test response. If you are mailing 15,000 questionnaires, you should probably make three versions, sending 5,000 to three Nth samples of your entire file. An Nth sample is an equally distributed sample created in such a way that the makeup of the recipients in each sample should be identical. Each version should vary the order, and the question wording to test which gets the best responses. The cost of printing different versions is seldom significant, but the results of a test can often be surprising. Sometimes, three versions can differ by as much as 20 percent in the response. You will learn a great deal by testing. You will learn very little if you don't test.

### A Survey that Produced Results

A national manufacturer with 120,000 retail outlets had never communicated directly with his retailers. Instead, he always worked through distributors. In 1991, faced with intense competition in this marketing outlet, he decided to try database marketing. He obtained the names of the retailers from the distributors, and a database of 120,000 was built for the first time.

A group of 17,000 was selected for a survey test mailing. The goal was to determine the attitude of the retailers toward the brand and to enlist their support in promoting the products with in-store displays. The survey forms included a free offer for respondents. The manufacturer followed up a sample of nonrespondents with a telemarketing test to determine the attitude of the nonrespondents.

The survey was a two-page questionnaire with 23 questions. They had 5,329 respondents, representing 31 percent of the 17,000 retailers surveyed—considered an outstanding response. All data received was coded into the database. From the responses, an algorithm written into the software quickly classified each retailer into one of five categories:

| | |
|---|---|
| Super satisfied | 45% |
| Very satisfied | 38% |
| Somewhat satisfied | 9% |
| Dissatisfied | 5% |
| Incomplete | 3% |

Each of the 266 dissatisfied retailers was contacted immediately by telephone to discuss the dissatisfaction. A number of those dissatisfied also were visited personally by marketing staff members. The goal was to take immediate action to correct whatever conditions existed that made the respondents dissatisfied.

Every respondent got a personal laser-printed letter thanking him or her and replying to every survey question response—good and bad—in a very unique and interesting way, based on some very elaborate software designed by an outside direct agency and prepared in advance by a database service bureau.

The software worked like this: Each of the 23 questions were numbered. Each had five possible multiple-choice responses, generally ranging from satisfied to unsatisfied. Different paragraphs were developed to respond to every one of the 115 possible answers that a respondent could give (23 times 5). The laser-printed letter was made up of these paragraphs. It spoke to the retailer as to a well-known old friend.

In many cases, the problems cited by the retailers and investigated by subsequent telephone follow-up disclosed significant errors in the handling of relationships with the retailers by the distributors or by the manufacturer itself. Marketing put pressure on the distributors and on the billing and product delivery staff to correct these problems immediately, so that the letters could report actual steps taken to correct the areas of dissatisfaction.

Figure 7-1 shows how the letter paragraphs were built:

### Figure 7-1: Building the Letter Paragraphs

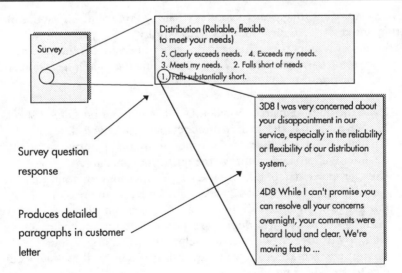

The success of the first year led to a mailing of 58,000 in the second year. In this mailing, there were three different surveys and cover letters. They were addressed to:

- Respondents to the first survey
- Nonrespondents to the first survey
- First time recipients

The purpose of this second-year effort was similar to that in the first year, but also to determine, as much as possible, the effect of the previous survey and subsequent follow-up on the attitude of the respondents.

This type of follow-up is exactly what should be done in the case of any customer survey operation. This is true database marketing! Many years ago, manufacturers were closer to their customers and could gauge their reactions directly. Today, of course, that is not possible. Database marketing, however, plus good surveying technique and well-planned and thorough follow-up can create a direct bond between the manufacturer and the customer who is purchasing the products.

The results of this effort were tabulated quite scientifically in terms of reduced attrition. A five-year slide in placement of the brand with retailers was arrested. The program was expanded and adopted as a permanent implement in the marketing tool kit.

## What Your Survey Should Look Like

How do you want to appear to your customers? Professional. Responsible. Caring. Interested in their responses. Trustworthy.

You can say a lot of these things in the way you create the questionnaire. There are some basic rules that work in conveying the right impression and improving response:

- Make the questionnaire a booklet. Don't send it out on stapled sheets. An organized booklet makes the document look well thought out—not hastily put together. In fact, the discipline of putting a booklet together will probably improve the quality of your survey.
- Use a proportional font. Don't use a typewriter font for your questionnaire. Times Roman 10 or 12 makes a much better impression.
- Use lots of white space. Cramming a lot of questions together can save printing costs, but will depress response. The questionnaire should look easy to answer. White space helps create that impression.
- Arrange answers vertically, not sequentially. Compare these two examples to see what I mean:

The most important requirement for word processing software is (a) cost (b) general use in industry (c) ease of use (d) convertibility into other formats (e) training and backup manuals (f) advanced features such as fonts, mail merge, etc.

The most important requirement for word processing software is:
(a) cost
(b) general use in industry
(c) ease of use
(d) convertibility into other formats
(e) training and backup manuals
(f) advanced features such as fonts, mail merge, etc.

The second version is much easier to read and understand, and can be answered much faster than the first.

- Don't include coding information. Most good questionnaires are designed with the key punchers in mind. It is important that the data be easily read and entered by your staff. But it will depress response if the form looks like a computer document.
- Make it look interesting. The most important single format point: make it look easy and fun to do. Give the impression that the responder will learn something just by filling it out. You can do this by using variety in your wording and in the way the questions are arranged. You can provide information while you ask for it:

Last year, 42 percent of American households used decaffeinated coffee. Ten years ago only 25 percent used decaffeinated. Which type of coffee is used in your household today?

## How to Structure Your Questions

As much as possible, you should use multiple choice questions. This is because such questions are easier to answer than fill in the blank and provide more options than true/false. Open-ended questions should be used only when you really feel that a dialogue is called for, and when you intend to read and act on the result.

For example, you may want to ask a question such as:

What problems did you have in getting the dealer to help you in the installation of your unit?
[ ] A. No problems. The dealer was very helpful.
[ ] B. No problems. I installed it myself.

[ ] C. I had some problems. They are: _____
Can we contact you later for suggestions on how these problems could be avoided in the future? [ ] Yes [ ] No

When you use such a question, you must do several things:

- Develop a coding system to categorize the problem. Your data entry personnel should be specially trained to use a two-letter dynamic coding system that can be added to as more kinds of problems crop up.
- Respond quickly to the problem. Customer service must be alerted within 24 hours after such a question is answered showing a problem. This is a golden opportunity. Once you get a customer to open up, a good customer service rep can get to the heart of the difficulty, solve the problem, and convert this person into a very satisfied customer.

### Opinion Questions

Most questionnaires ask people's opinions. The answers can be very valuable. But how you ask the question is vitally important if you want to get accurate answers and avoid turning off your respondents. Here are some tips on how to ask such questions:

- Balance your response possibilities carefully. Don't prejudice your answers by giving people a loaded group of possible responses. For example, here is a balanced method:

  Choose the response that best reflects your opinion:
  A. I agree strongly.
  B. I agree somewhat.
  C. I neither agree nor disagree.
  D. I disagree somewhat.
  E. I disagree strongly.

If you use the same answer format on the next page, repeat the list of answers. Don't make people go back to a previous page to find out what they are.

- Don't use leading questions. This is obvious, but tends to creep in without warning:

  Which software product is most helpful to you?
  [ ] A. Word Processing
  [ ] B. Spreadsheet

[ ] C. Database
[ ] D. Accounting
[ ] E. Presentation Graphics

This seems objective. But suppose the person does not have a computer, or does not use any of the software packages, or finds none of them helpful? Better to ask "Which of the following do you use most frequently?"—and include "None" as a possibility.

• Use a specific time period in the question.
    Bad:
        How often have you had to replace the motor on your compressor unit?
    Better:
        How often in the last two years have you had to replace the motor on your compressor unit?

• Don't require the respondent to calculate an answer to your question.
    Bad:
        How many miles do you drive to work in the average year?
    Better:
        How many miles do you drive to work in the average day?

• Check the value of the response by a fake choice. Sometimes, people fill in a questionnaire with crazy responses, either without thinking or to be deliberately difficult. In such cases, you will accumulate unreliable information in your database. One way of avoiding this is to ask factual questions that include some made-up answers:

    Which brand of dishwasher detergent is used the most in your house?
    [ ] A. Joy
    [ ] B. Electra-Sol
    [ ] C. Ivory
    [ ] D. Spotless
    [ ] E. Care-Free
    [ ] F. Other: _____

Some of these detergents don't exist. If the respondent picks these answers, other responses must be taken with a grain of salt.

## Details of Questionnaire Presentation

Obviously, a questionnaire should look inviting. Type should be large and easy to read with lots of white space. Here are some details that you might overlook:

- Keep a question on one page. Don't split a question between pages.
- Number your questions, and use letters for the responses.
- If you have to say "skip to ...", put it after the response. For example:

  How many dogs do you own? _____
  If you do not own a dog, skip to the next page.

  As I said before, if you know that the respondent does not have a dog, don't ask this question at all. Design your questionnaire to permit this type of personalization.
- Lead the reader into each section.

  The next group of questions asks about your employee benefits.

- Be sure to tell respondents the address and cut-off date for returning the response. In most cases, you will provide a return envelope and a letter, however, these easily can be separated from the questionnaire. At the end of all questionnaires, clearly print the return address and the deadline. You will get some responses that you might have missed.
- Be sure to thank respondents at the end. This is a dialogue. It is polite to say thank you in any exchange. Don't omit this step.

## Follow Through on Survey Results

Probably the least understood part of the survey process is what to do with the results. Hundreds of surveys are designed and sent out every year with little thought about what to do when the responses come in.

A plan for the handling of the responses is, if anything, more important than the design of the survey itself. You should make it an absolute rule that before any survey can be put in the mail, a carefully designed plan for handling the responses is not only written down, but operational. You need to know:

- Where will the responses be keypunched? Who will do it? How will the results be put into the database? Has the database been programmed to receive all this additional data? If not, delay the whole process until this vital step is completed.
- For each type of response to each question, what is your specific planned action?

## A Financial Services Example

Richard Courtheoux of Precision Marketing Corporation cited the methods used by a leading financial services company:

A survey was sent to a large number of the company's active card members. The survey made it possible to learn a great deal about the member's lifestyle and financial management needs. Some of the questions were quite interesting:

> Please check the statements that describe you:
> Lifestyle:
>> Starting to build the lifestyle I have selected
>> Approaching my biggest investment to date: buying a home
>> Planning to invest in a larger home or major home improvements
>> Providing for my children's education
>> Increasing my net worth
>> Structuring my assets to prepare for retirement
>> Living off the fruits of my labor
> Views on Financial Matters:
>> Covering my present needs and beginning some financial planning
>> Achieving my lifestyle goals now and paying over time
>> Seeking the right financial tools for me
>> Avoiding financial decisions whenever I can
>> Cautious, careful, slow to commit to new financial products
>> Enjoying managing my assets, reading about new products, and testing numerous financial products
>> Settled, happy with past financial decisions, not looking for alternatives
> How Financial Matters are Handled:
>> Making transactions by electronic means (e.g., automatic teller machines)
>> Depositing money by mail
>> Investing by mail
>> Applying for a loan by mail or phone
>> Requesting financial information by mail or phone
>> Making financial decisions based on information received by mail or phone
>> Using one financial institution for most of my needs
> Current Holdings:
> Which of the following products are part of your financial portfolio?

Savings account
Certificate of deposit
Low risk investments like mutual or money market funds
Higher risk investments like stocks, bonds, or securities
Secured loans like a mortgage or car loan
Insurance on property
Insurance on self

As a bank, stock broker, or insurance company, wouldn't the answers to these questions be ideal for targeting your marketing efforts to prospects?

## Including a Check with the Survey

Neil Walsh of the Ecocenters Corporation provided one method of communication that resulted in double-digit response rates.

A real estate developer was seeking prospective renters. To attract attention, he used a letter with a live perforated check that asked a number of important survey questions that the recipient had to answer in order to cash the check. Unlike surveys that contain actual money, nothing is wasted if the recipient throws out the envelope without opening it, and only those who respond are paid.

The survey pulled a 28 percent response rate. Eighty percent of the respondents completed all the questions on the check.

The $1 checks were processed by the banking system within a week. The savings from using checks, compared to a business reply envelope for the survey, was $290 per thousand. In addition, because the envelope contained checks instead of cash, the developer saved $720 per thousand since the uncashed checks cost nothing. A valuable database was created with the survey results.

## The Start of a Dialogue

Now that you have the names and addresses of a large number of people who have answered your questions, you can talk to them as individuals.

All the results—the responses to all the questions asked—must be stored in your database. I can hear your response: "We don't have space for all that data." Of course you do. The cost of data storage is coming down by about 10 to 15 percent per year. It is certainly much cheaper today while you are reading this than it was when I wrote it. If your Management Information Systems (MIS) department or service bureau can't store that much data, switch to a service bureau that can.

If you feel that it isn't worth it to store the data, then you shouldn't have asked the questions in the first place. Every survey should be designed with the database in mind. Every piece of information that you can learn from your customer, if it is intelligently obtained and intelligently stored and retrieved, can and should be used to build a relationship.

The survey also can be used to create profiles of customer types that will be the basis for further marketing. The 20,000 respondents to your survey can be broken down into small groups of customer profiles. Each profile should then receive individualized marketing promotions based on the information that they have supplied about themselves. You have a different message for people in their 20s from that for people over 65. You say different things to people who live in a high-rise than you do to those living in a single-family home in the suburbs. You speak differently to people who are very satisfied than you do to those who are somewhat indifferent to your product.

## Results from the Survey

Profiled and targeted marketing is the first result of the survey. The next result is the responsive personalized mailing.

Here is a family of four with an income of $60,000 and a life insurance policy of only $50,000. Your survey shows clearly that with $60,000 in income and two children, the policy should be more than $150,000. The survey is an excuse to inform people of the results, show them how they stack up against others, and begin your dialogue about insurance.

Next come the loyalty builders. The survey told you that a couple has bought your product for more than 12 years. It told you that they have a dog named Prince who has won prizes in two shows. A little congratulations are in order, along with an invitation to join the pet registry (complete with ID tag) and a chance to try (and provide opinions on) a new show-dog premium food, specially formulated for high stress pets.

You have hardly scratched the surface, but the payoff in relationships, loyalty, reduced attrition, and increased sales is well on its way.

## Summary

1.  Surveys are a good way to begin dialogues with customers or prospects. They provide more useful information than can be gained from overlays. To create a dialogue, however, you must react to a survey and modify your behavior based on the customer's response. Then you tell the customer what you have done and ask for further input. That is the beginning of real dialogue and the way to develop loyalty.

2. Market research is not database marketing. Customers like to talk and exchange opinions. That is not the same thing as providing data for a statistical report. If you want to build loyalty, keep the market researchers at bay.

3. You should make clear to the respondents and to yourself the purpose of the survey. Be sure to be honest with the respondents. If you say you are going to do something, you should be prepared to do it.

4. The first question to ask in beginning a survey is: Why would people want to fill out this survey? What's in it for them? If you don't have a good answer, you don't have a good survey plan yet.

5. Satisfaction surveys are great for building rapport. They should be entered into the database and used as a vital part of a relationship-building program as soon as they arrive.

6. There are several good ways of boosting response to a survey. They involve incentives of guilt and greed. A dollar bill enclosed with the survey relies on guilt. A sweep stakes entry supports greed. If your method is friendly, nondemeaning, and cost-effective, use it.

7. Surveys are best if personalized. Don't ask for information that you already know. It infuriates people. Also, avoid anonymous surveys. Better to get fewer results and have them signed than more results and have them anonymous and unusable.

8. In organizing surveys, make them fun and easy on the eyes. Put the soft questions first. Don't make customers calculate the answers. Make the survey a booklet with lots of white space. Use multiple choice questions throughout.

9. Respond quickly to information gleaned from surveys. Consider each survey as if it were a telephone call. Snap right back with action to correct any problems, and thank respondents for their attention.

10. All the data collected from surveys should be stored in the database and used as a basis for action. If you don't have space to store the data, you shouldn't ask for it. People assume that you are collecting the information for some valid reason. Don't disappoint them.

# Executive Quiz 7

Answers to quiz questions can be found in Appendix B. The quizzes are for fun. Do them if you enjoy quizzes. Ignore them if you don't.
*Choose the best answer to complete each statement or question.*

1. The Hawthorne effect showed that
   a. improved lighting boosts factory productivity.
   b. changing lighting systems is good for morale.
   c. workers produce more when others show an interest in them.
   d. management does not care about workers' opinions.
   e. None of the above

2. For a survey to be a success
   a. there must be a well-defined objective.
   b. the survey respondents must make a profit.
   c. data collection should not be the primary purpose.
   d. selling the results should not be the primary purpose.
   e. All of the above

3. Which of the following is the most likely to get a response to a survey?
   a. Promise of a copy of the results
   b. A $1 bill
   c. Two $1 bills
   d. Automatic entry in a valuable sweepstakes
   e. A premium sent by return mail

4. A survey should be personalized if
   a. it improves response.
   b. it helps build a relationship.
   c. it is not too expensive.
   d. it has been tested.
   e. All of the above

5. In a survey, the demographic questions should be
   a. at the end.
   b. at the beginning.
   c. buried unobtrusively throughout.
   d. in a separate message.
   e. None of the above

6. Using checks as a response device for a survey
   a. tends to depress response.
   b. violates banking laws.
   c. is more expensive than a business reply envelope.
   d. All of the above
   e. None of the above

7. Computing the effect of a survey program on lifetime value
   a. may prove that the survey is a loser.
   b. cannot be conclusive since data is lacking.
   c. is too complicated a process for a simple satisfaction survey.
   d. requires advanced modeling capability.
   e. None of the above

8. The response to a survey
   a. cannot be predicted in advance.
   b. requires an incentive for the customer.
   c. depends heavily on the day of the week it is dropped.
   d. falls off if the survey is more than one page.
   e. All of the above

# 8

# How Modeling Helps Build Profits

*Question: Show me some proof that these programs are working ...
What's the payback on investment in database marketing?*

*Answer: American Express has been very successful with target
modeling, as have other companies. But you know, I go to conferences, and I don't see any proof. Why haven't I seen proof? Because
we're all in competition, and showing proof is sometimes difficult.
To show an example where I succeeded, found something that has
really worked for American Express, and to present that to CIBC or
to the Bank of Nova Scotia is probably not a good idea.*
*—Bill Comeau, director market analysis, American Express Canada*

There are a number of very useful and sophisticated tools available to
marketers today that can help reduce marketing costs, improve marketing response, and build profits. These tools fall under the general
heading of modeling. Although many marketers still operate today without
the benefit of a model, this will soon change. In many cases, modeling
makes marketing so much more accurate and successful that competition
will soon sweep nonmodeling marketers aside. Just as farmers today have
learned that a computer is essential to successful dairy farming, marketers
are learning that models are essential to successful database marketing.

Modeling is the process of using mathematics and statistics to analyze a
database to determine some mathematical formulas that "explain" the
behavior of customers. Modeling is usually done with a statistical sample
(10 percent or less) of the entire database. These mathematical formulas
are then used to predict the response of customers and prospects to future
marketing promotions. The predictions, which can be ascribed not just to
the mass but to each individual customer and prospect, can be used to
reduce the number of promotions, cut the costs, increase the percentage
responses, and boost profits.

Here are some ways in which modeling is used:

- A department store with a proprietary credit card uses its database to create a profitability model that determines on a monthly basis the lifetime value of individual customers. It is used to identify and target various segments of the customer base.
- A regional airline develops and maintains a database with individual recency, frequency, and monetary information plus promotional response history. The database is used for targeting reactivation programs for the individual customer base of frequent flyers.
- A national catalog company enhances its customer file with response and purchase history, plus demographics and psychographics. The database is used to identify customers most likely to respond to off-season promotions, leading to an increase in sales.
- A national bank card company categorizes its prospect universe according to predicted promotional response rates and estimated net sales. The result is reduced postage costs and increased sales and profits by targeting only the top-ranked responders.
- A frequent flyer program profiles its member base using household level and individual usage information. It is able to identify the characteristics of the most frequent flyers allowing for targeted promotions on a regional basis.

## Mailing Smarter

Database marketing involves communicating with customers. When your customer base is large, each message often involves a considerable amount of money. The question naturally arises, "Is it worth it? Are we mailing the right thing to the right people, or are we just dumping more unwelcome junk mail on our customer base?"

A worthwhile question. This chapter is devoted to the idea of "mailing smarter," targeting our communications to people who want to receive them so that a meaningful and profitable dialogue can be created.

Mailing smarter involves testing and adjusting our subsequent communication plans based on the results of the test. This process relates one or more dependent variables, the desired outcomes, with almost any number of independent variables, such as customer behavior or demographics. The goal is to determine which of these variables will best predict the desired outcome. Examples of desired outcomes are: responses, purchases, and increased lifetime value.

To help us predict these outcomes, we could use hundreds of different aspects of customer behavior and lifestyle. The problem we face is this:

- To find out which of the possible variables are the most effective in predicting customer response
- To use the selected variables to modify our communications plan so that the customer is satisfied with the messages, and responds to them

The best method of mailing smarter to customers is using Recency, Frequency, Monetary (RFM) analysis (see Chapter 5, Building Profits with Recency, Freqency, Monetary Analysis), which is more accurate and less expensive than modeling. Unfortunately, RFM analysis works only with customers for whom you have compiled a fairly extensive purchase history. If you have such data, you absolutely must use RFM analysis, since it will pay dividends much greater than the efforts expended. When data is not available or when mailing to prospects, another way to mail smarter is through the use of a model.

With modeling, the prediction will not be as definite as with RFM analysis. It might work in some cases, and in other cases it might not be any help at all. You must test your file to determine its applicability.

## How Demographics Can Help

As explained in Chapter 5, RFM analysis makes use of behavior variables, such as purchases and responses. Modeling, however, makes use of both behavioral and demographic variables. The theory behind demographics is that the clue to behavior can be found in relevant facts: age, income, length of residence, presence of children, etc. Suppose you do a mailing to a test group that has been coded with demographic facts. By comparing the demographics of those who respond with those who do not, you should be able to identify some differences that explain the difference in behavior. This does take some work, however.

Chapter 6, Using Customer Profiles in Marketing Strategy, explained that customer files can be overlaid with internal or external demographics. Internal demographics come from surveys, application forms, credit histories, or some other customer source. External demographics come from census data, motor vehicle data, cluster coding, etc. Let's assume that you have obtained information and had it appended to the customer file, including such items as:

| | | |
|---|---|---|
| Age | Income | Cluster code |
| Home value | Length of residence | Home ownership |
| Presence of children | Educational level | |

Suppose that you conduct an initial test of 30,000 using the identical Nth across-the-board sample of your entire customer or prospect database. In this case, however, lacking RFM information, you must determine the characteristics of the successful responders by a form of modeling.

It would be nice to be able to analyze this type of data using a simple method such as an ad hoc cross tabulation, as shown in Table 8-1:

### Table 8-1: Response by Income Level

| Income | Mailed | Responded | %Response |
|--------|--------|-----------|-----------|
| $100,000 | 6,000 | 128 | 2.14 |
| $90,000 | 8,000 | 161 | 2.01 |
| $80,000 | 12,000 | 227 | 1.89 |
| $70,000 | 15,000 | 273 | 1.82 |
| $60,000 | 20,000 | 338 | 1.69 |
| $50,000 | 30,000 | 465 | 1.55 |
| $40,000 | 45,000 | 468 | 1.04 |
| $30,000 | 50,000 | 455 | 0.91 |
| $20,000 | 35,000 | 287 | 0.82 |

This shows that as income goes up, the response to this particular offer goes up. Similar cross tabulations can be run on other demographic factors to produce similar results.

In general, however, this is a pipe dream. Cross tabulations of response very seldom have this simple and straightforward relationship. The factors leading people to buy a particular product are complex and rarely related to such a simple factor as income, age, length of residence, etc. Moreover, the relationships between demographics and response—if they do exist at all—are often combinations of many factors that cannot be viewed on a simple table such as this one. This is why modeling is required.

## How Models Work

The basic idea behind models is the same as that of RFM analysis: to predict the future based on information from the present and the past. We take a known event, such as the response to a mailing to a test group, and look for characteristics in those who responded that separate them from those who did not respond. It may be recency, frequency, or monetary amount, or it may be other characteristics entirely: age, income, presence of children, or type of housing.

What makes a person buy a product? Impulse? Interest? Boredom? Spare cash? Temporary insanity? In my opinion, people buy products to remove personal subjective feelings of uneasiness that outsiders can seldom fathom. We all have bought products and been sorry afterwards. We have passed up items that we later wished we had purchased. I mention these possibilities to establish an important idea: We don't buy products because of our age or income (or similar demographic factors) alone. However, when we are considering large numbers (tens of thousands) of prospects or previous customers to whom an offer is made, it is possible that some demographic factors influence enough buyers to establish a trend.

As one example, consider my lifelong interest in books. I buy a lot of them. Ten years ago, my income was half of what it is today. I bought fewer books. Today, when I want a book, I don't have to ask how much it is. Income and age play a role in my book purchases. This is very likely true of millions of other people as well. That is why modeling works: There is some relationship between the market activity of customers and their demographics. The job of the model is to find out what that relationship is, quantify it, and apply it to the prediction of future responses and sales.

With our customers, we can collect a lot of information concerning their behavior and their demographics. This can be collected from sales records, application forms, and surveys. We can also purchase outside data about our customers [overlays for age and income, Standard Industrial Classification (SIC) code and annual sales for business customers, etc.]. Modeling of our customer files, therefore, makes use of a rich store of data inputs that often can enable us to do an excellent job of predicting response.

As mentioned earlier, the same is not as true of prospects. Since we have little or no behavioral history on prospects, we must rely on appended demographic information. This data may not be accurate—it seldom is— but it is usually all we have.

After determining which of the many factors available are important in predicting behavior, the next step is to quantify the influence of the important factors by establishing weights to be multiplied by each factor. The final step is to add together the product of each factor and its appropriate weight to arrive at a score. The score is, essentially, a number that predicts who will respond and who is not likely to respond. This score can be determined for any customer or prospect (for whom the same factors are available), so as to generate a prediction as to the response of a large and untested universe.

## Types of Models

Several modeling methods are in common use in marketing today. They include:

- Multiple regressions
- CHAID analysis

- Fractal modeling
- Fuzzy logic
- Expert systems
- Chaos classifiers
- Neural networks

Each of these methods has proved useful to some marketers. Multiple regressions were first used for direct marketing by the Reader's Digest in 1963. They have been widely used in marketing since the early 1970s. Use of regressions, however, is generally confined to professional statisticians who know how to apply the technique. Such people are rare and expensive, and must rely on experience, skill, and hunch for their success as well as on computer processing.

In this chapter we will concentrate on only one method: neural networks. Modeling using neural networks involves an iterative process of multiple regressions, testing different weighted inputs to determine the combination that best predicts behavior. We will focus on it for these reasons:

- It is the only system that marketing professionals without a strong background in statistics can use without a lot of outside assistance.
- It is becoming widely used and understood in marketing in the 1990s.
- It is nicely packaged so as to permit automatic functioning using an IBM-compatible personal computer, which is within the ability and price range of most professional marketers.

### A Brief History of Neural Networks

Ben Hitt of Advanced Software Applications Corporation in Pittsburgh, developer of ModelMAX, an automated modeling package based primarily on neural networking, supplied some interesting information on the history of this technique. Neural computing originated in 1943 in a single scholarly article in a professional journal by McCollogh and Pitts. Since computers did not exist at that time, their ideas could not be put into practice. All subsequent neural methods can be traced, however, to this original paper.

In the 1960s, Frank Rosenblatt devised the first successful neural network called the Perceptron, based on the visual perception of the housefly. It was a forward step, but lacked the ability to solve interesting problems.

In the 1970s, Bernard Widrow developed the Adaline, the first commercially viable neural network, still used today by the telephone company to compensate long-distance telephone lines.

Finally, in 1988, Fred Rumelhart developed the algorithm known as backpropagation, which is now used in more than 90 percent of all neural networks today. Backpropagation permits a computer to use the errors found in a single pass of a neural network model to make adjustments (backpropagations) in the inputs so that the next pass contains fewer errors. As a result of this development, a neural network can "train" itself to make better and better predictions. Practical neural networks, therefore, really began only in 1988.

## Modeling Steps

Let's see how a neural network would be used to create a model. Models begin with a test. An offer is made to a test group of customers who are representative of a much larger group. The model is used to predict the response of the larger group. To make sure that the test group is representative of the larger group, you should use an Nth—a computer-derived mathematically chosen sample. Both the test group and the larger group should have identical demographic or behavioral data in their database records: income, age, etc. These pieces of data are the independent variables used to construct the model.

The test group receives a promotional mailing (or telephone offer) to which they can respond, or make a purchase or donation. After the test, each individual in the test group is coded as being a respondent or a nonrespondent. They also may be coded by the amount they purchased, and any other data that resulted from the test.

Let's say that the test involved 40,000 individuals, of which 800 (2 percent) responded, and 39,200 did not. These 40,000 are then further divided into two equal groups of 20,000 with approximately 400 respondents in each. The first 20,000 (the neural network test group) will be used to "train" the model. The second 20,000 (the neural network control group) will be used to "validate" the model.

### The Input Variables

Let's say that there are nine pieces of data available in each of the 40,000 records. They might be such things as:

| | | |
|---|---|---|
| Age | Income | Gender |
| Marital status | Children | House ownership |
| Cluster code | Home value | Urban/suburban/rural |

A neural network software package should be installed on a fast personal computer, one with at least a 486 chip. Figure 8-1 is a schematic diagram of the network. Each of the input values is multiplied by a weight. The first

### Figure 8-1: Simplified Neural Network

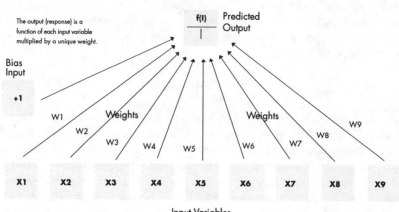

The output (response) is a function of each input variable multiplied by a unique weight.

f(I) Predicted Output

Bias Input

+1

W1  W2  Weights  W3  W4  W5  W6  W7  Weights  W8  W9

X1  X2  X3  X4  X5  X6  X7  X8  X9

Input Variables

time through, the weights are determined by a random number. It doesn't matter what values are used for the weights initially, since they will be corrected by the model. The processing element (in the diagram, the box on the top) computes the Internal Activation quantity (I), which is the sum of the product of each input and its corresponding weight. This Internal Activation is converted through a mathematical process called a nonlinear transfer function into a number between -1 and +1.

The model is run on every person in the neural network test group. Since the test mailing is already completed, we know the outcome for each person: either a response (+1) or no response (0). If the output of the model for an individual is 0.2 and the person's known value is +1 (a response), then there is an error of 0.8. The next person's error may be different: 0.3 or some other value. Each person, therefore, will have a different error (because of different inputs—age, income, etc.). The model then trains itself by recalculating the weights used for each input. It then reruns this process to produce a new prediction for each individual that will have, it is hoped, less error than the previous run.

## The Hidden Layer

The real neural network is more complex that the simple diagram shown above. Neural networks actually contain a hidden layer of nodes used to do intermediate processing. Figure 8-2 shows these hidden layers.

There can be one, two, or a large number of nodes in the hidden layer where intermediate processing is done. The more hidden nodes there are,

**Figure 8-2: Complex Neural Network with Hidden Layers**

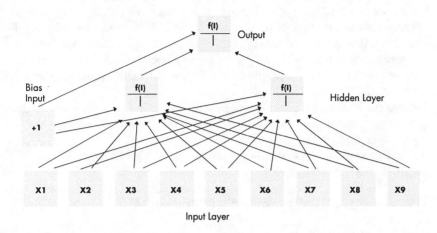

the more complex the network and the slower it runs, but the better it trains itself to understand the relationships in the data.

## The Training Process

Thus, a neural network is an iterative process. Each iteration consists of four phases:

1. A forward pass and computation of network output
2. A determination of error
3. Backpropagation of that error through the transformation functions of each node in the hidden layer and the output
4. Adjustment of the weights to reduce the error

Theoretically, a neural network could run forever, constantly minimizing its error and getting increasingly more accurate weights. In reality, on a fast personal computer, within about 45 minutes or 200,000 iterations, the law of diminishing returns sets in, and the amount of reduction in error in each pass becomes less and less significant. At that point, the model will stop the training process and validate itself.

## Scoring and Validation

With the training process completed, the model turns to the neural network control group set aside in the beginning (the other 20,000 who also received the test mailing). The weights derived in the training process are applied to the inputs of the records in the control group to arrive at a score for each person in the control group. The scores are usually from .000 to .999. In our terms, a person with a score of .999 is someone whom the model was just about absolutely certain would respond, and .000 is someone whom the model was positive would not respond. To make life easier, these scores are usually multiplied by 1,000, so they end up being numbers from 000 to 999.

Once the control group has been scored, the scores are compared to the actual response of the group. The scores should do a good job of predicting the actual response.

If the validation process is successful, the model is ready for use in making predictions on the larger group: the untested rollout.

## How Models Build Profits

Knowing what is likely to happen with a large untested group of customers and prospects is very powerful information. Here is what you can do:

- Mail only to those most likely to respond. Suppress the mailing to the others.
- Make better offers to those less likely to respond, and less costly offers to those most likely to respond. This reduces the cost of acquisition.
- Mail a second or third time to high scoring nonrespondents.
- Follow-up with telemarketing to high scoring nonrespondents.

Ben Hitt reported on the use of a model with four million names, each of which was scored with 150 variables including demographics and purchase history. A test mailing was made to 30,000. Eight weeks were allowed for the responses to be received. The mailing resulted in 574 buyers and 29,426 nonbuyers.

ModelMAX automatically selected 20 of the 150 variables for training, and 15 nodes were set up in the hidden layer. Preprocessing of the inputs took about an hour. Examples of the 20 variables that proved useful were:

- Length of time in residence
- Income
- Age
- Presence of children

Examples of the 130 variables that proved less useful and were not used were:

- Ethnic group
- Home-to-work driving distance
- Educational level
- Percent urban

Since the company had many different products, cross-product variables were created: those who had bought A and B were given a 1, and those who had bought A but not B were given a 0, etc.

Table 8-2 shows the simulated results of the mailing to the final universe, compared to the results if the model had not been used:

**Table 8-2: Mailing with and without a Model**

|  | Rollout w/o Model | Rollout w/ Model |
|---|---|---|
| Mailed | 4,000,000 | 2,200,000 |
| Responded | 76,400 | 53,480 |
| Nonrespondents | 3,923,600 | 2,146,520 |
| Response Rate | 1.91 | 2.43 |
| Sales ($85.05) | $6,497,820 | $4,548,474 |
| Mailing Costs ($0.551) | $2,204,000 | $1,212,200 |
| Direct Costs (66%) | $4,288,561 | $3,001,993 |
| Net Profit | $5,259 | $334,281 |

ModelMAX created the model in just under three hours, including the preprocessing time. The resulting model permitted the company to mail to only 55 percent of its audience and still reach 70 percent of the expected buyers. The response rate zoomed from 1.91 to 2.43, and the profits on the rollout climbed from $5,000 to more than $300,000.

## How to Select Variables

You may have been wondering throughout this discussion how to choose the input variables needed to create a successful model. This is a problem that all modelers have, and it is this sort of problem that has kept modeling an arcane subject whose practitioners command high fees.

Recent software innovations, however, have made selection of variables a less difficult task for marketers with products such as ModelMAX. In the above case history, ModelMAX automatically selected 20 variables for the 150 available in the customer records. Another example is the Database Mining Workstation (DMW) by HCN, Inc., of San Diego, California, one of the most widely used neural network marketing products. It offers an interesting solution to this problem of selection of variables.

As explained by Allen Jost, HCN's director of decision systems, the DMW consists of software installed on a PC in the form of interconnected modules. Of key importance is the Automatic Variable Selection Module, which determines the best variables to use for a model. Of the 100 or more variables (income, age, etc.) that you may have in an individual record, some duplicate the actions of others, and others are unimportant in predicting.

Since marketers may not know, in advance, which are the most important variables, it is useful to let the DMW software make that decision. The marketer puts everything that is known about customers into the model. The model pares down the list to what is really needed and constructs its final weighting system using only those.

For example, a marketer in financial services may assume that income is the key determinant of profitability or sales of certain bank products. When the model is run, however, it may show that "years in present home" may be more important in separating respondents from nonrespondents, and income may end up on the middle of the list of important variables, instead of at the top.

## The Impact of Desktop Modeling Systems on Marketing

Desktop systems like the HNC product signify that modeling has moved from the domain of the statistical specialist to becoming a standard marketing tool. In the 1980s, advanced marketing shops would hire an outside modeler who would construct a model using multiple regressions to help in predicting responses to a major company mailing. The model might take six months to produce and cost $50,000. It might save $100,000 or more.

Because of the time involved and the cost, the company would attempt to use the same model scores for several years and dozens of mailings. Problem: The market changes every day. A model built last year may be quite inefficient as applied to today's marketing situation.

With desktop modeling, however, that is no longer a problem. A desktop system can be purchased for about $80,000, including both the hardware and the software. Marketers can be trained to use it in a week. Thereafter, the marketing shop should build a model for every single mailing. Each mailing should be a learning experience leading to better customer dialogue and response in future mailings. There should be a test before every rollout, leading to model construction and a successful attempt to mail smarter on the rollout.

## Using a Model

Once you have begun modeling, you should use it often. In the banking world, for example, a model can predict which customer should have a home equity loan and the probable value of that loan, based on known information in the bank's files, including home value, when the current mortgage was taken out, credit rating, checking and savings balances, personal loans, age, etc. The most important single use of the model, from the standpoint of the bank's relationship with its customers, is to use it to determine qualification: to avoid offering a product, such as a home equity loan, if the customer is likely to be turned down when applying. Such a process—inviting an application, processing the application, and rejecting the application—is not only a very costly process for the bank, it is also likely to lose the customer for other bank business.

Prior review by bank personnel of every one of 20,000 home equity, credit card, auto loan, or personal loan invitations to be mailed is clearly impossible. Use of model scores in such situations is imperative.

## Linking Models Together

Ken Hartmann of Metromail points out that a number of models can be linked together to provide progressively pinpointed data on prospect and subsequent customer behavior. For example, a group of five linked models can predict:

- Response to solicitation for a loan
- Number of loans to a customer in his lifetime
- The average loan amount to this client
- The profitability of payments from loans from each customer
- The lifetime value of each new loan customer

The same reasoning can be used by a department store to determine to whom specialized catalogs should be sent or by an automobile dealer to decide when to vigorously promote a new model to an existing customer.

The most widespread use of such models, however, is in prospecting. Once a marketer understands the factors that influence response to a mailing, any marketer just itches to test the model on new outside prospects, selected using scores developed by the model.

## Testing

Because of their eagerness, however, many marketers make their biggest mistake. They do not set up control groups to test the validity of the model. The only way to prove that the model is successful in picking respondents from nonrespondents is to mail simultaneously to two groups:

one picked by the old method not using the model scores and a group picked by the model scores. It is useless to compare this month's mailing with last month's mailing—too many things change (the season of the year, the offer, the economy). The market changes much faster than most people realize. There are no "permanent" facts to be learned about how people react. What people did last month is what they did last month. It is not what they will do next month.

If you do your testing properly, the results should show that the group selected by the model scores performed better than the other group. But how much better? The results are seldom dramatic. Suppose the control group shows a 2 percent response, and the model group shows a 3 percent response. That is a 50 percent improvement in response. Against that, however, you have to balance the cost of getting the variable data needed for the model. Name rental agencies will seldom let you rent names according to detailed demographics, without a significant additional charge. The alternative to the extra charge is to rent lots of names, and do the selection yourself. Even then, however, you may face an additional charge from name rental agencies just for coded prospect lists with demographics.

After all the extra costs involved, the 50 percent improvement in response rate could actually turn into a net loss in profit—the control group might actually be more cost effective. Detailed cost analysis of the sort used in this chapter is required.

### Predicted Net Revenue

Some marketers use modeling to compute a Predicted Net Revenue (PNR) for each potential customer in a rollout mailing. The system works this way.

To begin, a test mailing is sent to a sample of the file. The file contains a significant number of variables (age, income, recency, etc.) that can be modeled. This model determines the weights to be assigned to each variable to predict who would accept the offer and who would reject it. The probabilities are calculated as follows:

- Response. The model calculates the probability that the promotion will result in a sale, based on the performance of the test mailing. The formula looks like this:

$$R \ (\text{Response}) = a_1 \times W_1 + a_2 \times W_2 + a_3 \times W_3 + \ldots$$

The $a$ values represent various demographic or other variables, and the Ws represent the weights assigned by the model to the variables.

- Rejects. A similar formula is used to calculate the probability of the offer being rejected by the individual.

$$J \text{ (Reject)} = b_1 \times W_1 + b_2 \times W_2 + b_3 \times W_3 + \ldots$$

The b values may represent the same or different variables from those used in computing the possibility of a successful sale.

- PNR. Once the model has calculated the two probabilities, the formula for the Predicted Net Revenue becomes:

$$PNR = R \times \text{(Value of order)} - J \times \text{(Cost of rejection)}$$

For a typical customer, the PNR could be:

$$PNR = (.2 \times \$12.45) - (.8 \times \$1.02)$$
$$PNR = \$1.67$$

This means that the net value of this prospect to you is about $1.67. The prospect should be mailed to for this offer. The formula is used to select or reject all customers or prospects for rollout promotions.

## Modification of PNR for Database Marketing

PNR is customarily used on a promotion-by-promotion basis. Database marketing, however, looks at the longer term value of a customer or prospect. Experience soon shows that prospects who become customers based on a single product offer may go on to buy other products and develop a long-term relationship. The probability of second, third, and subsequent purchases also can be modeled in the same way that PNR is modeled. When this is done, the lifetime PNR looks more like this:

$$PNR = \quad R \times \text{(Value of order)} - J \times \text{(Cost of rejection)} +$$
$$S \times \text{(Profit from subsequent sales)}$$

The advantage of this model is finding those prospects with a small PNR who might otherwise be overlooked. Through this model, they may be found to be profitable in the long run through subsequent sales. Astute readers will discern in this formula the same concept as the break-even formula used in RFM and modeling.

This type of analysis is particularly important to nonprofit organizations, which seldom break even on a prospect mailing. Their long-run profit comes from donations from respondents to subsequent mailings. Being able to predict who will respond a second time is vital for nonprofit financial success.

## Success Leads to Success

What has been overlooked in discussions of modeling in the past is the effect of repeated use of modeling on the improvement in customer lifetime value.

Lifetime value, as we know, is really based on several factors: the most important being average annual sales and average customer retention. Any improvement in one or the other will increase lifetime value. Mailing smarter means that people who are unlikely to respond will not be bothered with an unwanted solicitation. People who are likely to respond will be notified of the opportunity. What does this do for dialogue?

Nothing is more boring than a friend who babbles at you all the time about something in which you have no interest. I have a friend who will talk to me nonstop for hours about the details of government retirement systems, weather patterns, plant diseases, or other subjects I find very tiresome. I hide when I see him coming. How can you have a dialogue with someone who is directing a monologue at you?

On the other hand, I find other friends of mine really interesting to talk to. Why are they interesting? Because our conversations are an exchange of information, and they are sensitive to my feelings and interests.

That is what you have to be when you begin to create a customer dialogue: sensitive to the feelings and interests of your customers.

How can you do that when you have hundreds of thousands of customers? This is where the model comes in. Testing and response will tell you who is interested in your message and who is not. Modeling will help you to determine who, among the untested universe, will want to hear from you.

By communicating only to those who are interested, you will not only save money, you will begin to start a real dialogue. Several years ago, I was added to the mailing list of a large mainframe software company. After a week, I determined that this company could not do anything for me or my company. Since that time, they have written to me once a week. I must have received more than 200 letters from them to which I have never responded. I never open the envelopes.

Maybe something really interesting is in those envelopes, but the barrage of mailings has completely turned me off. I just don't care anymore.

On the other hand, I look eagerly for my copies of *DM News, Direct Magazine, Target Marketing*, and the *Canadian Direct Marketing News*.

They are filled with things that I want to hear about. I respond to their ads and articles.

The lesson: If you write to the right people with the right message, and if you respond properly and promptly when they write to you, you will create a dialogue that will result in better response to your promotional mailings. One way of finding the right people is the regular use of a modeling system.

## Summary

1.  When RFM is not an option, you can turn to demographics to explain behavior. In many cases, demographics and response rate are connected. Modeling is used to determine that connection.

2.  The neural networks modeling technique has become quite popular because nonstatisticians can use the technique. To begin the process, an Nth sample of the file is taken and given a test mailing. Those mailed are divided into a training group and a validation group.

3.  Neural network software begins with arbitrary weights in trying to decide which of a large number of input variables is most responsible for determining the dependent variable (response, sales, lifetime value, etc.). Neural network processes are run hundreds of thousands of times automatically. After each run, the error is calculated (erroneous predictions) and backpropagated into the model to revise the weights to get increasingly less error.

4.  When the model is completed, the model scores are validated on the control sample set aside earlier. If they correctly predict response, you are ready to use the model on your mailing universe. You create model scores for all people, and mail only to those who have a sufficiently high probability of response.

5.  Desktop neural network modeling programs should be used for each promotion to improve mailings, reduce costs, and build profits.

6.  Success with modeling will not only help on individual mailings, it will also build lifetime customer value. If you write to people who are not interested, they will learn to turn you off. After that, you can't get them to open your envelopes. On the other hand, if you target your mail, you can build a dialogue with benefits to both parties.

## Executive Quiz 8

Answers to quiz questions can be found in Appendix B. The quizzes are for fun. Do them if you enjoy quizzes. Ignore them if you don't.
*Choose the best answer to complete each statement.*

1. Profiling by intuition and ad hoc cross tab analysis
   a. can be done by any marketer with a customer base and ad hoc software.
   b. may be frustrating and useless with some files.
   c. demands a great deal of imagination and persistence.
   d. All of the above
   e. None of the above

2. Using an offer mailing to build a relationship at the same time
   a. may depress short run response but build long run.
   b. might have no effect on long run response.
   c. may increase the cost of the mailing.
   d. should be tested before the rollout.
   e. All of the above

3. Backpropagation, used in 90 percent of neural networks, has been around since
   a. 1943.
   b. 1964.
   c. 1972.
   d. 1988.
   e. 1992.

4. With each iteration of a neural network, the previous errors are
   a. backpropagated to correct the weights.
   b. used to adjust the input variables.
   c. used to correct the validation sample.
   d. used to predict the response rate.
   e. None of the above

5. A model that correctly predicts response should be
   a. not modified until it fails.
   b. continually revised with new tests.
   c. used for different product rollouts, since it works.
   d. viewed with skepticism, since models seldom work.
   e. None of the above

6. Modeling works best when
   a. the sample is very large—the entire universe if possible.
   b. there is a test group and a control group.
   c. the sample is chosen by income level.
   d. the sample has not yet been mailed.
   e. very little is known about the sample chosen.

7. In mailing to a customer file where extensive purchase history over several years is available, the best method for increasing response to future promotions is
   a. modeling of demographic factors.
   b. an affinity matrix analysis.
   c. RFM analysis.
   d. a survey of customer intentions.
   e. neural network analysis.

# 9

# Strategy Verification: Testing and Control Groups

*I think that without numbers there is no future. You cannot measure your progress unless you've got benchmarks against which to evaluate costs and profits. So ROI [Return on Investment], RFM [Recency, Frequency, Monetary analysis], and lifetime value are the minimal critical benchmarks you must now establish if you want to measure the profitability of your business today. Those same benchmarks then become the standards by which you measure your business's future growth and the justification for the database tools you must have to get that growth. Without the numbers, you don't have a future.*

*—John Travis, manager, business development,
Hudson's Bay Company*

**D**atabase marketing cannot achieve its objectives without constant testing. Some will argue with that idea. After all, if you are building a solid relationship with your customers, isn't that, on the face of it, good? Why do you need a test?

Wrong thinking. Some relationship building may not pay off in the short run or the long run either. You must test to be sure.

Let's go back to basics. Why are we engaged in marketing activities, anyway? To return a profit for the enterprise. Successful marketing increases profits by more than the money expended in marketing—or why do it? Testing is the only way that you can learn whether you have been successful. Testing has two objectives:

- To determine the effectiveness of each marketing program
- To improve our performance

The author gratefully acknowledges the assistance of Annette Champion of Arthur D. Little, Inc., who developed many of the concepts in this chapter.

The first objective is the most basic: It tells you whether you are reaching your overall marketing goals.

Every activity in a company has to justify its existence. It has to prove that what is being done contributes to making company profits. Fortunately, database marketing is in a much better position to test and prove its contribution to profits than advertising, customer relations, corporate planning, research and development, or most other staff functions. We just have to go about it in an organized way.

## Marketing Objectives

The first step in any testing program is to determine what you are trying to accomplish. The goals of database marketing programs usually are:

- Increase sales to existing customers
- Reduce attrition
- Gain new customers

The statement of objectives should always be specific with a percentage and a date (e.g., increase sales by 4 percent within the next two years). Use the specific percentage so that you can relate this objective to your estimated costs before you start. A 4 percent increase in sales may represent, for instance, a $1 million increase in gross profits from those additional goods sold. If your new marketing program costs more than $1 million, however, the marketing program has lost money for the company, even though sales have gone up. You will have to refine your strategy: Shoot for a loftier goal, cut your costs, or do something differently.

The best method, of course, is to define your customer lifetime value and test the effectiveness of various alternate ways of increasing lifetime value. Building lifetime value thus becomes a measurable goal. Once you have defined consistent goals, you should set up—in advance—the controls necessary to ensure that your marketing program is properly tested. In this chapter, we will go through the steps necessary to test several types of marketing programs. Let's begin by devising a test for a department store.

### Creating a Controlled Test

Let's assume that your department store has a house credit card tied in to a customer database. This house card permits you to capture data about purchases. You are planning a new offer to increase sales. The question: How much will the offer actually increase sales, and what is its effect on lifetime value?

To set up a test, you need two groups of customers: a test group that receives the offer and a control group that does not. Without the control group, you really know very little. If you don't have a control group and sales go up, is it because of the offer or because of some other factor unrelated to the offer? You can't be sure. If overall sales go down, perhaps they would have gone down *more* without the offer.

## Setting up Test and Control Groups

Assume that your department store has one million customers who use the store credit card. You have a new line of high fashion clothes for women being promoted through print ads. You want to test, in addition, the effectiveness of a direct mail offer to female customers. For the purpose of the test, you have decided to mail your offer to 100,000 women.

As a first step, you query your database to see how many women have credit cards in their names. There are 400,000. You must select two groups: a test group of 100,000 who will get the mailing and a control group of 100,000 who will not get the mailing. How big should your test and control groups be? Cost considerations say make them small. Statistical accuracy says make them large. A good rule of thumb: each test and control group must be large enough so that there will be a minimum of approximately 500 responses. If you anticipate a 2 percent response rate, then your test group must have at least 25,000 people in it. If you have two few respondents, the number of responses could be so small as to give you invalid results for future predictions. The control should be similar to the test group so that you get a fair comparison.

To create these two groups, you can take an Nth of the 400,000 using a software function that assures that you get an exact representative sample in each group selected. An Nth works this way: If you have a file of 800,000 records and you want a test file of 20,000, you would select every 40th record to create your Nth (800,000 ÷ 20,000 = 40). If you want a test file of 24,000, you will select every 33rd record, etc.

Most modern database software systems permit marketers to create these test groups with a PC connected to a mainframe for large files or just with a PC for small files. In earlier times, the creation of these groups would have required a programmer to select the customers for each group, put codes in their records indicating that they had been selected, and store the records back in the database. Today, all these functions are performed by nontechnical marketers working at their PCs without a programmer using such software as MarketVision.

When the test and control groups are set up, the promotional offer is made to the test group. Nothing is mailed to the control group. Since both groups use the store's credit card, their purchase behavior is registered in the marketing database. A month later, the purchases of the two groups are compared. The effectiveness of the promotion is measured by the purchasing differences between the test group and the control group.

Suppose that 5,000 of the 100,000 test households (5 percent) took advantage of the offer, buying a net average of $150 of promoted items plus $80 of nonpromoted items during the month. The remainder of the test group (95,000 households) bought an average of $30 of nonpromoted items during the same month. Let's assume that during the same month, households in the control group bought an average of $2 of the promoted items (even though they were not promoted to them) and $22 of nonpromoted items during the same month. How successful was the test? Table 9-1 shows the result:

### Table 9-1: Sales to All Groups in First Month per Customer

|    | Group Name | Number | Promo Items | Non-Promo Items | Total Items | Total Sales |
|----|------------|--------|-------------|-----------------|-------------|-------------|
| T1 | Test-Resp. | 5,000 | $150 | $80 | $230 | $1,150,000 |
| T2 | Test-Non-Resp. | 95,000 | $0 | $30 | $30 | $2,850,000 |
| T3 | Controls | 100,000 | $2 | $22 | $24 | $2,400,000 |
| T4 | Total (T1+T2+T3) | 200,000 | | | | $6,400,000 |
| S1 | Normal Sales without Promotion (Double T3) | | | | | $4,800,000 |
| S2 | Net Increased Sales from Promotion (T4–S1) | | | | | $1,600,000 |
| S3 | Marginal Profit from Sales (@10% of S2) | | | | | $160,000 |
| C1 | Cost of Promotion ($600/M for 200,000 test & control) | | | | | $60,000 |
| P1 | Net Profit from Promotion (S3-C1) | | | | | $100,000 |

Why did sales of nonpromoted items increase in responding households? Because when customers went into the store to get the discount, they saw other items and bought them too.

Why did sales of nonpromoted items to nonresponding test households increase over sales to control households? Because some of the nonparticipating customers went to the store because of the promotion, failed to find promoted items that they wanted, but bought something else anyway.

The net result of this test, therefore, was a $100,000 profit over the cost of the promotion itself. The promotion now can be repeated to the control households with presumably equal success. Figure 9-1 shows the procedures involved in measuring results of the test promotion.

## Figure 9-1: Measuring Promotion Results

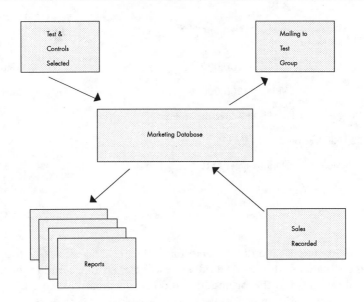

## Monitoring Results

Clearly, the test was a success because it increased profits over the cost of the test. That is not the end of the test, however. Good testing measures the results on the test group in the following months. After all, the test resulted in bringing many more than 5,000 women into the store: the 5,000 respondents plus an unknown number of nonrespondents.

In following months, those in the test group who were motivated to act because of the offer may visit the store again. This is normal behavior. The customer most likely to buy from you is someone who has just made a purchase. This subsequent behavior also can be measured, as seen below in Table 9-2:

Total sales this month are down. Why were sales to controls only $2 million during the second month? Who knows? This was a slower month, for reasons unrelated to the test. If the controls had not been followed, however, and only the test group measured, one could have concluded that the test promotion depressed sales in the following month, which, of course, was not true. The testing shows that even in a slow month, the test helped overall sales.

Thorough testing programs will follow the test and control groups for

**Table 9-2: Sales to All Groups in Second Month (per Customer)**

|  | Group Name | Number | Sales/ Cust. | Total Sales |
|---|---|---|---|---|
| T1 | Test-Resp. | 5,000 | $30 | $150,000 |
| T2 | Test-Non-Resp. | 95,000 | $21 | $2,000,000 |
| T3 | Controls | 100,000 | $20 | $2,000,000 |
| T4 | Total (T1+T2+T3) | 200,000 |  | $4,150,000 |
| S1 | Normal Sales without Promotion (Double T3) |  |  | $4,000,000 |
| S2 | Net Increased Sales (T4-S1) |  |  | $150,000 |
| S3 | Marginal Profit from Sales (@10% of S2) |  |  | $15,000 |
| C1 | Cost of Promotion (None – promotion is over) |  |  | $0 |
| P1 | Residual Effect of Promotion in Second Month |  |  | $15,000 |

the following 12 months to determine the residual effects of the test. In some situations, the residual effects can be even more important than the initial response to the promotion, and can, in themselves, be the justification for the marketing effort itself. The next step, of course, is to determine the effect on the lifetime customer value from the promotion. Lifetime value, rather than the immediate short-term payoff, should be the real goal of marketing database strategy. Lifetime value calculations without the promotion are shown in Table 9-3.

**Table 9-3: Lifetime Value of Store Control Group without Promotion**

|  |  | Year1 | Year2 | Year3 | Year4 | Year5 |
|---|---|---|---|---|---|---|
|  | **Revenue** |  |  |  |  |  |
| R1 | Customers | 100,000 | 70,000 | 49,000 | 34,300 | 24,010 |
| R2 | Retention Rate | 70 | 70 | 70 | 70 | 70 |
| R3 | Average Yearly Sale | $300 | $310 | $320 | $330 | $340 |
| R4 | Total Revenue | $30,000,000 | $21,700,000 | $15,680,000 | $11,319,000 | $8,163,400 |
|  | **Costs** |  |  |  |  |  |
| C1 | Cost Percent | 80 | 80 | 80 | 80 | 80 |
| C2 | Total Costs | $24,000,000 | $17,360,000 | $12,544,000 | $9,055,200 | $6,530,720 |
|  | **Profits** |  |  |  |  |  |
| P1 | Gross Profit | $6,000,000 | $4,340,000 | $3,136,000 | $2,263,800 | $1,632,680 |
| P2 | Discount Rate | 1.00 | 1.20 | 1.44 | 1.73 | 2.07 |
| P3 | NPV Profit | $6,000,000 | $3,616,667 | $2,177,778 | $1,308,555 | $788,734 |
| P4 | Cumulative NPV Profit | $6,000,000 | $9,616,667 | $11,794,444 | $13,102,999 | $13,891,734 |
| L1 | **Lifetime Value (NPV)** | $60.00 | $96.17 | $117.94 | $131.03 | $138.92 |

The assumption made here is that on the average, the store retains 70 percent of its cardholders each year while 30 percent drop out, and that the average sale of the remaining cardholders gradually rises because these customers are the loyalists. No assumptions are made here about inflation. The discount rate is taken as 20 percent per year, which breaks down into 10 percent interest costs and 10 percent risk factor. Annette Champion of Arthur D. Little, Inc., an international management and technology consulting firm, uses a much lower discount rate that does not include the risk factor. You will have to decide on the appropriate rate for your case.

From Table 9-3, we see that after five years, the present discounted lifetime value of the control group members is $138.92 per person. Let's see the effect of the single promotion described above on the test group. The results are shown in Table 9-4:

### Table 9-4: Lifetime Value of Test Group with Promotion

| | Revenue | Year1 | Year2 | Year3 | Year4 | Year5 |
|---|---|---|---|---|---|---|
| R1 | Total Customers | 100,000 | 75,000 | 52,500 | 36,750 | 25,725 |
| R2 | Retention Rate | 75 | 70 | 70 | 70 | 70 |
| R3 | Average Yearly Sale | $320 | $310 | $320 | $330 | $340 |
| R4 | Total Revenue | $32,000,000 | $23,250,000 | $16,800,000 | $12,127,500 | $8,746,500 |
| | **Costs** | | | | | |
| C1 | Cost Percent | 80 | 80 | 80 | 80 | 80 |
| C2 | Direct Costs | $25,600,000 | $18,600,000 | $13,440,000 | $9,702,000 | $6,997,200 |
| C3 | Promotion Costs | $700,000 | $0 | $0 | $0 | $0 |
| C4 | Total Costs | $26,300,000 | $18,600,000 | $13,440,000 | $9,702,000 | $6,997,200 |
| | **Profits** | | | | | |
| P1 | Gross Profit | $5,700,000 | $4,650,000 | $3,360,000 | $2,425,500 | $1,749,300 |
| P2 | Discount Rate | 1.00 | 1.20 | 1.44 | 1.73 | 2.07 |
| P3 | NPV Profit | $5,700,000 | $3,875,000 | $2,333,333 | $1,402,023 | $845,072 |
| P4 | Cumulative NPV Profit | $5,700,000 | $9,575,000 | $11,908,333 | $13,310,356 | $14,155,429 |
| L1 | **Lifetime Value (NPV)** | $57.00 | $95.75 | $119.08 | $133.10 | $141.55 |

The assumptions made here are these: The one-time impact of the promotion increases the average annual sale to this test group from $300 to $320—an increase of $2,000,000. This was the original $1,500,000 plus residual effects of $500,000 during the remainder of the year. The assumption is that the increased sales effect (of this one promotion) would have disappeared by subsequent years.

There is a secondary effect, as well. The promotion caused a large number of women to visit the store, and undoubtedly had an effect of retaining some of them who otherwise might have dropped out. The first-year retention factor is shown as 75 percent instead of 70 percent. Subsequent years are kept at the original 70 percent.

The bottom line: Lifetime value in Year1 is down from $60 to $57 because of the increased cost of the promotion. Lifetime value by Year3 is up to $119.08, and by Year5 to $141.55. Without the promotion, lifetime value in Year5 was only $138.92, meaning that the promotion caused a lifetime value increase of $2.63 per person. Multiplying $2.63 by the 100,000 customers gives a net long-term lifetime value increase of $263,000 from this one promotion—after all promotion expenses are paid. Without this detailed analysis, a promotion costing $700,000 might be difficult to justify.

Conclusion: This one promotion can be shown to increase the long-term lifetime value of the test group by a specific amount (after all the costs of the promotion are included). This analysis assumes that there was no further promotional activity. This assumption is correct, from a testing point of view. Each test should stand on its own, and make a positive contribution to lifetime value.

Testing like this can really put a marketing staff on the map within an organization. Few groups in any organization can have such a powerful justification for their existence. Few marketers, unfortunately, know how to take advantage of this opportunity. If you want to try it yourself, see the Technical Assistance section in Appendix A for additional help.

### Measuring Sales

The examples in this chapter are, of necessity, easy ones. It is easy to measure sales made through a credit card, or to a bank or utility. These sales are all posted to a marketing database used for the needed computations.

Unfortunately, many manufacturers do not have any way of getting direct information on the sales of their products. A packaged goods company can measure coupons redeemed, but cannot effectively measure product sold to coupon redeemers versus nonrespondents. How do we solve this problem?

Every marketer will have to come up with a solution. One idea is to measure monthly wholesale sales over a period to time to identifiable areas for which these sales can accurately be recorded (ZIP code, state, or region). Knowing average household annual consumption of your product, estimate the number of participating customer households by dividing annual wholesale shipments to the area by the annual household consumption. Once this base is known for both the test and control groups, run your test. After one, two, and three months, compute the sales per household in your test (promoted) and control (nonpromoted) areas.

Is this an accurate measure? No, but it may be all that you've got. You must have some way of measuring your success.

## Testing in Credit Card Sales

The next few pages provide a second example of testing, this one by a bank offering its own credit card to its customers. From a bank database of checking account and savings account customers, a test group and a control group are selected as prospective new credit card members. The two groups are selected, excluding customers who already have the credit card. With modern software, this selection can be performed in a minute or two using a PC connected with the bank's marketing database located in the bank's database service bureau.

Before any telemarketing is done, the customers must be prequalified. The bank sets up certain criteria for qualification for each credit card. For example, let us suppose that the offer is a $5,000 maximum line of credit, 16 percent interest rate, and $40 annual fee, waived for the first year. Only about 20 percent of the bank's customers would qualify for this offer, based on its underwriting requirements. The bank's marketing database software should permit the marketer to select from customers on the bank's marketing customer information file, using such criteria as:

- Income
- Minimum balance during the previous 12 months
- Age
- Date when account first opened
- Credit history

The prequalification must be performed for both the test group *and* the control group, even though there will be no promotion to the control group. Why waste time qualifying the control group? The reason is, of course, that we want to compare similar groups. If the control group is not selected in the same way as the test, any conclusions reached from the test will be invalid.

Once two groups of 40,000 each have been selected, there can be several tests performed:

- 20,000 with a letter followed by a telephone call
- 20,000 with a telephone call without the letter
- 40,000 with nothing (the control group)

The sequence of the promotion is shown in Figure 9-2.

Testing and evaluation of this program is quite complex and interesting. First, the basic offering method can be tested: mail versus phone. Phone

**Figure 9-2: Credit Card Promotion Sequence**

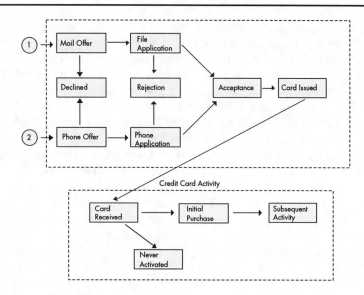

calls usually produce more sales, but cost much more to carry out. In each case, the cost of the entire promotion is measured against the number of people who sign up. The cost per new cardholder is calculated. These tests will tell which method is the most cost-effective. This, however, is only the beginning.

The real issue is not whether people take out a card, the issue is how much profit can be made from them as cardholders after they take out the card. This can be learned without the control group. The control group becomes important in relating their card ownership to their use of other bank products.

Does a card owner who uses a plastic card with the bank name on it several times a week tend to make greater use of other bank products as a result: money market funds, certificates of deposit, home equity loans, traveler's checks, etc.? Is the card ownership just the entrée to a whole new world of banking services for the customer? In such case, the money spent on acquiring the card membership needs to be judged not against the subsequent card activity alone, but also against the use of other products.

To determine the incremental sales that result from these additional uses of bank products, the subsequent history of the test group and control group members needs to be tracked over a period of time as they make additional purchases, make payments, pay annual fees, pay finance charges, take out loans, or fall into default. The control group also should be used to evaluate the success of the promotion by estimating the number and timing of the incremental accounts opened by the test group.

Annette Champion points out that we are borrowing from the future here. The test group members open accounts they would have opened anyway but at an earlier point in time. As these accounts are opened sooner, they are worth more.

The real test is lifetime value of the customer, not of the cardholder. Before the promotion, these were, after all, bank customers who already had their own lifetime value as owners of checking or savings accounts (or other bank products). One way of testing would be to divide both the test group and the control group into various customer profiles:

- Checking account customers
- Savings account customers
- Home equity customers
- Checking and savings customers
- Checking and home equity customers

Customers would have their own lifetime value before and after the acquisition of a credit card. The change in the total lifetime value of the test group measured against the control group would provide an overall test of the value of the original marketing effort.

## Long-Term Testing Difficulties

Testing seems so simple when described in the pages of a book; however, real life is much more complicated. In the first place, a credit card promotion such as the one described above is not the only marketing activity at the bank, by any means. During the average year, the bank is conducting promotions on a monthly basis for various products. Some of the same people who served in a test group for one promotion are in the control group for another, and the test group for a third promotion. How do you measure the long-term impact of any one promotion, when people are constantly involved in many different promotions, all of which can affect their attitude towards the bank and lifetime value?

This is what makes database marketing so interesting, so complex, and so sophisticated as compared to direct marketing or general advertising. The possibilities for creative thinking about the bank's relationship to its customers are rich with a wealth of detail that enables intelligent marketers to learn a great deal about the bank's customers and about the best way to improve overall relationships.

Several years ago, I took out a home equity loan with the Chevy Chase

Bank in Maryland. The program was widely advertised; the rates were low. I used the loan to finance the building of a barn, a swimming pool, and an addition to my house.

Some time after I took out the loan, Chevy Chase sent me a preapproved invitation for a Master Card at low interest rates. I have received dozens of others over the years, which I routinely toss in the trash. I responded to Chevy Chase because I had formed a favorable opinion of the bank from the home equity experience, and I canceled my American Express Card. (The American Express people, by the way, did an excellent job of trying to keep me. They just couldn't accept the idea that anyone would voluntarily drop the card. I got three different telephone calls and more than four letters on the subject before they finally gave up.)

A couple of years later, I noticed that my broker was handling Chevy Chase bonds. They were selling at about 40 percent of par, due to the national savings and loan problem. I asked the broker to buy some for me, because I had such good feelings about the bank. Since that time, the bonds have come up to 104 percent of par value, besides paying a 13 percent rate of interest. I have become a loyal Chevy Chase customer.

The point of this personal story is to illustrate the way in which customer lifetime value builds up based on the way that the customer is treated by an institution. Chevy Chase, if they calculate lifetime value at all, should see me as a cardholder, home equity customer, and bond holder, each of which contributes to overall bank profits.

In fact, Chevy Chase is not doing much of a job in profiling its customer base. A very persistent Chevy Chase telemarketer called me at dinner time one night telling me that "as a long-time cardholder with an excellent record" I was being awarded two months free life insurance with no preconditions. After the two months, the policy would be charged to my credit card at the rate of $14.40 per month unless canceled by me. I asked how much the policy paid, and was told $2,000—a ridiculously low amount for that rate. Chevy Chase knows that I have more than $200,000 worth of insurance for which I pay about $180 per month. How do they know? Because I had to tell them in my credit application. Question: Is the $2,000 insurance offer good database marketing? Does it tend to reinforce my sense of loyalty and identification with Chevy Chase?

Keeping track of the long-term effects of any one promotion, therefore, is almost impossible, since there are many different promotions. How do we database marketers sort all this out?

The answer is a straightforward one: lifetime value. The lifetime value of every customer in your database should be calculated and maintained at all times. Every time money is expended on a customer: a promotion, a newsletter, a satisfaction survey, etc., the lifetime value effects should be calculated, and the revised lifetime value inserted in the customer record. The new values can be compared with lifetime values in the control group to determine long-term effects of any marketing activity.

## How to Calculate Return on Investment

In addition to the measurements already discussed, marketers should perform several other calculations to analyze their work. In any campaign, a methodology must be devised to determine the return on investment from marketing dollars invested. Here is one method of calculation, based on the use of a control group. To use this method, you have to know with some accuracy the number of people in both the test group and the control group, and be able to measure their total sales.

|   |   |
|---|---|
| A. Test Group Sales Rate | $8 per thousand |
| B. Control Group Sales Rate | $3 per thousand |
| C. Incremental Test Sales | $5 per thousand |
|    (A – B) | |
| D. Number in Test Group | 100,000 |
| E. Incremental Sales from Test Group | $500,000 |
|    (C x D) | |

### Marginal Profits

It is important that marketing be able to measure the incremental profit rate from incremental sales. Incremental (marginal) profits are usually higher than average profits because the calculation for average profits takes into consideration all overhead and developmental costs, whereas marginal profits takes into consideration only the extra (incremental) costs.

For example, consider a company manufacturing and selling a 50-foot garden hose that retails for $20 and wholesales for $10. The first 100,000 hoses may cost $9 each to make, covering all expenses including general advertising, manufacturing, overhead, storage, delivery interest, etc. The average profit is $1 per hose.

If sales pick up, and manufacturing doubles production to 200,000 per year, the company can probably produce this extra output for $7 per hose. Why? Because the basic costs (plant, machinery, overhead, etc.) are paid for in the first 100,000. The extra hose requires only materials and a second shift of labor. This second 100,000 produces a net profit of $3 per hose.

If we are going to measure the return on investment from our marketing campaign, should it be measured against the average profit of the first 100,000 ($1) or the marginal profit of the next 100,000 ($3), or an overall average profit ($2)? From a marketing point of view, the $3 (30 percent) is the correct answer, especially if the marketing program is incremental (additive) to the normal sales of the company. Let's continue our example to show how the return on investment is calculated:

| | | |
|---|---|---|
| E. | Incremental Sales from Test Group | $500,000 |
| F. | Incremental Profit Rate | 30% |
| G. | Incremental Profits | $150,000 |
| | (E x F) | |
| H. | Direct Marketing Costs ($100 ÷ 1,000) | $100,000 |
| I. | Program Profitability | $50,000 |
| | (G – H) | |
| J. | Return on Investment | 50% |
| | (I ÷ H) | |

## Why Incremental Profit Rates Are Important

The method of calculation of incremental profits is not just an academic exercise. If incremental profits are computed as average profits and not marginal profits, the same marketing campaign that has seemed so successful, becomes a loser. This is shown in Table 9-5 below:

### Table 9-5: Profit Computed with Average Profits

| Incremental Sales | Incremental Profit Rate | Direct Costs | Program Profit |
|---|---|---|---|
| $500,000 | 30% | $100,000 | $50,000 |
| $500,000 | 20% | $100,000 | $0 |
| $500,000 | 10% | $100,000 | – $50,000 |

Don't let some financial type tell you what the incremental profit rate is. Calculate it yourself. If you don't, a highly successful marketing program can be written off as a loss.

## Lifetime Value Calculations

One other point to consider: Should each promotion stand on its own, as we have been suggesting here, or should the long-term implications of promotions and database activity be the prime consideration of each action?

Everything, really, depends on everything else. Any promotion that brings people into the store is likely to have long-term implications. Some of those new people will come back again and again and again. If these people are further cultivated by database activity (newsletters, notices of special sales, membership cards, credit cards, etc.), there will be a long-term effect on any daily activity.

Let's look at a garden supply business viewed in the long term. Without any promotion, 1,000 people wander into our garden supply store and spend an average of $100 per person in a year. Half of those people come back next year, spending another $100. This continues for five years. The net present value of the lifetime value of those original 1,000 people, thus, is $33.86 each, as shown in Table 9-6.

### Table 9-6: Lifetime Value of Garden Supply Customer Control Group

|    |                      | Year1     | Year2    | Year3    | Year4    | Year5   |
|----|----------------------|-----------|----------|----------|----------|---------|
|    | **Revenue**          |           |          |          |          |         |
| R1 | Customers            | 1,000     | 500      | 250      | 125      | 63      |
| R2 | Retention Rate       | 50        | 50       | 50       | 50       | 50      |
| R3 | Average Yearly Sale  | $100      | $100     | $100     | $100     | $100    |
| R4 | Total Revenue        | $100,000  | $50,000  | $25,000  | $12,500  | $6,300  |
|    |                      |           |          |          |          |         |
|    | **Costs**            |           |          |          |          |         |
| C1 | Cost Percent         | 80        | 80       | 80       | 80       | 80      |
| C2 | Total Costs          | $80,000   | $40,000  | $20,000  | $10,000  | $5,040  |
|    |                      |           |          |          |          |         |
|    | **Profits**          |           |          |          |          |         |
| P1 | Gross Profit         | $20,000   | $10,000  | $5,000   | $2,500   | $1,260  |
| P2 | Discount Rate        | 1.00      | 1.20     | 1.44     | 1.73     | 2.07    |
| P3 | NPV Profit           | $20,000   | $8,333   | $3,472   | $1,445   | $609    |
| P4 | Cumulative NPV Profit| $20,000   | $28,333  | $31,806  | $33,251  | $33,859 |
|    |                      |           |          |          |          |         |
| L1 | **Lifetime Value (NPV)** | $20.00 | $28.33 | $31.81 | $33.25 | $33.86 |

Now let's vary the situation. Try a promotion, followed by database activity that costs $8 per customer per year. Eight dollars per customer is expensive. The lifetime value in the first two years drops. In the long term, however, the value goes up to $41.87. If the store has 100,000 customers, the net present value of the five-year profit increase is $801,000. This difference is shown in Table 9-7.

The assumptions are that as a result of the database activity, the retention rate increases from 50 percent to 60 percent. Customers refer other customers at the rate of 5 percent of the remaining customers per year. Average spending by the average customer goes up from a flat $100 per year to $120, $140, etc.

In the long run, database activity seems very beneficial in our example. To determine whether all these things *really* happen, however, it is vital to have a control group that does not get the database activity. Only in that way can you be sure that the things shown above are happening. Too many marketers are quick to rope everyone into their database without building in any control groups. The danger? When the company suffers a

### Table 9-7: Lifetime Value of Garden Supply Customer Test Group

| | Revenue | Year1 | Year2 | Year3 | Year4 | Year5 |
|---|---|---|---|---|---|---|
| R1 | Referral Rate | 5 | 5 | 5 | 5 | 5 |
| R2 | Referred Customers | | 50 | 33 | 21 | 15 |
| R3 | Total Customers | 1,000 | 650 | 423 | 296 | 207 |
| R4 | Retention Rate | 60 | 60 | 65 | 65 | 70 |
| R5 | Average Yearly Sale | $120 | $140 | $160 | $180 | $200 |
| R6 | Total Revenue | $120,000 | $91,000 | $67,680 | $53,280 | $41,400 |
| | **Costs** | | | | | |
| C1 | Cost Percent | 80 | 80 | 80 | 80 | 80 |
| C2 | Direct Costs | $96,000 | $72,800 | $54,144 | $42,624 | $33,120 |
| C3 | Database & Promo Cost | $8,000 | $5,200 | $3,384 | $2,368 | $1,656 |
| C4 | Total Costs | $104,000 | $78,000 | $57,528 | $44,992 | $34,776 |
| | **Profits** | | | | | |
| P1 | Gross Profit | $16,000 | $13,000 | $10,152 | $8,288 | $6,624 |
| P2 | Discount Rate | 1.00 | 1.20 | 1.44 | 1.73 | 2.07 |
| P3 | NPV Profit | $16,000 | $10,833 | $7,050 | $4,791 | $3,200 |
| P4 | Cumulative NPV Profit | $16,000 | $26,833 | $33,883 | $38,674 | $41,874 |
| L1 | **Lifetime Value (NPV)** | $16.00 | $26.83 | $33.88 | $38.67 | $41.87 |

downturn, the database will be one of the first things to be dropped, if it has no hard and fast way of proving its value. Control groups are essential.

## Summary

To know if a marketing program is successful, you must test it properly. The steps are:

1. Determine the objectives of the marketing program, and in the design phase, be sure that it will result in a positive return on investment.
2. Develop a controlled test design, including both test and control groups. Make sure that both groups are as exactly equal as possible, in every respect.
3. Determine the incremental profit rate that applies to your sales.
4. Develop a method to measure sales. This may be easy or may be the most difficult part of the whole effort. It has to be done, however.
5. Carry out your marketing program to the test areas. Do not do anything to the control areas.
6. Measure the incremental sales by comparing sales in the test groups with those in the control groups.
7. Calculate the direct costs of your program.
8. Figure the short-term net profitability of your program and the return on your investment.
9. Figure the long-term net profitability of your program based on change in lifetime value of your customers.

## Executive Quiz 9

Answers to quiz questions can be found in Appendix B. The quizzes are for fun. Do them if you enjoy quizzes. Ignore them if you don't.

*Choose the best answer to complete each statement.*

1. Control groups are
   a. for market research, not database marketing.
   b. for promotions, not for long-term testing.
   c. a waste of marketing dollars.
   d. not useful when sales go down.
   e. None of the above

2. Nonrespondents should act
   a. the same way as a control group.
   b. the same way as respondents.
   c. better than the control group.
   d. better than the respondents.
   e. None of the above

3. The results of a given promotion can best be measured for
   a. one month.
   b. three months.
   c. six months.
   d. 12 months.
   e. None of the above

4. For credit card promotions, qualification is needed for
   a. all who respond.
   b. all who respond plus a control group.
   c. all who are promoted.
   d. all who are promoted plus a control group.
   e. the control group alone.

5. Measurement of the lifetime value of bank credit card holders should cover
   a. credit card profits in first year.
   b. credit card profits in first five years.
   c. five-year activity in all products.
   d. five-year credit card activity plus one year other products.
   e. None of the above

6. When banks run multiple promotions, the results should be calculated based on
   a. response to each promotion.
   b. lifetime value updated for each promotion.
   c. response by test groups compared to lifetime value of control groups.
   d. annual average customer activity.
   e. return on investment from each promotion.

7. Building a close customer relationship
   a. is worthwhile, regardless of the cost.
   b. helps profitability in ways that cannot be measured.
   c. must be done if competitors are doing it.
   d. must be measured by lifetime value analysis.
   e. is rarely justified for seldom purchased items.

8. Database marketing is harder to cost justify than
   a. advertising.
   b. corporate planning.
   c. research and development.
   d. customer relations.
   e. None of the above

# Part Three: Profiting by Experience

# 10

# Database Strategy for Retailers

*The "mass market" approach is a way of thinking many retailers have used to focus both their merchandise and advertising strategies. Two parts of the traditional retailing equation have been:*

*First: Mass market to the broad "middle market"—The retailer provided a wide selection of goods and advertised in the mass media to attract a large homogeneous customer group.*

*Second: Compete on price and selection—To be able to do this, the retailer purchased smart, in large quantities and maintained low overhead. This has led to homogeneous merchandise, very similar price points, and an overabundance of "on sale" items in many retail stores in virtually every region of the country.*

*That is how it has been. But the mass market is gone. Homogeneity in consumer goods marketing is a thing of the past. Successful retailers from now on must look at the consumer in a new way— as small groups of individuals, with individual wants and needs. In every case, information-based target marketing is a large part of the solution.*

*—Timothy J. Keane, Retail Target Marketing Systems, Inc.*

**D**uring the past decade, many national retailers have gone under. The pressures on them are tremendous and come from several different directions:

- Many of the central hub stores have been closed, forced out of central cities by the flight to the suburbs.
- "Anchors" in large suburban malls have seen many of their customers spending time in small specialty shops rather than in their departments. These shops, collectively, offer more personal services and nonhomogeneous products than the department stores can afford.
- Retailers have found themselves trumped in on-sale offers by Wal-

Marts and factory outlets that offer increasingly attractive merchandise at rock bottom prices.
- The growth of the specialty catalog industry has hit retailers especially hard. Affluent, fashion-conscious, busy, working women spend their few moments at home scanning high-fashion catalogs and ordering high-priced merchandise, rather than visiting department stores.

### How to Compete?

Retailers have at last fallen back on the one group that was nearby all along, but which they had been neglecting: their customers. Instead of concentrating on products and how to move them, they are now looking at their customers and figuring out how to move *them*. They are learning how to build loyalty and repeat sales by appealing to the hearts and minds of their customers. Their solutions focus on a number of neglected areas:

- Increasing the number of people who hold and use the store credit card as opposed to those who use Visa, MasterCard, check, or cash, so that stores can build their customer databases
- Learning more about their customers through surveys and appended data, so that they can market better to them
- Using selective inserts in their monthly statements to target special offers to particular groups
- Teaming up with external specialists to make targeted solo mailing offers to their customer base, drawing on their name and reputation to get the envelope opened and the sale made
- Following up customer purchases with special personal services—thank-you letters, follow-up surveys and telephone calls—and becoming specialists in customer service
- Keeping track of birthdays, anniversaries, and other key personal events in customers' lives and communicating one-on-one when they occur, so that they can become a family friend, not just another store
- Understanding the geodemographics of their store trading areas so that they can do a better job of locating branches, and do a better job of bringing customers into their stores
- Profiling customers into profit groups and marketing differently to each group
- Experimenting with their own catalogs

Brian Woolf, president of the Retail Strategy Center, Inc., of Greenville, South Carolina, has been conducting an extended study for the supermarket industry on electronic marketing. Brian provided these examples:

- Sam's, a division of Wal-Mart, Inc., is typical of most players in the warehouse club industry. For six weeks prior to opening one of its 100,000 square-foot warehouses, the company sends a team into the area to contact all the small businesses, government agencies, etc. to invite them to become members of Sam's for an annual $25 to $30 membership fee.

  Business members typically spend three times the amount of individual members, and therefore receive preferential treatment. For example, the warehouse is open several hours earlier each day just for these business members.

  Each club member is issued a membership card with his or her photograph on it. At the beginning of each transaction, the card is given by the customer to the cashier at the check stand and keyed into the register. From this process, Sam's has built an enormous database on their customers.

- Shop Rite is the supermarket arm of Wakefern Food Corporation in New Jersey. In 1990 Shop Rite introduced its Price Plus Club. In exchange for the free membership, members fill out an application form providing information on birth date, household size, ages of children, and household income.

  After applying for membership, shoppers receive a plastic scannable Price Plus Club card with their unique member number. Throughout the store on any given day there are about 150 items with a special savings sign. The discounts, which range from $0.10 to $2, are for members only, with a limit of four discounts per item per visit.

- Staples, Inc. was the originator of the office supply super store industry. It focuses on the office supply buyer in smaller companies. Staples treats all customers like warehouse club members, issuing them an identification card so that customer activity can be tracked. When the company began, rather than giving a discount to members, it charged all nonmembers an additional 5 percent over the list price in the store. Now they offer discounts on selected items to members.

- Waldenbooks has a Preferred Reader Program that entitles members to a 10 percent discount on all purchases with additional $5 gift certificates sent from headquarters for every $100 of purchases. In effect, this means a 15 percent discount on all purchases for an annual fee of only $10. To pay for the program, Waldenbooks reduced the number of weekly specials offered to all shoppers, and applied those savings to their best customers, who spend 70 percent more than other shoppers. In addition, Waldenbooks markets directly to its members based on what they are buying.

Let's discuss some of these initiatives to see how database marketing is helping retailers to compete.

### Building the Cardholder Base

Where does your business come from? Who is buying your products? Strangely enough, most retailers do not really know. The only thing that they can tell for sure is the percentage of their sales that come from store cardholders, as opposed to those who pay by other means.

Once shoppers use their store credit cards, it is possible to keep track of them, find out what they buy, learn about their interests, and market to them. The effectiveness of these marketing efforts can be measured. Customer lifetime value can be calculated with precision. But all this can happen only if people will apply for and use the store card. How can you get that to happen?

Many techniques are being used. Some stores offer a special substantial discount (10 percent on top of all other discounts) for first-time card applicants. Helena and I purchased a $360 set of china from the Hecht Company. The set was on sale at a 20 percent discount, which reduced it to $288. Because we did not have a store card, the clerk asked us to fill out an application, offering an additional 10 percent reduction as an inducement. That reduced the price by an additional $29.

Why hand out $29 to a card applicant? Because Hecht's has done its homework. It knows the lifetime value of a cardholder and calculated it as considerably more than $29. The application form asked us for some demographics (age, income, occupation) in the process of establishing credit. That information, which in most cases is discarded once the credit is established, will, if Hecht's is doing the job right, find its way into a marketing database. It knows something about the Arthur Hughes family that can be used in profiling us and targeting future offers. Having an additional card holder is not worth $29, or even $1, if you don't know how to exploit the opportunity. We will see what the Hecht Company does with it.

### Building the Retail Database

Any retailer who has begun to create a customer marketing database has come up against a significant obstacle: the size of the file. To be useful, a marketing database has to have purchase history. Retail purchases can cause a database to run into the billions of bytes.

For example, one retailer has more than 10 million cardholders, who over a two year period ring up more than 200 million transactions. They are maintaining an operational database (using an IBM mainframe and DB2 software) that gets out the monthly bills. This system, together with the inventory, payroll, and general ledger system, keeps a stable of programmers and a half acre of disks fully occupied.

The marketing department wanted to profile these customers and target specific offerings to selected groups. For example, it wanted to find men who had purchased more than $X in three key departments over a six-month period. The management information systems (MIS) department made a heroic effort to satisfy the marketing request. It took two weeks and the full-time efforts of two people to produce the 60,000 names. The cost of the operation, as calculated by MIS, was about $16,000. There was no way that the promotion to the 60,000 (with all its costs and uncertainties) would pay for the $16,000 select cost. A rented list of names (at $80 per thousand) would have cost only $4,800.

This experience, and many like it, convinced marketing that they needed a marketing database, separate from the operational billing files. Marketing needed Recency, Frequency, Monetary (RFM) analysis put in each record. The operational MIS file could not do that for several reasons, the most important of which was that it only kept a few months worth of data, whereas marketing wanted to go back two years.

All the information needed in a marketing database for the store would consume about 40 gigabytes of disk or, alternatively, scores of individual tapes. The disk was prohibitively expensive. The tape was too cumbersome to use for production of ad hoc counts, reports, and selects. The store was at an impasse.

As a solution, a plan was developed for the marketing database whereby:

- It would retain full purchase history for 90 days.
- Thereafter, purchases would be "rolled up" by department by month.
- Two year's worth of data would be stored on tape.
- Data from prior years would be summarized and kept with customer records indefinitely.
- Daily access to the complete data would be created using MarketVision software with PC access that linked the marketing department to the mainframe data.

This approach would enable the marketing department to carry out ad hoc counts, reports and selects, RFM analyses, customer profiles, and have the results available on their PCs, linked to the mainframe, in a few seconds. With the new system, the 60,000 men could be selected in about 30 seconds, at a marginal cost of less than $10.

## How Can Retail Databases Be Used?

Since all retailers have to grapple with problems very similar to those faced by the retailer described above, it is worth spending a few minutes examining how the database can be used and maintained.

### Personal Communications

The Nordstrom department stores are legendary in the services provided to their upscale clientele. Their clerks are trained to send a personal thank-you letter to all customers who make significant purchases. In particular, they take pains to acknowledge all orders that require personalization, a gift message, or other special orders. The message is written in a narrative sequence in a conversational tone. The message provides an opportunity to reinforce Nordstrom's image and commitment to customer satisfaction. They have a library of prewritten correspondence used to respond to a wide variety of customer service requirements.

As Nordstrom has learned, a letter from a major department store in which you have a current personal interest (such as a credit card) is worth a look. It can help build a relationship, particularly if the letter, when opened, turns out to be a personal communication to you, with real data:

> Thank you, Mr. Hughes, for your purchase of the Italian china last month. I hope that you are enjoying it, and that you received the $29 discount in your most recent statement. If you find any defect in the product, please contact me immediately.
> Since you like fine china, you may be interested in a special selection of Venetian crystal that has just arrived and is on sale until March 15th. Please ask for me, Hang Nguyen, when you come in. I will be glad to show it to you.

Will such a communication have an impact and produce results? In the right situation and handled correctly, such communications can do more to generate traffic than any number of discounts, sales, or space advertisements. How is the database used to create such correspondence?

- The product SKU, date, quantity, dollar amount, and sales clerk are recorded for each transaction.
- Special discounts and rebates are coded as well.
- The delivery method for products may be another key database element, according to Jeff Parnell of Overton's. People who request and

pay for next day delivery are often impulsive buyers for whom money is no object. Find out how many of these buyers are on your database, and figure out unique ways to cultivate them. They will appreciate it, and so will you.

- Event-driven software pulls out large purchases (over $X) in which a rebate or a special offer occurred. The merchandise department has created affinity groups (see Chapter 6, Using Customer Profiles in Marketing Strategy) for each major sale item: china and crystal, tires and tune-ups, pool chemicals and patio furniture. When there is a large purchase and the computer finds an affinity group on a look-up table—bingo! A letter is generated.
- Special software formats personal laser letters from individual sales personnel to the customers they served, on a weekly basis. Thousands are sent out from a central mail shop.
- At the same time, individual lists are created for all sales clerks noting the letters sent in their name: who the customers were, what they bought, when they bought it, and what offer was made in the clerk's name, so that when a customer does return, the clerk can respond knowledgeably and responsively.

This is complex follow-through, but not at all impossible if you have a marketing database. Will it get results? You have to test it to see.

The letters can be generated and put into the mail for about 50 cents each including software selection, formatting, printing, and postage. The effect on the lifetime value of customers can be tested very precisely by creating a control group of cardholders to whom no such letters are sent.

### Getting Shoppers to Come Right Back

Another use for a retail database is a repeat customer program. We all know that the person most likely to buy from you again is someone who just bought from you yesterday. It is one thing to know that and another thing to make the idea pay off. Jennifer MacLean of Direct Marketing Technology, Inc. worked with a retailer that developed a winning program. The program worked like this:

As soon as a customer made a purchase, the customer database generated a thank-you letter. Included with the thank-you letter was a dated coupon, the value of which was based on past purchasing behavior. The customers were divided into two groups: test and control. The test group got the letter. The control group got no letter.

The first experiment was to determine the best value for the coupon. Two were tested: a high value coupon and a moderate value coupon.

Figure 10-1 shows the results from coupons in thank-you letters.

**Figure 10-1: Increased Sales over Nonpromoted Customers**

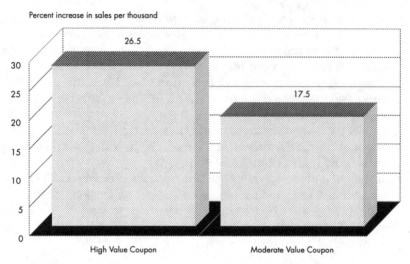

Percent increase in sales per thousand

Graphic courtesy of Jennifer MacLean.

What this shows is that those in the test group that received a high value coupon increased their sales per thousand during the next six weeks by 26.5 percent over the sales of the control group in the same period. The moderate value coupon's "lift" was 17.5 percent. Which was better? To answer that, you have to compare the cost of the coupons with the profit from the increased sales.

That is the short-run approach. The long-run approach—which is much better—is to look at the effect of these coupons on lifetime value. Will the coupons increase the lifetime value of the test group over the control group? That analysis was not done. My guess is that it won't. Why? Because giving out coupons to existing customers sends the wrong message. It says, "We know the only reason you shop here is price, so here is another little sweetener." If they don't get another coupon after their next visit, they may be disappointed. ("What have you done for us lately?")

The experiment also was measured by looking at the effect of the coupons on shoppers of different frequencies before the test started. These results are shown in Figure 10-2.

The more frequent shoppers increased their sales per thousand over the control group more when they received a thank-you coupon than did the less frequent shoppers.

**Figure 10-2: Increased Response by Frequency of Shopper**

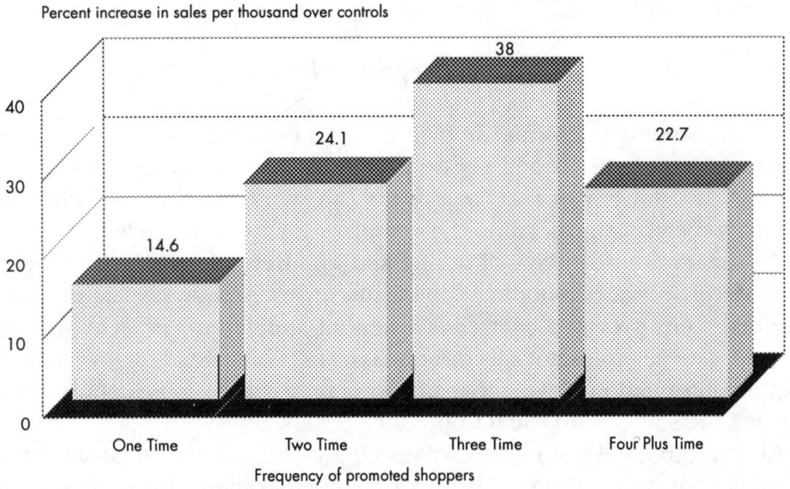

Percent increase in sales per thousand over controls

Frequency of promoted shoppers

Graphic courtesy of Jennifer MacLean.

This is the type of experiment that any retailer can try with a customer database. With really creative thinking, it also should be possible to get a comparable response with an excellent thank-you letter and no coupon! A personal letter that refers to a recent purchase and suggests an affinity item, such as the one from Hang Nguyen, costs much less than the coupon since no discount is offered. It is also more likely to be considered seriously since it is so personal. To be sure, however, you have to test.

## Incentives for Frequent Shoppers

What else can you do to reward frequent shoppers? Brian Woolf of the Retail Strategy Center has a number of practical suggestions:

- Special member checkout lines. Supermarkets today offer express lines for people buying only a few items, while their heavy buyers have to wait in long lines. Why not set up special lanes for cardholders? This benefit will cost the store far less than the discounts, yet be worth more to the shoppers.
- Gold club membership available for an annual fee (regular membership is free). Benefits are express checkout lanes and discounts on all purchases. Double discounts for Gold club members over regular member discounts.

- Monthly personalized newsletter with recipes and food tips. Personal thank-you letters from the store manager to the 10 largest customers each month.

### Marketing Special Events

Retail marketers also can use their PCs and databases to select customers for special promotions and create profiles to learn more about their customers. In addition to that, marketers can work out a list of scheduled events to be programmed into the computer for automatic selection.

For example, birthdays of adults and children can be derived from a number of sources, including application forms. Anniversary dates can be gleaned from previous occasions when an anniversary present was purchased. The key to use of this information is encouraging employees to collect the information, developing an easy way to store it in the database, and writing the software to use it to produce results.

Keeping track of such information requires a great deal of advance planning. Recall how Thomas Lix recommended solving this problem (see Chapter 2, "The Vision Thing") with personal letters to the husband at his place of business, reminding him of his wife's birthday, and making specific suggestions for items that the store knew she liked. A similar message can be dispatched well in advance of the couple's anniversary.

Even more elaborate communications can be devised for the birthdays of mothers, sisters, brothers, aunts, uncles, grandparents, and grandchildren. The people of today are all working. They are all busy. Few have time to shop. Many are affluent. Intelligent and imaginative retailers make use of their resources and build their sales and their bottom line.

All this means that retailers today have to build very complex and productive databases, filled with useful information. Places have to be found for birthdays and anniversaries, together with information on whose birthday it is, the sex and date of birth, the relationship to the card member, the income and budget of the card member, and the lifestyle of the recipient. Is capturing all this data possible? Yes, but it may be difficult. How can you get it?

Figure 10-3 provides an example:

Some stores may experiment with the direct approach: send out survey forms to their customers asking for birthdays, ages, names, and addresses, with some suitable reward for compliance. Store clerks can be armed with appropriate forms to fill out at the point of sale whenever a husband comes in seeking a suitable birthday present for his wife or relative, or when a woman comes in looking for apparel for herself.

Is this being too nosy? Yes, if it is done in a pushy way. If the store has a

**Figure 10-3: Building Personal Data in Customer Records**

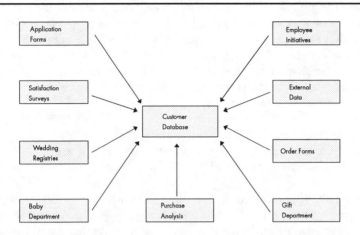

gift department or a bridal department, the collection of this type of information can be made to seem routine and matter of fact.

Will consumers accept this kind of assistance? Some of them will love it. Some will not. The store must experiment and test on a small scale, learning as it goes, dropping false starts, and expanding on successes. For a customer who likes this kind of personal attention, the result can very important in building loyalty. For this customer, it is much more useful to have a suggestion for what to get for his anniversary (in plenty of time) than it would be to have a discount coupon. The store trades something that it can easily afford (personal service and information provided by a database and computer software) for something it badly needs (loyalty and repeat sales). The customer trades something he badly needs (help in remembering his anniversary, suggestions of what to buy, and time savings) for something that costs him practically nothing (buying the gift from this store rather than from some other store). It is a win-win situation for both.

Will collecting and using this information in a database be too expensive and complicated? Yes and no. A good plan, with well-constructed software, can produce a smooth weekly flow of communications from the store to its card members with regular reminders of birthdays and anniversaries that will be genuinely appreciated and rewarded with increased patronage.

How can you be sure? Do lifetime value analysis. Let's try an experiment.

### Effect of Anniversary or Birthday Program on Lifetime Value

Once a database is set up to receive anniversary or birthday information and the forms are ready to receive it, make efforts to enroll a large number of card members in the birthday or anniversary club. An equal number of nonparticipating but active card members will be set aside as the controls.

Experiment for a two-year period with a stream of personal communications to the test group on the occasion of birthdays and anniversaries, monitoring closely the sale of recommended items and the purchases of all other merchandise by the test and control groups during the test period. The controls should receive no similar mailings. The test should have significant measurable effects on:

- The average amount spent per month by the test group
- The percentage of the test group that continues active use of the store card, i.e., reduction in attrition

Why have the control group? Because without them, it will be impossible to know whether the increased sales by the test group are due to the birthday program or just normal growth due to other factors. If, for example, sales are down all over, the test group could possibly show a lower reduction than the reduction by the control group, thus proving the value of the test.

Let's visualize the typical situation of a retail chain without a marketing database. Assume about one million active customers with annual sales of $300 million. The sales per customer are $300. Of 1,000 customers in Year1, about 45 percent shop there a second year. Thereafter, the retention rate is about 50 percent. Table 10-1 is a lifetime value calculation of each customer, assuming an expense rate of 80 percent of gross sales.

**Table 10-1: Lifetime Value of Cardholders without Database Activity**

|    | Revenue | Year1 | Year2 | Year3 | Year4 | Year5 |
|----|---------|-------|-------|-------|-------|-------|
| R1 | Customers | 1,000 | 450 | 203 | 102 | 51 |
| R2 | Retention Rate | 45 | 45 | 50 | 50 | 50 |
| R3 | Average Yearly Sale | $300 | $300 | $300 | $300 | $300 |
| R4 | Total Revenue | $300,000 | $135,000 | $60,900 | $30,600 | $15,300 |
| | **Costs** | | | | | |
| C1 | Cost Percent | 80 | 80 | 80 | 80 | 80 |
| C2 | Total Costs | $240,000 | $108,000 | $48,720 | $24,480 | $12,240 |
| | **Profits** | | | | | |
| P1 | Gross Profit | $60,000 | $27,000 | $12,180 | $6,120 | $3,060 |
| P2 | Discount Rate | 1.00 | 1.20 | 1.44 | 1.73 | 2.07 |
| P3 | NPV Profit | $60,000 | $22,500 | $8,458 | $3,538 | $1,478 |
| P4 | Total Lifetime Value | $60,000 | $82,500 | $90,958 | $94,496 | $95,974 |
| L1 | **Lifetime Value (NPV)** | $60.00 | $82.50 | $90.96 | $94.50 | $95.97 |

The net present customer lifetime value rises to $95.97 after five years. Adding a database marketing program brings some real cost increases.

Let's assume that it costs an average of $25 per customer (including the incentives) to acquire the names and add them to the database. The cost of the database (of one million names) is about $1.50 per name per year. It is assumed that an additional $3 per customer is spent per year in cultivation resulting in increased sales.

The increased average sales in the first year is $50 per customer, with an increase of $10 each year for the remaining customers. One important effect of the database marketing program is that the retention rate is markedly higher. Instead of losing 55 percent the first year, only 35 percent are lost. Thereafter, the database retains 60 percent of the remainder, rather than 50 percent without the database.

In total, the database results in increasing the lifetime value of the customers from $95.97 to $113.44, an increase of $17.47 per customer, or $17,470,000 total, after all expenses of the database are met. Table 10-2 shows the lifetime value with database activity.

### Table 10-2: Lifetime Value of Cardholders with Database Activity

|  | Revenue | Year1 | Year2 | Year3 | Year4 | Year5 |
|---|---|---|---|---|---|---|
| R1 | Total Customers | 1,000 | 650 | 423 | 275 | 193 |
| R2 | Retention Rate | 65 | 65 | 65 | 70 | 75 |
| R3 | Average Yearly Sale | $350 | $360 | $370 | $380 | $390 |
| R4 | Total Revenue | $350,000 | $234,000 | $156,510 | $104,500 | $75,270 |
|  | **Costs** | | | | | |
| C1 | Cost Percent | 80 | 80 | 80 | 80 | 80 |
| C2 | Direct Costs | $280,000 | $187,200 | $125,208 | $83,600 | $60,216 |
| C3 | Acquisition ($25) | $25,000 | $0 | $0 | $0 | $0 |
| C4 | Maintenance ($1.50) | $1,500 | $1,500 | $1,500 | $1,500 | $1,500 |
| C5 | Promotions ($3) | $3,000 | $1,950 | $1,269 | $825 | $579 |
| C6 | Total Costs | $309,500 | $190,650 | $127,977 | $85,925 | $62,295 |
|  | **Profits** | | | | | |
| P1 | Gross Profit | $40,500 | $43,350 | $28,533 | $18,575 | $12,975 |
| P2 | Discount Rate | 1.00 | 1.20 | 1.44 | 1.73 | 2.07 |
| P3 | NPV Profit | $40,500 | $36,125 | $19,815 | $10,737 | $6,268 |
| P4 | Cumulative NPV Profit | $40,500 | $76,625 | $96,440 | $107,177 | $113,445 |
| L1 | **Lifetime Value (NPV)** | $40.50 | $76.63 | $96.44 | $107.18 | $113.44 |

Is this realistic? Will your retail chain be able to duplicate these increases in lifetime value? That is up to you and your situation. Some things work, some things don't. You have to experiment and test constantly. What is definitely true is that you can do the calculations presented here with your customer base. You can figure out most of the numbers needed to do these calculations. You can test on a small scale with control groups whether each of your strategies will work. With a database, all this is possible. Without a database, you will never know.

## Fighting Duplicates

Once your database is in place, you need to continually monitor your records to try to eliminate duplicates. One letter from a familiar retailer is likely to be opened—particularly if the recipient has had a successful experience with correspondence from the store. Two or more similar letters in one day, however, make it clear that a computer is generating the letters. The second letter destroys the effect of the first. Your file must be reviewed by households to ensure that you mail only one letter per house.

Your job is made more difficult by the fact that customers may hold more than one credit card—especially when you get a rebate for doing so. Figure 10-4 shows the process used to update the customer database:

### Figure 10-4: Processing the Retail Database

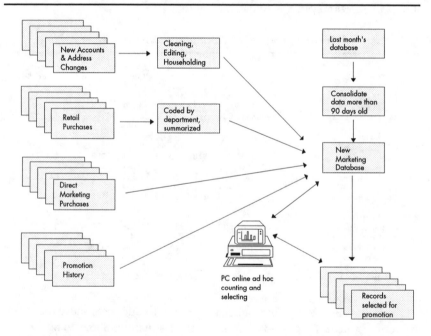

New accounts and changes of address must be matched against the existing database to consolidate people into households so that there will be only one letter per house. Addresses are the primary matching device, but telephone and social security numbers also can be used if available.

The householding process has to be done every month, because duplicates keep appearing. The point of householding is not to save money in mailing—although it will—but to prevent the destruction of the one-on-one relationship with the customer through multiple messages.

## Adding Noncardholders to Your Database

Once you experiment with these strategies, it will become obvious that there is a definite cash value for every name retained in the database. Profits will be a function of the number of customers (not necessarily credit cardholders) in the database. How can you get at the anonymous majority who pay with cash, check, or nonhouse credit card?

One method, of course, is to provide applicants with a noncredit check-cashing card that speeds up the acceptance of checks. Supermarkets use such cards routinely. Department stores can do the same.

Jennifer MacLean reported on how one retailer added thousands of customer names to his database in a short space of time. All cash and nonhouse credit card customers were asked to supply their telephone numbers as part of the transaction. The numbers were keyed into the point-of-sale device.

By capturing the information on 304,427 transactions, the retailer discovered that 28 percent were repeat buyers. The unique telephone numbers were sent to a service bureau where the numbers were looked up through an electronic reverse telephone directory system. The names and addresses of 129,623 customers were identified through this process.

The resulting file was checked against the house credit card file. It turned out that 36 percent of these customers were house credit card holders: two-thirds were active, and one-third were inactive. The remaining 82,869, of course, were new names that were added to the store's marketing database.

The fact that many card holders, previously thought inactive, were actually making purchases at the store came as a pleasant surprise and added to the store's knowledge about its customer base.

### Reactivating Lost Customers

Every retailer with a house card knows that fully half of the cards issued are never used. I am unlikely to use the card I received when buying the Italian china, for example. Why? Because it is a damn nuisance to carry a wad of cards around with me all the time. My driver's license, a couple of gasoline credit cards, health insurance, library card, MasterCard, Admiral's Club, and Giant Food check cashing card just about cover my lifetime needs. Every additional card further distorts my wallet. So the retailer will soon assume that I am a lost shopper.

What can a retailer do to reactivate people like me who appear not to have shopped at the store for nine months or more? Will direct mail to these "lost" customers be more cost effective than "accidental" reactivation due to general advertising?

Jennifer MacLean explained an experiment in which a retailer used a VIP reactivation letter, measured against an unpromoted control group, to bring back these lost sheep.

The results, as shown in Figure 10-5, were very interesting. The high dollar customers were harder to reactivate than the low dollar customers. The frequent shoppers were harder to reactivate than the less frequent shoppers. Why would this be so, when these two categories (high dollar and frequent) are usually the best respondents to any promotion? While no one can be sure, of course, it seems probable that the high dollar and frequent shoppers in the control group reactivated themselves due to general advertising. Since these better performing shoppers reactivated themselves spontaneously, this reduces the apparent "lift" in the test group.

### Figure 10-5: Reactivation of Lost Shoppers

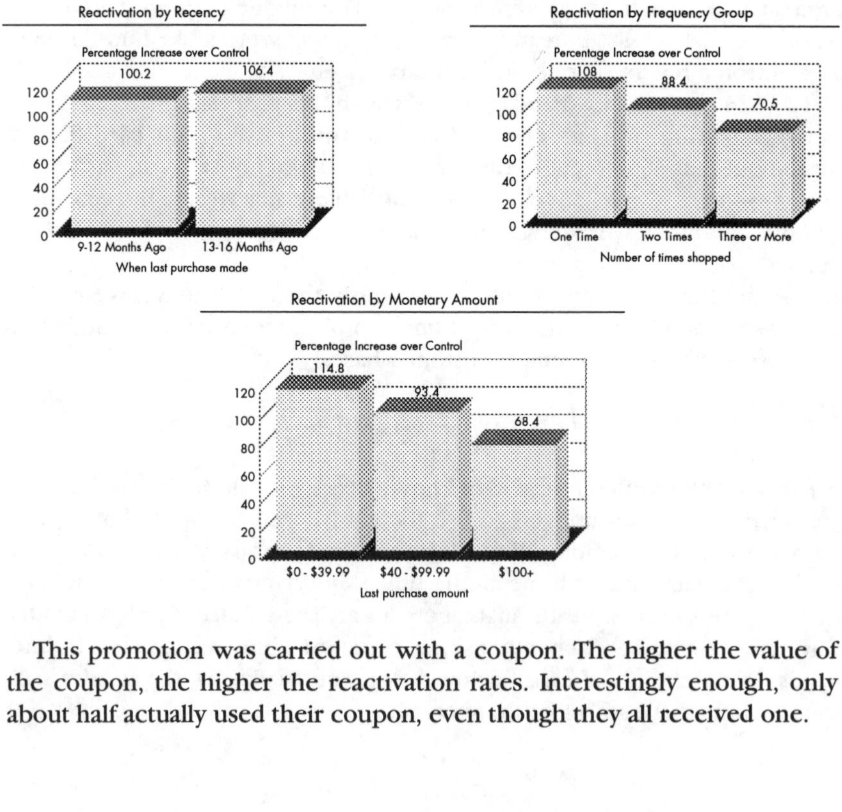

This promotion was carried out with a coupon. The higher the value of the coupon, the higher the reactivation rates. Interestingly enough, only about half actually used their coupon, even though they all received one.

What would have been the effect of reactivating these shoppers with a more personal message, such as a birthday or anniversary message rather than using a coupon? Testing would determine that. It is certainly possible that the overall cost of such a reactivation program could have been substantially reduced by offering recognition and personal attention (a cheaper method) rather than dollar value coupons (more expensive).

## Building Up Traffic in a Retail Store

What do you do when a new store fails to perform as planned? How can database marketing help? Let's assume that you, as a marketer, have a budget of $250,000 and three months to prove yourself. Here are some options suggested by Steve Gasner of North American Integrated Marketing:

- A media blitz: This is what most people would do. Unfortunately, such blitzes usually produce short-term gains. They must be repeated to maintain patronage. It is an expensive strategy.
- In-store publicity: Using a celebrity as a draw also is short term. Can you sustain business without the celebrity?
- Research through point-of-sale interviews: Sounds good, but in fact, is unlikely to tell you anything. The problem is that you want to know about people who are *not* there, rather than about those who are. The possibility of such research telling you anything you don't know is fairly remote.
- Telephone interviews in the trade area: Calls that reach both customers and noncustomers might well tell you something that you don't know. It should be on your list.
- Database analysis to see what people are buying: If the database contains complete customer data (from the store credit card) and an inventory of the products that you actually have in stock, it is possible to see who is buying what. Some inventory lines may be selling well and others poorly. Why? Could the answer be in the lines themselves, or in the type of customer coming to your store? It is possible that with creative research using data already in your possession, you can figure out your weaknesses and strengths and devise a program to solve the problem within budget and time constraints.

## Profiling Retail Customers

Once the database is up and running, there are all sorts of things that you can do that would be impossible without it. One of your first steps should be to study behavior by applying Recency, Frequency, Monetary (RFM) analysis, described in detail in Chapter 5. With customers divided into RFM cells, the lifetime value of each specific group can be determined.

In addition to RFM cells, customers can be profiled into lifestyle groups. You can develop separate marketing programs for mothers of small children, working women, senior citizens, new homeowners, etc. Each customer would be placed in a defined profile group. Within the profile group, their profitability can be determined by RFM and lifetime value.

This kind of knowledge can lead to the testing of each marketing promotion before even $1 is spent. Using a spreadsheet, you can test each strategy by making assumptions about the effect of the strategy on the lifetime value of the customer segment you are addressing. What will it do to the retention rate? What will it do to the average annual purchases? What will be the database and promotion costs? All this can be determined with some precision. In some cases, you can see, before any money has been spent, that your strategy will be a loser. In other cases, you can get enough ideas from the analysis so that you can say, "This might work. A test of 10,000 customers will prove if it will be a success." You will become a real professional at your craft.

### Testing the Store Trading Areas

So far, we have talked about profiling customers by purchasing habits and by demographics. There is another dimension: geography. Looking at a map of your customer residences may tell a retailer a great deal about how to market to them.

Once the database is established, it is possible to use it to determine such things as:

- The trading area for each store
- The penetration rate for each store trading area
- The best location for future branches
- Why some products do better at some locations than others

## Profits from Promoters

Another, less obvious use for a retail database involves a partnership with a product promoter. Consider what your name is worth. A retailer name carries an image that sends a message: Sears, JC Penney, Bloomingdale's, Nordstrom, L.L. Bean. As you read each of these names, an image is formed in your mind of the store: what it stands for, what a message from that store is likely to mean to you.

American Express spent years cultivating its name with its slogan "Mem-

bership has its privileges." An envelope from American Express or Bloomingdale's is more likely to be opened than one from an unknown retailer.
The name alone, in other words, is worth money.

Some retailers have put their names to effective use by working with
small promoters to make special offerings to their cardholders.

The way it works is shown in Figure 10-6:

### Figure 10-6: Working with a Promoter

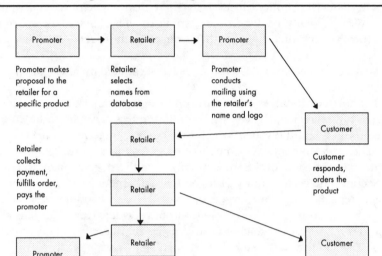

1. The promoter comes to the retailer with a product and an idea. Let's
   say it is a cellular phone that fits into a woman's pocketbook.
2. Together, they figure out the demographics and purchase behavior of
   the store customers most likely to respond to such a product.
3. The retailer does an ad hoc search of the store's cardholder database
   to identify the likely prospects.
4. The promoter prepares direct mail materials describing the offer. A
   contract is signed with the retailer indicating the percentage of sales
   going to the retailer and the percentage to the promoter.
5. The promoter carries out the mailing using a list provided by the
   store, letterhead and envelopes from the store, and the promoter's
   own resources. The store pays nothing for the mailing. Alternatively,
   the offer can be included in the store's monthly statement mailing to
   customers. This is a less costly method; however, it has a much lower
   response rate.
6. Fulfillment is carried out by the store's fulfillment department. Pay-

ment is made to the store's accounting department. Once a month, the promoter is reimbursed for the promoter's share in the venture.

What are the advantages in such an arrangement?

- Knowledge: The retailer gets to experiment with direct marketing for very little cost. Valuable knowledge is learned about the customers, their responses, and their propensity to buy certain products.
- Profits: The profits can be far greater than any similar retail venture. With virtually no investment, some retailers have made more total profits from such a system than from their entire retailing operation.

Is there a downside? Will customers feel exploited by having their names used in this way?

The answer involves the entire philosophy of marketing. In the first place, the retailer must scan each of these offers carefully to be sure that the products and the way in which they are presented fully reflect the standards that customers have come to expect from the store. The promotion of trash in the name of the store will cheapen the store in many ways.

Second, the retailer must do a good job of targeting its mail to the right customers. Picking your targets is not only good economics, it is also a favor to the customers. If every letter from your department store is loaded with merchandise in which a customer has no interest, the customer will soon lose interest in the store and in opening its envelopes.

Assuming that the promotion involves a quality product, well targeted to the right customers, retailers can only gain from such a system. If customers are buying, they must be happy: They have made a profit from their transactions. Making customers aware of profitable opportunities is doing them a favor.

## Summary

1.  It is true that retailers today are in serious trouble. Database marketing offers them a real solution. They have an established name, and millions of customers who recognize them and what they stand for. They can use their name and customer list to provide personal and special services for the customers, to build real relationships that will pay off for them, and to make their customers happy.

2.  The first step is usually to boost the number and percentage of customers who use the store's credit card. This forms the basis for the database.

3.  Retail database files can be very large. The solution to the size problem can be found in keeping detailed data for a short time only, rolling up older data by department, and using modern PC marketing software that provides access to mainframe customer files for ad hoc counts and selects.

4.  The database can be used to generate personal communications and thank-you letters from store employees to customers. These personal communications can often do more to bring in traffic than any number of discounts, sales, and space advertisements.

5.  Event-driven software can automatically pull out data from the database to generate personal communications, using look-up tables for affinity products produced by the merchandising department.

6.  To generate personal correspondence, the database has to be designed to hold a wealth of personal detail, and methods must be devised to see that store personnel, order forms, application blanks, and surveys are used to keep the data flowing into the database.

7.  An anniversary or birthday program can be a useful way to use the database to build a relationship with retail customers. Such as program can affect the lifetime value of retail customers by altering two factors: the retention factor and the average amount spent per year.

8.  Noncardholders can be added to the database by learning the names and addresses of cash, check, and credit card customers.

9.  Half of the store credit cards issued are never activated. Retailers can develop programs to get the dormant cards reactivated. When this happens, the high dollar and frequent shoppers have a lower reactivation rate than low dollar and less frequent shoppers.

10. The database can be used to determine the store trading area and the penetration rate. The database can be used to find the best location for future branches.

11. Retailers can combine with external promoters to market directly to retail customers. The result can be very profitable for the retailer.

## Executive Quiz 10

Answers to quiz questions can be found in Appendix B. The quizzes are for fun. Do them if you enjoy quizzes. Ignore them if you don't.
*Choose the best answer to complete each statement or question.*

1. Which one of the following is not commonly used to build retail customer loyalty?
   a. special personal services
   b. solo mailings
   c. incentives for store card members
   d. fast checkout for card members
   e. rewarding customers on their birthdays

2. Sam's business members spend what percentage of the spending of individual members?
   a. 50 percent
   b. 100 percent
   c. 200 percent
   d. 300 percent
   e. 400 percent

3. Since creation of its database, Waldenbooks weekly specials have
   a. decreased.
   b. stayed the same.
   c. increased 10 percent.
   d. increased 20 percent.
   e. increased 30 percent.

4. With modern database software, retail stores find that their marketing databases can store two years' data on customer
   a. purchases by product SKU.
   b. purchases by week by department.
   c. monthly purchases by customer.
   d. annual purchases.
   e. None of the above

5. Birthday and anniversary reminders and gift suggestions
   a. can be easily programmed into database software.
   b. are very expensive to set up.
   c. are always more trouble than

they are worth.
   d. require data that is difficult to obtain.
   e. cannot be tracked using lifetime value.

6. In calculating the effect of database activities on lifetime value, the value in the first year tends to
   a. go down.
   b. stay the same.
   c. go up by a small amount.
   d. go up by a large amount.
   e. There are no general rules.

7. In store credit card lost-shopper reactivations, which group had the highest percentage of reactivations?
   a. low monetary customers
   b. medium monetary customers
   c. high monetary customers
   d. Monetary amount irrelevant.
   e. This cannot be measured.

8. Which method does Steve Gasner suggest for building up retail traffic?
   a. using database information to revise inventory
   b. a media blitz
   c. in store publicity
   d. point-of-sale interviews
   e. None of the above

# Packaged Goods Databases: Don't Lose Your Shirt

*In recent years, I have had phone calls—mostly from little kids in big agencies—asking for sample mailings for such things as frozen TV dinners, dog food, shampoos, baby food, breakfast cereals ...*

*I asked [one] kid how much frozen dinners sell for. The answer: about $2.50 in the supermarket. Of that, the supermarkets get half and the manufacturer gets half. Send out a solo mailing for $350 per thousand persuading consumers to go into the supermarket and get a frozen dinner, and enclose a $1 off coupon with the mailing, and the net revenue to the manufacturer is $.25 ($250 less 50 percent markup = $1.25 less the $1 coupon = $.25).*

*You have to sell 1,400 frozen dinners to pay for the cost of the mailing; that doesn't include the cost of the dinners. That's an impossibly high response. Plus, there's the cost of maintaining the name in a database—if the name can be captured at all. The entire concept is preposterous.*

*What's going on? Big agencies are in trouble. Direct marketing is the fastest-growing advertising medium. Database marketing and relationship marketing are buzzwords. In order to pry more money out of the clients, the big agencies are conning these poor suckers into trying solo mailings for packaged goods when they haven't a clue as to what they are doing or how the cost structure works.*

*—Denison Hatch*, Target Marketing

**D**oes database marketing work for packaged goods? There is no clear-cut answer to this question. Many manufacturers have tried it. Some have succeeded. Some have failed. Does that mean that it can't be done, or does it mean that they didn't go about it correctly? That is the key question. Strategy is very important here. If you don't have a really good idea and execute it well, you will lose your money trying to do database marketing with packaged goods.

Why is that? It is because brand loyalty has been seriously eroded by billions of coupons available from every conceivable source: Carol Wright, local co-op programs, Sunday newspapers, in-store coupons, etc. Millions of people plan their shopping trips around the coupons they collect.

Coupons can be placed in a Sunday newspaper for $6 per thousand. Coupons sent directly to targeted homes by mail cost a minimum of $300 per thousand. Your package, offer, and concept will have to be outstanding to permit your targeted offer to overcome this cost differential. Few companies know how to do it.

## Recognize the Risks

Because it is so difficult, no packaged goods company should undertake a risky venture like database marketing without the assistance of a direct response agency with experience in this area—or a really good idea of how to go about it. In virtually all cases, you will need to call on some outside direct response genius who brings some experience to the table.

Let's explore the strategies that others have used that might be effective in building up customer loyalty for your product.

### Setting the Goal

The first step, of course, is determining what you are trying to accomplish. What can you reasonably achieve with database marketing?

Consider what others have accomplished:

- Kraft General Foods has been able to preserve and increase usage of Crystal Light among users in its one million member club database, with a profitable return on investment for several years.
- Stash Tea has been able to increase total sales by 30 percent per year for seven years in a row.
- The Wacky Warehouse program increased Kool-Aid sales over several years to 83 percent of the powdered drink market and, at the same time, reversed youngsters' preferences for Pepsi and Coke to Kool-Aid.

### How to Begin

Determine the goal in numerical terms with a specified time period. For example:

To increase sales of product X by 4 percent during the next four years.
To hold market share at 11 percent or above during the next three years.

Note that database projects usually have a long payout period. Two years is a minimum. It takes a long time to get them going, and even longer for them to make a measurable dent. Whatever your product and situation, you must begin with a specific goal: a number and a three- or four-year plan for achieving the number. This goal will drive all the rest of your calculations and planning.

## Developing a Great Strategic Idea

There is no simple formula for packaged goods database marketing. There is, by now, for airlines. Every airline has a frequent flyer program, and they are all more or less alike. There is an established formula for software databases. Most large software companies are building a customer database that they use to sell upgrades and cross-over products. They are quite similar. Packaged goods programs, however, have not settled into a nice secure formula that you can use for your product.

You need to come up with a plan for a club, referral program, magazine, continuity scheme, catalog, or something that will catch the imagination of your customers and make your product soar.

Let's look at each of these possibilities:

- User clubs
- Affinity groups
- Preferred customer programs
- Retailer co-op programs
- Continuity programs
- Referral programs

## User Clubs

Kraft General Foods has pioneered with user clubs for packaged goods, but it is not alone. Clubs for gardening, sports, gourmet cooks, automobiles, children, computers, dieting, travel, or nature can be created for users of your products. The club can be centered on a newsletter or magazine that focuses on activities using your product.

The idea in such clubs is to provide customers with something unusual that does not involve price, but the use of the product. Examples are:

- Italian food recipes (or French, Spanish, Indian, Chinese, etc.)
- Dieting ideas: fitness, exercise, weight loss
- Children's activities: coloring books, games, toys
- A club for sufferers of diabetes, heart disease, obesity, etc.

In such a club, the idea is to build the interest in the activity, not your product. The product, instead of being the central feature, is an assumed fact. Of course, everyone uses Contadina Italian products when serving a meal. But look at these great Italian aprons you can get for the chef! Look at these tours of Rome and Naples sponsored by Contadina!

If your club provides enough benefits for members, it can eventually become self-supporting through sales of services and merchandise (other than your immediate product) or paid ads in the club magazine.

The club par excellence is the *Nintendo Power* magazine, which built up a readership of two million customers eager to learn more about how to use the product. A 900 telephone number (paid by customers) is used by 10,000 kids a week. Up to 40,000 letters are received every month by readers, all of whom get an answer. Such a club, once established, is ideal for the launch of a new product. When Nintendo introduced its Game Boy, it sold five million in the first year and 20 million cartridges in follow-up sales.

Can you copy this example and build a club? It is a strategy that, if done well, will never go out of style. Done poorly, or half-heartedly, it will just drain your treasury:

- Ask Mattel what happened to the Barbie Pink Stamps Club. Members of this club sent $2 along with membership forms packaged in Barbie merchandise. Members received hair accessories, fashion posters, T-shirts, and the Barbie Fashion Guide, complete with beauty tips, stories, games, puzzles, and order information for mail-order premium items, to be purchased with Barbie pink stamps or cash. A great idea. It was discontinued in March 1992 after a three-year run.
- Ask McCormick-Schilling what happened to the Society to End Dull Meals Forever, which provided a quarterly newsletter and 12 recipe cards every six months. The club was canceled in 1992 because the cost of maintaining and mailing the magazine exceeded the benefits from increased sales.
- Ask the Miller Brewing Company what happened to the Lite Beer Athletic Club founded in 1987. Members paid $2 per year to receive a quarterly magazine. It ended shortly thereafter. As late as 1993, Miller had no functioning customer clubs. The idea did not work.

On the other hand, the Shiseido Club has 10 million members in Japan. The club helps Shiseido sell $2 billion worth of cosmetics to Japanese women. It has its own magazine. The Woolworth Kids Club in the U.K., launched in 1987, has more than a half million members. Its quarterly comic book helps to sell Woolworth toys. Birthday cards to kids and a newsletter for adults rounds out the Woolworth Club offerings.

Conclusion: Clubs are a great idea if well thought through, if the economics are there, and if they are well managed. They are hard to do properly for packaged goods.

## Affinity Groups

An identified affinity group, to which you can mail a newsletter and invitations to purchase the product, is slightly less demanding than a club.

The average baby consumes more than $1,400 worth of disposable diapers per year. Kimberly Clark spent more than $10 million to set up a database for Huggies diapers that covers 75 percent of the expectant mothers in the United States.

Affinity groups often involve database marketing to existing customers, a decision that is usually based on incremental profits. You are already making a profit selling your product or service, or you wouldn't be in business. The idea in considering database marketing is that you could somehow make additional profits: you could increase trial, retention, referrals, annual sales, etc. To decide whether database marketing would work for you, there are two steps involved:

1. Determine how much incremental profit you could make per customer per year through database activities.
2. Balance that against the incremental costs that you will incur by building a database and engaging in database marketing activities.

Let's take a specific example. Suppose your company is selling baby food in supermarkets. A jar of baby food sells for about $.79. Let's assume that your profit on a jar is about $.10.

By doing some creative thinking, you can envision an affinity group like that created by Kimberly Clark. You could obtain a list of parents of new babies and send them a welcome kit and a baby nutrition newsletter prepared by a noted pediatrician on a quarterly basis during the first two years of every baby's life. The newsletter includes personalized checks that can be used only for the purchase of your baby food. You can use these checks to measure usage of the product by newsletter recipients. On-pack offers to control groups (which deliberately do not receive the newsletter) track usage by nondatabase customers.

To reinforce your newsletter, you could set up a toll-free baby nutrition hotline with technical information and advice. Your expert could answer personal letters from worried parents. You may even try infomercials to publicize your expert and your product. All this is good database marketing. Essentially, the purpose of your database marketing program is to get people to use your product in the first place and to keep on using it for two years.

### Estimating the Incremental Usage

To sell your current product, you are using awareness and direct response advertising in newspapers, baby magazines, television, etc. You have a 15 percent market share. You compute that the average family in your market area with a one-year-old baby is buying about 8.4 jars per month:

| | |
|---|---|
| Lunch and dinners in a month | 56 meals |
| Market share in your area | 15% |
| Average family buys per month | 8.4 jars |

How much can database marketing increase these sales? Here you must do some creative thinking. The effect of the database marketing can be felt in two ways:

1. Increased number of families try the product for the first time
2. Increased retention and purchases by user families due to the newsletter, plus a certain amount of referral business

To give meaning to these two effects, let's plug in some numbers. First consider increased trial usage. By giving the welcome kit to every family with a new baby, let's assume it is possible to assure 60 percent trial, whereas at present you have about 45 percent trial. Of those 45 percent who try the product now, one-third (15 percent) become regular users. Of the 60 percent who try the product with the welcome kit, if one-third become users, the market share will rise to 20 percent, a one- third increase in market share (from 15 percent to 20 percent).

There is only one flaw in this reasoning: most of your competitors already have a database marketing program to parents of newborns. Next to confirmed gamblers and new movers, parents of newborns are probably the most overworked affinity group in the United States. Because of this competition, you will probably increase your market share by much less— say an increase of two percentage points from 15 percent to 17 percent. This will translate to an increased sale of 1.12 more jars per family per month (2 percent of 56 meals).

Let's look next at increased retention, referral, and sales. Here, the database program again comes up against entrenched competition. To succeed, your welcome kit and newsletter have to be very well done. You will have to offer something considerably better than your competition, since all families will have several competing products arriving in their mail boxes at approximately the same time. The results depend on successful execution more than anything else.

Assuming you do a good job, let's say that you can increase your market share here by another 3 percent, or 1.68 jars per month. In total, therefore, your database marketing has increased sales by 2.8 jars per family per month. That is an incremental profit of $.28 per family per month.

### Measuring the Costs

How much will it cost to send welcome kits and newsletters, build a database, maintain a customer information hotline, provide technical support, distribute checks and coupons, fund your infomercials, and pay your expert to answer letters? I would be surprised if you could accomplish all of this for as little as $.25 per family per month. But, let's say you do it for $.22. That is a monthly profit of $.06 per family per month ($.28 – $.22). Multiplying that by about two million families with babies on your database (parents with children up to 24 months), that $.06 is an incremental profit of $120,000 per month or about $1.4 million per year.

The figures are relatively close, however. A slight upward shift in costs, and a slight downward shift in the success rate will leave you with a net loss from database activities.

### Other Revenue

There is one other source of income, however, that might put your database project firmly in the black. Database marketing activities are usually carved out of the advertising budget. It is possible that the database program, which is targeted directly at the only consumer audience interested in your product, can replace much of your current advertising without loss in sales or market share. In this case, your profits will be much greater. In any case, however, the case for database marketing in this situation is a very shaky one that depends on many uncertain factors.

## Preferred Customer Programs

For the last 50 years, packaged goods companies have built up loyalty programs tied to proof of purchase. This is particularly useful if you have many different products under the same brand, such as Kellogg's, Lever, General Foods, Quaker, and Nestle.

In general, most customers are not conscious of the ownership of the products they buy. Who owns Hellmann's mayonnaise? Who makes Friskies cat food? Each product is looked on by the customers as an independent brand. As such, a preferred customer program can be costly.

Such a program may be more successful if you can promote the idea of wholesomeness, purity, diet-consciousness, or some other central theme with a whole line of related products (Campbell's soups, Jell-O, Quaker). Each individual product can include a proof-of-purchase coin or label, which, when sent to a collection point, can earn the customer a preferred status, qualifying for specific bonus prizes or benefits—just as the famous S&H Green Stamps did in the 1960s.

The database serves as the repository for data about customer use of products. Quarterly mailings to members can build the loyalty, just as the mailings from American Airlines do to frequent flyer members.

Are the economics there to support such a program? Are the margins on product sales sufficient to provide a big enough incentive to members to make it worth their while to mail in the proof of purchase? When American Airlines sells a seat from Washington to Chicago for $700, there is enough margin there to give away a few air miles. How much margin is there in multiple purchases of Kellogg's Frosted Bran?

Before you begin such a preferred customer venture, get out your calculator and figure out how the customer will make enough profit to make it interesting to join. If you get a good answer, then figure out how you can boost lifetime customer value enough through such a system to justify the expense. The key is changing the retention rate, and through it, the lifetime value. If you can do so, go to it. If not, pass this idea up. Keep your eye on the bottom line.

## Retailer Co-op Programs

In 1990, a manufacturer worked with a number of retailers to test the effectiveness of a specific offer to a group of households.

The test was made on the purchase of liquid and powder cleaning products in a mature category with no significant growth. The manufacturer was a market leader with the dominant brand, who was introducing a new related brand in the same field. The objective was to increase sales by expanding total consumption with the new specialty product, without reducing overall sales of the dominant brand.

The test targeted 150,000 existing users of the dominant brand with promotional offers of the new product, designed to generate trial and increase overall consumption. A control group of 90,000 regular shoppers was picked at random to test against the trial groups. Half of the households received a letter with a $1 off coupon. The other half received a $.25

coupon that involved an entry into a sweepstakes. The results of these two tests are shown in Figure 11-1.

### Figure 11-1: Test of $1 Vs. $.25 + Sweepstakes

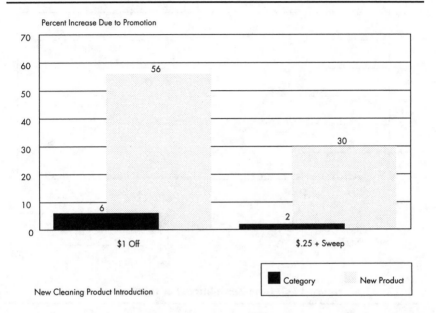

Percent Increase Due to Promotion

New Cleaning Product Introduction

Category          New Product

Overall, after 12 weeks, the $1 off promotion of the new brand increased total sales in the category by 6 percent while it increased sales of the new brand by 56 percent. The $.25 off plus a sweepstakes entry did not do as well. This increased the category by 2 percent and the product by 30 percent.

One obvious question: did sales of the new brand hurt sales of the manufacturer's other product, the dominant brand. Figure 11-2 shows that there was no impact on the dominant brand at all; its sales were basically stable (up by 1 percent). A final question: What was the long-term impact of the promotion of the new product? Figure 11-3 shows that even after 36 weeks, there was still a big increase in sales of the new product—in other words, it was successfully launched.

Can you duplicate these results with your database? The answer is yes and no. The database being used here was the retailer's database. Retail customers had frequent shopper cards that they used every time they shopped. The data on all their purchases was captured by the point-of-sale system and sent nightly to a central processing point.

The program that ran this test no longer exists. Today there are hun-

### Figure 11-2: Effect on the Dominant Brand

Percent Increase Due to Promotion

[Bar chart with y-axis 0 to 70. For "$1 Off": Dominant = 1, New Product = 56. For "$.25 + Sweep": Dominant = 1, New Product = 30.]

$1 Off                              $.25 + Sweep

New Cleaning Product Introduction

Legend: ■ Dominant        New Product

### Figure 11-3: Long-Term Impact of the Promotion

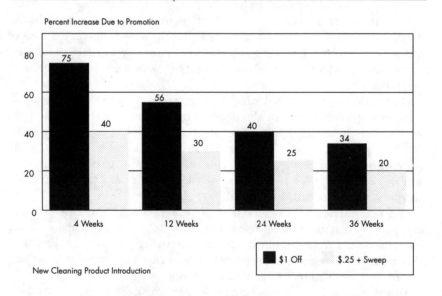

Percent Increase Due to Promotion

[Bar chart with y-axis 0 to 80. 4 Weeks: $1 Off = 75, $.25 + Sweep = 40. 12 Weeks: $1 Off = 56, $.25 + Sweep = 30. 24 Weeks: $1 Off = 40, $.25 + Sweep = 25. 36 Weeks: $1 Off = 34, $.25 + Sweep = 20.]

4 Weeks        12 Weeks        24 Weeks        36 Weeks

New Cleaning Product Introduction

Legend: ■ $1 Off        $.25 + Sweep

dreds of stores that have frequent shopper programs, however. The data they collect belongs to them. Some, undoubtedly, would be willing to run such tests as the one described—for a fee. It is their database, not the manufacturer's, that will be used for the testing, however.

## Continuity Programs

Americans love continuity programs. Few manufacturers have realized this yet. The Book of the Month Club and the Columbia Record Club have been going strong for decades. Carnation launched the idea with Perform Pet Food in 1989.

The Perform program involved the introduction of a premium pet food delivered fresh to your door by UPS. You do not have to be home to receive it, since it is charged to your credit card. Dog and cat food requirements are fairly consistent, so Perform was able to set up a system whereby the dog or cat food could be delivered automatically once a month (or at other intervals) without the need for a telephone call. Thousands of pet owners solved the problem of regular replenishment of their pet supplies by making one telephone call.

Continuity programs are particularly good for developing niche markets where the product is too specialized to command the shelf space needed in a supermarket, but strong enough to make a profit, and regular enough in consumption requirements that continuity would work. What products other than pet food could there be? How about swimming pool chemicals, diapers, allergy or diabetes medicines, coffee, tea, beer, wine, fruit, candy, steaks, records, videos?

## Referral Programs

There is a progression that most customers go through: awareness, trial, user, advocate, regular user. Once some people become hooked on your product, they want to tell their friends about it. They become advocates.

In most cases, there is little that advocates can do, except to tell a couple of friends at the office or a neighbor. Why not capitalize on this brief phase of infatuation, before they become blasé regular users, by giving the advocates something positive that they can do to promote the success of this wonderful product; to spread to others the joy and satisfaction that they feel every time they use it?

This is where referral programs come in. If you can use your database to encourage advocates to spread the word in a positive way, you can boost your own sales and make your customers happy.

Carnation's Perform program did this. Members were encouraged to recommend friends and neighbors who might want the product. When these friends and neighbors purchased, the recommender received a thank-you letter together with a $2 reduction on the next pet food bill. MCI also does this with its Friends & Family Program. MCI, of course, is not a packaged good, but the concept still applies.

Packaged goods programs can do the same with on-pack referral programs, inviting people to send in names. You can build a database of recommenders and their referrals, with benefits accruing to recommenders when their referrals take some recorded action (proof of purchase, enrollment in a club, etc.)

Such a program can be quite inexpensive. On-pack offers have a delivery cost that is almost zero (compared to direct mail or advertising). The customer pays the postage. You pay only when you receive a response—and this is the kind of payment that is really worthwhile because you are dealing with a customer, not a prospect.

Stash Tea built its database using on-pack offers. Stash, a small tea company in Portland, Oregon, founded in 1972 by David Leger and Steve Lee, sold its tea at first to health food stores and restaurants. Once the company began packing the tea into foil-sealed tea bags, it got the idea of putting a catalog offer on the back of the foil packet. As many as 2,000 tea customers per month call Stash's toll-free number or write in for the quarterly catalog, which sells a wide variety of products and gives out information about the history of tea, the name Stash, the Stash Tea foster child, stores that carry the product, and letters from readers. This catalog has lasted. It produces 35 percent of the company's net profits from only 10 percent of its sales.

Why has Stash Tea been successful when so many others have failed? Because the company had an idea, a theme (exotic teas and tea lovers), a sound economic program (an interesting catalog), plus excellent execution of the idea. The catalog goes only to people who ask for it. Since Stash Tea is sold only in upscale restaurants and specialty stores, the customers are, in general, more affluent and in a position to buy the products in the catalog. It is niche marketing at its best.

## Weight Watchers Success with Packaged Goods

One outstandingly successful use of database marketing with packaged goods is the Weight Watchers program, created by Targetbase for the H. J. Heinz Company. Heinz's Weight Watchers International includes two separate businesses:

- A weight-loss program with four million members who meet in 6,200 distinct locations each year

- A group of 250 "lite" foods sold in supermarkets

In the late 1970s Heinz became a leader in the "lite" foods category due to Weight Watchers success. After a six-year meteoric rise, however, intense competition in this category eroded Heinz's market share. Heinz was attempting to market 250 products across 78 categories through traditional brand-by-brand and category-by-category structure.

By 1990, Weight Watchers food sales declined by 10 percent while "lite" foods as a whole increased by 5 percent. A major reorganization in marketing strategy was required to save the business. A new management team was assembled to staff a new Weight Watchers Food Company with a totally new marketing strategy.

Weight Watchers turned for assistance to Dennis Gonier, senior vice president of Targetbase Marketing of Las Colinas, Texas. With his help, the team reviewed Weight Watchers resources and determined that:

- The food sales dynamics showed that a majority of the sales came from a small percentage of the users who were dieters in the Weight Watchers weight loss programs.
- Despite this fact, no system existed for the rapid collection of the names of weight loss program members.
- Many of the weight loss center franchisees did not actively promote the use of the food; some found the two businesses incompatible.
- The current mass promotion program was not turning current users into high-volume loyal customers through cross-selling and trial inducement.

The new marketing strategy combined the existing Weight Watchers franchises, a form of a user club, with a continuity program that offered incentives to buy Weight Watchers food products. The team defined the objectives for a new program to be called WINNERS!:

- Increase the buying rate (the number of units purchased) for widely used products, such as frozen entrees.
- Expand penetration (trial usage) of other products like cheese and mayonnaise.
- Make active use of the Weight Watchers membership list—a previously underused asset.
- Work to change the attitude of the franchisee managements by using the program to promote *both* the food sales and center attendance.

The team decided to:

- Build a system for accessing membership names in a timely fashion
- Enlist franchisee support in promoting Weight Watchers brands
- Use multiple contacts, promotional purchase incentives, and frequent-use rewards to build a relationship with each member

WINNERS! was designed to contact Weight Watchers weight loss program members at key strategic points over the course of their participation, which generally averaged eight weeks. Research indicated that the most effective contact periods were in weeks three, five, and eight. WINNERS! mailings were timed accordingly.

Upon enrollment into the weight loss program, each individual was handed a welcome kit to the WINNERS! program. This outlined the tangible and intangible rewards for participation, and coupons to invite trial of several products.

In week three, members received their first mailing, including a welcome letter from their local area meeting center and additional coupons.

In week five, they received a second mailing with a letter of encouragement, bonus point offers, and more coupons.

The final mailing arrived in week eight, with information on premiums, coupons, another encouragement letter, and an offer rewarding continued meeting attendance.

Figure 11-4 shows an overview of the WINNERS! program:

### Figure 11-4: WINNERS! Program Overview

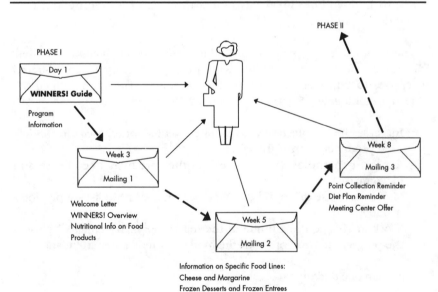

Using their experience in similar programs, Targetbase professionals set aside a control group that did not receive the promotional mailings to test the program's effectiveness. They used three evaluation systems:

• Receiver reaction studies
• Response analysis
• Program return on investment tracking

The volume and profitability measurement of the success of the program showed that those enrolled in the WINNERS! program overall bought 66 percent more product than the control group.

Figure 11-5 shows the effect of the WINNERS! program on individual product categories.

#### Figure 11-5: WINNERS! Purchases Compared with Control Group

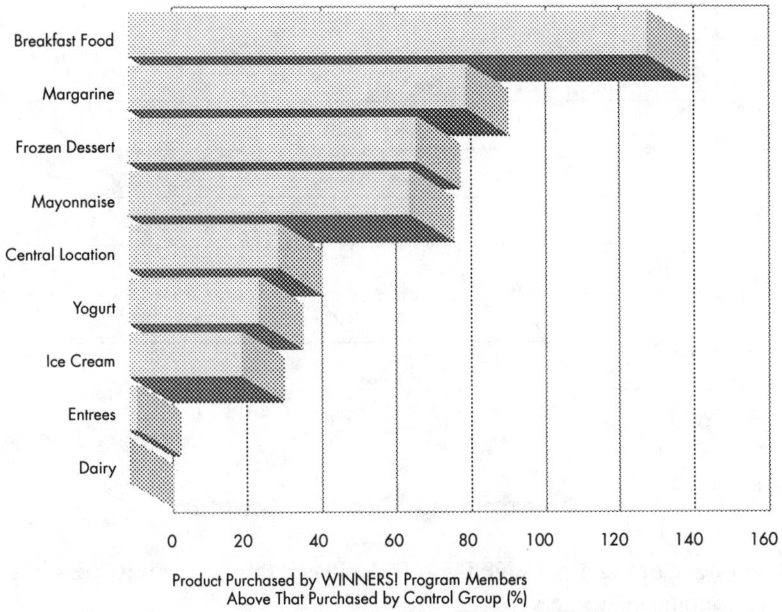

Product Purchased by WINNERS! Program Members
Above That Purchased by Control Group (%)

The real test, however, was the behavior of the people after the program was over. The second three months is the time after a member leaves Weight Watchers. Those who had been enrolled in the WINNERS! program still purchased at levels that were twice as high as those who were not in the program. Targetbase matched actual purchase behavior against real-time Weight Watcher member files over the nine months preceding, during, and following the program mailings.

A Targetbase proprietary model was used to determine return on investment by matching the change in volume purchase with shifts in attitudes and behavior. In computing each product line's profit, less the cost of the program, it was determined that WINNERS! paid for itself in 90 days and delivered a 45.5 percent return on investment. Franchisees also benefited. They received an average of one extra week in classroom fees from WINNERS! participants over the control group.

In summary, after 18 months of a declining business, the Weight Watchers WINNERS! program turned things around. Using a database marketing program, the company increased overall volume by 66 percent. Figure 11-6 shows the long-term effect of the WINNERS! program on sales of entrees.

**Figure 11-6: Effect of WINNERS! on Sales of Entrees (% Change)**

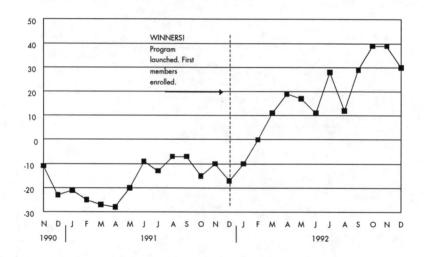

## Determining Member Benefits

When developing a packaged goods database, the profit must be sufficient to encourage customers to be loyal.

Profits are not necessarily in cash. Profits can be a magazine, membership in a club, access to a technical hotline, or a coloring book—anything that people cannot easily get elsewhere that is perceived as a benefit.

If you cannot come up with an adequate profit level for the customers, stop right there and drop or revise your project. The database will fail if the customers do not benefit from being in it.

## Developing a Budget

Once you have a goal for your packaged goods database marketing program, a great strategic plan, and have calculated the customer profit level, you need to do your homework: cost out the plan, locate the resources, and figure out where the money will come from to run the program.

There are many potential sources of revenue:

- Renting database names
- Catalog sales
- Club membership or magazine subscription
- Direct sales
- Brand credit (brand manager credits marketing program with specific dollar amounts based on demonstrated performance in boosting sales)
- Savings in the advertising budget
- Co-op advertising in your magazine
- Marketing budget

Put these together into a sound budget, and get it approved within your organization.

## A Contadina Lifetime Value Calculation

Let's do a packaged goods lifetime value calculation. For analysis, I have chosen Contadina Products, a family of Italian foods from Carnation/Nestle. I have no inside knowledge of Contadina and have contacted no one in the company. My calculation is based solely on my experience as an enthusiastic consumer of Contadina products and my knowledge of lifetime value.

In the typical supermarket, Contadina has two dozen products, ranging in price from $.40 to $2.59. They all revolve around the idea of tomatoes, pasta, and Italy. There is a definite bond of affinity that exists between the product and the customers. The idea: Build a database of Contadina customers with a quarterly newsletter featuring Italy, Italian food, Italian recipes, and associated gifts and products.

The newsletter, if well done, could be very interesting, and could offer ideas and products not found in stores or in general interest magazines and newspapers. The idea: We are a special group—we Italian lovers—and we have our own thing here. The newsletter also could feature Contadina aprons, chef's hats, bibs (for spaghetti lovers), and, why not, Contadina Club tours of Venice, Rome, and Naples.

In the long run, if successful, the newsletter could be self supporting with paid advertisements. In the short run—the first three years—it will require funding. Let's suppose that a database of one million names is created, and the newsletter gets out the door including postage for $.80 a copy, four times a year. The second and third years, the sales of related products and advertising could bring the per copy costs down to $.70 and $.60 respectively.

### Contadina Revenue Effect

The next step is to consider the club's effect on revenue. How much could such a club build sales of Contadina products? We will assume that all club members are already Italian food lovers. They already buy a lot of Italian food products. The club members would have to increase their purchases. Let's assume that the marginal increase in retail purchases of Contadina products by club members would be $.50 per week, about a $26 million increase in retail sales. If Contadina's incremental profit is 10 percent of the retail price, this works out to an annual increase in profits of $2.6 million.

That sounds good, until we consider the costs of creating such a club. The club will have expenses, as outlined below in Table 11-1:

**Table 11-1: Contadina Club First Year Budget**

| | |
|---|---|
| Number of Members | 1,000,000 |
| Monthly Costs | |
| Direct Response Agency | $15,000 |
| Database Maintenance | $17,417 |
| Four Newsletters @ $.80 | $266,888 |
| Telephone Communications | $20,000 |
| Marketing Management | $10,000 |
| Total | $329,083 |
| First Year Costs | $3,948,996 |
| First Year Costs per Customer | $3.95 |
| First Year Increased Revenue | $2.60 |
| Net Loss per Member from Database | ($1.35) |

If these figures are correct, the Contadina club would be a big loser. The increase in revenue of $.50 each for one million families is certainly quite speculative, and depends on market factors that no one can anticipate, plus extremely creative execution of the newsletter. The costs of the entire project do not seem promising.

Looking at the lifetime value, however, the picture is somewhat brighter.

To begin, let's set up a control group of one million customers who are regular users of Contadina products today without any special inducement.

We will assume that each family spends about $2.50 per week on Contadina products. What is their lifetime value? Table 11-2 works it out to a net present value, after five years, of $19.99.

**Table 11-2: Customer Lifetime Value without the Club**

|  | | Year1 | Year2 | Year3 | Year4 | Year5 |
|---|---|---|---|---|---|---|
| | **Revenue** | | | | | |
| R1 | Customers | 1,000 | 450 | 203 | 102 | 51 |
| R2 | Retention Rate | 45 | 45 | 50 | 50 | 55 |
| R3 | Average Yearly Sale | $125 | $125 | $125 | $125 | $125 |
| R4 | Total Revenue | $125,000 | $56,250 | $25,375 | $12,750 | $6,375 |
| | **Costs** | | | | | |
| C1 | Cost Percent | 90 | 90 | 90 | 90 | 90 |
| C2 | Total Costs | $112,500 | $50,625 | $22,838 | $11,475 | $5,738 |
| | **Profits** | | | | | |
| P1 | Gross Profit | $12,500 | $5,625 | $2,538 | $1,275 | $638 |
| P2 | Discount Rate | 1.00 | 1.20 | 1.44 | 1.73 | 2.07 |
| P3 | NPV Profit | $12,500 | $4,688 | $1,762 | $737 | $308 |
| P4 | Cumulative NPV Profit | $12,500 | $17,188 | $18,950 | $19,687 | $19,995 |
| L1 | **Customer lifetime value** | $12.50 | $17.19 | $18.95 | $19.69 | $19.99 |

This calculation assumes that of the present customers about 55 percent will drop the product next year, and about half of the remainder will drop out in each of the subsequent years.

Now let's introduce the Contadina Club. We are assuming that the club will affect customer behavior in two ways: Customers will tend to stay with the product and they will purchase more. The retention rate for club members goes from 45 percent to 65 percent and rises after five years to 75 percent, as shown in Table 11-3. The assumptions are these:

- This chart is a picture of the behavior of 1,000 club members during the first five years of their membership. Existing members bring new people into the club at the rate of 5 percent per year.
- The club will have the effect of increasing membership purchases of Contadina products from $125 per year to $135 per year in the second year. Thereafter, the remaining members will increase their purchases by $10 per family per year.
- The incremental profit on a retail Contadina product is 10 percent.
- The newsletter cost will drop from $.80 to $.60 over the first three years due to advertising and sales of specialty products.

An initial investment of $3,000 per 1,000 members will be needed to get the club started. Names will be accumulated by means of on-pack enrollment forms, coupon enrollment forms, print ad coupons with toll-free number enrollment, and existing promotional results.

### Table 11-3: Customer Lifetime Value with the Club

|     | Revenue | Year1 | Year2 | Year3 | Year4 | Year5 |
|-----|---------|-------|-------|-------|-------|-------|
| R1 | Referral Rate | 5 | 5 | 5 | 5 | 5 |
| R2 | Referred Members |  | 50 | 35 | 25 | 18 |
| R3 | Club Members | 1,000 | 700 | 490 | 368 | 276 |
| R4 | Retention Rate | 65 | 65 | 70 | 70 | 75 |
| R5 | Average Yearly Sale | $125 | $135 | $145 | $155 | $165 |
| R6 | Total Revenue | $125,000 | $94,500 | $71,050 | $57,040 | $45,540 |
|     | **Costs** |  |  |  |  |  |
| C1 | Cost Percent | 90 | 90 | 90 | 90 | 90 |
| C2 | Direct Costs | $112,500 | $85,050 | $63,945 | $51,336 | $40,986 |
| C3 | Newsletter ($3.20) | $3,200 | $2,240 | $1,568 | $1,178 | $883 |
| C4 | Database ($0.74) | $740 | $518 | $363 | $272 | $204 |
| C5 | Startup Costs | $3,000 | $0 | $0 | $0 | $0 |
| C6 | Total Costs | $119,440 | $87,808 | $65,876 | $52,786 | $42,073 |
|     | **Profits** |  |  |  |  |  |
| P1 | Gross Profit | $5,560 | $6,692 | $5,174 | $4,254 | $3,467 |
| P2 | Discount Rate | 1.00 | 1.20 | 1.44 | 1.73 | 2.07 |
| P3 | NPV Profit | $5,560 | $5,577 | $3,593 | $2,459 | $1,675 |
| P4 | Cumulative NPV Profit | $5,560 | $11,137 | $14,730 | $17,189 | $18,864 |
| L1 | **Customer lifetime value** | $5.56 | $11.14 | $14.73 | $17.19 | $18.86 |

The net effect of the club will be to decrease net present lifetime value of Contadina club members from $19.99 after five years to $18.86. The club would not be a certain winner for Contadina.

Side by side, Table 11-4 shows the lifetime value calculations from the previous two charts.

### Table 11-4: Lifetime Value Comparison

| | | | | | |
|---|---|---|---|---|---|
| Value without the club | $12.50 | $17.19 | $18.95 | $19.69 | $19.99 |
| Value with the club | $5.56 | $11.14 | $14.73 | $17.19 | $18.86 |

Net Loss: $1.13 per memeber, or $1,130,000 over five years

This is a somewhat discouraging picture. It is possible that Contadina could not make money with such a really great creative idea. Despite the company's enthusiasm, its numbers do not show a profit. This reminds me of an incident that happened some time ago.

In 1957, I sent out contracts for construction of my house. I got four bids at $36,000 and one at $21,000—all for exactly the same house. I took the low bid. After construction began, I realized that the builder was way over his head. His price was much too low. He was building eight other houses simultaneously and apparently losing money on them, too.

"How can you survive if you lose money on every house you build?" I asked him.

"I'll make it up on volume," he replied.

The builder went bankrupt six months later. But before that, he finished my house.

## Am I Wrong?

Suppose that perhaps my conclusion about a database for Contadina is wrong. Maybe there are benefits that I have not been able to visualize. What could they be?

- Club members might be able to increase their purchases by more than I have shown here.
- The retention rate could be higher (but this seems really unlikely).
- More referred members could sign up.
- Members might buy products in bulk direct from Contadina, reducing the direct cost percentage from 90 percent to about 60 percent.
- The newsletter might become so popular it could sell ads and become self-supporting. This happened with the Burger King Kids Club. It is not impossible. It depends on the ability of the direct response agency that creates the newsletter.

But, realistically speaking, all these things are a long shot. The margin on Contadina and other packaged goods is so very thin that there is very little slack for a database program. So we live and learn. Or rather, calculate and learn. Do your homework. Don't get carried away. Don't lose your job promoting a wonderful idea that bombs.

## Some Heroic Assumptions

Despite the numbers we have just seen, suppose we go all out on Contadina. Let's really try to make the club idea work. Let's assume that we can make four things happen:

- Rent the names on the Contadina database for $1 per name per year.
- Establish catalog sales through the club that average a net return to Contadina of $15 per club member per year.
- Secure co-op advertising in the membership newsletter that averages $1 per member per year.
- Get the Contadina brand manager to carve $1 per club member out of the advertising budget to donate to the cause.

What could this do to the club? Table 11-5 provides an indication.
Here is a possible solution. The lifetime value after five years will grow

**Table 11-5: Customer Lifetime Value with Heroic Assumptions**

| | Revenue | Year1 | Year2 | Year3 | Year4 | Year5 |
|---|---|---|---|---|---|---|
| R1 | Referral Rate | 5 | 6 | 7 | 8 | 9 |
| R2 | Referred Members | | 50 | 42 | 35 | 31 |
| R3 | Club Members | 1,000 | 700 | 497 | 383 | 299 |
| R4 | Retention Rate | 65 | 65 | 70 | 70 | 70 |
| R5 | Average Yearly Sale | $125 | $135 | $145 | $155 | $165 |
| R6 | Total Retail Sales | $125,000 | $94,500 | $72,065 | $59,365 | $49,335 |
| R7 | Name Rental $1/yr | $1,000 | $700 | $497 | $383 | $299 |
| R8 | Catalog Sales $15/yr | $15,000 | $10,500 | $7,455 | $5,745 | $4,485 |
| R9 | Co-op Advertising $1/yr | $1,000 | $700 | $497 | $383 | $299 |
| R10 | Brand Credit $1/yr | $1,000 | $700 | $497 | $383 | $299 |
| R11 | Total Revenue | $143,000 | $107,100 | $81,011 | $66,259 | $54,717 |
| | **Costs** | | | | | |
| C1 | Cost Percent | 90 | 90 | 90 | 90 | 90 |
| C2 | Direct Costs | $128,700 | $96,390 | $72,910 | $59,633 | $49,245 |
| C3 | Newsletter ($3.20) | $3,200 | $2,240 | $1,590 | $1,226 | $957 |
| C4 | Database ($0.74) | $740 | $518 | $368 | $283 | $221 |
| C5 | Startup Costs | $3,000 | $0 | $0 | $0 | $0 |
| C6 | Total Costs | $135,640 | $99,148 | $74,868 | $61,142* | $50,423 |
| | **Profits** | | | | | |
| P1 | Gross Profit | $7,360 | $7,952 | $6,143 | $5,117 | $4,294 |
| P2 | Discount Rate | 1.00 | 1.20 | 1.44 | 1.73 | 2.07 |
| P3 | NPV Profit | $7,360 | $6,627 | $4,266 | $2,958 | $2,074 |
| P4 | Cumulative NPV Profit | $7,360 | $13,987 | $18,253 | $21,210 | $23,285 |
| L1 | **Customer lifetime value** | $7.36 | $13.99 | $18.25 | $21.21 | $23.28 |

to $23.28 instead of the $19.99 it was without the assumptions. If the club has one million members, that is an increase in profits of about $3 million. Would you risk your job on these assumptions?

## Accumulating the Names

Let's move on from Contadina and back to the general subject of a packaged goods database. By now, you should have done your homework and determined if your packaged goods database has a possible benefit. Next, you will need customer names, of course. Most packaged goods companies already have accumulated millions of names of which they are unaware. These names are located in fulfillment houses, telemarketing companies, and customer service computers. They result from sweepstakes, promotions, check redemptions, and on-pack rebate offers, to mention a few.

To get only the customer's name and address is, in most cases, of little value. For packaged goods, it is better to get this type of data:

- Name and address
- Date and type of offer (sweepstakes, rebate, phone call, etc.)
- Product acquired and size of product
- Value of the offer

- Media used plus response rate
- Answers to two vital questions: What brand of X do you usually buy? (Don't leave this open-ended: Let the customer check off one of the five or six most popular brands, with blank as the last choice.) How many boxes (or pounds, etc.) of this product does your family use in a month? Give them possible answers to check.

Why these questions? Because you want to distinguish if the customer is a regular user of your brand, a competitive brand, or a switcher, and if the customer is a heavy user of the product or a light user.

Once you know these things, you can plan your database strategy much more intelligently. You can design offers to heavy users of competing brands; you can design offers to switchers. The more you know about the recipient of your promotions, the better job you will do.

## Where Did the Name Come From?

The media is important. If the name comes from a sweepstakes, it may be almost worthless. Many sweepstakes entrants are gamblers, not serious product purchasers. Size is also vital: If a person bought a five-pound can, they are probably a more serious customer than a six-ounce trial size purchaser. People who sent in proof of purchase (showing that they bought the product) are often more serious than casual coupon users.

If the names available are skimpy, you might want to round out your database with the purchase of names from a company such as National Demographics and Lifestyles (NDL). NDL is the recipient of more than 100 different company ownership registration forms that include scores of lifestyle questions. Their database contains detailed information on more than 25 million households with such information as: marital status, sex, age, children, income, occupation, house type, hobbies, and interests.

The customer registration forms that come with products covered by NDL ask a number of common questions that provide valuable information about the customer. Figure 11-7 shows part of the form packed with a Norelco razor that is used to build the Norelco customer database.

## Cleaning and Enhancing the Names

Once the names are collected, you should have a service bureau put them together in a common format (retaining all the above information), and do a merge/purge to find and consolidate the duplicates. Duplicates, of course, are very valuable. They are your multibuyers—serious purchasers of your or your competitor's product.

**Figure 11-7: Sample Customer Registration Form**

Since many of the names will be old—two or three or more years old— the addresses in many cases will be obsolete. You should have a National Change of Address (NCOA) run on the file to correct these addresses. You may want to geocode the file (to determine the census block) and add cluster coding and demographics (see Chapter 6, Using Customer Profiles in Marketing Strategy). These additions will mean that you know a lot about the income, education, age, and lifestyle of these customers that you can use in your database marketing. Geocoding also can be helpful in determining trade locations. If you run a promotion with a tie-in to a specific chain of stores and the file is geocoded, you can match your marketing plan to the areas where the chain has sales or marketing territories. You also can match your names to media markets (radio, TV, or cable station areas).

Your database should be up and running at a service bureau that gives you hands-on access by means of a PC on your desk, linked to the database on a mainframe.

## Developing Profiles

Before you consider any serious marketing efforts, you should use the database to learn more about who is buying your products, and who is using the competition. A profile of heavy and light users of your product and your competitor's product can give you a lot of information before you begin to do any marketing.

Using modern software, you can, for example, compare heavy and light users of your product by the type of car they drive or the type of house that they live in, as shown in Figure 11-8.

**Figure 11-8: Heavy Users of Product by Type of Housing**

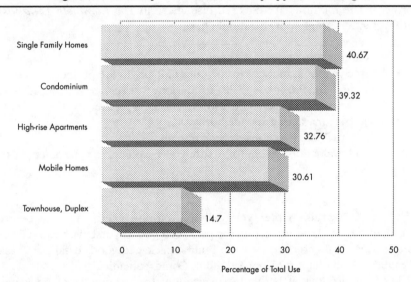

Single Family Homes — 40.67
Condominium — 39.32
High-rise Apartments — 32.76
Mobile Homes — 30.61
Townhouse, Duplex — 14.7

Percentage of Total Use

This shows that most people in the database are light users of the product; however, those who live in townhouses and duplex apartments are very light users compared to people in any other type of home. You should exclude townhouses and duplexes from any mailings intended to seek out heavy users.

This type of profiling can help to:

- Identify varying degrees of product and brand loyalty
- Identify the most profitable segment of your database
- Look at urban versus rural users
- See how the presence of children affects brand loyalty

This type of profiling can help to determine the target for your strategy. For example, if you want to distribute samples to competitive brand users, you should use your samples only on those who indicate that they are not loyal brand users of your product or a competitor's product.

You can do other profiling of this sort with the data that you have used to enhance your database. When you are sure that you understand your customers, you are ready to take the next step: testing some ideas for marketing strategy.

## Implementing the Strategy

With all the planning out of the way, you are ready to begin your database project. The methods are covered elsewhere in *The Complete Database Marketer.* As a minimum you should have:

- An external direct response agency
- A three-year commitment from your company to the project
- A Request for Proposals (RFP) for an external service bureau, leading to the selection of such a bureau as a business partner
- A database marketing service bureau
- An external telemarketing service bureau
- A good evaluation system to be sure you are attaining your objectives

## Recapitulation

If, after reading this chapter, you feel I am warning you to go slowly before rushing into database marketing for packaged goods, you have received the message. A really creative idea can build a packaged goods database. Stash Tea did it. Could Lipton? Kool Aid did it. Could Contadina?

My feeling is that it is tough to surmount the economics of packaged goods. The database, in almost all cases, will make only a modest incremental increase in sales. Will that modest increment be sufficient to provide enough benefits to the members of the database that they will want to be members of whatever affinity group you establish, and will develop a loyalty to your product and company? Will the modest increment be sufficient not only to pay the benefits to the customer, but also to pay all the expenses of the database?

The answer can be found in lifetime value analysis. Before you spend any money at all on a database, do your homework.

## Summary

1.  Database marketing for packaged goods is particularly difficult because margins and loyalty have been seriously eroded by the billions of coupons issued yearly. Many companies who have entered this field have failed to build a satisfactory long-term database system.

2.  Coupons in a newspaper cost $6 per thousand. Any type of direct mail costs a minimum of $300 per thousand. You have to prove that direct mail is better, or give up the project.

3.  User clubs have been successful, although most fail. The club must be self-supporting, or you should not start it. An affinity group (horse lovers, new parents, fishermen) can work, if the economics are there.

4.  A preferred customer group that uses returned proofs of purchase also can work if there is enough profit for the customer. Make sure that the customer will be satisfied. If so, then figure out how you can make money with it. Just having the names of your customers is worthless unless you have a profitable plan for using the names.

5.  Retailer co-op programs have worked in some cases. Find a retailer that will work with you. If the retailer has a frequent shopper program, and will let you use the data, you may have a perfect match—if your idea contains sound economics.

6.  A continuity program works for books and records and dog food. Why not try it for your product? It is worth trying now that supermarkets are so big that they are not worried about the competition from direct sales? Diapers, prescription medicine, coffee, videos?

7.  Referral programs can be very cheap to organize and very profitable. On-pack offers provide an almost costless transmission vehicle. By getting customers to nominate other customers, you let the customer do all the work. Be sure that the economics are there to support a profit for the suggester, and for you.

8.  In computing your revenue from packaged goods projects, figure in extra revenue sources including renting the customer names, magazine subscriptions and ads, catalog sales, and brand credit. There are lots of sources of profit that should be figured in to come up with customer lifetime value calculations.

## Executive Quiz 11

Answers to quiz questions can be found in Appendix B. The quizzes are for fun. Do them if you enjoy quizzes. Ignore them if you don't.
*Choose the best answer to complete each statement or question.*

1. Coupons can be placed in a news-paper for $6 per thousand. What is the minimum price for coupons delivered by targeted mail?
   a. $6
   b. $12
   c. $36
   d. $72
   e. $300

2. Which one of the following is not suggested as a possible successful packaged goods database strategy?
   a. continuity programs
   b. targeted coupons
   c. referral programs
   d. user club
   e. preferred customer program

3. Which one of the following was not suggested for a continuity program?
   a. swimming pool chemicals
   b. coffee
   c. light bulbs
   d. steaks
   e. medicines

4. How did Stash Tea build its database?
   a. direct response TV
   b. print ads
   c. direct mail
   d. on-pack offers
   e. in-store promotions

5. Which of the following was not sug-gested as a means of financing a packaged goods marketing database?
   a. ads in member magazine
   b. rental of database names
   c. direct product sales
   d. brand credit
   e. retailer co-op

6. In the Contadina example, why might the database not succeed?
   a. idea would not appeal to customers
   b. implementation too difficult
   c. margin on products not sufficient
   d. club would not increase sales of product
   e. referral system would not work

7. Names derived from a sweepstakes offer are normally
   a. less valuable than other names.
   b. no different from other names.
   c. more valuable than other names.
   d. harder to get than other names.
   e. None of the above

8. Why does the Norelco customer registration form ask about your children?
   a. to sell them a razor
   b. to market to the whole family
   c. to learn the demographics of its customer base
   d. form design error
   e. None of the above

# Business-to-Business Database Marketing

*There is no direct marketing program that promises more but delivers less than lead generation ... Most often, the direct marketing program isn't the problem. It's measuring the results. How do you get the sales force to give accurate feedback on the quality of the leads provided? ...*

*Most companies apply pressure on the salespeople to return lead information and chastise them when information isn't returned ... The more pressure that is put on the organization to return the lead information, the more likely the data will be inaccurate. The sales force might react to the pressure by taking all the leads and coding them as bad leads.*

*Lead management is frustrating and difficult. Many companies give up and send leads to the sales force without any attempt to measure the results. We have found that lead tracking is used in less than 50 percent of lead generation programs.*
*—Bernie Goldberg, Direct Marketing Publishers*

*When the Federal Express courier enters my office, she should see $180,000 stamped on the forehead of our receptionist. My little 25-person firm runs about a $1,500 a month Fed Ex bill. Over 10 years, that will add up to $180,000.*
*—Tom Peters, author and management consultant*

This chapter is loaded with information about business-to-business database marketing strategy. To keeping you from getting lost, here is a road map for what you will find inside:

- Lead generation theory
- Lead qualification through telemarketing
- Dealer development and training

Omitted from this chapter is any extensive treatment of the methods of maintaining customer loyalty in a business-to-business situation. Leaving it out does not mean that it is not important. It is. It is the most important part of database marketing. I assume that business-to-business marketers, if they have read the other chapters in this book, will have gained an appreciation of how to go about this vital task. This chapter focuses on lead generation and qualification simply because the subject does not come up in the same way in most consumer marketing, and therefore, it needs separate attention here.

## Lead Generation Theory

Most marketing database literature is devoted to consumer databases, and treats business databases as an afterthought. There are good reasons for this: from the standpoint of the service bureau or the creative agency, there is more money in a consumer database because it is much larger.

On the other hand, a business-to-business database has one redeeming feature for anyone working with it: it usually covers big-ticket or high-volume items that provide the margin necessary to do a first-class job building relationships, loyalty, and repeat sales. In this chapter, we will explore the strategy for using a database in business-to-business marketing.

In most cases, your database will help you achieve two overall goals:

- To build customer loyalty and repeat business by getting existing customers to buy more, to buy new products, and to upgrade and trade in their existing products
- To serve as a lead generation and lead tracking system by finding new prospects that match the profiles of the most profitable customers, marketing to them, and qualifying them before handing them over to a sales representative

Several units usually stand between the marketing staff and the ultimate business customer. These units include the sales representatives, agents, or dealers who have the real contact with the customers. These people are seldom willing to give up the names of their customers for fear that the customer will be "stolen" from them. It is a perfectly reasonable fear.

Travel agents, for example, don't like to give airlines and hotels addresses of their customers—even though they have to provide the names.

You may think that getting customer names is not that much of a problem—just consult your billing department. You are in for a shock. The billing department's names consist of a bunch of accounts payable clerks in your customers' companies. The shipping department is of no help either;

it has the addresses of the loading docks. Neither of these groups have the decision makers' names: the people who actually place orders for your products. To get this information, you have to deal with the sales force.

Before you begin to develop a business-to-business marketing strategy, therefore, you have to come to grips with the question: How are you going to handle your sales force? Let's begin with this.

## What Does the Sales Rep Need?

Marketing and salespeople seldom get along. There are good reasons for this. They are fundamentally different types of people.

Sales reps are people types. They hate computers, lead tracking systems, and reports. They know how to drink with the client, how to ask for the order, and how to close. Sales reps are what keep any company afloat.

Marketers are above all that. They like computers, statistics, and reports. They have probably never asked for an order and would be embarrassed to have to do it. They see business as a middle-class game, with customers as data that can be manipulated to achieve a desired result.

The database, perhaps for the first time, will bring these two dissimilar types together on a common project.

As the marketer, the designer of the project, it is important for you to be sure that sales is comfortable with the system you set up. If they fight it, they will win, and your whole database project will be a big waste of time.

Sales reps and dealers—whether independent or on your company payroll—can be pretty independent guys. They distrust any central marketing program that they think will rope them into a computer-based system. If you don't find a way to cooperate with them, they will refuse to turn their names over to you, they will ignore your leads, and they will refuse to tell you what happened to any leads you have generated for them.

They will be especially concerned that your database will somehow deprive them of commissions—particularly by servicing existing customers directly and not through the sales force.

### How to Get Sales Help in Planning

Before you start creating a database, work out in your mind, and in direct discussions with representatives of your sales force, just how the database will fit in with their sales program. Some suggestions:

- Try to include your sales reps or dealers in the planning phase—to get their ideas and participation from the beginning.
- Figure out, and put in writing, a policy on what happens to commis-

sions once the database program is underway.
- If the database includes telemarketing, get the sales force to help in the training of the telemarketers. In some cases, having the telemarketers working directly out of the regional sales office is a good plan.
- Make sure that leads generated are *qualified* before they are routed to a sales rep. Nothing is more discouraging for all concerned than to have the sales force flooded with so many unqualified leads that the really good ones get buried and lost.

## Prospect Classifications

There are four classifications of businesses that you might have to deal with: suspects, prospects, leads, and customers. A suspect is a name on a list. A prospect is a suspect who you believe may be interested in your services for some reason. A lead is a prospect who has volunteered a real interest in your product or service. Leads, however, are not necessarily qualified. Many so-called leads are just brochure collectors, not real leads. Sales reps know this; marketers often do not. Figure 12-1 shows the universe of suspects, prospects, leads, and customers.

### Figure 12-1: Prospect Classifications

The world in general

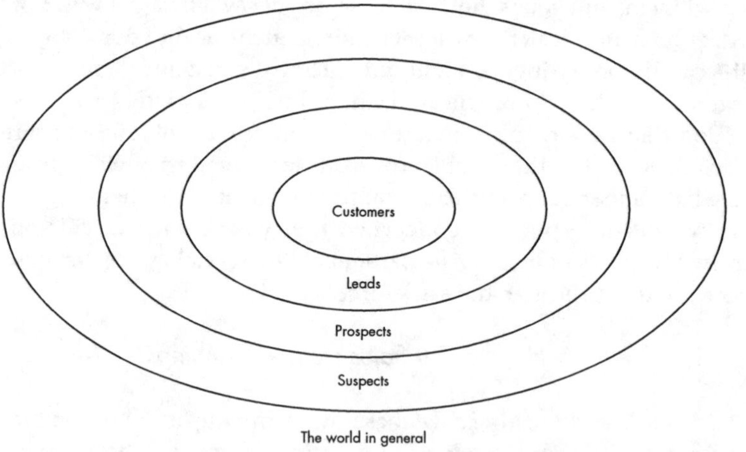

Set up a foolproof system for feedback from dealers and sales reps on what happens to leads. It must be simple. If it is going to work, it must involve an incentive system with significant rewards for participation. People do what is in their economic best interest. Sales reps are not only no exception to the rule, they *wrote* the rule. To get sales reps to do anything, you have to reward them in terms that they can understand.

To design the rewards, you must figure out: What is feedback on the status of leads worth to the company? The answer to that comes from the answer to a more important question: What are leads worth?

## The Value of a Lead

Calculation of the value of leads depends on the percentage of leads that result in a sale. This percentage in turn depends on two factors: the quality of the lead and the aggressiveness with which the lead is investigated. The best lead in the world is of no value at all if the sales rep handling it drops the ball. On the other hand, most leads generated from business cards dropped in a basket at a trade show are usually not worth the time it takes to enter them into a computer. This may be true of leads generated in a hundred other ways.

Many marketers fool themselves into thinking that most of the leads they produce in their marketing programs are worth pursuing. That is because marketers usually don't have the job of doing the follow up, and do not rely on commissions from these leads for their livelihood. If they did, their attitude would be entirely different.

### Money, Authority, Need, and Desire

How can you tell the difference between a valuable lead and a worthless one? There are a great many ways, none of which are universally valid. In general, leads can be distinguished from prospects by four factors, according to Bernie Goldberg, one of the most thoughtful experts on this subject and co-author of *Business to Business Direct Marketing*.

According to Goldberg, a lead is someone who has money, authority, a need for your product, and a desire to purchase it. It is the marketer's job to ascertain these things before the lead is sent off to a sales rep. Without marketing help, a sales rep will spend 90 percent of his or her time on non-sales activities before actually closing the sale. These activities include:

- Prospect identification
- Prospect qualification
- Marketing to the prospect
- Receiving a response
- Qualifying the respondent as to money, authority, need, and desire

If marketing is doing its job, it can take over these first five jobs almost entirely, and can hand over to sales a lead that meets Goldberg's description. Figure 12-2 illustrates this process:

### Figure 12-2: Qualification of Leads

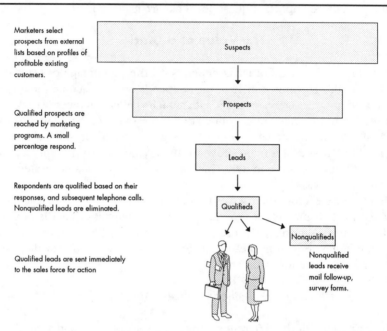

Marketers select prospects from external lists based on profiles of profitable existing customers.

Qualified prospects are reached by marketing programs. A small percentage respond.

Respondents are qualified based on their responses, and subsequent telephone calls. Nonqualified leads are eliminated.

Qualified leads are sent immediately to the sales force for action

Nonqualified leads receive mail follow-up, survey forms.

Business-to-business database marketing has to come to grips with the capacity of the sales force at any given time. Whether sales reps or telephone sales personnel are used, there is a limit to what any one person can do during a day. The marketing program generating leads must be careful not to generate more leads than sales can handle.

## Lead Value Calculation

Let's look at what a lead is worth using this simple method.

First, determine lifetime customer value. For an illustration, let's look at a typical business situation. A manufacturer, Surgical Products, Inc. (SPI), sells supplies and equipment to hospitals, clinics, and HMO groups. It has 20,000 customers and annual sales of $240 million. SPI uses a sales force to visit the bigger customers and a tele-sales unit to handle the supply orders and the smaller customers. SPI has just built its first customer database and is using it for the first time to compute customer lifetime value. This is shown in Table 12-1.

**Table 12-1: Customer Lifetime Value with Database**

| Revenue | Year1 | Year2 | Year3 | Year4 | Year5 |
|---|---|---|---|---|---|
| R1 Customers | 1,000 | 600 | 360 | 234 | 152 |
| R2 Retention Rate | 60 | 60 | 65 | 65 | 70 |
| R3 Average Yearly Sale | $12,000 | $12,500 | $13,000 | $13,500 | $14,000 |
| R4 Total Revenue | $12,000,000 | $7,500,000 | $4,680,000 | $3,159,000 | $2,128,000 |
| **Costs** | | | | | |
| C1 Cost Percent | 80 | 80 | 80 | 80 | 80 |
| C2 Direct Cost | $9,600,000 | $6,000,000 | $3,744,000 | $2,527,200 | $1,702,400 |
| C3 Commission | $1,200,000 | $750,000 | $468,000 | $315,900 | $212,800 |
| C4 Total Costs | $10,800,000 | $6,750,000 | $4,212,000 | $2,843,100 | $1,915,200 |
| **Profits** | | | | | |
| P1 Gross Profit | $1,200,000 | $750,000 | $468,000 | $315,900 | $212,800 |
| P2 Elapsed Time | 0.5 | 1.5 | 2.5 | 3.5 | 4.5 |
| P3 Interest Rate | 8 | 9 | 10 | 10 | 10 |
| P4 Risk Factor | 1.2 | 1.5 | 2 | 2.5 | 3 |
| P5 Discount Rate | 1.05 | 1.21 | 1.58 | 2.18 | 3.26 |
| P6 NPV Profit | $1,146,241 | $620,251 | $296,683 | $144,665 | $65,347 |
| P7 Total Lifetime Value | $1,146,241 | $1,766,492 | $2,063,175 | $2,207,840 | $2,273,188 |
| L1 **Lifetime Value (NPV)** | $1,146.24 | $1,766.49 | $2,063.18 | $2,207.84 | $2,273.19 |

This chart, unlike the others in this book, has a considerably more complex determination of the discount rate. The elapsed time (Line P2) is varied because of the assumption made by the company that they must wait an average of six months for the payments for their products to materialize, due to the complexities of the healthcare system. They have assumed some changes in the interest rates (Line P3) looking ahead for five years. The risk factor (Line P4), in addition, is considerably modified. Instead of a flat doubling of the interest rate, it assumes a gradually increasing risk factor as sales are projected into the future. The resulting discount rate becomes much more sophisticated. I should point out that it is also possible to use the discount rate to apply separately to the revenue and to the costs, rather than just applying it to the profit. In a particular situation, that degree of detail might be important, particularly in business-to-business transactions. Whether your situation requires this detail is entirely up to you. You can, of course, use the same system in consumer databases. For assistance in this area, see the Technical Assistance section in Appendix A.

The assumptions made here are:

- The average customer spends $12,000 per year, with annual increases of $500 for those who stay as customers. This can be derived by dividing total sales by total customers.
- The retention rate is 60 percent, increasing with loyal customers. This can be determined by choosing 1,000 customers from several years back, and seeing how many were left one, two, and three years later.
- The direct cost percent is 80 percent and the average sales commission is 10 percent.

The resulting lifetime value of a customer after five years is $2,273. This is the start of our analysis.

Now, let's look at the lead conversion rate. From your experience, determine how many leads result in conversion to paying customers. Suppose that of the *qualified* leads furnished to your sales force (leads with money, authority, need, and desire), your sales force manages to convert one of 10 into a paying customer. This means that the value of each lead is $227 ($2,273 ÷ 10).

If this is the value of a lead, then it gives you an idea of the maximum amount that you can spend through marketing efforts to acquire that lead.

Let's use this information on the value of a customer to evaluate a promotion program designed to bring in more customers. The details are shown in Table 12-2.

### Table 12-2: Results of Prospecting Program

|  | Item Quantity | Unit Dollars | Total Dollars |
|---|---|---|---|
| Prospect Mailing | 40,000 | $1.00 | $40,000 |
| Responses | 1,200 | $0.50 | $600 |
| Telesales | 1,200 | $11.00 | $13,200 |
| Sales Visits | 120 | $220.00 | $26,400 |
| Total Costs | $80,200 | | |
| | | | |
| Cost of Customers Signed Up | 48 | $1,670.83 | $80,200 |
| Lifetime Value of Customers Signed Up | 48 | $2,886.00 | $138,528 |
| | | | |
| Long Term Profit from Promotion | 48 | $1,215.17 | $58,328 |
| Return on Investment | 172% | | |

This is the type of analysis that you can and must do to justify your business-to-business database marketing to prospects. It will solidify your budget proposal and assure funding for your program.

Figure 12-3 shows the final steps of the lead conversion process.

These figures are also very useful when you are talking to the head of your sales department about the disposition of your leads. If these figures are accurate, it means that every time you discard a qualified lead without investigating it, you are throwing away $227, of which $45 has already been spent, and the rest is anticipated profits.

## Getting Sales Reps to Report on the Status of Leads

As we have said, people respond to what is in their economic best interest. If you want sales reps to report on the status of leads, make it worth their while. If you do, they will do it. If you don't, they won't. It is that simple.

### Figure 12-3: Lead Conversion

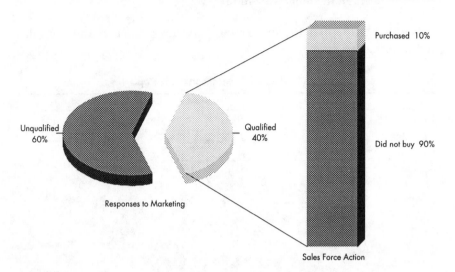

Purchased 10%

Unqualified
60%

Qualified
40%

Did not buy 90%

Responses to Marketing

Sales Force Action

In the case of lead processing, you now know what a lead is worth. If you want sales reps to process them and report to you on the status of processing, you will have to find a way to transfer some of that lead value into the sales rep's wallet. The figures we have just developed can provide you with a justification for giving the sales reps $5 or more just for reporting on the status of each lead. "Money wasted," you say? Not at all. If you don't determine the status of leads, you are just fooling around with lead generation. You are not a professional database marketer.

Every day, companies come up with methods for getting sales reps to do what they want. Only a few of them actually work. Those that do are more likely to be based on economics than chastisement (the most common system). Some of the ones that do work include something like this:

Simple system: Provide a simple system for returning information on the status of each lead provided—such as a peel-off copy of the lead card, self-addressed for internal office (or post office) routing and postage paid.

Incentive reward: Announce that each lead card copy returned earns a reward, either $X in cash or an entry into a sweepstakes with a significant prize (such as cash) awarded every quarter.

In this system, sales reps who have received a lead must provide at least two different responses:

1. An acknowledgment that the sales rep has received the lead—sent in as soon as the lead is received

2. Final disposition of the lead (either a sale or determination that no sale will occur in the immediate future)

Figure 12-4 depicts the interaction between marketers and the sales force during this process:

**Figure 12-4: Lead Assignment and Reporting**

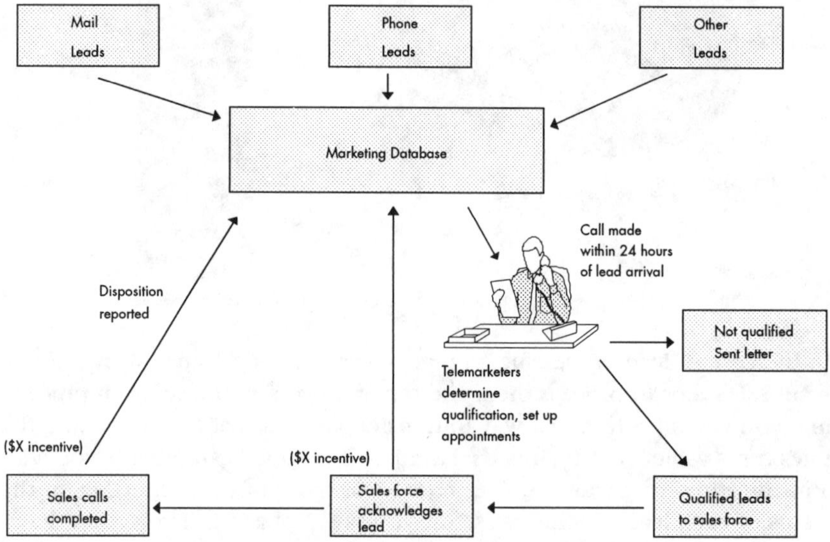

Each communication with the central database must be simple and rewarded. Any failures to make a sale must be accompanied by a survey completed by the sales rep. After all, if one lead in 10 is converted, you must find out what was wrong with the other nine. Your money, authority, need, and desire lead qualification system cannot be doing its job. Each unconverted lead costs you $45. If your survey discloses defects in your qualification efforts that can be corrected, the survey is worth real money.

Suppose by changing the telemarketing scripts, sales reps can get better leads and can convert one in nine, instead of one in 10. What is that worth? This is a savings to you of $45 from every 10 leads furnished to sales reps. In a year, the survey form alone could be worth several thousand dollars.

All the above suggests that to be successful in developing a business-to-business strategy, you have to look at your database system from the sales rep's point of view. You have to say, "I am a sales rep looking at this new system. What's in it for me?" If you can't come up with a logical, winning answer, rethink your whole program before you go further.

## What Does the Customer Want?

After working out the sales rep's role in your database, you next have to put yourself in the shoes of your customers. Let's say you are selling computers. As a customer, what kind of a relationship do I want with you—my computer supplier?

As a customer, I would like to know that, if something goes wrong, there is someone I can call, someone who remembers what I bought and will tell me how to get it fixed: where to take it, how long it will take, and how much it will cost. Ideally, it should be someone who can say, "Hey, you're in luck! You still have two and half months left on the factory warranty, so any parts are free! We will pick it up tomorrow, and have it back to you in four business days."

As a customer, I would love to know about upgrades to the software I buy. I would like to know about the tape backup attachment that just came on the market. I would like to know that I could trade in my present model for a more powerful one.

To learn about the customer's desires, have several brainstorming sessions with sales reps and focus groups with actual customers, and find out what they would like to have.

The road to customer loyalty is a two-way street. It starts with offering customers the things that they want. It ends with getting the things that you want. But the customer comes first.

## The Value of Inquiries

How important are inquiries about your products? It depends on the source of the inquiry and the nature of your business. In general, inquiries resulting from magazine reader response cards have a very low probability of producing sales. Surveys made several months after a business-to-business inquiry show that more than a quarter of those people inquiring have actually bought the product in question from someone. One reason why these buyers did not choose what they inquired about could be the lack of sales follow-up. A national survey showed that only 12 percent of leads received by a sample of all companies were followed up by the sales force.

If prospects have responded to your ad, you have one try to get their business. This try should not be wasted, and thus should have these features:

- Your response must be immediate—within 24 hours of receipt. If you organize your marketing program properly, you should be able to get even low-priority inquiry responses out that fast. If someone complains that 24-hour turnaround is too expensive, determine the value of each inquiry (based on conversion rate to leads). This value will quickly tell you how much you can spend on inquiry follow-up. Let's say that of 1,000 inquiries, 50 become leads. These 50 leads are worth $11,350 ($227 times 50). Each inquiry, therefore, is worth $11.35. Learn the value of each piece of information you work with. It will teach you to respect the information and treat it appropriately.

• Your response must be cost-effective—fax, letter, overnight, telephone response, or personal visit—depending on the situation. Now that you know the cash value of an inquiry, you can decide the most cost-effective way to follow up. It is a good idea to develop an algorithm for classifying the value of different types of inquiries, so that you don't waste resources (telephone calls or overnight letters) on unlikely ones, but you do put whatever it takes into responding to potentially profitable ones. The database needs software that automatically classifies inquiries into cold, warm, or hot, and produces a cost-effective response.

• Your response creates a continuing dialogue. It makes it easy for the prospect to answer, because it has the prospect's name, address, and company printed on the response device, it is easy to fill out, and the postage is paid.

• Your response serves to qualify the lead. The more information you can get at an early stage, the better you can deal with the inquiry.

### How to Qualify Leads

As already noted, if a business-to-business lead tracking system is going to work, leads have to be qualified as to money, authority, need, and desire. How can you do that? One method is to ask them, in the form of a reply card, a toll-free number response, or an outgoing call.

How do you make this process happen quickly enough? Ideally, the qualifying data should go directly into your database, entered by the tele-sales operators or data entry clerks opening your mail. The database should have software that immediately determines the qualifications of this customer, and routes the hot leads directly to outgoing telesales for final qualification before being routed to the correct sales rep for action.

### The Value of Advance Telemarketing

The face of sales is changing under the impact of database marketing. The old idea of turning sales reps loose with a territory is shifting to an eight-step process:

1. Building a customer database
2. Determining the profile of the profitable customer
3. Finding prospects that match the profile of the profitable customer
4. Sending direct mail to the selected prospects
5. Telemarketing to respondents (or all prospects, depending on the size of the project and the cost of the product)
6. Determining the "hot leads" based on the phone calls
7. Making appointments with the hot leads
8. Sending sales reps to the appointments

Following are three examples of the way advance telemarketing can make the sales force more effective, provided by Susan Hancock of Hancock Information Services.

### Example 1: Mainframe Software

A software company sold mainframe software for purchasing and materials management automation. The software cost about $60,000. The company had been prospecting by direct mail, followed up by a sales visit. Before it began telemarketing, the cost per lead using direct mail was about $150.

As a test, Susan Hancock's telemarketers tried calls to likely prospects on the direct mail list. After 133 hours of calls, they completed 617 "research survey" interviews, averaging 4.5 interviews per hour. The total cost of the calling was $6,650.

The results: 19 percent of the survey calls were considered hot leads—a total of 117 leads. The cost per lead was $57, or about one-third the cost of direct mail prospecting.

### Example 2: $2 Million High Tech Equipment

A high-tech equipment company had a very narrow and finite market for its $2 million plus product with only 200 prime prospects in the entire United States. How could the company reach these prospects?

The problem was that the ideal recommenders were highly technical engineers buried in the bowels of the prospect companies. Calling the top executives would not do the trick.

Susan Hancock's staff called up to 17 levels deep in each of the 200 organizations, spending about $200,000 in all. The results: The leads they uncovered resulted in 23 sales amounting to $46 million dollars. A good ratio for the $200,000 investment.

## Example 3: $200,000 Accounting Software

An accounting software system cost $200,000. The target market for such a product was top finance executives. To sell the product, an elaborate campaign was developed including advertising and four targeted direct mail pieces of 15,000 each offering a free software evaluation package.

The response rate to the offer varied between 3 and 6 percent, depending on the list used.

The 600 responders were called by a special high-tech telemarketing group under Susan Hancock's direction. Their objective was to qualify the leads after they had received the evaluation package.

The result of the telephone calls was a 34 percent ratio of hot leads. Eleven sales reps followed up on these hot leads and were able to convert 10 of them into sales, for a total incremental revenue of $2 million.

The total cost of the program, including creative, evaluation packet, advertising, direct mail, telemarketing, and internal support was $250,000.

## Dealer Development and Training

Most marketers must do their customer contact thirdhand, working through a retailer, a wholesaler, a dealer, or an independent agent in addition to a sales rep. That does not mean that you cannot have a customer database. You can, and you should (if the lifetime value supports it). But there is something extra that you can do to improve your customer contact, and that is to train your dealers. These people, after all, are your front-line troops. If you are going to build a relationship with your customers that inspires loyalty to your products and your company, you simply must have good loyal people out there representing you. Many companies do not realize that they can play an active role in training their front-line troops, rather than hunkering down and expecting the worst.

Jeffrey Geibel, managing partner of Geibel Marketing Consulting in Belmont, Massachusetts, is one of the real experts in dealer development and training. Good dealers are usually hard to come by, he points out. Most companies recruit dealers, hope for the best, and drop the worst. Some companies use the 10 out of 100 approach—recruiting 100 dealers and getting rid of 90 to get the 10 best ones.

There is a better way. Instead of assuming that dealer quality is fixed, it is possible to train the dealer to do what you want. By means of careful selection, it is possible to keep up to 90 percent of your dealers, by devoting the resources to training the ones you recruit. The steps are these:

Treat the dealer as a partner. Instead of seeing dealers as contractors who carry on a series of small transactions, make it a long-term partnership. A partnership creates an environment in which both parties are committed to the success of the relationship. Of course a partnership won't work if both parties are trying to maximize profit opportunities on each transaction. Both must take a long-term view.

Agree on mutual rights and obligations. The margin should be agreed on, plus your obligation to provide state-of-the-art products, technical support, and an aggressive marketing and lead generation program (not skimming the good leads for your "inside sales").

Develop a profile of the ideal dealer. Study the dealers you now have who are the most successful. Determine their areas of specialization, staffing depth and quality, overall experience, and revenue levels. If your product and services make up less than 30 percent of dealers' revenue, you probably can't expect them to become serious partners.

Locate dealers who match this profile. Design a letter of introduction with a response device. Your response rate will be less than 2 percent, even from a good list.

Qualify the responses received with a long telephone call. Ask your prospective dealers why they're interested in you, why they think they'd be a good dealer, and questions from your ideal dealer profile. If the answers are not good enough, stop there. This is a qualification step to develop a partnership. If they don't seem like a partner, don't waste your (and their) time.

Have them fill out a formal application form. This step is very important. Ask them how many people they will devote to your product and how much time these people can give to training and support. Also ask them to provide a detailed business plan explaining how they will develop the market. Generally, no plan means no results. The application form is actually a marketing document for you. In it, you have to sell your company and your products. If you request financial information, you must supply similar information to your partner as well. In many cases, up to half of the resellers in the software industry, for example, are technically insolvent at any point in time. Find this out early before you become burned with worthless accounts receivable.

Develop a few strategic dealers. A strategic dealer is one who can support a large market area in a key location. These dealers must possess the potential to eventually realize a significant percentage—up to half—of their revenue from your products and services. Concentrate on these strategic dealers before worrying about others.

Begin a dealer skills training program. This is a formal process with definite stages, designed to bring dealers and their staffs up to a defined skill level before they can move on to the next higher stage. Examples of these stages are:

1. Basic training and product familiarity. Goal: The dealer must be able to give a competent demo and master troubleshooting skills.
2. Joint sales calls with your current sales staff. During these calls, dealers could function as demo assistants, receiving comprehensive post-call debriefings from your sales staff. Goal: The dealer must make a positive contribution to a sales call.
3. Sales calls with roles swapped. The dealer takes the lead, with your sales staff becoming assistants. In some cases, the dealer may make mistakes and even lose the sale. The sales staff must give the dealer an opportunity to learn by doing. Make sure that the dealer knows how to close. Goal: The dealer must achieve satisfactory close rates.
4. Weekly telephone briefings. These involve discussions of sales problems and issues covering each sales call, pre and post. Goal: The dealer must meet or get close to pre-agreed sales targets.

### Sales Staff Responsibilities

To do all this, you must have a first-class sales staff that can function as trainers, not just as sales reps. Have a trainer follow a dealer through each step so that the trainer develops a sense of community with the dealer.

Professional dealer development programs are a signal of your commitment to establishing a productive partnership relationship.

## Summary

1.  One of the best summaries of business-to-business database marketing philosophy is provided by Hunter Business Direct. They say that to do successful business-to-business direct marketing:

    • You market to individuals, not corporations
    • You address unique sets of needs
    • All contacts must be of value to the customer or prospect
    • The best technology is transparent
    • A strategic relationship with the client is essential
    • Planning is critical
    • Testing is mandatory
    • Integrated direct marketing is a continuous improvement process, capable of implementing business strategy

2.  There are two overall goals for business-to-business marketing databases: to build customer loyalty and repeat business, and to serve as a lead generation and lead tracking system.

3.  Sales reps, agents, and dealers will often resent the database and refuse to cooperate with it. You must win them over, or your database will fail.

4.  The first step in business-to-business database strategy is to figure out how to deal with your own sales force members. You should include them in the planning phase to get their participation; get a written policy of the relationship between the database and sales force commissions; make sure leads are qualified before they are routed to sales reps; and set up a foolproof system for lead tracking.

5.  To get sales force participation you have to make it worthwhile to process leads. To determine how to compensate the sales reps, you have to figure out what a lead is worth to you.

6.  Lead value is based on long-term customer value plus the aggressiveness with which leads are pursued. To be valuable a lead must be qualified in terms of money, authority, need, and desire for the product. Marketers must qualify leads in these terms before they are sent to a sales rep.

7.  The number of leads that marketing supplies has to be geared to the ability of the sales force to process them. It is wasteful to supply leads faster than they can be acted upon for two reasons: the wasted promotional money and the poor reputation generated in the minds of possible leads that do not get contacted.

8.  Leads should be valued based on long-term customer value rather than number of customers converted: the value of a customer can vary depending upon the way in which that customer was acquired.

9.  To get sales reps to report on the status of leads, you must provide them with incentives to do so. The technique is to make the reporting system simple and to provide them with a valuable premium. The value of the premium has as its upper bound the value of the lead and as its lower bound what it takes to get sales reps to act.

10. The database should be designed to serve the sales reps, the customers, and customer service. To get customers to give you data, you can use surveys, with suitable incentives. For the sales reps, you use the database to remind them of customers that they should call on, upgrade dates, etc.

## Executive Quiz 12

Answers to quiz questions can be found in Appendix B. The quizzes are for fun. Do them if you enjoy quizzes. Ignore them if you don't.

*Choose the best answer to complete each statement or question.*

1. The chief obstacle to building a business customer marketing database is usually
   a. finding a service bureau.
   b. getting customer names.
   c. working with MIS.
   d. finding a direct agency.
   e. enhancing the data.

2. Which of the following must be qualified before being given to a sales rep?
   a. prospect
   b. lead
   c. suspect
   d. customer
   e. None of the above

3. The value of a lead depends on
   a. lifetime customer value.
   b. sales force aggressiveness.
   c. quality of the lead.
   d. money, authority, need, and desire.
   e. All of the above

4. Marketing should not be responsible for
   a. prospect qualification.
   b. prospect identification.
   c. customer profiling.
   d. making the sale.
   e. selection of prospect names.

5. Your mailing cost is $1 per piece. Response rate is 5 percent and costs $3 each. Qualification rate is 20 percent. Telemarketing costs $12 per call. What does each qualified lead cost you?
   a. $35
   b. $75
   c. $100

   d. $175
   e. $225

6. The customer lifetime value is $3,600. The qualified lead conversion rate is 20 percent. What is each qualified lead worth?
   a. $72
   b. $180
   c. $360
   d. $720
   e. $1,200

7. What is the best method for finding out what sales reps do with leads?
   a. Make it company policy to report promptly.
   b. Design a simple reporting system.
   c. Pay sales reps for reporting.
   d. Use a database system.
   e. None of the above

8. If the lifetime customer value is $4,800, the lead conversion rate is 25 percent, and the inquiry to lead conversion rate is 2 percent, what is an inquiry worth?
   a. $12
   b. $24
   c. $120
   d. $240
   e. $1,200

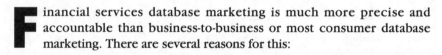

# 13

# Financial Services Database Marketing

*In many organizations, the marketing, sales, and service organizations have evolved their own separate ways. While there is an undeniable commonality of purpose among these three functions, it is often the case that they do not share a unified information strategy ... It is customer information that suffers the most in this environment. Customer data is probably the organization's most widely shared data, yet are treated by each department and each system as if it were the sole owner. As a result, companies have created "islands" of customer information that are split across systems, media, business units, and branch offices. Information about the same customer ends up being replicated, duplicated, and corrupted ...*

*What is needed is a business partnership that focuses the organization on the customer, and on the integration and sharing of information resources across functional areas. Together, the result is a better equipped and happier frontline that can dedicate more of its efforts to attracting new business and increasing the lifetime value of its customers.*

*—Darrell H. Burns, president, Frontline Systems, Inc.*

**F**inancial services database marketing is much more precise and accountable than business-to-business or most consumer database marketing. There are several reasons for this:

- More data: A bank, insurance company, or brokerage house has more hard information on its customers than most other types of businesses.
- Relevant data: The demographic variables that are easily obtained from prospect files (age, home value, presence of children, income, automobile) are often *more relevant* to purchasing behavior for financial services than they are for most other types of products and services.
- Identification: Letters from banks or brokerage houses have a greater

265

chance of being opened and read than letters from most other commercial enterprises.

As a result, most financial services, including banks, brokerage houses, and insurance companies began database marketing long before it was fashionable in other industries.

## Construction of the Customer Information File

In banking, the first step is the construction of a Customer Information File (CIF). While the system differs with each bank, in general the CIF idea is to set up a single database that has information on all the bank products available to customers: checking and savings accounts, money market funds, certificates of deposit (CDs), mortgages, home equity loans, auto loans, personal loans, credit cards, etc. There are lots of uses for a CIF, but one of the most important is to cross sell, meaning to find people who have a large checking account, but no money market, CD, or savings account; people with a mortgage, but no home equity loan, etc.

Figure 13-1 shows the process involved in the construction of the CIF.

### Figure 13-1: Creation of the CIF Database

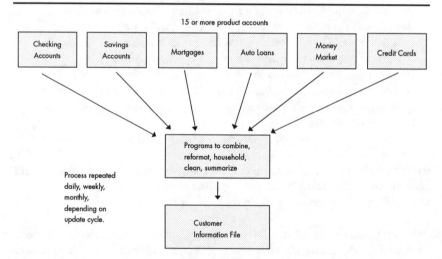

The biggest stumbling block to financial services database marketing, however, is this construction of the CIF. Why is it so difficult? Because most banks, for historical reasons, keep their individual product accounts on different computers using different software. The whole philosophy is based on the product: keeping track of every account and having it balance to the penny at all times. Checking accounts are seldom stored on the same software that keeps automobile loans or home equity loans. Building the CIF requires that the central focus of the data be the customer, not the product or the account. It requires not only putting all this information together using the customer as the focus, but maintaining and updating it month after month using inputs from a large number of different sources.

Some of the difficulties are these:

- Householding: Ideally, the bank wants to group all accounts in a family together. There are some keys to make that easier: social security number and telephone number, in addition to the street address. But the accounts (both single and joint) remain separate and independent and often difficult to group properly.
- Platform: Should the CIF be built on the bank's mainframe, or somewhere else? The bank's management information systems (MIS) department often argues for keeping it in-house because of data security reasons, or (really) because the department doesn't like to lose business. On the other hand, if the CIF is built in-house, it may take years of development time since it is always of lower priority than the urgent business of getting out the monthly statements. Some banks have spent more than five years trying to build a CIF without ever producing a usable product.

Northwestern University Professor Don Schultz pointed out:

*There'll be a conflict in most cases between the MIS department and the marketing people. MIS people want to create the database of all databases. Marketing people want information quick and dirty, and they don't care how you get it.*

*Some companies are adding a position to run interference between the computer and marketing departments and to act as a translator for both. But it really should be the marketing people who oversee the database because they are responsible for customer response, sales, and customer service.*

- Different inputs: Different software systems, often under different bank executives, are often so hard to combine that banks just give up.

On the other hand, competition from banks that have successfully built functioning CIFs is pressing on those who have not done it yet. The 1990s is certainly the decade of the customer where banks are concerned.

## A Bank that Succeeded

Darrell Burns, president of Frontline Systems, Inc. in Pittsburgh, has a lot of solid experience with bank database marketing. Darrell's company has worked with a number of banks to help them improve their management of customer information and their marketing to customers. He spent 14 months at each of two different banks helping them build large integrated database systems that involved thousands of bank employees. Darrell explained how this was accomplished:

*One of the banks had more than 300 branches in a single state. Half of the many thousands of bank employees were located in three departments that accounted for most of the customer contacts: Account Managers, Customer Service Administrators, and Marketing.*

*There were several core applications that kept the books on deposit accounts, loans, and other products. These were run separately using different software systems, with some on different computers. They had all been engineered to cooperate, however, with a central real-time operational customer information file (CIF).*

- CIF System: When Darrell's group began working with the bank, the operational CIF had been in use for two years, resident on an IBM mainframe using DB2 software. The CIF contained the common customer-related data (e.g., name, address, social security number, etc.) shared by the customer's checking, savings, loan, and other accounts. All day, bank officers could access this file using PCs on their desks linked to the mainframe. This system kept track only of customers, not prospects, and provided direct access to data on their active accounts. Besides this file, there were two other customer-based databases in active use: branch-level call tracking files and a central marketing file. The other two systems had no direct connection to the CIF system.
- Branch-level call tracking: Each branch maintained a separate PC system on a local area network (LAN). Using this system, branch personnel kept track of sales activity with both customers and prospects. The data, however, were entirely independent from the CIF, consisting mainly of names, addresses, and notes such as "Call Webster in January re: expansion loan."
- Central marketing summary: This PC database also operated on a LAN. It took data from the CIF that had been compiled at the customer level for each branch and downloaded it once a month. The data summa-

rized the customer's monthly balances, profitability, and percentage change from last year by product group.

Figure 13-2 illustrates the relationship between these multiple bank customer systems.

### Figure 13-2: Multiple Bank Database System

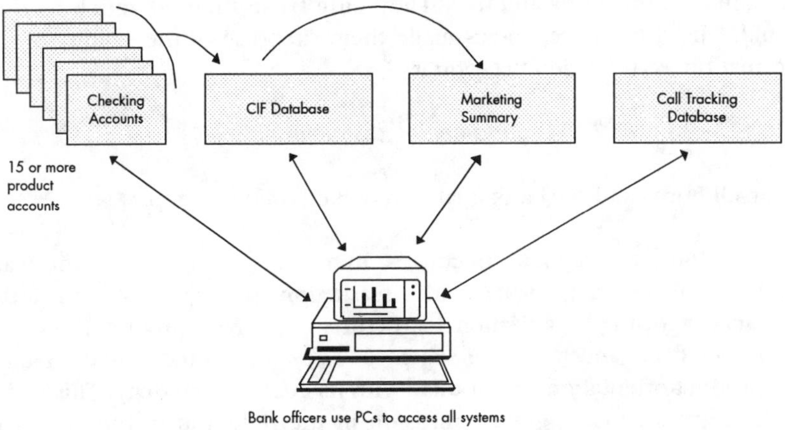

Bank officers use PCs to access all systems

## Problems

These three systems provided lots of customer and prospect data to help the account managers and service reps understand their customers. Unfortunately, the employees were not at all happy with the arrangement. What were the problems?

- Redundant and inconsistent data across systems: The customer on the CIF customer profile screen is named Doe John M, while the customer on the prospect screen of the call tracking system is named Jack Doe. They have different addresses, but the same phone number. Are they the same person? The answer is yes, but since the two systems formatted the name and address differently, the data looks different. There is no synchronization. When Jack moves, his address may change on only one system, depending upon the department that is notified.
- Duplicated data: The CIF has additional customer profile screens on which Jack Doe also appears, but with slightly different data—the social security number has a different last digit. This data was created

intentionally by a different account manager who wanted to get credit for a mortgage sale to Jack.
- Data not shared: Users would love to have call tracking, marketing, and CIF data together, but they can't. Even though all three are available on their PCs, the users must log off one to access another, and can't transfer data.

As a result of these problems, the users found accessing three systems very tedious and unproductive. They didn't use them as much as they should. The data discrepancies made them skeptical of the validity of the information, so they didn't rely on it.

## Fundamental Restructuring

Darrell Burns and the bank finally embarked on these steps:

- Customer strategy and incentives: In a series of interviews, the team began to understand the bank's marketing strategy and how it interfaced with the organizational structure, objectives, product lines, customer base, and incentive schemes. They discovered that the bank's product orientation was at odds with its customer strategy. This difference was causing great confusion in the field and in the database. There were conflicts between the head office's sales goals and the way in which the field was given incentives. The bank was unable to reach a consensus on such fundamental definitions as customer, client, and household, and who should manage them.
- Who manages the customer: The entire incentive system was based on the idea that every customer is managed by one and only one employee. That being the case, once a single account executive was named for a customer, no one could benefit by passing on leads or information. Valuable profit opportunities were being ignored on a daily basis, because of this business concept. After realizing this, the team was able to shift the bank thinking to the idea that more than one employee could manage a customer, with the database keeping track of who did what. The database could be designed to capture referrals and to allow a team selling approach, while at the same time enforcing the business rules. Result: Everyone began to do more to build business.

As a result of the 14-month effort to build an integrated customer database system, the bank realized very significant and measurable results, in each of the three key areas: Account Management, Customer Service, and Marketing. These are explained in more detail below.

## Account Management Results

Account managers secure new customers and expand the profitability of existing ones. Their job was to call on new prospects, qualify prospects' needs, submit proposals to the credit committee, open new accounts, etc.

Using the new system, account managers were able to:

| | |
|---|---|
| Increase client contacts | 100% |
| Increase sales of new accounts | 25% |
| Reduce loan proposal rejections | 10% |
| Reduce acquisition costs | 50% |
| Increase profitability of their portfolio | 10% |

## Customer Service Results

Eighty percent of the contact that customers have with the bank is with the customer service personnel, who execute deposits and withdrawals, verify checks, open new accounts, extend credit limits, investigate discrepancies, and transfer funds. Originally, customer service personnel were not given access to the CIF, since their job dealt with operational account systems. In their work, however, these people came across innumerable product and service sales opportunities. Without an incentive system in place, they rarely took the time to provide leads to the account managers.

When they were given access to the new CIF system they were able to:

- Set up referrals and get credit for resulting sales
- Reduce the number of complaints
- Reduce their research time
- Speed up account-opening time
- Eliminate unnecessary steps

Using the new system, the customer service administrators were able to:

| | |
|---|---|
| Reduce the number of lost customers | 5% |
| Increase customer lifetime value | 20% |
| Reduce operational costs | 20% |

## Marketing Results

The marketing department ran about 25 campaigns per year. They used mostly rented lists, because the process of extracting data from internal lists was too cumbersome.

A high percentage of the direct mail was either returned as undeliverable or sent to customers who already had the product. Most of the literature directed people to the nearest bank branch. There was no system for tracking whether they actually did. Even when marketing did generate response data, there was no place in the CIF to store the information.

Once the new system was in place, marketing was able to:

- Identify their best customers
- Identify their best prospects
- Avoid undesirable prospects
- Coordinate promotions
- Avoid over-solicitation
- Anticipate customer needs

Using the new system, marketing was able to:

| | |
|---|---|
| Reduce direct mailing costs | 33% |
| Increase the response rate | 100% |
| Increase the new accounts signed up | 33% |
| Increase profitability of new accounts | 32% |

I would conclude that:

- The strategy behind database marketing is to build a relationship with the customer that increases lifetime value.
- That relationship is built best by the frontline troops: the customer service personnel and account managers, rather than the marketing staff.
- Giving these frontline troops better data enables them to improve their services to customers, create warmer relationships, and do more to retain and build business than any number of marketing messages.
- Marketing's job is to turn up leads. What happens to those leads should be marketing's prime concern. The new database system helped tremendously with the job of lead qualification and tracking.

### The Importance of Prequalification

One improvement made by Darrell Burns was to allow marketers to better determine the qualifications of customers and prospects before they were solicited for new business.

When marketing to financial services prospects, you should carefully prequalify your prospects for two reasons:

- Mailing to an unqualified prospect is a waste of money. This is true of all marketing programs.
- Mailing to an unqualified prospect can be very annoying to the prospect. For example, if you are offering a credit card with a $5,000 line of credit, you may have to reject the application if a credit check shows that the financial status of the customer cannot support a credit line of that size. Why put thousands of people through the humiliation of filling out your unsolicited forms only to be rejected? Why incur the expense of processing them?

### How to Prequalify Prospects

What kinds of data can you collect on a prospect that will help you to prequalify them? Steve Gasner of North American Integrated Marketing, one of the leaders in credit card marketing concepts, provided a number of useful suggestions:

- Credit scores reflecting wealth and ability to pay: If you are selling a product, this can be converted into "open to buy," a measure of whether the prospect has the resources to buy your product. These scores also can tell you about possible response levels, since people who cannot afford your product are unlikely to respond to your offer.
- Pays interest on credit cards: Some people pay their balance in full every month. These are usually more wealthy clients. They are also usually not very profitable customers, since the card company receives no interest. "Pays interest" denotes a downscale lifestyle with limited resources and a certain amount of risk, but possibly a more profitable customer for the bank.
- Date account opened: Long-time customers tend to be more loyal to a firm. On the other hand, new additions to a file tend to be more likely to respond to direct mail than old accounts. Why is that? Mainly because they have received less mail from the bank and are more curious about what you might have to offer.
- Recency: Recent purchase behavior is the most important single piece of information you can get on any prospect. The fact that prospects just made a purchase from you makes them more likely than any other customers or prospects to make another purchase right away.
- Frequency: Frequent purchases are another clue that a person is worth pursuing. Every database record should have a frequency indicator.
- Monetary amount: The size of a person's previous purchases has a real bearing on the type of offer you should make. Don't send a person who buys $1,000 at one time an offer for $10, and vice versa.

- Date of birth: This tells a lot about lifestyle. The offer to a 60-year-old man should be quite different from that made to a 25-year-old. If your program does not take age into consideration, you are probably wasting money.
- Gender: Any service bureau can gender code your file. Once this is done, your marketing programs may be different for men and women. The difference will be appreciated by the customer, as well as being more profitable for the bank.
- Home and automobile ownership: These often have a relevance for lifestyle and purchasing behavior that the marketer should observe when designing promotions.
- Length of residence: The longer individuals reside at a single address, the better credit risk they usually are. However, there is another side to long residence: People staying for a long time at a single address are very unlikely to respond to direct mail. New movers are the most likely to respond to almost any offer. Length of residence, therefore, is a powerful indicator. You should get it on any file and learn how to predict response and qualifications with it.

### Who Are the Best Financial Services Prospects?

As a result of the above principles, Steve Gasner suggests dividing all prospects into three groups:

- Good credit risks
- Medium credit risks
- Barely acceptable credit risks

Which of these three will respond best? In all cases, the barely acceptable credit risks are the best respondents. Mailing to the good credit risks is a waste of your mailing dollar. They rarely respond—and that is one reason why they have such good credit.

When I was in my 30s, I had very little capital. I opened bank accounts in a number of banks that offered me a $2,000 or more line of credit. I drew each account up to the limit, using the funds to invest, quite profitably, in the stock market. I responded to every financial services offer I received. Now, I have plenty of capital. I have a $5,000 line of credit on my bank account, which I never use. I get several offers for lines of credit a month. I throw them all away.

If you are going to market to good credit risks, you have to offer them a gold card or some premium offer to get them to respond at all.

## Penetration Rates

One interesting way to estimate response is first to measure penetration rates. From census data, you can find out the population in every census tract. By geocoding you can find out how many of your customers are in each census tract. Comparing the two gives you the percentage of penetration of each tract. Penetration can be compared to "awareness" of the financial institution. If the prospects have never heard of you, they may not respond as well.

Figure 13-3 shows an area of census tracts coded by penetration rates.

**Figure 13-3: Penetration Rate by Census Tract**

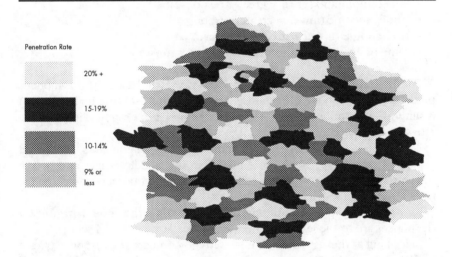

When penetration rates are taken into account, will prospects in census tracts with similar penetration rates tend to respond in similar ways? Not necessarily. Wealthy prospects will respond poorly. Less affluent areas generate a high rate of response because they are more credit needy.

## Modeling to Predict Response Rates

Table 13-1 shows the result of a mailing with the results organized by a model that predicted response rates based on a combination of different factors including:

• Risk (higher risk = greater response)

### Table 13-1: Mailing Using Model that Predicts Response Rate

| Model Scores | Number Mailed | Number Responders | Response Rate | Cum. Number Mailed | Cum. Number Responders | Cum. Response Rate |
|---|---|---|---|---|---|---|
| 900 | 674 | 220 | 32.64 | 674 | 220 | 32.64 |
| 800 | 33,982 | 5,379 | 15.83 | 34,656 | 5,599 | 16.16 |
| 700 | 252,104 | 22,387 | 8.88 | 286,760 | 27,986 | 9.76 |
| 600 | 1,118,350 | 67,325 | 6.02 | 1,405,110 | 95,311 | 6.78 |
| 500 | 1,212,396 | 52,860 | 4.36 | 2,617,506 | 148,171 | 5.66 |
| 400 | 1,197,450 | 37,480 | 3.13 | 3,814,956 | 185,652 | 4.87 |
| 300 | 927,938 | 16,796 | 1.81 | 4,742,894 | 202,447 | 4.27 |
| 200 | 15,142 | 161 | 1.06 | 4,758,036 | 202,608 | 4.26 |
| Total | 4,758,036 | 202,608 | 4.26 | 4,758,036 | 202,608 | 4.26 |

- Length of residence (short = greater response)
- Penetration ratio (great = greater response)
- Family income (lower = greater response)
- Home value (lower = greater response)
- Type of dwelling unit (rental = greater response)

The first column shows the model score values, based on the model's prediction of likelihood of response. Names scoring 900 (the highest value) resulted in a response rate of more than 32 percent. Overall, the response rate was 4.26 percent.

Both in terms of number mailed and number of respondents, the model produced bell curves, with most people in the middle ranges and only a few at the extremes. Figure 13-4 shows the mailing numbers and response rates ranked by model score.

The actual responses did slightly better than the model predicted (responses are to the left of the number mailed at each model score).

In looking at these responses, it is useful to compare the response rate of each segment with the average for the group as a whole. For the entire group, the response rate was 4.26 percent, a very good response. The segments with a model score below 500, however, did much worse than the average. Overall, it would have been better if the model had been trusted, and the worst of these segments had not been mailed at all.

### How to Stop Card Dropping

Let's focus now on one particular financial service: credit cards. Credit cards have become highly competitive. Not only is there competition between MasterCard, Visa, Discover, and American Express, but there is active competition between different banks offering Visa and MasterCard. The average middle-class family is deluged with several competing credit card offers per year.

**Figure 13-4: Mailing and Response Ranked by Model Score**

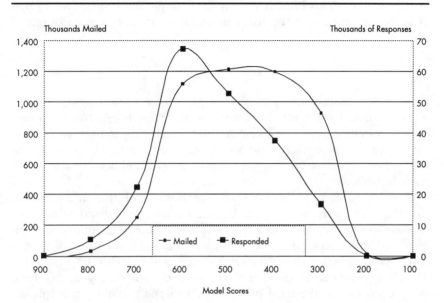

Viewed from the standpoint of a card issuer, how do you retain the customers you have, and get them to use their cards? For solutions to this generic problem, direct response agencies are increasingly advising their clients to use the power of database marketing.

Steve Gasner developed an innovative way to keep the most valuable credit card customers from dropping their cards. The process uses a database and modeling to make the most effective use of the bank's relationship marketing budget.

## The Cost of Acquisition

It costs an average of $80 to add a new credit card customer. This money is spent for list rental, profiling, qualification, direct mail, processing the application, and issuing a new card. Once this kind of money has been spent for acquisition, it is highly important that efforts be made to keep these customers. Ignoring the possible attrition is like tossing money down the drain.

The annual voluntary attrition rate of credit card customers runs between 10 percent and 20 percent. For a card issuer with a half million customers, that means losing as much as $8 million per year in acquisition costs. Most banks are taking steps to see that some of these losses are reduced by proactive loyalty building activities. Studies show that a 5 percent reduction in attrition costs can increase portfolio profits by 75 percent. Better targeting of the attrition reduction efforts can increase profits even more.

## Retention Budget

Since card cancellation is a common problem in banks that issue cards, many of them have created promotional budgets designed to keep customers from dropping their cards. The size of the budget varies by bank, by the size of their cardholder base, and by the level of recognition within the bank of the possibilities and importance of retention activities for long-term profitability.

The idea in retention is to build a relationship with the cardholders so that they are aware of the card, the bank, and their individual interest. Retention activities can be included in the monthly statement, or programmed as a separate letter or even a telephone call. The issue, of course, is to whom do you write? Everyone? Those most likely to drop the card? The most profitable customers? The most likely droppers who also have the potential to be the most profitable? By carefully thinking through the answers to these questions (plus planning an innovative series of relationship-building activities), the successful banks are separated from the less successful ones.

## Retention-Building Programs

What can you do to keep a credit card customer from leaving you? There are a number of techniques, each of which is used with different types of customers with varying levels of success. They are:

- Increasing the customer's credit line
- Upgrading the card to a gold card
- Sending out cash advance checks
- Reducing the annual percentage rate (APR)
- Reducing, rebating, or waiving the annual fee
- Setting up a co-op spending initiative with a local merchant

Properly applied, these initiatives can reduce attrition by a very significant percentage. The problem is that each has a built-in cost. Success lies in determining which of the bank's cardholders should receive promotional relationship-building incentives to reduce the possibility of attrition. Spending money on people not likely to drop the card is actually money wasted, as is spending money on people whose card use is not profitable for the bank. Finding the right customers to promote is the secret of success. This can happen by using a customer marketing database and developing a satisfactory model of cardholder behavior.

The first step is building an attrition model. The idea is to profile the attrition history of cardholders who have dropped the card and those who have not dropped it, using an enriched database that contains demographic and financial data. For example, customers who have voluntarily dropped their card in the last two quarters can be compared with those who did not, to determine characteristics most likely to distinguish the two groups.

After running a neural network model, it is possible to assign a score to each account ranking each in terms of its percentage likelihood of canceling the account, going from 100 percent to 0 percent. The score is inserted into each database record.

Table 13-2 shows the scores assigned by a hypothetical model to 502,624 credit card customers. The scores range from 95 (very likely to drop the card) to 15 (not likely to drop). A total of 3,315 customers received a score of 95. Of these, 1,619 customers actually dropped the card. This was an actual attrition rate of about 49 percent, showing the power of the model.

### Table 13-2: Cardholders Ranked by Likelihood to Drop the Card

| Score | Total Base | Actual Attrition | Percentage Attrition | Cumulative Base | Cumulative % Attrition |
|---|---|---|---|---|---|
| 95 | 3,315 | 1,619 | 48.84 | 3,315 | 48.84 |
| 90 | 15,014 | 3,974 | 26.47 | 18,329 | 30.51 |
| 85 | 26,378 | 4,858 | 18.42 | 44,707 | 23.38 |
| 80 | 39,923 | 7,139 | 17.88 | 84,630 | 20.78 |
| 75 | 32,874 | 5,226 | 15.90 | 117,504 | 19.42 |
| 70 | 33,926 | 6,182 | 18.22 | 151,430 | 19.15 |
| 65 | 53,536 | 6,992 | 13.06 | 204,966 | 17.56 |
| 60 | 71,594 | 9,274 | 12.95 | 276,560 | 16.37 |
| 55 | 74,870 | 5,814 | 7.77 | 351,430 | 14.53 |
| 50 | 24,314 | 1,178 | 4.84 | 375,744 | 13.91 |
| 45 | 20,646 | 662 | 3.21 | 396,390 | 13.35 |
| 40 | 21,168 | 1,104 | 5.22 | 417,558 | 12.94 |
| 35 | 29,203 | 883 | 3.02 | 446,761 | 12.29 |
| 30 | 41,373 | 1,325 | 3.20 | 488,134 | 11.52 |
| 25 | 13,994 | 442 | 3.16 | 502,128 | 11.29 |
| 20 | 464 | 0 | 0.00 | 502,592 | 11.28 |
| 15 | 32 | 0 | 0.00 | 502,624 | 11.28 |
| Total | 502,624 | 56,672 | 11.28 | 502,624 | 11.28 |

## Targeting Your Program

Suppose that a bank sets aside an annual budget of $650,000 to use for retention programs with current cardholders. If it were to divide that budget across all 502,624 customers, it would be able to spend about $1.29 per customer for retention programs. With that kind of budget, it would be able to make each customer a maximum of a two offers per year, picking one of the techniques listed above.

Instead, using the model scores, Gasner advises targeting only those customers most likely to drop the card. This can be done by focusing on the 276,560 customers with an attrition score of 60 or higher, ignoring those with a lower attrition score.

Figure 13-5 shows the division between cardholders promoted and ignored, as well as the percentage of those who actually dropped the card.

**Figure 13-5: Selecting the Most Likely Card Droppers**

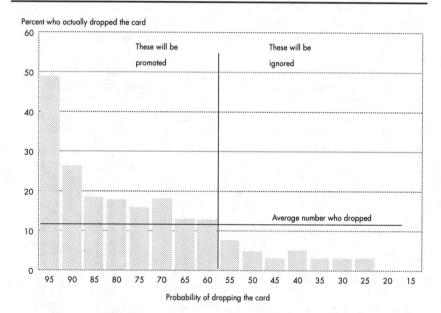

The obvious question is why were those 276,560 selected? Why was a score of 60 chosen as the cut-off? The answer can be found in the database. Overall, the actual attrition rate for the entire database is 11.3 percent. Those 276,560, with scores of 60 and above, were predicted to have an attrition rate higher than 11 percent. Customers with scores below 60 had lower attrition rates and, thus, were ignored.

This concentration on the 276,560 most vulnerable increases the amount that can be spent per cardholder to $2.35. Four mailings per year can be squeezed out of this kind of a budget, which puts the money where it will do the most good.

## Taking the Model One Step Further

Many banks stop there. When they know who is most likely to drop, they begin programs corresponding with these cardholders, encouraging them to use their cards, and offering benefits for continuing. This may not be the most profitable avenue, however.

Some customers are worth more than others. This is where lifetime value comes into play. If you have a good estimate of the lifetime value of each customer, you can use that estimate to target your promotions to the most valuable, giving the less valuable customers little or no attention at all. The result: a further increase in the bottom line.

A series of lifetime values can be calculated for each group of customers, ranked by their relative wealth, age, lifestyle, and the propensity of people in each profiled group to make use of their credit card. After these values are inserted in each card member's database record, the overall values are produced in a table of ranges. The ranges for the 276,560 people most likely to drop the card are shown in Table 13-3 below. For simplicity, those with lifetime values above $600 are grouped together and assigned a value of $600.

*Table 13-3: Lifetime Value of Cardholders Most Likely to Drop the Card*

| Lifetime Value | Number Members | Cumulative Members | Percent Members | Percent Cum. Value | Lifetime Value | Cumulative Life Value |
|---|---|---|---|---|---|---|
| $600.00+ | 18,823 | 18,823 | 6.81 | 15.73 | $11,293,800 | $11,293,800 |
| $550.00 | 10,234 | 29,057 | 10.51 | 23.57 | $5,628,700 | $16,922,500 |
| $500.00 | 12,833 | 41,890 | 15.15 | 32.51 | $6,416,500 | $23,339,000 |
| $450.00 | 13,433 | 55,323 | 20.00 | 40.93 | $6,044,850 | $29,383,850 |
| $400.00 | 15,534 | 70,857 | 25.62 | 49.59 | $6,213,600 | $35,597,450 |
| $350.00 | 18,556 | 89,413 | 32.33 | 58.64 | $6,494,600 | $42,092,050 |
| $300.00 | 20,356 | 109,769 | 39.69 | 67.15 | $6,106,800 | $48,198,850 |
| $250.00 | 25,543 | 135,312 | 48.93 | 76.04 | $6,385,750 | $54,584,600 |
| $200.00 | 31,456 | 166,768 | 60.30 | 84.81 | $6,291,200 | $60,875,800 |
| $150.00 | 35,993 | 202,761 | 73.32 | 92.33 | $5,398,950 | $66,274,750 |
| $100.00 | 41,789 | 244,550 | 88.43 | 98.15 | $4,178,900 | $70,453,650 |
| $50.00 | 26,578 | 271,128 | 98.04 | 100.00 | $1,328,900 | $71,782,550 |
| $0.00 | 5,432 | 276,560 | 100.00 | 100.00 | $0 | $71,782,550 |
| Total | 276,560 | 276,560 | | | $71,782,550 | $71,782,550 |

This table shows the lifetime value calculation for each of the 276,560 most likely to drop the card. The amounts range from zero to $600 plus. The reason for doing this analysis is to focus our loyalty-building programs on those with the greatest overall lifetime value.

## Cost Calculations for Three Methods

Let's assume that we have a budget of $650,000 to spend on retention activities. What is the best way to spend this budget to get the best return on our investment? Below, we have analyzed three methods:

1. Divide the money equally among all cardholders.
2. Mail only to those who are ranked 60 percent or better in a list of those most likely to drop the card.
3. Mail to this group, but concentrate our effort on the 55,000 who have the highest lifetime value. Table 13-4 shows the results of using these three methods:

### Table 13-4: Three Methods for Attrition Reduction

| Method | Members | Amount Spent | Percent Reduced | Attrition Estimated | Attrition Reduced | Lifetime Value | Total Gain Lifetime Value |
|---|---|---|---|---|---|---|---|
| All Members | 502,624 | $1.29 | 0.08 | 56,672 | 4,534 | $259 | $1,174,244 |
| Top Rank | 276,560 | $2.35 | 0.16 | 45,264 | 7,242 | $259 | $1,875,740 |
| Top Rank/High Value | 55,323 | $9.00 | 0.56 | 9,960 | 5,578 | $531 | $2,961,706 |
| Remainder | 221,237 | $0.68 | 0.04 | 35,305 | 1,412 | $191 | $269,730 |
| Total | 276,560 | $2.35 | 0.15 | 45,265 | 6,990 | $259 | $3,231,436 |

We have made some arbitrary assumptions, namely that the reduction in attrition will be proportional to the amount of money spent on retention activity. Spending $0.68 will reduce it by 4 percent, and $9 will reduce it by 56 percent.

Table 13-5 shows the net lifetime value gain for each of these methods:

### Table 13-5: Net Lifetime Value Gain

| | |
|---|---|
| Method One | $524,244 |
| Method Two | $1,225,750 |
| Method Three | $2,581,436 |

Clearly, in our example, the third method—selecting those most likely to drop with the highest lifetime value—seems to bring about the most profitable results.

## Summary

1. Financial institutions have a greater opportunity to do database marketing than most commercial businesses, because they have more

valuable data about their customers, and customers tend to identify with their banks more than with other commercial institutions.

2.  On the other hand, building a CIF is a very complex undertaking, which few banks have managed adequately. Account managers and customer service require individual customer record look-up capability to do a good job. Marketing, however, does not.

3.  Modeling can be much more sophisticated in financial institutions than it is in other situations. Credit card or home equity modeling can result in quite accurate predictions of response and prequalification.

4.  Since the techniques of database marketing are so much better refined for banks than for most institutions today, those banks that do not engage in active database marketing in the 1990s will soon begin to lose significant market share.

5.  The biggest marketing problem in financial services marketing is qualification: finding people who are qualified for the products and who want the products. The more risky the customer (and less qualified), the greater the customer response to promotions—and vice versa.

6.  A model can be constructed that will quite accurately predict response rates to credit card mailings. This model is based on: risk, length of residence, penetration, family income, home value, and type of dwelling unit.

7.  It costs more than $80 to acquire a new credit cardholder. When a customer drops his or her card, the bank loses the $80 investment. For this reason, banks have retention budgets designed to provide incentives for people to keep them from dropping their cards.

8.  Who should get such mailings? People shown as most likely to drop the card by a model score. The usefulness of this retention effort can be further increased by promoting to only those with a high customer lifetime value.

## Executive Quiz 13

Answers to quiz questions can be found in Appendix B. The quizzes are for fun. Do them if you enjoy quizzes. Ignore them if you don't.

*Choose the best answer to complete each statement.*

1. Financial services marketing has an advantage over other database marketing for all but one reason:
   a. Customers identify with their banks.
   b. More customer data is available.
   c. Customer data is relevant to purchase decisions.
   d. Banking data is usually on one central computer.
   e. Mail from a bank is more likely to be opened and read.

2. Householding of bank accounts involves
   a. changing the bank accounting system.
   b. convincing customers to merge accounts into one household account.
   c. setting up a separate marketing database.
   d. putting all bank product accounts on one computer.
   e. None of the above

3. In banking, MIS and marketing
   a. seldom agree on how to manage a marketing database.
   b. usually try to do all marketing on the bank's mainframe.
   c. agree that bringing in new business is the bank's top priority.
   d. would not need an officer to mediate between them.
   e. agree that customer data should be highly accurate.

4. In most banks, the reward structure and organization is based on
   a. service to the customer.
   b. meeting the needs of a household.
   c. marketing individual products.

   d. improving penetration ratios.
   e. transfer of data across departments.

5. In most banks, field incentives are
   a. consistent with central sales goals.
   b. focused on customer needs.
   c. determined on a product by product approach.
   d. designed to build a relationship with customers.
   e. None of the above

6. Account managers in large banks usually
   a. provide islands of stability in a changing situation.
   b. keep detailed records of contacts in a central database system.
   c. spend much of their time chasing information instead of selling.
   d. get most of their leads from internal bank referral.
   e. have less than 5 percent rejection rates on loan proposals.

7. Bank marketing departments
   a. need access to individual customer records.
   b. find it difficult to track customer response.
   c. prefer keeping data on the central MIS computer.
   d. store marketing data in the CIF.
   e. All of the above

8. One of the following is not a typical sign that a credit card might be dropped:
   a. anniversary date is near
   b. complaint about annual fee
   c. very high card usage
   d. complaint about credit line
   e. no card usage

# 14

# Why Databases Fail

I just received my copy of *Great Shakes,* the Burger King Kids Club magazine. I joined the Kids Club (as an interested marketer) three years ago. It is still going strong. At first, Burger King Corporation mailed out a personalized membership card, letter, stickers, and a poster featuring Kids Club characters. A four-page color newspaper with games, puzzles, and movie reviews was published five times a year and distributed free of charge in the restaurants.

In 1993, Burger King expanded the Kids Club to include a quarterly magazine that sells advertising to national advertisers. The magazine is published in three editions: *Small Fries* for zero to five year olds, *Great Shakes* for six to eight year olds, and *Have It Your Way* for ages nine to 10. The circulation in 1993 was 3.8 million and growing at the rate of 100,000 per month.

What has been the result of the Burger King Kids Club? When the program was launched, children's meals accounted for about 1 percent of total sales. By 1994 the sales had grown by a very significant percentage. Most of this growth can be attributed to the Kids Club. Unfortunately, coupons in the magazines are not personalized, therefore Burger King Corporation does not know which of their members are using them. However, since the coupons appear only in the magazine, they know that they are being used by club members. The Burger King Kids Club has almost everything that successful database marketing requires:

- A practical idea with a realistic goal: Sell more children's meals by reaching the kids directly.
- A concept based on lifetime customer value that permits calculations of growth due to the database.
- Farsighted management that continued funding for several years to get the benefit of experience and accumulated acceptance by members.
- A willingness to experiment and innovate.

The only thing that it lacks is real dialogue. There is no toll-free number. The coupons are not personalized, so Burger King Corporation does not know who is reading the magazine and using the coupons. They only know that sales are going up. That, however, is plenty. It's wonderful; it's a great success story.

But not every great idea results in a long-term profitable experience. In many cases, an idea that sounds good ends up by being discontinued because it isn't paying off.

## Unsuccessful Attempts

A number of promising, yet unsuccessful database marketing projects were mentioned in a dinner conversation at one of the database marketing conferences. One woman described Citicorp's Reward America, probably the largest such project ever tried. Another brought up the Quaker Direct project, which was widely publicized beforehand, but withdrawn after the first mass mailing.

"Does anyone remember the Barbie Pink Stamps Club?" one of us asked. "That club was set up to build a database of the names and ages of Barbie owners, their parents, their buying habits, and the other children in the household. It was a long-term project, but they canceled it in 1992 at the end of three years."

"My favorite was the Society to End Dull Meals Forever," someone exclaimed. "McCormick, the spice people, built a database of more than 200,000 cooks who were going to receive regular mailings of coupons and product samples. I called them to get on the list, but they told me that it was dropped in 1992 because of mailing costs. It's a shame because it was a great idea."

"There are more canceled projects than you realize," said one veteran. "Somebody should write a book about why database projects fail. All the books and articles you read are about success, success, success, but really, there are a lot of flops too. You often learn more by studying the mistakes than you do by reading about the triumphs."

The fact is that many database marketing projects fail. It is not all win-win. Some projects are lose-lose. The purpose of this chapter is to explore in some detail why databases fail, and what can be done by marketers to assure themselves that they do not start something that will bomb in a few months or years.

Database marketing, properly conceived and executed, can bring your company customer loyalty, repeat sales, reduced costs, cross sales, improved identification of prospects, and a continuing boost to your bottom line.

But if you go about it in the wrong way, it will not bring you any of these things—it could be a costly failure.

## The Nine Mistakes

In this chapter we are going to discuss the following nine fundamental mistakes, any one of which can serve to doom your database project:

1. Lack of a marketing plan
2. Focusing on price instead of service
3. Building the database in-house
4. Building models instead of relationships
5. Taking too long to become operational
6. Getting the economics wrong
7. Failure to follow through
8. Failure to track results
9. Lack of a forceful leader

## Mistake 1: Lack of a Marketing Plan

Database marketing has at last caught on. There isn't a corporation that isn't discussing it. Many have positions devoted to it. All over the United States, marketers are collecting names of people who have bought their products. "When we get enough," they say, "we will have a marketing database!" But what they seldom think through is what they are going to do with the names once they have them. How can they turn a list of names into profits? That is a tough question to answer.

A marketing plan using a database aims at building a relationship with each customer: making him or her feel recognized and special. You become an old friend. You provide things the customer wants—recognition, information, and service—and the customer gives you what you want—loyalty and repeat sales.

But how are you going to do that? To go from a list of names and addresses to building a relationship is a giant leap. Somewhere in your plan there must be a practical program for using the names that accomplishes a definite objective.

These services need to be organized around certain definite elements:

- An achievable numeric goal that can be translated into profits
- A long-range plan with a budget that is long enough to show results
- A series of practical steps that modify customer and company behavior to reach the goal. The list of possible steps might contain: member-

ship cards with points and credits, newsletters with coupons, surveys and responses, personal letters and telephone calls, or recognition and special services.

Many, many database projects have been undertaken without marketers spelling out the goals, having the budget, or working out what the practical steps should be.

### Constructors and Creators

By now you are familiar with the concept of constructors and creators. A constructor is interested in building a database: collecting and cleaning the names, designing the computer access, planning instant retrieval and segmentation. A creator figures out how to make money with the database by designing practical relationship- and sales-building programs.

You need both kinds to have a successful database. The creators are the hardest to find. Without them, you are doomed to failure.

A major national corporation collected the names of seven million of its customers through a number of promotional activities for baby food, pet food, and adult food products. Marketing executives decided that this pool of names constituted an important corporate asset. Money was found to merge/purge these names and put them in a common format. The National Change of Address process updated the addresses. A database was created.

The only problem was that no one knew what to do with the names once they were ready. None of the brand managers had any promotions planned that could use the names. There was no newsletter or other vehicle in the works. As a result, the seven million names hung on a tape rack for three years, while the names got stale.

No one was willing to admit it, but every penny spent on this database was totally wasted.

Before any database project is undertaken or any money is spent to put a database together, you need to draft a document that states:

- The goal of the database project—a numeric achievable goal
- The method whereby the database will achieve that goal
- The time frame necessary to achieve the goal
- The budget required to accomplish the goal

Then, of course, you need to sell your plan to whomever approves multi-year budgets.

How do you go about creating such a plan? Each situation is different. Experience suggests, however, that such plans come most easily from the top strategists of direct response agencies. If you don't have a direct response agency on retainer for your marketing program, now is the time to take that step. Marketers alone in a giant corporation are often defenseless. An agency can help by:

- Coming up with the plan
- Fleshing it out with mockups of the creative, research, and graphics
- Bringing experience from other database projects to bear
- Helping you sell it to your top executives

The agency is the beginning of your database team. Other members, of course, will include:

- Customer service department
- Sales force
- Management information systems (MIS) department
- Your database service bureau
- Your telemarketing service
- Market research

Using ideas from the direct response agency, the support of your team, and a lot of effort on your part, you can sell your program. Then, get started building the database.

## Mistake 2: Focusing on Price instead of Service

What do you offer a customer to build a relationship? A discount is the last thing you should consider. Before most neighborhood stores went out of business in the 1970s, people kept coming back to them because they liked the owner, the employees, and the friendly atmosphere at the stores. The store was convenient. The owner recognized you and did favors for you. You would not think of asking the owner to cut a product's price. The relationship was built on trust and service.

That is not true today. Mass marketing stores are based on price, not on relationships. Databases are built on relationships. Once you begin talking discount, it sends the wrong message.

A discount is what everyone else offers. Discounts do not build loyalty or relationships. They make people forget about quality, service, and loyalty, and think about the price.

If all you want to do with your database is use it to offer discounts, your database will fail. Why? Because a database costs money. There are many cheaper ways to provide discounts, particularly coupons. Once you begin to play the discount game, any competitor with a deeper discount can rob you of your customers.

The Quaker Oats Company provides one example of what happens to a major national database program built on the idea of discounts.

Quaker Oats began a major database marketing effort in September 1990. After a test mailing, with a budget of $18 million, Quaker Direct sent co-op mailings of coupons to 20 million households carefully selected from Computerized Marketing Technology's compiled database, Select and Save. Unlike free-standing insert coupons, the Quaker coupons were bar coded with a Quaker household number so that data could be collected from the responses of each of the 20 million households.

The central idea in the promotion, according to Dan Strunk, the director of the Quaker program, was to gain knowledge of the market and to begin a dialogue with a select group of confirmed Quaker users, thereby building brand loyalty.

Although the program cost approximately four times as much as the cost of sending the same coupons in a Sunday newspaper, and twice as much as the cost of Donnelley's Carol Wright co-op program, Quaker Direct reasoned that because of the correct targeting, the redemption rates would be much higher. The net effect, therefore, would be a reduction in overall costs by "mailing smarter." Another means of reducing the cost of the promotion was enlisting national advertisers who paid to share the mailing with Quaker.

Quaker hoped to achieve a real one-to-one bonding with the consumers of their brands through the dialogue created by the receiving and redemption of coupons. After the first mailing, however, the entire project was canceled, and the director was terminated. Quaker did not comment on the reasons.

Quaker Oats is a household word in the United States, with an excellent reputation with the public. Why did its database project fail?

First, Quaker marketers did not get as many co-op advertisers as they had hoped, so the program was more expensive than they had assumed. Their failure to get other co-op partners stemmed from the second problem.

Second, coupons do not build a relationship. People love Quaker because of the wonderful wholesome food that Quaker is famous for, not because the company discounts its products. No customers will love Quaker more because they got a coupon in the mail giving them $0.50 off. The entire basis for the Quaker program was mistaken. They were smart to stop it before more money was wasted.

Contrast the Quaker fiasco with what Kraft General Foods does with the Crystal Light program. Beginning in 1987, John Kuendig, director of direct marketing, created the Crystal Light Lightstyle Club. Crystal Light is a low-calorie artificially sweetened drink powder, selling for less than $3 per box. Heavy users buy 10 or more boxes during the summer.

There are about a million members in the club at any given time. These are medium-to-heavy users of the product. The goal is to preserve this group and increase their usage.

Members receive a package that contains a club newsletter on diet and fitness, discount coupons for General Foods products, a cover letter, and a catalog. The catalog is part of the club image, because it offers watches, mugs, jogging suits, and other gear that bears the Crystal Light emblem. Catalog items can be purchased with cash plus proof-of-purchase seals from Crystal Light boxes.

Each year, market research is used to measure the effectiveness of the program in building and maintaining sales of the product.

How does this program differ from the ill-fated Quaker Direct? It is built upon three key concepts, all of which were missing from Quaker:

- A theme (fitness, exercise, weight loss, diet)
- A club (with a logo, clothing, a newsletter)
- Exclusivity (a very focused group of consumers interested in the club and the theme)

Of course Crystal Light uses discount coupons, but the program is not based on the coupons. They are not the main idea. They are a sweetener that supports the program and facilitates the dialogue. I would venture to say that if Kraft mailed out coupons alone, the program would soon die.

Where mailing programs are built on discount coupons as the core, instead of building a relationship focused on the product or the manufacturer's established name and reputation, they are doomed to failure.

Solid relationships built through database marketing are immune to discounts. Your customers prefer you because you are an old friend who recognizes them, who provides personal services, and delivers a well-known quality product. You would be insulted if a friend gave you a tip for doing a favor. A database should aim at that same kind of friendship.

## Mistake 3: Building the Database In-House

Many companies believe that they have to build their marketing databases in-house on their own mainframes. Some have been successful. Kraft General Foods, for example, has built its huge customer base on its internal mainframe. The majority of large corporations, however, have outsourced their customer databases, and even Kraft has been getting bids on outsourcing. Why is that?

- Few company computer systems are built for marketing. They exist for payroll, inventory, billing, and manufacturing. These operations pay the bills, and control the data processing priorities of the company. Marketing must sit in the dugout when these heavy hitters step up to the plate. Marketers will soon find that they cannot get the priority attention to their functions that they need to do their job.
- In-house MIS staffs seldom have the specialized software and experience needed to do database marketing. Merge/purge, geocoding, statistical modeling, on-line access, ad hoc counting and selecting are a few of the skills needed for database marketing, and seldom available on in-house company computers.
- Most computer operations, like payroll or inventory, are stable systems that run for years without change. Marketing is dynamic. The software requires constant testing, modification, retesting, and shifts in approach. MIS will not understand devoting hundreds of hours of program development time on a monthly basis to your marketing database. "Why can't you guys make up your mind?" is the MIS refrain.
- As a result, it will take you much longer to get your database up and running, and *cost you much more* to build your system in-house.

The answer, of course, is to find an external experienced service bureau to build your marketing database. If you get the right one, they will have built databases for many others, and can bring a wealth of experience to the table. Develop a tight contract that puts you, as the marketer, in control. You will be able to specify and hold your contractor to timetables and quality standards that you could never do with your in-house MIS staff.

Once your database is successfully built and running, it always can be migrated to your in-house computer. But in the crucial formative years, you cannot afford to rely on a part-time job by an inexperienced in-house crew.

Consider the following scenario: The marketing staff of a large telephone company wanted to build a database of its one million yellow page subscribers. The plan was to have the database up and running in six months so that they could use it as a lead generating and tracking system for their sales force. The marketing staff received funding approval for a pilot test of the idea. The database was built by an outside service bureau in a three-month period. It enabled the marketers, for the first time, to know who their most profitable customers were, and to compare the level of advertising by different industrial classifications. It worked and provided the marketing staff members with exactly what they wanted.

The next step was a long-term contract to keep the database updated on a monthly basis using a tape from the MIS billing file as the key input. Seeing a reduction in its key role in the company, the in-house MIS group said it could build such a database itself, and what's more, could do it cheaper. The external contract was canceled.

To build the database in-house, MIS staff members had to install new and unfamiliar database software, new merge/purge software, and postal pre-sort software. They had to create a new on-line access system so that users could work directly with the database. Millions of dollars were spent on acquiring this new software and learning how to use it. The work went slowly because MIS had many other higher-priority projects that took pro-grammer time and funding away from the marketing database. Four years later, the database had not been built. The key marketing individuals who had initiated the program had left the company. The project was canceled.

This experience is not at all unique. Contrast this story with the experi-ence of companies such as Microsoft, Pizza Hut, Western Union, and Carna-tion. All have large mainframes, yet they have elected to have their market-ing databases built and maintained at outside database service bureaus.

## Mistake 4: Building Models instead of Relationships

Some marketers look on a customer database as an opportunity for multi-ple regressions: model building to determine which of the demographic, lifestyle, and psychographic variables that can be appended to a household are the key determinants of response and purchasing behavior.

This school of marketers overlays the database with quantities of exter-nal data: assumed income, age, home value, presence of children, educa-tional level, psychological profile, media interests, etc. Since this work is expensive and time consuming, they often work with a statistically repre-sentative sample (such as 10 percent) of the file, and assume their conclu-sions hold for the entire file.

The goal of their work is a set of simple statements: "People who buy our product have qualities B, C, and D. We can, therefore, write our copy to emphasize these qualities, and seek in our prospecting programs to find others who have these same qualities."

There is value in this work. It can help write copy. It can help in select-ing mailing lists. But it is not database marketing. A few years ago one of these modelers accepted a large contract from a liquor firm to model its customer base. His conclusion was that most bourbon drinkers were white males more than 50 years of age—hardly an earthshaking discovery!

Perhaps this mistake comes about through failure to understand the dif-ference between market research and database marketing. Database mar-keting aims at building a profitable individual relationship with each cus-tomer. Modeling rests on the assumption that purchase behavior can be deduced from demographic and psychographic data. Sometimes this is true. But in many cases it is either not possible, or—like the bourbon case—obvious and hardly worth the money and effort.

The fact is that what people decide to do in the marketplace varies from day to day based on their own subjective values, the products they have already acquired, their family needs, and their hopes and fears.

My wife, Helena, and I used to go out to a restaurant once a week. We loved it: exploring a different section of the city each time and trying out exotic foods from different countries. Then we found that we were getting too fat. We cut out the restaurants altogether. We only go out now when we have company visiting us.

The point: We are the same people, with the same income, home value, presence of children (none), educational level, and age as before, but our behavior is entirely different. Can our behavior (restaurant goers or stay-at-homers) be deduced from any demographic factors? Obviously not.

Here's another example: I used to rent two videos every week. We love watching movies. Then Helena's job became much more demanding. She gets home after 9 P.M. most nights. We cut out the movies.

Everyone reading this book has had a similar experience: We sometimes change our spending habits without a corresponding change in externally measurable demographics. For this reason, it is safe to say that your market activities cannot be predicted with any precision based on static demographic data. But this is the only data available to modelers that can be applied to unknown prospect lists.

What can help in predicting customer behavior or known prospects is previous behavior when combined with demographics:

- If I buy a compact disc (CD), I am much more likely to buy another CD recording right away than someone who has not bought a CD in the last year.
- If I buy a CD, am more than 60 years of age, and have an income over $100,000, I am probably more likely to buy another CD right away than if I had an income of only $15,000.

Modeling can help in deciding which individuals should receive promotions from the universe of those you could conceivably contact. Using modeling, you can reduce the cost of your mailing and still maintain sales.

This type of analysis, however, is on the fringe of database marketing. Real database marketing occurs when I buy another CD recording because I bought the first one, and I therefore receive a catalog of new CDs together with a message thanking me for my purchase and suggesting that I check out the additional Beethoven symphonies listed in the catalog.

*Us Versus Them*

Excessive reliance on modeling will divert database marketers from their main objective: building an individual relationship with each customer. Rather than spending money on appending external data (which may be inaccurate), it is better to use the same money to survey your customers and ask them why they bought your product, what they would like to see in the way of new products and services, what their plans are for next year. Once you know these things, you can really build a relationship, and your bottom line.

The conduct of modeling and market research tends to perpetuate the "us versus them" psychology of marketing: looking at customers as a mass of data instead of as a group of individuals with loyalties, desires, and personalities. It gets marketers thinking "How can I move this product?" instead of "How can I make these people love our company?" Moving product seldom builds lifetime value. Winning the hearts and minds of customers does.

## Mistake 5: Taking Too Long to Become Operational

How long should you take to build a marketing database? One year, at the most. Many unsuccessful databases are the result of a long-range plan—and no action. Why should you move fast?

- Technology is racing ahead. If you take too long to plan, your database will become obsolete.
- Your marketing database will teach you a lot about your customers, and how to market to them. It will build your bottom line. None of this will happen during the planning phase—only after you have gotten started.
- You need funding and top-level support for a marketing database. If you wait too long, the funding will dry up, and the top-level supporter will transfer to a new job. Good-bye, database.
- Waiting causes you to lose money. A successful database earns money. Without it, those customers will keep slipping away.
- Your competition is probably experimenting with a database right now. It takes several years to build relationships and get the database system working correctly. You are losing out in a competitive race if you wait too long to get started.

A major bank had a long-range plan for building a marketing database on its mainframe in three years. A large committee from all parts of the bank met every two weeks to plan the system. At the end of two years, committee members decided to shift to a five-year plan, since the bank had just bought two other banking systems and needed time to absorb its new branches. Their five-year plan is now in its fourth year. They have decided to postpone the database again due to some recent acquisitions.

The bigger the corporation, the longer it takes.

In early 1991, a retailer with 13 million credit card customers, who generated 200 million transactions over a two-year period, decided to create a customer marketing database. The company had several large IBM mainframes that were used for its billing system. As a first step toward creating its marketing database, the retailer's marketers drew up a detailed set of flowcharts of their customer record system. This work was finished in November 1991. Building on this success, they proceeded to develop a strategic plan for the information they would need for the database. This was completed in January 1992.

After review of this document, the marketers embarked on a three-month feasibility study for the database, which was completed in April 1992. This resulted in a contract with an outside firm to draft a general design document for the system.

The general design document was completed in July 1992. With this in hand, the company began the search process to find the right service bureau to build the database.

In March 1993, the retailer selected the service bureau and asked it to do an information survey designed to lead to the building of the database. This report was completed in April 1993.

In July 1993, a decision was reached to begin a seven-month process of building the database. It was finally set up and operational in March 1994.

Steady progress from 1991 to 1994, of course, but during those three and a half years, the marketers still had no database. They could not select customers by purchase behavior or demographics. They could not build relationships, other than by sending the same message to everyone in monthly statements. They were not building their bottom line.

This is typical of many companies. The good news in the retailer's story is that it finally got a database to show for three and a half years of planning. Most companies are not that lucky. The proponents of database marketing seldom remain in the same job for that length of time. The new executives are interested in another project. The database is put on hold.

What should the marketers have done? The answer is clear. They were frightened by the number 213 million (13 million customers plus 200 million transactions). They saw thousands of dollar-eating disks spinning endlessly, and choked with data. Storing and processing 213 million records is a major challenge for any data processing system anywhere. They should have started small: created a database of their top one million customers, retaining data on only one year's worth of transactions. The result would be one million customers and eight million transactions.

Drawing up plans for this database could have been a pilot for the larger one. Get it running in six months. Experiment with it. Market to these one million households, while learning more, building relationships, and making money. After a year, expand the database to include everyone.

How many other companies are making this same mistake right now? Hundreds.

## Mistake 6: Getting the Economics Wrong

If you sell a bar of soap for less than $1, it is hard to see how a list of five million of your customers can possibly do you any good. The margin isn't there. The economics are wrong.

On the other hand, if you sell automobiles, rental cars, insurance, power tools, vacation cruises, software, or computers, your customer list could be turned into a valuable database.

Big ticket items, repeat sales items, cross-brand possibilities: these are the lifeblood of marketing databases. Too many companies rush into building a database without thinking about the economics. Say to yourself: "How am I going to make money with these names?" Your answer must be simple and practical—for example, something that you can explain to your parents so they can understand it.

A major package goods company compiled a list of six million names of its customers. Executives of the company were repeatedly asked how they were going to use the names to build relationships and sales. Their answer was a simple one: "The boss wants a database." They continued to spend efforts maintaining the names. No one has yet been able to figure out how they can use these names to make money.

Citicorp, one of the nation's largest banks, became a major entrant into the database marketing field for retailers in the middle 1980s. Its idea, called Reward America, was to help grocery chains build up a valued customer database, with each customer having a family membership card. When the family came to shop, they would bring their card and present it for scanning before their shopping cart contents were rung up. As a result, the computers in each cash register would have a record of all the purchases made by that family: the date, the time of day, the product SKU, the quantity, the price.

The idea caught on fast. Several chains were signed up, and the software was installed. Every night, the cash registers were electronically polled, with the data on the day's transactions being fed over the telephone lines to each chain's central computer. From there, on a weekly basis, Citicorp retrieved each member household's purchasing data for storage on its mainframe in Connecticut.

With detailed information on the shopping habits of millions of Americans, Citicorp figured it would be able to realize a profit from the sale of this household data to manufacturers: who was using Camay, Pampers, Kraft General Foods products, Quaker products.

It was a great idea. The stores would use the data to learn more about their customers: where they lived, when they shopped, what they bought. They could use the data to pursue members who stopped buying, and to reward loyal member customers with daily specials and premiums.

There were many different types of discount arrangements made by the different chains who installed the system. For example, in some systems, members using their card to purchase goods that were on special would receive $2 for buying eight cans of this juice, or $1 for buying three boxes of that cereal. The system would keep track of purchases, so the products did not have to be bought on the same visit. Each month, members could receive a mailing including a purchase summary and a certificate for the amount they had earned so far. In other systems, the reward would be instant—with a discount for special items with each visit, and no retention of credits.

Citicorp made retailers a deal that they couldn't refuse: a free system. The bank planned to make its money on the other end by selling the purchase data to manufacturers. It hoped to build a database of 40 million households.

Most of the dozen chains that signed up for the system did so because the program was free and offered a way to learn about frequent shopper programs. Unfortunately for Citicorp, many things went wrong.

What happened?

- Rewards must be instant. The concept of rewarding customers three months down the road for purchases just didn't go over. If you are going to give grocery shoppers money, they want it now, which explains the success of the instant discounts and electronic coupon programs—such as those run by Catalina marketing.
- The data problems were immense. Citicorp's central computer choked on the data. Company executives didn't realize how huge the volume of grocery chain purchase data could be and did not have adequate software in place. After the program was canceled, they had thousands of unprocessed tapes stored in their computer center.
- Few companies wanted the names. Manufacturers did not jump at the chance to buy the names of their customers, as Citicorp expected.

- Costs exceeded revenues. The program cost too much to support. Citicorp spent $200 million and generated about $20 million in revenue. In November 1990, it canceled the program and fired 174 employees, leaving many retail chains with no way to maintain systems that they had been promoting to their customers.

Looking at the broad picture, what lessons can we draw from the Citicorp experience?

- Test first. Before you do something big in the database field, you should test, test, test. Citicorp, a very large and successful bank, approached this project the same way they successfully approached credit cards and other projects: pour in money and get a national foothold before competitors know what is going on. It may have paid off in credit card acquisitions, but it certainly did not work in retailing. If they had been prepared to start on a small scale with one or two chains, experimenting and learning (with just a few employees on the project), Citicorp could have gotten the bugs out of the concept at a modest cost—such as $10 million—and been ready for a successful national rollout in two or three years.
- Compute the costs. Don't underestimate the data processing aspects of database marketing. When you compute the data on one household's grocery purchases in a year, you may be talking 6,000 or more items purchased by a family of four. Multiply that by 40 million households and you have 240 billion transactions in one year alone. Without really efficient software, the costs and time consumed will bring even the most powerful data center to its knees in no time.
- Work out lifetime value. Put yourself in the customer's shoes. Successful database marketing is relationship building: one-on-one with the customer. Some marketers might be thinking, "How can we make money selling data about these rubes?" instead of saying, "Why would anyone want to join a frequent shopper club?" You have to start with the basics. Profits should be created by having built a relationship with the customer that is satisfying to all concerned.

Know your market. The economics were wrong for the manufacturers, the customers for the names. Few packaged goods manufacturers today know what to do with a database of their own customers. Most of them have millions of names stored in their data centers from previous promotions. They haven't yet figured out how to turn these names into relationships, loyalty, repeat sales, cross sales, and profits. If that is the case, why would they go out and pay money for more customer names?

If there were a demand for the names because the manufacturers had a way of making money from them, the profits would have solved all the other problems. But, alas, the demand was not there.

A satisfactory economic solution to database marketing won't come looking for you. You have to find it. And if you can't, maybe it isn't there!

## Mistake 7: Failure to Follow Through

Most marketers fail to appreciate how complicated the follow-through is in database marketing. What does a small country store owner do to build relationships with his customers?

People ask him to save them a fat turkey next week; they ask him to get in some stick ginger; they ask him to remind them when peaches come in; they ask him to deliver a basket of fruit to a sick aunt. He has to remember all this, and do it. He has to decide what to charge for this service and how to get paid for it. He has to remember to ask if the aunt has gotten better, and if the daughter is happy in college.

That is what database marketing is all about. It is listening to customers and recording what they say, and then acting on that information to provide a lifetime of personal services.

Too many marketers think that database marketing is segmenting the files, sending out a few cute letters or targeted offers, and raking in the sales. Would that this were true!

Successful database marketing involves careful, painstaking, advance planning of each step. When the customer says A, what do you do? When she says B, and possibly A, how do you react? When she says, "Can I have C?"—something that you haven't thought of—what do you tell her? Small shop owners make it up as they go along. But you can't do that with 100,000 or more customers writing and phoning. The advanced planning for follow-through can make or break your system. Few database marketers are skillful enough to have mastered this aspect of the job.

Even the best idea can be ruined by poor execution. Look at these bloopers:

Sample distribution: A program involved samples of a new product being sent out to persuade customers to buy the product itself. After the beginning of the program, more than half a million samples had been requested, while only 100,000 products were purchased. The real problem was that virtually none of the people who ordered the samples converted to being customers. After six months, the marketer running the project investigated. He found that the fulfillment house had never gotten around to distributing the samples, being so swamped with orders for product. The fulfillment house was fired, and the program was almost ruined. Fortunately, the sale of product was sufficient to keep the program going.

Tape mix-ups: To be sure that mailing addresses were correct, a large tape was sent out for National Change of Address correction. The tape came back with the old address in one part of each record, and the new, corrected address in another part. The corrected tape was sent to the mail shop for the rollout mailing.

Compared to the earlier test, the rollout was a failure. The response was terrible. Thousands of dollars were lost on what should have been a winning program. Weeks later, trying to piece together what had gone wrong, the marketers asked the mail shop how it had processed the outgoing tape. It turned out that no one had told the mail shop which of the two addresses was the corrected one, and which was the bad one. It had picked the one that seemed correct and guessed wrong.

Admirals and brothers: In a half-million name nonprofit mailing, title codes were used. Instead of Mr. and Mrs. in the tape, there was a one-byte code: 1 = Mr., 2 = Ms., 3 = Mrs., 4 = Dr., etc. There were more than 20 different codes, including Rev. and Mrs., Bishop, Captain, Colonel, etc. A stood for Admiral and B stood for Brother (a religious title). Through a mix-up in the title table, 1 and 2 were interchanged with A and B. Most of the men were given the title of Admiral, and most of the women were called Brother. The mailing was a disaster.

Envelope errors: A mail shop was given one million letters to insert in envelopes with response devices and business reply envelopes (BREs). The BREs were late in arriving, which delayed the job. When the truck with the BREs arrived, the envelopes were immediately fed into the inserter so that no time would be lost. It later turned out that the envelopes were the wrong ones. Those who responded had their mail delivered to a company that had nothing whatever to do with the promotion. Fortunately, the second company was nice about it. It received the 6,000 responses, paid the postage, and turned them over to the correct fulfillment house, which reimbursed the company for its trouble—and paid for printing one million new BREs.

This is a small sample. Any experienced direct-mail veteran can regale you with a dozen similar experiences of amusing slip-ups or unmitigated disasters caused by sloppy execution of mailing programs. The opportunity for error is tremendous. Why is this?

- Inexperienced personnel: Most agencies doing massive direct mail or database marketing for the first time are simply unaware of what can go wrong. They put junior, inexperienced personnel on the mundane tasks of execution. These people are often ignorant of the risks and unwilling to show their ignorance. They assume that everything will go all right (and it doesn't), and don't know the right questions to ask.

Experienced personnel in the mail shops or fulfillment houses find that they cannot get answers when they call, but are simply told, "Mr. Rivers is in travel status for the next week. He left word, however, that the job has to get out on time."

- Vendor status: Good results come from treating participants in the database program as partners. Poor results come from treating them as vendors. A partner is someone who has a personal stake in the success of the promotion. A vendor is simply supposed to follow orders. Vendors are engaged by giving out each job to the lowest bidder, who has no interest in the success of the promotion at all. Partners are signed on for a year or more, and know that their future business depends on their understanding of the mission of the marketing program and their ability to support it.

### Successful Execution

On the other hand, good follow-through is highly possible. Look how one company solved the problem:

A manufacturer with 45,000 retail outlets nationwide had never had direct contacts with its customers: the retail dealers. Instead, it had always dealt with distributors. Trying to boost sales by romancing a distributor is like kicking around a 400-pound sponge. The manufacturer decided to try database marketing.

Getting each distributor to furnish the names was difficult, but not impossible. The database was constructed, cleaned, and ready. The program was designed by a direct response agency. It involved a detailed relationship-building survey form sent to the retailers twice a year. The survey asks the retailers to rate (from 1 to 5):

- Equipment reliability
- Variety and popularity of brands offered
- Promotions and merchandising
- Service provided
- Quality of the product
- Delivery service
- Management support
- Quality control

To assure dealer response, the survey contains free display materials, plus a premium (such as a T-shirt). Respondents are entered into a sweepstakes offering free tickets, travel, and accommodations at the World Series. The results show who is satisfied and who is not. Telemarketing takes over with the dissatisfied dealers, who receive a telephone call and often a personal visit to determine the cause of the problem. Direct action is taken to rectify it.

What happens with the others, however, is even more interesting. Event-driven programs are written for the database to provide individual letters to each survey respondent. The direct response agency writes letter paragraphs to answer each of the possible responses. The database software composes a personal letter to each dealer saying thank-you for the response and discussing in detail what the company is doing to improve service or products in each of the areas checked by the respondent as being below par. The program thus becomes a personal one-on-one dialogue with several thousand dealers, using a combination of mail, telephone, and personal visits.

The result of the program has been a measurable increase in sales and a reduction in the rate of attrition. More display materials are requested and used. Morale among the respondents is considerably higher (measured by survey responses over several years).

This is database marketing at its best. A detailed dialogue is maintained with several thousand different customers with a minimum of expense, but a measurable impact on the bottom line.

Making this program work requires a great deal of follow-through on the part of the direct response agency and the manufacturer. Most companies, today, simply send out survey forms and tabulate the responses. With this database, the tabulation is a minor part of the whole exercise. Personal action and reaction is the name of the game. It can be done because the agency understands the power of modern database software, and the manufacturer understands the benefits of a long-term commitment to building a relationship with the customers. Not 1 percent of the companies in the United States are making this type of commitment. They will do a one-time survey, note the results, and scrap the project, remarking that, "This database marketing relationship-building stuff is really overrated!"

## Mistake 8: Failure to Track Results

At a database conference, one gets a picture of success stories. We marketers are all ad people at heart. We warm to the superlative. It comes naturally to us. But when we get back to the office, we know, deep down, that we are always operating on the brink of disaster.

Computers are marvelous. They make it possible to communicate with millions of customers in very personal ways. There is another side to the computers. They make it possible to botch relationships with millions of customers through very simple mistakes that don't get caught on the way out, but seem so obvious after the communications hit the fan.

Rather than give you a book filled with success stories and exhortations to go out and build relationships (which generally this book does), I would like to provide a little balance, by warning those who don't know that database marketing is not all downhill. Things can go wrong—sometimes seriously wrong.

Forewarned is forearmed. Read and heed. If you look for these things, you can avoid them.

### What Can Go Wrong with Source Codes?

Most new database marketers don't think about details like source codes. They plan great campaigns that produce wonderful responses, but fail to get accountable results. There have been many very good campaigns designed and run that could not be tracked at all because the planners neglected to construct a useful source-code tracking system.

The list of failures is endless and universal.

- Failure to start with an organized system. Most companies that have participated in direct marketing for several years have failed to set up a well thought through source code system. They begin, for example, with one set of marketing campaigns (such as a direct mail program using many lists, offers, segments, and packages). Then they undertake an entirely new program (such as a telemarketing or catalog mailing campaign) that is really incompatible with the first system. In the course of trying to patch several different systems together, they run out of numbers or letters.

- Failure to design the mailing piece to include a space for the source code or ID number. Quite often the creative design of a mailing piece is designed by someone other than the database marketer planning the overall campaign. This creative designer works out an eye-catching promotional piece or letter, complete with a response device. There have been many cases in which the designer did not know about the mail code and did not leave space for it. At the last minute, the mail shop has to cram it in somewhere on the printed piece where it does not exactly fit, and can be lopped off when the customer tears off the coupon to mail it in.

- Failure to capture the source code in the data entry process. It will happen more often than you realize. A well-designed campaign includes source codes on the tape and printed on the response device. Someone forgets to tell the fulfillment house to punch the source code in addition to punching the name, address, and order information.

Thousands of orders are fulfilled before anyone notices that none of them contain a source code. Tracking is lost, and it is too expensive to rekey all the responses over again to learn the source codes.

### Solutions

- Set up a foolproof, universal, long-range, source code system.
- Put the source code definitions in the database and in a notebook.
- Have the database manager check the design of mailing pieces and the keypunching format (used by fulfillment houses) rather than leaving these matters to production people.

## Mistake 9: Lack of a Forceful Leader

Too many databases fail through the lack of a strong leader to head the project. Leadership is vital: There is so much to be coordinated within the company and with outside suppliers who are required to make a database possible. Successful databases usually have outside telemarketers, a service bureau, a creative agency, and a fulfillment house; inside, they need the coordination of marketing, market research, sales, billing, customer service, and MIS. To pull the team together, you must have a forceful leader. The committee system will never work here. Decisions are needed on a daily basis to keep the database going, responsive, dynamic, building customer relationships, and making sales.

If you are planning a database in your company, be sure you have found a strong leader, and that he or she has been given the responsibilities and authority to make it work. Without this, your database will never get off the ground.

### A Failure of Leadership

As of 1994, one of the biggest failures in database marketing continues to be the U.S. auto companies. They have all the prerequisites necessary to do an excellent job, yet they have failed. What are these prerequisites?

- A product with a large enough margin to finance database activities— and a clearly delineated lifetime value that can be modified by relationship-building activities.
- An easy way to keep track of the identities of their customers: registrations and dealer service calls.
- A product that has a well-known cyclical purchase pattern that can be predicted with some precision.

• A product in which the average customer is intensely interested: Cars speak for the customer's lifestyle, income, age, and family composition. People identify with their cars. They would like to identify with the manufacturers.

Yet, in spite of all these advantages, in general, U.S. automobile companies have not succeeded in building solid, lasting relationships with their customers. Why not?

I recently met with the marketers responsible for creating the customer database for one of the big three companies. They have a database of 25 million names of owners of their products. They are working on the problem. From what I could see of their activities, I believe that they will fail. Why can't they succeed?

All the marketers that I talked to from this company were constructors. They were awed by the huge size of the database. They were exploring technical solutions to store and access the names. Should they use UNIX-based workstations? How much data should they keep? How can they do ad hoc searches with such a large file?

Successful databases cannot be built by constructors. You must have a creator leading the pack: a man or woman who has a vision, a drive, and a practical idea of how to build a profitable customer relationship. A person who is thinking every day, "What can the customers gain from being in our database? What can we give them that will solidify their identification with our company? How can we build loyalty? How can we include dealers in the relationship loop?"

A friend of mine has owned automobiles made by this same company for the last eight years. In all that time, he has received only one letter from the company. It was a federally mandated recall to repair the engine emission system.

Here was a wonderful opportunity. They had to write to him by law. The money for the communication had to be spent. They could have used the opportunity to consult with him, build a relationship, and start a dialogue. They could have included an owner survey, an announcement of new models, an invitation to take a test drive. What did they do? Nothing. Why?

The recall probably came from the legal department. The company is too large and bureaucratic to consider letting marketing participate in the recall effort. Database marketing, in this company at least, is a technical problem involving computers, disks, workstations, and sophisticated software. Relationship building, if there is ever to be any, has been relegated to a committee that is holding monthly meetings. It is a failure of leadership.

What would I do if I were in charge of sales at the automobile company? I would tell the database director to forget about the 25 million, and concentrate on one million current customers. I would tell him to find an external direct response agency with great ideas about how to build customer loyalty and repeat sales. I would tell him to contract out the database to an external service bureau, and to stop playing around with computer hardware and concentrate on marketing. I would tell him to make a specific quantifiable increase in the lifetime value of those one million customers within the next three years, which would translate into a big boost in the bottom line.

But, of course, I am not in charge, and whoever is in charge does not understand database marketing.

Let's look at some figures shown below in Table 14-1:

**Table 14-1: Lifetime Value of Auto Owners without Database Marketing**

|    |                       | Year1 | Year2 | Year3 | Year4 | Year5 |
|----|-----------------------|-------|-------|-------|-------|-------|
|    | **Revenue**           |       |       |       |       |       |
| R1 | Customers             | 1,000 | 500 | 250 | 138 | 76 |
| R2 | Retention Rate        | 50 | 50 | 55 | 55 | 60 |
| R3 | Annual Sales          | $12,000 | $1,000 | $4,000 | $6,000 | $2,000 |
| R4 | Total Revenue         | $12,000,000 | $500,000 | $1,000,000 | $828,000 | $152,000 |
|    | **Costs**             |       |       |       |       |       |
| C1 | Direct Cost Percent   | 80 | 80 | 80 | 80 | 80 |
| C2 | Total Direct Cost     | $9,600,000 | $400,000 | $800,000 | $662,400 | $121,600 |
| C3 | Advertising @10% Rev. | $1,200,000 | $50,000 | $100,000 | $82,800 | $15,200 |
| C4 | Total Costs           | $10,800,000 | $450,000 | $900,000 | $745,200 | $136,800 |
|    | **Profits**           |       |       |       |       |       |
| P1 | Gross Profit          | $1,200,000 | $50,000 | $100,000 | $82,800 | $15,200 |
| P2 | Discount Rate         | 1.00 | 1.20 | 1.44 | 1.73 | 2.07 |
| P3 | NPV Profit            | $1,200,000 | $41,667 | $69,444 | $47,861 | $7,343 |
| P4 | Cum. Profit           | $1,200,000 | $1,241,667 | $1,311,111 | $1,358,972 | $1,366,315 |
| L1 | **Lifetime Value (NPV)** | $1,200.00 | $1,241.67 | $1,311.11 | $1,358.97 | $1,366.32 |

Let's explain some of these numbers. Automobile companies today spend a fortune on advertising. We are estimating that this company spends $0.10 of every retail sales dollar on advertising. We are also assuming that, with no database marketing, half of their customers are retained because of the product and the general advertising.

From the sales figures, we are assuming that the average retail price of a car is $12,000, and that in the second year after purchase, a small percentage (8.3 percent) purchase another car or a replacement car. In the third year, one third purchase a replacement car, and in the fourth year 50 percent buy a new car. The remaining customers buy a new car in the fifth year. These numbers account for the annual sales figures.

The lifetime value of a new car purchaser is $1,366.32. Table 14-2 shows the effect of a database on lifetime value.

In these figures, we are assuming that the advertising budget is unchanged from the original picture (the same amount each year), but that

**Table 14-2: Lifetime Value of Auto Owners with Database Marketing**

|     |                    | Year1 | Year2 | Year3 | Year4 | Year5 |
|-----|--------------------|-------|-------|-------|-------|-------|
|     | **Revenue**        |       |       |       |       |       |
| R1  | Referral Percent   | 5     | 5     | 5     | 5     | 5     |
| R2  | Referred Customers |       | 50    | 30    | 20    | 14    |
| R3  | Remaining Customers | 1,000 | 600  | 390   | 274   | 206   |
| R4  | Retention Rate     | 55    | 60    | 65    | 70    | 75    |
| R5  | Annual Sales       | $12,000 | $1,000 | $4,000 | $6,000 | $2,000 |
| R6  | Total Revenue      | $12,000,000 | $600,000 | $1,560,000 | $1,644,000 | $412,000 |
|     | **Costs**          |       |       |       |       |       |
| C1  | Direct Cost Percent | 80   | 80    | 80    | 80    | 80    |
| C2  | Total Direct Cost  | $9,600,000 | $480,000 | $1,248,000 | $1,315,200 | $329,600 |
| C3  | Advertising        | $1,200,000 | $50,000 | $100,000 | $25,000 | $12,600 |
| C4  | Database           | $20,000 | $12,000 | $7,800 | $5,480 | $4,120 |
| C5  | Total Costs        | $10,820,000 | $542,000 | $1,355,800 | $1,345,680 | $346,320 |
|     | **Profits**        |       |       |       |       |       |
| P1  | Gross Profit       | $1,180,000 | $58,000 | $204,200 | $298,320 | $65,680 |
| P2  | Discount Rate      | 1.00  | 1.20  | 1.44  | 1.73  | 2.07  |
| P3  | NPV Profit         | $1,180,000 | $48,333 | $141,806 | $172,439 | $31,729 |
| P4  | Cum. Profit        | $1,180,000 | $1,228,333 | $1,370,139 | $1,542,578 | $1,574,308 |
| L1  | **Lifetime Value (NPV)** | $1,180.00 | $1,228.33 | $1,370.14 | $1,542.58 | $1,574.31 |

$20 per customer is added for major efforts at database marketing: satisfaction surveys, telephone calls, personal letters, event-driven communications, user clubs, etc.—the kind of activities that Land Rover has been doing for years.

The effect of the database is to increase the retention rate from 50 percent to 55 percent—a very modest increase, with further increases in future years from the loyalists who stay with the company. In addition, satisfied customers are able to bring in some new customers (as a result of database marketing activities). About 5 percent of the active customers do so each year.

The net effect of database marketing, therefore, is to increase the lifetime value of the average customer from $1,366.32 to $1,574.31, an increase of $207.99. If the company has a half million customers, this means a net increase in profits of $103,995,000, a tremendous increase.

Can an automobile company actually increase lifetime value by a hundred million dollars through spending $20 per year per customer on database marketing? Probably not. These figures are probably wildly optimistic. However, there is enough evidence from other databases that a significant gain can come through database marketing. Some automobile companies, notably Ford, are already doing some active experimentation. The profits are there; it just takes some effort to unearth them.

## Summary

These are the nine deadly mistakes of database marketing:

1. Lack of a marketing plan
2. Focus on price instead of service
3. Building the database in-house
4. Building models instead of relationships
5. Taking too long to become operational
6. Getting the economics wrong
7. Failure to follow through
8. Failure to track results
9. Lack of a forceful leader

What should you do to avoid them?

Here are a few simple steps that you can take to be sure that you go about building your database properly:

- Put yourself in your customer's shoes. Don't think of what you want to sell, think of what a customer would want from your company. It may not be primarily a product at all—it may be recognition, attention, information, helpfulness, service, friendship. If you can deliver on these things, the sales will follow. A database may be the best way to provide these things.
- Build a database team. Successful databases have a strong, creative, imaginative leader who has pulled together a team composed of marketing, sales, the service bureau, the creative agency, MIS, customer service, outside telemarketers, brand managers, fulfillment, and billing.
- Think small and think fast. Start your database with a small elite group of customers. Start soon. Make every action a test. Conduct your test, and evaluate your results. Build bigger as you accumulate experience.
- Keep your eye on the bottom line. Database marketing is supposed to *make money*. Plan your economics. Calculate lifetime value. If you can't quite see how what you're doing will be profitable, then don't do it! Rack your brains and find a way to turn your customer relationship into a profitable customer relationship.

## Executive Quiz 14

Answers to quiz questions can be found in Appendix B. The quizzes are for fun. Do them if you enjoy quizzes. Ignore them if you don't.
*Choose the best answer to complete each statement or question.*

1. The Burger King Kids Club had all but one of the following:
   a. farsighted management
   b. willingness to innovate
   c. real dialogue with members
   d. a realistic objective
   e. acceptance by its membership

2. Which of the following is not essential to a successful database?
   a. a marketing plan
   b. constructors
   c. creators
   d. a numerical goal
   e. a five-year plan

3. A direct response agency does all but one of the following:
   a. provides the budget
   b. develops the strategy
   c. does the creative
   d. brings experience
   e. helps to sell top management

4. Successful database marketing is based primarily on
   a. discounts to members.
   b. recognition and service.
   c. awareness of the product.
   d. the computer used.
   e. the software.

5. Coupons for database members
   a. help to build a real relationship.
   b. are an elevated form of dialogue.
   c. are cheaper to deliver than free-standing inserts.
   d. are the real profit for members.
   e. None of the above

6. Databases should be built in one year or less because
   a. funding may dry up.

   b. technology is racing ahead.
   c. waiting loses money.
   d. the competition may be building one without your knowing it.
   e. All of the above

7. Source codes on outgoing mail pieces
   a. should always be eight bytes long.
   b. are sometimes overlooked in mailings.
   c. seldom cause problems.
   d. are standard throughout the industry.
   e. are never stored in database records.

8. Citicorp's Reward America suffered from all but one of these:
   a. People will not use membership cards when shopping.
   b. The volume of grocery transactions are a data problem.
   c. Manufacturers won't pay much for the names of their customers.
   d. People won't wait three months for cash refunds.
   e. The economics of the scheme were wrong.

# 15

# Database Types that Succeed

*The U.S. version of the Air Miles loyalty program, launched in April 1992, came crashing to earth a year later, although the more successful Canadian and British programs continued uninterrupted. The U.S. program had 40 corporate sponsors and 2.2 million members, less than half of whom actively collected Air Miles. The Canadian program had 56 corporate sponsors, and about four million consumers signed up.*

*The differences: In the U.S. program, consumers had to clip out proofs-of-purchase and mail them in to receive credit. In Canada, a mag[netic] stripe, UPC code, and embossing on the Air Miles membership cards allows members' purchases to be tracked the same way credit card purchases are tracked. "In Canada, we created a card that makes collecting easy," said Joanna Fuke, Loyalty Management Group Canada's director of consumer marketing. "In the U.S. they took a packaged goods strategy and had a clip-and-snip program ... That probably made it a little tougher for consumers to play the game, and depressed the activation rate."*

*—Stephen P. Lloyd,* Canadian Direct Marketing News

**B**y now, you are aware that database marketing is zooming ahead in some areas and failing in others. It is not all win-win. Some marketers have lost their jobs by betting on database marketing in areas where it did not work.

Before you risk your career, let's see if there are some rules that will guide us to success and steer us away from failure in this new marketing mode. To begin with, you must pick the product situation in which database marketing is likely to work.

There are really two separate (but related) forms of database marketing: relationship-building with current customers and marketing to prospects selected by developing profiles of the most profitable customers. This second technique is much easier to succeed in than the first. It is described at length in Chapters 6, 8, and 9. Marketing to prospects, when done right, always involves a test. Before a rollout of one million, you do a 20,000 test, use a neural network to determine the factors leading to response, and mail smarter on the rollout. If you follow the rules, you can't fail. There is no problem in this area.

Relationship-building database marketing is the area where most mistakes are made. Why? Because it is much harder to see the immediate results. It takes months or years before relationship building begins to pay off. By the time you discover that it doesn't pay off, millions of dollars may have been wasted. That's why this chapter is so important.

## Relationship Marketing

Why would I want to have a relationship with the makers of my shirts, shoes, or soap? I really don't. I don't care enough about these products to want to waste time corresponding with their manufacturers. But, at heart, the main reason that I don't want to be on their databases is that I can't visualize any particular benefit to me in the relationship.

If the shirt manufacturer could come up with something really personally interesting, I might listen. If he offered to sell me a high-quality shirt that said "Hughes" on the pockets or "AMH" on the cuffs, I might listen. But, life is too short to spend it corresponding with the makers of the 1,000 or more different products that I use in any given month.

As I look around my office, I see that I am using Dixon pencils, a Swingline stapler, a Texas Instruments calculator, a Westclox clock, a Radio Shack diskette case holding 3M diskettes, a LUI desk, and a Rubbermaid wastepaper basket. I don't want to hear from any of these people. I can't imagine what they could say to me that would be worth the time it would take me to open the envelope and read or to answer their telephone call. Not all customer relationships can result in a mutual profit. Most of them, in fact, probably cannot.

On the other hand, I am typing on a computer from Advanced Computer Systems and using a Hewlett Packard printer. I certainly hope that they have me on their databases and correspond with me about upgrades and accessories. I can see how I could profit from a relationship with them.

When American Airlines writes to me, I pay attention. I have earned two free trips to Chile on American, and I am working on my next two. I can see the profit to me in the relationship. When Harvard Graphics, Wordstar, Lotus, or Microsoft send me notice of an upgrade because I am in their databases, I will read it and probably buy it.

I have bought three Dodge Colt Vistas with four-wheel drive in the last six years. I am about ready for a new one. If I were to get a letter from Dodge about the new models, you can bet that I would read it and would probably go for a test drive, if one were offered. But, of course, Dodge does not have a database. There is no danger of Dodge marketers writing to me because they don't write to anybody. I would love to have a relationship with them, but they don't want to have a relationship with me.

Database marketing designed to maintain a relationship works wonderfully in some areas and does not work at all in others. Let's take a few examples, limited to consumer products, and see how they illustrate our general principles. These are areas in which relationship marketing might work if handled correctly:

| | |
|---|---|
| Auto service | Automobiles |
| Baby products | Banks and financial services |
| Beverages | Books, records, videos |
| Children's food products | Communications |
| Computers | Credit cards |
| Department stores | Diet and health centers |
| Diet food products | Drug stores |
| Entertainment | Florists |
| Fuels and utilities | Gasoline and car care |
| Gardening supplies | Heating and air conditioning |
| Home maintenance services | Hospitals and physicians |
| Insurance | Lawyers |
| Lumber and hardware | Magazines |
| Medical care and glasses | Membership and nonprofits |
| Pharmaceuticals | Restaurants |
| Sewing and knitting supplies | Sporting events |
| Supermarkets | Travel industry |
| TV and radio | |

On the other hand, these are areas in which it is harder to make relationship marketing work:

| | |
|---|---|
| Apparel and upkeep | Appliances and electronics |
| Building supplies | Carpets |
| Contractors | Electricians |
| Food (exceptions) | Furniture and home furnishings |
| Glass and mirrors | Home remodeling and additions |
| Linen and draperies | Locksmiths |
| Movers | Office supplies and equipment |
| Packaged goods (exceptions) | Painters |

Paving                          Pest control
Real estate                     Roofers
Towing                          Toys and sporting goods
Wallpaper                       Water treatment

It is dangerous to publish a list like this. I am sure that some marketers with products on the "won't work" list will write to me or call me and tell me of a very successful case in which a profitable relationship was built with one of these "won't work" products. An imaginative marketer can easily prove me wrong. My purpose in the two lists is simply to alert you to the problems and encourage you to think carefully—especially if you have a "won't work" product—about how you are going to make money with your database.

Underlying these two lists is a general principle:

Relationship marketing works when the provider can supply sufficient benefits to the receiver to make it worthwhile for the receiver to respond. At the same time, the average receiver has to be in a position to reciprocate with benefits to the provider that exceed the provider's costs in creating and maintaining the relationship.

I will be willing to play my part in a relationship with a supplier of products and services if I can see some benefit greater than the work I have to do or the money I have to pay: filling out survey forms, answering the telephone, buying products, etc. As a customer, I have to make a profit from the relationship or I won't play.

Suppliers, on the other hand, have to be able to increase the lifetime value of their customers by means of the relationship-building activity. Let's take a specific case: my Swingline stapler.

I have had this stapler on my desk for more than five years. It is a heavy, solidly built, excellent product that is still working as well as when I bought it at an office supply store. It probably cost about $25. Swingline, as far as I know, does not have a database, and if it does, I am not on it. I don't need another stapler. I need staples occasionally, which I buy from the office supply store. Would I buy them direct from Swingline if the company wrote to me? Perhaps. But I buy them once a year, and spend less than $5. Swingline's profit on the sale would not justify the cost of the database and the communication costs.

The person who *should* be on the Swingline database is the owner of the office supply store. The owner, more than I, is responsible for this piece of equipment on my desk. I bought the best thing that the store had. If it had featured some other brand at the time, I would have bought that.

The conclusion: There are thousands of products that find their way into consumer's hands for which the manufacturers should not create consumer marketing databases because the consumers cannot profit by being on the databases. Since that is so, neither can the manufacturer profit by maintaining it.

### Alternate Database Uses

On the other hand, there are circumstances in which the customer database for such mundane objects as a high-quality stapler might be profitable after all.

If Swingline has a broad line of office products grouped in a catalog, it might send me the catalog since my ownership of an expensive stapler probably indicates that I have an active business in need of office supplies.

If Swingline does not have such a catalog, but it has captured the names and addresses of the owners of its top-of-the line staplers, it could rent these names and addresses to someone who needed a list of likely office supply prospects.

In the absence of such alternate uses, there are many products like my stapler for which a relationship-building consumer database will probably never have any economic value to either party.

## Further Criteria for Success

Just being on the "might work" list does not guarantee that such databases will be profitable. There are other criteria. Databases for relationship-building purposes are more likely to be profitable if some or all of the following are true:

- The provider has a well thought through marketing program. Such programs are hard to create. There must be a direct response agency or a creative marketing director who has designed a program that will return real benefits to the customer in exchange for the customer furnishing real benefits to the provider: loyalty and repeat business resulting in increasing long-term value.
- The payment system for the product or service makes it easy to get names, addresses, and purchase behavior. This is true in utilities, transportation, communications, banks and financial services, insurance, magazines, credit and gasoline cards, etc. The providers of these products and services have to have the name and address of the customer to provide the service in the first place. Many of them mail monthly statements. This type of activity leads very easily into the building and maintenance of a customer database. Unfortunately, with most products, purchase behavior is much more difficult to capture.

This is the central idea behind point-of-sale membership programs, in which customers at a supermarket, hardware chain, office supply store, or department store use their membership cards when making purchases. The membership database record in the store then begins to accumulate records of all purchases.

A great idea in theory. In practice, few people have been able to find a sufficiently profitable use for the data to pay the cost of capturing and storing it. We are talking about billions of transactions made by the U.S. public every week. Just retaining that data is a multimillion dollar enterprise. What are the profitable payoffs that will come from using the data?

"Aha! Arthur Hughes has just spent $3.59 for a box of staples for the Swingline stapler he bought five years ago." Think about it: who can make any money from that piece of information? I can't think of anyone, and neither can you.

If I had just bought a pair of skis, a recreational vehicle, a baby crib, or a saddle for a horse, I can think of many profitable uses for the data. But these items are needles in the point-of-sale haystack. There are less expensive ways of capturing them than vacuuming up all the data in all the transactions in the United States every night and storing it in computers.

- The product or service involves periodic, repeat purchases plus name capture at point of sale. This is true for automobiles, auto servicing, medical care, pharmaceuticals, diet and health centers, and home services (such as heating and air conditioning, plumbing, lawn care).
- There is a definite affinity group from which a database can be constructed. This applies to parents of new babies, sports enthusiasts, nonprofits, gardening supplies, knitting, sewing, music, etc.
- The provider can construct a frequency reward system with significant benefits for both parties. This applies, of course to the travel industry, to department stores, supermarkets, and the entertainment industry.

### Why the "Not Successful" List Exists

What is wrong with the products and services on the second list that make them unlikely candidates for relationship-building database marketing? Several factors apply to most of these products and services:

- The product is a commodity with a mark-up that is too narrow to finance relationship-building activity. Most packaged goods are simply too competitive and inexpensive to make a database work. What could you do with the names and addresses of all the purchasers of Ivory Soap? Nothing, really. There is no money for relationship building. Because of the competition for shelf space in a supermarket, the availability of store brands, and the commodity nature of the products, the margins for such manufacturers are paper thin.

Look at the bar soap industry. It is highly competitive and widely discounted. In general, it is dirt cheap (if you will pardon the expression). In 1993, Ivory bar soap was selling four bars for $1.29. Soap is a commodity; any bar is perceived by the public as washing equally well. The only difference is the price and the scent. While an expensive bar may be nice to have in the guest bathroom, most household shoppers grab whatever appeals to the teenagers (the pickiest consumers in any home) for family washing. Would a nice letter in the mail from Ivory change family buying habits? It seems unlikely. A coupon included with the letter might well be redeemed—but there are competing soap coupons in every Sunday newspaper, delivered to homes at a fraction of the cost of a personal letter.

There are exceptions to this rule. In some cases, manufacturers have been able to create an aura surrounding certain products that enables them to command a margin sufficiently high to let them to finance relationship marketing. Neutrogena soap falls into that category. Other examples are diet foods and children's foods.

Kraft General Foods has promoted the Wacky Warehouse club, which has successfully built Kool-Aid sales for years, even though the product sells for as little as $0.25 in the supermarket.

The Wacky Warehouse, the brainchild of Kool-Aid category manager John Vanderslice, is a mythical place run by the Kool-Aid man, which contains children's merchandise that can be earned by Kool-Aid proof of purchase points. A prospect database of four million households with children ages three to 12 is the target audience for mailings of comic books and other materials. The database mailings are coordinated with local advertising and promotions. Since the program began in 1987, Kool-Aid has been able to hold its own against Coke and Pepsi with the younger market.

Kraft General Foods also pioneered with the Crystal Light Lightstyle Club, which promotes its presweetened drink powder to diet-conscious adults. It sells for less than $3 a box. The average user will buy 10 boxes in a season.

- The purchase is made seldom and unpredictably. Furniture is a good example. A family pays $2,000 for dining room furniture. It may last five years, 10 years, 20 years. Furniture is usually purchased from a dealer who displays the products of many different manufacturers in one location. Can a relationship be developed by the manufacturer of one specific brand of furniture and the customer that will assure that the manufacturer's furniture is considered when the next major purchase takes place? It seems like a long shot to me.

The furniture manufacturer's database should be a business-to-business one used to market to all the furniture dealers of America (both large and small). On the other hand, furniture retailers (not manufacturers) can use a consumer prospect database to good advantage (see below).

In the case of lumber and hardware, there are hobbyists who spend their lives puttering and fixing up a house or boat or car. If the retailer can locate such people and build a database of them, a profitable relationship can ensue. Can the manufacturer of these products profit from building a relationship?

In some cases, yes. Black and Decker or Skilcraft, which offer a wide line of power tools, could build a relationship by using surveys combined with catalogs or a newsletter on carpentry. There are always new tools coming out that hobbyists want to learn about. A few years ago, one company made a good business of selling nuts, bolts, and screws by direct mail to such people. From what I could tell, no attempt was made to build this into a database. Could Armstrong develop a relationship with individuals who bought floor covering once, which would lead to them buying floor covering a second time? Who knows?

To illustrate why the second list is something to worry about, consider the case of a vacuum cleaner company that might try relationship marketing with its customers. It could get the customer's name from a registration form inside the shipping container and could initiate a direct mail program, selling replacement bags and attachments and leading to announcements of new models when they become available. How would this work?

Let's start by looking at customer lifetime value for this vacuum cleaner company without a database, as shown in Table 15-1.

Customers buy a vacuum cleaner for $200. Without a database, half of the customers leave the company every year, and never come back. Five years later, the few loyalists still remaining buy a replacement model.

The database is designed to change all that with relationship building, friendship, communication, direct sale of attachments. Table 15-2 shows what happens.

We spend $5 per customer per year on the database. It finances some very creative programs. The result: The retention rate goes from 50 percent to 60 percent. Existing customers recommend other customers who are added to the customer base. As a part of the database, bags and attachments are sold directly to customers (at a reduction in cost from 70 percent to 40 percent).

But despite all these wonderful things, the lifetime value of the vacuum

### Table 15-1: Customer Lifetime Value *without* Database

|   |   | Year1 | Year2 | Year3 | Year4 | Year5 |
|---|---|---|---|---|---|---|
| | **Revenue** | | | | | |
| R1 | Customers | 1,000 | 500 | 250 | 138 | 83 |
| R2 | Retention Rate | 50 | 50 | 55 | 60 | 65 |
| R3 | Annual Sales | $200 | $12 | $12 | $12 | $200 |
| R4 | Total Revenue | $200,000 | $6,000 | $3,000 | $1,656 | $16,600 |
| | **Costs** | | | | | |
| C1 | Cost Percent | 70 | 70 | 70 | 70 | 70 |
| C2 | Total Cost | $140,000 | $4,200 | $2,100 | $1,159 | $11,620 |
| | **Profits** | | | | | |
| P1 | Gross Profit | $60,000 | $1,800 | $900 | $497 | $4,980 |
| P2 | Discount Rate | 1.00 | 1.20 | 1.44 | 1.73 | 2.07 |
| P3 | NPV Profit | $60,000 | $1,500 | $625 | $287 | $2,406 |
| P4 | Cum. Profit | $60,000 | $61,500 | $62,125 | $62,412 | $64,818 |
| L1 | **Lifetime Value (NPV)** | $60.00 | $61.50 | $62.13 | $62.41 | $64.82 |

### Table 15-2: Customer Lifetime Value *with* Database

|   |   | Year1 | Year2 | Year3 | Year4 | Year5 |
|---|---|---|---|---|---|---|
| | **Revenue** | | | | | |
| R1 | Referral Rate | 5 | 5 | 5 | 5 | 5 |
| R2 | Referred Customers | | 50 | 33 | 21 | 15 |
| R3 | Remaining Customers | 1,000 | 650 | 423 | 296 | 222 |
| R4 | Retention Rate | 60 | 60 | 65 | 70 | 75 |
| R5 | Annual Sales | $200 | $12 | $12 | $12 | $200 |
| R6 | Total Customer Revenue | $200,000 | $7,800 | $5,076 | $3,552 | $44,400 |
| | **Costs** | | | | | |
| C1 | Cost Percent | 70 | 40 | 40 | 40 | 70 |
| C2 | Total Direct Cost | $140,000 | $3,120 | $2,030 | $1,421 | $31,080 |
| C3 | Database Cost @$5 | $5,000 | $3,250 | $2,115 | $1,480 | $1,110 |
| C4 | Total Costs | $145,000 | $6,370 | $4,145 | $2,901 | $32,190 |
| | **Profits** | | | | | |
| P1 | Gross Profit | $55,000 | $1,430 | $931 | $651 | $12,210 |
| P2 | Discount Rate | 1.00 | 1.20 | 1.44 | 1.73 | 2.07 |
| P3 | NPV Profit | $55,000 | $1,192 | $646 | $376 | $5,899 |
| P4 | Cum. Profit | $55,000 | $56,192 | $56,838 | $57,214 | $63,113 |
| L1 | **Lifetime Value (NPV)** | $55.00 | $56.19 | $56.84 | $57.21 | $63.11 |

cleaner customer falls from $64.82 to $63.11—a loss of $1.71, or $1,710,000 if the company has one million customers. Relationship marketing is not a winner in this case.

Is this a rule? Can vacuum cleaners be ruled out of database marketing? Answer: probably, but not definitely. It is possible that a really aggressive database program could build the retention rate up to 70 percent or higher, which could make a significant improvement.

But don't count on it. The database that the vacuum cleaner company should be counting on is the retail store database. Retailers are the ones who tell their customers, "You know, there are a lot of good ones out there, but nothing beats a Hoover." That sentence alone can make or break the company's future.

How do you get the dealer to say that? Study Jeffrey Geibel's dealer training program in Chapter 12, Business-to-Business Database Marketing. Database marketing can work in this area. Let's not get too optimistic about what it can accomplish with consumers.

I think that the reader can see that there are no definite lines that can be drawn. For any product that you select, it is possible to visualize how a profitable relationship-building database *might* be constructed. Whether it *can* be constructed depends on the economics of the product and the creativity of the marketers involved.

## Summary

1.  Relationship marketing is much more difficult than using a database to find new customers. The reason: How can you offer your customers a profit from the after-market relationship? There are thousands of products for which a profitable customer database is very unlikely.

2.  Relationship marketing works when the provider can supply sufficient benefits to the receiver to make it worthwhile to respond. At the same time, the average receiver has to be in a position to reciprocate with benefits to the provider that exceed the provider's costs in creating and maintaining the relationship.

3.  For relationship marketing databases to be profitable:

    - The provider must have a well thought through marketing program.
    - The payment system for the product or service must make it easy to get names, addresses, and purchase behavior.
    - The product or service should involve periodic repeat purchases plus name capture at point of sale.
    - There should be a definite affinity group from which a database can be constructed.
    - The provider should be able to construct a frequency reward system with significant benefits for both parties.

4.  Products for which after-market relationship marketing is unlikely to be profitable are those in which:

    - The product is a commodity with a mark-up that is too narrow to finance relationship-building activity.
    - The purchase is made seldom and unpredictably.

5.  Lifetime value analysis may show clearly that the costs of the relationship building will exceed the incremental profit created by the loyalty generation activities. Do your analysis before you spend a lot of money on a dream.

## Executive Quiz 15

Answers to quiz questions can be found in Appendix B. The quizzes are for fun. Do them if you enjoy quizzes. Ignore them if you don't.
*Choose the best answer to complete each statement or question.*

1. The U.S. Air Miles program was inferior to the Canadian program because
   a. of proof of purchase clipping and mailing.
   b. of the mag stripe and UPC code on the Canadian card.
   c. the U.S. strategy was a packaged goods strategy.
   d. All of the above
   e. None of the above

2. Why are more mistakes made in relationship building than in profiling and prospecting?
   a. In relationship building results take longer to show up.
   b. Tests are seldom possible in relationship building.
   c. Neural networks are of no use in relationship building.
   d. In large prospect mailings, mistakes are seldom made.
   e. All of the above

3. Successful relationship marketing requires that
   a. the buyer makes a profit from being in the database.
   b. the seller makes a profit from the database.
   c. there is communication between the seller and the buyer.
   d. All of the above
   e. None of the above

4. Which of the following is an unlikely area for successful relationship marketing?
   a. sewing and knitting
   b. prescription drugs
   c. apparel manufacturing

d. gasoline
e. insurance

5. For which of the following products is the building of long-term consumer loyalty through a database the least likely?
   a. automobiles
   b. canned soup
   c. software
   d. wine
   e. vacuum cleaner bags

6. What is not required for a profitable relationship database?
   a. a valid marketing program
   b. benefits to the consumers
   c. an easy way to get names and addresses
   d. all retail transactions stored in the database
   e. an affinity group from which the database can be built

7. To create a successful relationship building program, it is best if
   a. the markup is rather small.
   b. the product is highly competitive in price.
   c. the product is identical to the competition.
   d. the date of a future purchase is predictable.
   e. All of the above

8. Successful database activity usually affects all but one of the following:
   a. discount rate
   b. retention rate
   c. annual sales rate
   d. referral rate
   e. lifetime value

# 16

## Database Marketing and the Internal Struggle for Power

*In a market economy at any given time, an enormous amount of ignorance stands in the way of the complete coordination of the actions and decisions of the many market participants. Innumerable opportunities for mutually beneficial exchange ... are likely to exist unperceived. Each of these opportunities also offers an opportunity for entrepreneurial profit. Each of the potential parties to each of these unexploited exchange opportunities is, as a result of the imperfection of knowledge, losing some possible benefit through the absence of coordination represented by this situation.*
—*Israel Kirzner, professor, New York University*

Inside every company, contests are always being waged between different individuals and units seeking larger budgets, personnel, programs, and power. There is only so much money to go around at any given time, and each unit believes it needs more to accomplish its vital functions.

For many years, marketing—particularly database marketing—has had a real struggle to get any funding at all. Sales and advertising are usually much more successful in their efforts. Sales can point to the revenue it generates. The results of advertising can be seen by everyone in the company when they look at magazines, newspapers, and television. Database marketers, on the other hand, operate out of the limelight on obscure programs that most people don't understand.

The money for any new program—like a marketing database—has to be taken out of someone else's budget. Those who stand to lose seldom take a cut lying down. Only when the CEO decides to make the customer the focus of the company marketing strategy will database marketing get a chance to show what it can do. When that happens, the database marketers have to produce something useful fast, or they will be swept aside. The attention span of top management for any new program seldom exceeds 12 months.

Database marketing is faced with a catch-22 problem: Database marketing cannot prove itself unless it receives enough funding over a three-year period to permit the building of the database, the launching of a group of relationship-building programs, and the measurement of lifetime value change after those three years to prove the long-run effect. But no one is going to give database marketers sufficient funding for that unless they can first prove that it works. What is the answer?

There are really two ways that database marketers can get the resources they need to begin their work: by educating top management and by demonstrating results by successful experiments. Successful experiments are described throughout this book. Let's concentrate here on educating management.

## Educating Management

It is a commonplace of economics that the most successful production techniques are usually the most roundabout. For a primitive man to be successful at hunting, he first has to build a bow and arrow, which usually involves much experimentation with different types of wood and different materials for the cord. Such a primitive man does not look as if he were engaged in hunting, but he really is going about it in a very intelligent and roundabout way. Database marketing is also very roundabout.

To be successful at building customer loyalty and repeat sales, we must first build a marketing database that involves much experimentation with lists, software, data cleaning and correction, construction of reports, and customer profiles. None of this looks to outsiders as if it were connected with the generation of customer loyalty or repeat sales, but it really is an intelligent way of beginning the process.

Early man probably had a family that was demanding that he bring home some food and asking him why, instead of attempting to catch an animal for supper, he was experimenting with pieces of wood and cord. Database marketers have these same disbelievers looking over their shoulders wondering what all this data processing activity has to do with the generation of profitable sales.

Because database marketing is so roundabout, marketers have to conduct a major educational campaign within the company. Such campaigns are really directed at influencing top management, even though they begin by educating people at lower levels.

Management involvement is necessary, because management has to understand the process before it will be willing to commit the funds necessary to make it a reality. How do you educate management?

- You can send top management executives to conferences on database management.
- You can send marketing executives to training courses on database marketing, getting them certified in this new profession so that they can help in the sales and execution process.
- You can hire a direct response consultant or agency with database experience to advise you and brief top management.
- You can form a database marketing planning committee that meets regularly to lay out the groundwork for a database system, providing regular progress reports to top management.

All of these methods are useful, and in most cases, all of them should be attempted.

### Database Conferences

It is amazing how much progress is made at national database conferences. I have been to two dozen such meetings in the last five years. I learn a great deal from each one. The speakers are usually executives from direct response agencies, service bureaus, or marketing departments of companies. Many of the exhibits enable you to get a good idea of what is available. There is no better way to learn the state of the art. The conferences not only educate, they also bring marketers into direct contact with service providers. The National Center for Database Marketing devotes a considerable amount of time and effort to networking: getting people together. I had a very interesting experience at one of its conferences in Orlando.

In the opening session, the conference chairman, Skip Andrew, asked all 700 attendees to stand up, introduce themselves, and shake hands with the person behind them. I did so, meeting a woman from Michigan, an account executive from a small direct response agency. She had come to the conference seeking help in building a database for one of her clients, a large pharmaceutical firm. I had come to the conference to speak and to find account executives just like this delightful woman. In the 60 seconds that Skip Andrew gave us to talk, we found out about each other and arranged to meet for breakfast the next day.

At the "all you can eat" buffet breakfast the next day, she and I spent two hours together. I ate six scrambled eggs, 14 sausages, french toast, and mounds of rolls. I also persuaded her to come to visit us in Reston, Virginia, to meet our staff and discuss her pharmaceutical database. A month later, we had a signed contract and were creating a fascinating marketing database. I have had other equally rewarding conferences, but this was the one at which I gained the most weight.

This conference, which is held twice a year, is probably the best single event for finding out about the science and practice of database marketing. If you can get your senior executives to go to such an event, you are halfway on your journey to introduce database marketing to your company.

## Hands-On Training

Most professions have training programs providing nuts and bolts instructions in the technical details of the work. For example, financial planners, association executives, travel agents, and real estate professionals undergo extensive training. Database marketing is just beginning to get such training. York University in Toronto and the Database Marketing Institute, Ltd., in Arlington, Virginia now offer two-day hands-on training sessions for database marketing executives. The training includes case studies and practice in lifetime value calculation; Recency, Frequency, Monetary analysis; modeling; profiling; database construction; strategy development; testing; and control theory. If you are serious about database marketing and want to become a true professional, two days in such a seminar is time well spent.

## Enlisting a Direct Response Agency or Consultant

The hardest part of database marketing is developing an intelligent and productive strategy that uses the database. Building a database is comparatively easy. Making money with one is the real trick.

The famous economist Joseph Schumpeter drew an important distinction between an invention and an innovation. Inventions, he pointed out, are really not worth very much unless someone has invested some capital in their development. Once money has been invested in them, inventions become innovations; they change the course of human events. Leonardo da Vinci invented the airplane and a great many other things, which were, essentially, ahead of their time, but nothing much came of them. They came long before the Industrial Revolution. Capitalists were not available to take advantage of them.

Today many companies are resting on their past laurels, and simply won't go out on a limb for some new marketing idea. There are others, however, that are still struggling to get to the top, that are looking for ideas that they can turn into successful innovations. For database marketing to be converted from an invention to an innovation requires these two ingredients: a profit-making idea and a company with the capital resources and the entrepreneurial spirit needed to take advantage of the idea. Where do such ideas come from?

Ideas, of course, can come from anywhere. Many people have the ability to think up a better way to do the job that fate has assigned to them. With any luck you, the reader, will hit on a winning concept that will enable your company to make its customer happy and build the bottom line with database marketing.

I believe that direct response agencies and consultants are one of the best places to look for profit-making database ideas that can lead to successful innovations. My reasons are:

- Direct response agencies and consultants have usually helped several companies build successful (or unsuccessful) databases. Either way, they have learned something valuable that you don't know, which can help make your company's road to profitable database marketing a little easier.
- Such agencies and consultants must live by their wits. If they lose an account, they may lose their jobs. The entrepreneurial spirit is strong. In large corporations, on the other hand, marketing employees can count on a paycheck whether they win or lose. The entrepreneurial spirit is weak or nonexistent. Large corporations tend to stifle innovators and reward people who go along.
- Outsiders, like agency executives and consultants, can often go right to the top with an idea. Top corporate managers often listen to ideas from a relatively young account executive from Earl Palmer Brown or Ernst and Young, while the same person might never get a hearing as a junior in the company marketing department.
- Outside agencies usually have major resources that can be used to shape your particular strategic plan: copywriters, graphic artists, statisticians, and skilled presenters. Few corporate marketing staffs have many of these things.

For these reasons, you should have the assistance of an experienced and creative outside database marketing strategy agency in building your program and selling it to the top.

### Forming an In-House Team

Database marketing is different from any other marketing program. It requires building a lasting relationship with your customers. They will come to see your company as a friend who listens to them, asks their opinions, and reacts to what they say. How can you deliver on that concept?

The only way is to get a large number of internal groups actively involved in the relationship building:

328 of STRATEGIC DATABASE MARKETING

- Customer service
- Technical support
- Sales
- Dealer support
- Advertising
- Corporate communications
- Fulfillment and delivery
- Accounts receivable
- Management information systems (MIS)
- Marketing research
- Your outside direct response agency
- Your outside database service bureau
- Your outside telemarketers at your toll-free number
- Your outside data entry and fulfillment house
- Your outside list manager

Few companies have all these groups, but all companies have some of them. Your job, as a marketer, is to pull all these units together as a working team that coordinates policies and activities relating to the customer. For example:

- If you classify customers into blue, gold, and platinum categories, how are you going to assure that the appropriate groups within your organization work to treat these different levels differently, recognizing the privileges of the gold and platinum customers?
- If you promise 24-hour turnaround, how are you going to assure that this happens?
- If you ask people to bring one of your promotional letters to your branches, how are you going to assure that the branch personnel react properly to the letter and let you know that they have received it, noting the customer's ID number?
- If you have a customer with a 10-year buying history and a lifetime value of $2,000, how are you going to assure that Accounts Receivable takes that into consideration when the customer falls 60 days behind in payments because of travel in Europe?

Looking at the above, you can see that you, as a marketer, must become the leader of a relationship-building team that completely restructures the communications between your customers and your internal units.

Getting these in-house and outside people lined up in support of the plan is a major job. But it is also a source of your strength. If and when you form such a team, they will see the value of what you are doing. They will appreciate the importance of customer lifetime value and the part that they can play in making it grow. Once they understand your plan, they will be your key allies in selling your program to top management and getting the multiyear funding that you require.

## Knowledge of the Market

How can you learn what is in your customers' minds, and what your competition is doing? Economists who assume that all knowledge of the market is shared by the participants just don't understand the market. The fundamental problem that all marketers face is ignorance: lack of knowledge of what is out there, of what customers want, of how to let them know what we have to offer. Every piece of knowledge about the market, about how to price our products, about what the customer is thinking is valuable and can be converted, by alert marketers, into profit opportunities.

The difference between those who are successful marketers and those who fail can largely be attributed to the ability of the former to gain knowledge about the attitudes and plans of existing and possible customers, and to put that knowledge to work in a productive way. Successful marketers are alert to opportunities, but they also have developed ways of making the opportunities turn up by increasing their knowledge of the market.

Building a successful marketing database is one of those ways. Just as a chief financial officer (CFO) can look at a balance sheet and an income statement, and determine a profitable direction for company activity, so an alert marketer can look at the information stored in a customer database and learn of profitable marketing opportunities. Such knowledge, in the hands of a skillful marketer, is market power. It is also internal power in the struggle for success within the corporate hierarchy.

The data in a customer database is still rarely understood. Analysis of sales figures, however, are well known and widely studied. Income and expense reports, inventory, stock prices, balance sheets: These are all common management tools. They give the CFO power and influence to control the destinies of most units of the company.

Customer data, on the other hand, is an entirely new breed of information, which many on the corporate ladder do not yet understand. Certainly, customers' ideas about current products and services and their desire for changes can be, in the right hands, one of the most powerful marketing tools imaginable. Let's take an example from real life.

### Knowledge of How to Bring in New Business

What inducements are needed to get existing customers to persuade a neighbor to become a customer as well? Of those new customers brought in by such a program, how long will they remain customers—what is their lifetime value? From the answers to these two questions, how much can the company afford to spend on such a program?

These are detailed questions. The answers are far from universal. Success depends a great deal on the specific product, the offer, the method of selection of the customers, and the timing. If the marketer is alert to opportunities and able to experiment and test, the database can provide very useful answers to these questions. These answers, in the right hands, represent real market power. Larry Hawks of Marketing Communications, Inc. provided an interesting example:

> *A major propane gas distribution firm with more than 500 district offices nationwide had a customer base of more than 500,000 households and businesses, located mainly in rural areas.*
>
> *Several years ago, a marketing executive launched a referral program to generate new customers. The referral package offered either a $15 credit on the customer's next statement or a flannel-lined jacket as the premium. Existing customers were asked to supply three referral names, which were then followed up with personal sales calls by the district office. District managers loved the program because the conversion rate to customers was quite successful.*
>
> *The letters to customers inviting their participation were highly personalized, bearing the digitized signature of the local district manager. The envelopes containing the responses went directly to the local office, instead of to the headquarters that sent out the letters. The marketer believed that making the program appear to be a very local affair would improve the participation rate and hence the overall success.*
>
> *In the first year of operation, the program signed up 3,000 new customers who generated more than $3 million in revenue. One year later, more than 80 percent were still buying gas at the same rate. The total cost of the program in terms of mailings and premiums was less than $350,000.*

What does knowing how to create such a program mean to the propane gas company? Market power. What does the ability to use that knowledge to generate $3 million give to the marketer? Internal power.

Is the propane gas company spending too much or too little to acquire new customers? How much should it spend? Lifetime value calculation will answer the question.

## Uses for Market Knowledge

Marketers who have built marketing databases and who know how to use them, as in the case of the propane gas marketer, have very powerful knowledge in their possession. They can use it to win customers away from oil and electric heating in the marketplace. They also can use it to justify their marketing budget within their organizations. Here, for the first time, is a chance to stand up to the CFO and argue for a higher allocation for marketing in terms that the CFO can understand. This is powerful. It is more than the advertising chief can do—yet, because of tradition, advertising budgets are always many times larger than direct marketing budgets.

In time, this type of market knowledge will make its mark within most companies. The logic and precision of this type of calculation is unassailable. But to get to a position where marketers have that knowledge, they first must get the resources to build their databases, and learn how to use them. There are many steps necessary to the position of power within the corporation that most database marketers will attain in the future.

## Steps to Knowledge

To gain market knowledge, leading to market power, the database marketer must:

- Build a customer marketing database, complete with purchase history and demographics.
- Develop an active marketing program that uses the database to gain new customers, and to retain and increase sales to existing customers.
- Use the database to analyze marketing activities with precision and predictive capability so that the database marketer becomes the master of the marketplace.
- Use the knowledge gained within the company to obtain sufficient resources for the database marketing program so that it becomes the most powerful marketing force in the organization.

## Obstacles to Database Realization

These are exciting ideas. They are powerful ideas. But realization of the potential of database marketing is not going to be easy for anyone. Here are some of the obstacles:

- Brand managers and the ad agencies that they work with are not going to roll over and play dead when a marketing database comes along. Every dollar for a database is one less dollar for the advertising budget. It will be tough.

- The CFO and the MIS department that reports to the CFO are used to being the information resource. A customer database—they will begin to realize—will, in time, represent an independent source of knowledge and power. This independence will rival the power the CFO has gained through cash flow reports and balance sheets.

Some CFOs have caught on to this and are requiring such information as customer visitation frequency and the retention rate in the monthly reporting system throughout the company.

Power within a corporation tends to be a zero sum game. For everyone who gains internal influence, the dominance of other groups tend to be lessened. Few leaders will take the loss of power lying down. To the extent that consumer databases confer authority and influence on the marketing staff, there will be a counter reaction from other parts of the corporation that feel their positions threatened by this new technique. In many cases, there has been and will continue to be, active opposition to database marketing as a threat to established centers of internal power. Ultimately, top management will have to intervene or a potentially potent source of sales and profits will be sabotaged by internal bickering.

How does this opposition manifest itself? Let's look at a couple of examples of real situations in major companies today.

### Example 1: No Junk Mail

In the early 1980s, the product design department of a growing company began to pack registration cards inside every unit that it manufactured. The cards were quite detailed in the information they requested of the registrant. The idea was to figure out who was using the product, and what they were doing with it so that the product design department could anticipate market trends, and come up with features that were most in demand.

The project was a great success. Thousands of cards were received and poured over by designers who soon learned a great many things that they hadn't known before. For example, they learned that large numbers of people went out and bought—from external vendors—hardware that they plugged into the product to make it more useful. In effect, this highly successful product was carrying a dozen other companies, like parasites, on its back, whose existence depended on inadequate product design! Gradually they redesigned the product to incorporate these features so that the profits from these extras came to the company, not to the outsiders. The existence of the built-in features also provided a very useful selling point that contributed to the growth of overall sales.

So many cards were received that the product design team couldn't handle them all. After reviewing them, they shipped them in cardboard boxes to the company librarian. This enterprising woman knew a professor at a local university whose speciality was public opinion surveys. She persuaded him to take the boxes off her hands. A local data entry firm keypunched the cards into tapes then sent them back to the professor.

Within a few months, the professor was able to furnish the librarian with printed reports that summarized the findings from the cards. The company library soon became a haven for internal researchers who wanted to learn more about the uses of their rapidly expanding product. There were several problems, however. The computer printouts were very bulky and hard to read, particularly the carbon copies. Even though the professor presented the information in a dozen different cross-tabulations, it always happened that the exact relationship sought by the researchers was not on any of these. There was a demand for additional reports. The professor and the university programming staff soon grew months behind in their ability to keep the librarian satisfied.

The librarian drew up a Request for Proposals, which was sent to three service bureaus, one of which was selected to take over the growing database. The change in the library was dramatic. Reports were now printed on easy-to-read laser copies. There were 56 different cross-tabulations for each of the new models, which came out four times a year. There was so much information that the librarian became an essential resource in all company meetings involving the product or public reaction to it. Her growing status increased the power and prestige of her job, to which two assistants were soon added, and that of her supervisor who was given a substantial raise and a new title. In effect, without realizing it, they had created a powerful consumer database.

It wasn't long before the marketing department learned of this valuable resource. After studying the reports, they tried to get tapes from the system to do test mailings. They were firmly rebuffed, being told: "Our customers are not going to be bombarded with junk mail. If we did that, the flow of customer cards would soon cease." The marketing department's pleas fell on deaf ears within the company, because for the next six years, the company had more orders for products than it could handle. Marketing was almost irrelevant, and database marketing was never attempted.

The scene shifts to the present. Intense competition in the industry has brought this company its first loss after years of growth. New management determined that this would be "the year of the customer." The marketing department was told to begin active marketing operations. They began to rent outside lists of names. The one source they could not tap was the company's customer base, which by this time included more than one million names. These million people had each purchased a by-now obsolete model. Marketing wanted to get these customers to "trade up." Selling to satisfied customers is the easiest sell in the world, but the company did not attempt it. Why? The protection of the fiefdom of the database manager. As he saw it, if he gave up his database to the marketers, his monopoly of information would be at an end—and so would his power and position within the company. He successfully fought any use of the customer base for marketing, alluding to a "sacred understanding with the customers that we will not use their names."

Needless to say, this company, which has one of the finest and most comprehensive consumer databases in the world, is not doing any database marketing. Internal opposition has effectively killed this possible marketing route.

Is this attitude unique? Not at all. It is quite common. The General Electric Answer Center receives three million calls a year from customers who usually provide their names, addresses, and telephone numbers, and interests in specific GE products. Are these names placed into a marketing database? Not at all. They are destroyed 90 days after the telephone call is made. Customer service, you see, considers itself as a higher calling than mere sales. Customers do not want to be bombarded with sales literature, just because they called to inquire about a GE product—that is the rationale for not turning these names over to the marketing department.

Conflicts between marketing and market research or customer service are not rare at all. Market research, in particular, is often staffed by statisticians whose interest is to discover "truth" rather than to increase sales. They see themselves as researchers not marketers, and resent the implication that they have a responsibility for the bottom line.

Sales organizations also oppose database marketing, as explained in Chapter 12, Business-to-Business Database Marketing. Database marketers want to get their hands on customer names to put them in the database. Once this happens, the next step, as sales sees it, is direct marketing to the customers, cutting the sales staff out of its commissions. Database marketers find that the names of customers in many companies are denied to them.

The fact is, information is power in corporate America. Those who have gained information seldom like to give it up to others and risk losing their source of power. This is shown clearly in a second example.

### Example 2: Job Security?

The XYZ company maintained ongoing records of the monthly service use of its one million customers. Augmented by credit data compiled during the customer's application process, the database represented a tremendously valuable resource for marketing, market research, financial analysis, customer service, product design, technical support, and dealer relations. In the early days, no one knew how to get information out of the database. An enterprising researcher began using the software package FOCUS, which enabled him to extract data and produce useful reports. His services were soon in great demand on all sides. His boss soon told the researcher to drop all other work so that he could become an information resource to the entire company.

Demand for reports led the researcher to a much deserved promotion, and the appointment of a full-time assistant. Two years later he hired another assistant. Despite the staff increase, the team consistently maintained a six-month backlog of requests for reports and data.

Realizing it was time that the company entered the database marketing world, top management approved a Request for Proposals for an outside service bureau. The choice was eventually narrowed down to two firms. The first one would keep the data on a mainframe, but transfer it monthly to a PC with huge disk capacity that could be used by the researcher and his staff to service data requests much more rapidly than at present. The second contender would also keep the data on a mainframe, but provide direct access by telephone linkup to PCs from all the departments that needed information, thus largely doing away with the need for the researcher and his staff.

The decision making process was an agonizing one for the company. The researcher maintained that giving users direct access to the data would be a disaster. Inexperienced users would not know how to interpret their results correctly, leading to erroneous conclusions, disputes over data, and mistaken marketing decisions. Users argued that their programs were hampered by inability to get information. They had no faith that the researcher's famous six-month backlog would be reduced by the new system, as it represented a cushion for him at budget time to assure him of continued support for his operation.

What can we conclude from this?

- Knowledge derived from a consumer database confers significant market power on the company that possesses it and uses it appropriately.
- Failure to use the knowledge confers no power at all.
- Ability to capture and use the knowledge also confers internal power in the quest for advancement inside the company.
- Companies that allow this knowledge to be centralized to a limited group—for its own advancement—are weakening their market power

and denying themselves the benefits that come from proper use of a consumer database.

- Every company should: assure that all relevant sections have access to the data and build a strategy for its use.

## Winning over Top Management

You want to build a marketing database. You need to convince top management. Here is a strategy that will work:

- Determine lifetime customer value using the present system.
- Create a picture of lifetime value with the database.
- Show the effect on the bottom line.

Can you back up your numbers against the holes that will be poked in them by other executives, particularly the advertising staff (supported by their agency)? It will be tough. You will have to do your homework. If you can run some small scale tests, it might help. Show them this book, and hit them over the head with it. Get your direct response agency to help you.

However you do it, of course, is up to you. The steps you will have to go through are certainly going to be similar to those described above.

Good luck.

## Summary

1.  Database marketing has a struggle to obtain funding. Programs take many years to show real results. The money must come from some other unit's budget. Programs can be funded only by persuading top management.

2.  Methods include sending top management to database conferences, enlisting the help of a direct response agency, and forming an in-house database marketing planning committee.

3.  Direct response agencies are essential because they usually have broad experiences building databases for others, they have entrepreneurial spirit, and they can gain access to your top management more easily than you can. In addition, they have large creative staffs that can really flesh out an idea.

4.  An in-house team is essential for database marketing. There are a dozen different disciplines that are needed to craft a relationship-build-

ing program with customers. It is hard to get such a team together, but it is also a source of strength for the marketing staff.

5.  In-house coordination is needed to assure that preferred customers get preferred treatment, that turnaround time is given as promised, that customer contacts are reported to the database.

6.  Most company executives know how to compute customer lifetime value and relate it to the bottom line. Marketers have to get on top of this discipline if they want to succeed.

7.  Experience in database marketing plus precise calculation of lifetime value can be powerful tools in getting database marketing budgets approved.

8.  There are many obstacles: Brand managers and ad agencies will fight any cut in their budgets. MIS will fight marketers getting their own independent sources of information.

9.  Information about the company's customers can provide market power. Too often, however, this information is locked away inside market research, customer service, or some other unit where it cannot be used to build market share. Companies that allow this to happen are throwing away money.

## Executive Quiz 16

Answers to quiz questions can be found in Appendix B. The quizzes are for fun. Do them if you enjoy quizzes. Ignore them if you don't.
*Choose the best answer to complete each statement or question.*

1. Database marketing usually has difficulty getting adequate initial funding because
   a. it is hard to do cost benefit analysis for relationship building.
   b. rivals seek to keep budgeted funds for their own programs.
   c. advertising is usually more productive of sales.
   d. database marketing is an unproven technique.
   e. many databases fail.

2. Which method is not suggested for educating management on database marketing?
   a. making them read this book
   b. sending them to conferences
   c. enlisting the help of a direct response agency
   d. building an in-house team
   e. constructing a lifetime value analysis table

3. The conferences of the National Center for Database Marketing provide
   a. a way for vendors and companies to meet each other.
   b. high level briefing on marketing techniques.
   c. exhibits from practitioners.
   d. All of the above
   e. None of the above

4. Which of the following was not suggested as a member of the in-house database marketing team?
   a. chief financial officer
   b. MIS
   c. database service bureau
   d. customer service
   e. sales

5. Database marketing in the early 1990s is
   a. taught in most advanced business schools.
   b. taught in most marketing programs.
   c. available as a correspondence course.
   d. learned only on the job.
   e. given as a certificate course by the Direct Marketing Association.

6. Which of the following is unlikely to oppose database marketing within a corporation?
   a. market research
   b. MIS
   c. sales
   d. advertising
   e. None of the above

7. Why are market research and database marketing often in conflict?
   a. Market research has different goals.
   b. Database marketing cannot use models.
   c. Database budgets usually come from market research.
   d. MIS sides with database not with research.
   e. Customer service wants market research as one of its functions.

8. Companies that keep customer data exclusively in research or customer service staffs
   a. protect their customers from junk mail.
   b. feed internal corporate power struggles.
   c. gain major marketplace power.
   d. help to build a corporate asset.
   e. None of the above

# A Farewell to the Reader

Congratulations on getting this far. As we say farewell to each other, let's review the main strategic database marketing concepts that I hope you have learned:

- Database marketing does not always work. It is generally quite useful in direct marketing to prospects, where it usually permits reduction in marketing costs and improvements in response and profits. It is more difficult to carry out successfully in marketing to existing customers. In the right situations, it will create loyalty, reduce attrition, and build your bottom line. There are some product and service situations in which a database may not be economically justified.

- The biggest difficulty in making database marketing work is the development of an effective and profitable marketing strategy using the database. Typically, too much attention is focused on hardware and software, and not enough on marketing.

- The way to estimate the possibilities of proposed database marketing strategies and to evaluate the effectiveness of existing ones is to create test and control groups and calculate the lifetime value of both groups. Lifetime value is the net present value of future profits to be received from the average customer.

- In free-market transactions, both the buyer and the seller always make a profit. The way to increase your sales, therefore, is to find a way for the buyer to make a profit. In today's market situation, a profit may not necessarily be a low price. Instead, it may be recognition, helpfulness, service, information, convenience, and an opportunity to identify with a friendly and reliable organization. A database program may be the ideal way to provide those things at the least cost.

## Conclusion

Let us end with the words we started with in the Introduction: Database marketing is not just a way to increase profits by reducing costs and selling more products and services, although that is, and must be, one of its results. It is a tool that provides management with customer information. That information is used in various ways to increase customer retention and increase customer acquisition rates—the essence of business strategy. The database provides both the raw information you need and a measurement device essential for the evaluation of strategy.

Viewed from the customers' point of view, database marketing is a way of making customers happy: of providing them with recognition, service, friendship, and information for which, in return, they will reward you with loyalty, reduction in attrition, and increased sales. Genuine customer satisfaction is the goal and hallmark of satisfactory database marketing. If you are doing things right, your customers will be glad that you have a database and that you have included them in it. They will appreciate the things that you do for them. If you can develop and carry out strategies that bring this situation about, you are a master marketer. You will keep your customers for life and be happy in your work. You will have made the world a better place in which to live.

# Appendix A: Keeping Up with Database Marketing

To keep up with the many new innovations and developments in this field, you will have to read, talk to people, and attend conferences. Since publication of *The Complete Database Marketer,* many readers have called me to talk about their database marketing experiences. I have used much of the knowledge gained from these talks in this book. As a reader, you should feel free to contact me if you think that the call would be useful for both of us.

## Magazines

You should subscribe to the following magazines and newsletters:

- *The Cowles Report on Database Marketing,* 470 Park Avenue South, New York, NY 10016, (800) 775-3777.
- *DM News,* Mill Hollow Corporation, 19 West 21st Street, New York, NY 10010, (212) 741-2095, Fax (212) 633-9367.
- *Target Marketing,* 401 North Broad Street, Philadelphia, PA 19108, (215) 238-5300.
- *Canadian Direct Marketing News,* 1200 Markham Road, Scarborough, Ontario M1H 3C3, (416) 439-4083.
- *Direct,* Six River Bend Center, Stamford, CT 06907, (203) 358-9900.
- *Direct Marketing,* 224 Seventh Street, Garden City, NY 11530, (800) 229-6700.
- *American Demographics,* P.O. Box 68, Ithaca, NY 14851, (800) 828-1133.
- *Sales and Marketing Management,* Bill Communications, 633 Third Avenue, New York, NY 10017, (212) 630-1549.
- *Strategy: The Canadian Marketing Report,* 366 Adelaide St. West, Toronto, Canada M5V 1R9, (416) 408-2300.

## Books

You should read the following books:

- *The Complete Database Marketer,* Arthur M. Hughes (Chicago: Probus Publishing Company, 1991).
- *The Complete Direct Mail List Handbook,* Ed Burnett (Englewood Cliffs, N.J.: Prentice Hall, 1988).
- *After Marketing,* Terry Vavra (Homewood, Ill.: Business One Irwin, 1992).
- *MaxiMarketing,* Stan Rapp and Thomas L. Collins (New York: McGraw Hill, 1986).
- *The Great Marketing Turnaround,* Stan Rapp and Thomas L. Collins (Englewood Cliffs, N.J.: Prentice Hall, 1990).
- *The New Direct Marketing,* David Shepard (Homewood, Ill.: Dow Jones-Irwin, 1990).
- *Business-to-Business Direct Marketing,* Tracy Emerick and Bernie Goldberg (Hampton, Conn.: Direct Marketing Publishers, 1987).

## Conventions

The following convention is probably the best two days you could possibly spend on learning about database marketing. The sessions are held every six months in Chicago and Orlando. They are attended by more than 700 people each time, with about 70 speakers. They will give you a chance to hear about new things and to meet all sorts of people in the business:

- Database Marketing, National Center for Database Marketing, 911 Hope Street, Box 4232, Stamford, CT 06907-0232, (800) 927-5007.

The following conference is also of great interest to database marketers in the business-to-business arena:

- Direct Marketing to Business and Industry, sponsored by Federal Express and Dun's Marketing Services, P.O. Box 1161, Ridgefield, CT 06877, (203) 438-2318.

There are also other valuable database marketing conferences called from time to time by such institutions as *Canadian Direct Marketing News* (see above) and *Target Marketing* (also above).

## Hands-On Training

Some institutions in Canada and the United States are now offering hands-on training in database marketing techniques. The courses, limited to a maximum of 40 executives per session, include practical training in creating lifetime value tables; Recency, Frequency, Monetary (RFM) analysis; modeling; profiling; database construction; and strategy development. The two-day sessions are taught several times a year by leading database marketing professionals, including Professor Paul Wang of Northwestern University, David Foley of York University, and Arthur Hughes of the University of Maryland. The following organizations can provide more information about these hands-on training courses:

- York University, Division of Executive Development, North York, Ontario. For information call Peter Zarry, director, (416) 736–5079.

- The Database Marketing Institute, Ltd., Arlington, Virginia. For information call Sarah Cooper Associates, (703) 908-9309.

## Technical Assistance

The strategic thinking in this book is rooted in mathematical analysis, as is all of database marketing. You simply cannot be successful in database marketing unless you can learn to manipulate lifetime value, RFM analysis, and response analysis. Advanced marketers will probably also need to become proficient at neural network modeling and affinity analysis.

To do these things, you need two basic tools: the ability to work comfortably with a spreadsheet, such as Lotus 1-2-3 or Microsoft Excel, and the ability to do ad hoc cross-tabulations with your database software, which will provide you with the data to put into your spreadsheet. To do neural network modeling, of course, you will need a modern neural network software package such as HNC's DMW or Software Application's ModelMAX. These two packages come with user training.

The ability to do ad hoc cross tabulations is available from a number of different mainframe and PC packages. I am, understandably, somewhat fond of the ACS package MarketVision, since I was one of the designers of this product. There are, however, other good products out there that can do a good job of ad hoc analysis, and you should look into these as well. MarketVision comes with two days of user training. Other ad hoc programs also include training.

Spreadsheet analysis can be learned in organized courses or from a man-

# 344

ual (which is how I learned it). If you are not good at it, you should begin to learn it now. You cannot be a good database strategist if you have to leave all the calculations to someone else.

Once you can use a spreadsheet, you should be able to duplicate all the analytical work that you find in this book (except for neural network modeling). Even so, working out the formulas and constructing the tables will take you some time (it took me about three weeks).

To make it easier, Automated Systems Associates, Ltd., provides a diskette that has many of the formulas constructed, ready to be loaded into either Lotus 1-2-3 or Microsoft Excel. The diskette does not have spreadsheet software on it. You have to have your own copy of 1-2-3 or Excel and know how to use it in order to make any use of the diskette. The diskette will not teach you how to use a spreadsheet. It simply consists of ASCII data that can be copied by you, as an experienced user, on to your hard disk and manipulated with your spreadsheet to produce the tables found throughout this book.

I don't want to encourage you to send for the diskette if you have already figured out how to do the analytical tables in this book. There is nothing new in the diskette that you cannot find in these pages. It contains mainly data and formulas that you can construct on your own without it. But if you want to save yourself a few days' time in getting started, you may find the diskette worth the investment.

I have a second reason for encouraging you to send for the diskette, however, which I should disclose here. I like to keep in touch with people in the industry like yourself. I learned about many of the case studies and new ideas that you have read about in this book from readers of *The Complete Database Marketer* who have contacted me during the last three years. I hope to continue to do this in the future. If you do send for the diskette, therefore, you might include in your request a little background about yourself, your company, and your database plans, so that we can begin a dialogue. That is what database marketing is all about.

The IBM compatible 3.5-inch PC diskette (there is no Macintosh version), for use with Lotus 1-2-3 or Microsoft Excel, is available from Automated Systems Associates, Ltd., 4141 North Henderson Road, Suite 1219, Arlington, Virginia 22203. The cost is a check or money order for $36 plus $4 for shipping and handling. Outside the United States add $2.

# Appendix B: Answers to the Executive Quiz Questions

| Chapter 2 | Chapter 3 | Chapter 4 | Chapter 5 | Chapter 6 |
|-----------|-----------|-----------|-----------|-----------|
| 1. c | 1. b | 1. c | 1. d | 1. 95 |
| 2. a | 2. d | 2. a | 2. b | 2. 80 |
| 3. c | 3. c | 3. d | 3. c | 3. 190 |
| 4. a | 4. b | 4. c | 4. d | 4. 2.0 |
| 5. e | 5. b | 5. a | 5. c | 5. $116,076 |
| 6. a | 6. d | 6. e | 6. e | 6. $173,880 |
| 7. b | 7. c | 7. c | 7. e | 7. $57,804 |
| 8. d | 8. e | 8. a | 8. c | 8. e |
| 9. c | | | | 9. c |

| Chapter 7 | Chapter 8 | Chapter 9 | Chapter 10 | Chapter 11 |
|-----------|-----------|-----------|------------|------------|
| 1. c | 1. d | 1. e | 1. d | 1. e |
| 2. e | 2. c | 2. c | 2. d | 2. b |
| 3. c | 3. d | 3. d | 3. a | 3. c |
| 4. e | 4. a | 4. d | 4. b | 4. d |
| 5. a | 5. b | 5. c | 5. a | 5. e |
| 6. e | 6. b | 6. b | 6. a | 6. c |
| 7. a | 7. c | 7. d | 7. a | 7. a |
| 8. b | | 8. e | 8. a | 8. c |

| Chapter 12 | Chapter 13 | Chapter 14 | Chapter 15 | Chapter 16 |
|------------|------------|------------|------------|------------|
| 1. b | 1. d | 1. c | 1. d | 1. b |
| 2. b | 2. e | 2. e | 2. a | 2. a |
| 3. e | 3. a | 3. a | 3. d | 3. d |
| 4. d | 4. c | 4. b | 4. c | 4. a |
| 5. e | 5. c | 5. e | 5. e | 5. d |
| 6. d | 6. c | 6. e | 6. d | 6. e |
| 7. c | 7. b | 7. b | 7. d | 7. a |
| 8. b | 8. c | 8. a | 8. a | 8. b |

# Index